# Menu Planning, Design, and Evaluation
## Managing for Appeal and Profit

Jack D. Ninemeier

*The School of Hospitality Business, Michigan State University, East Lansing, Michigan*

David K. Hayes

*Managing Owner, Clarion Hotel and Conference Center, Lansing, Michigan*

*McCutchan Publishing Corporation*
3220 Blume Drive #197
Richmond, California 94806

ISBN 0-8211-1313-5
Library of Congress Catalog Card Number 2003109954

# Dedication

This book is dedicated to the thousands of hospitality students with whom we have come in contact during our teaching careers. In our foodservice management classes we consistently emphasize, "*It all starts with the menu!*" We know that simple statement to be a fact, but we also recognize that the menu's importance is reaffirmed for the students after they have become managers in all types of food and beverage operations. We have also confirmed the accuracy of this statement as we consistently read about the menu's importance in the ever-increasing body of knowledge applicable to the hospitality industry, including books and articles in trade magazines and in more scholarly publications.

Our admonition to students is that they must recognize the importance of the menu and incorporate its effective management into day-to-day operations. Our concern provided an incentive to develop this book for today's and tomorrow's hospitality students. As well, we want to recognize those who were students "yesterday" and who are now practicing the "art and science" of food and beverage management. They have taught us much about the menu, and we are anxious to share what we have learned with the readers of this book.

# Table of Contents

# List of Figures

# Preface

Today, especially with the advent of the Internet and other computer technologies, students of foodservice and hospitality management and industry practitioners who want information about menus (or almost any other topic!) have lots of information readily available. Why, then, is additional information about menu planning—which is already extensively discussed in many other venues—still necessary?

The authors believe that this text puts a special emphasis on the topic. For example, all of the information presented in this book is *practical*; students and those working in the industry will appreciate the extensive and comprehensive information presented here, and will realize associated benefits from using the information. Second, the information in this text consistently focuses on the consumers of food and beverage products and services (that is, guests in a hotel or restaurant, employees of a business or industry, patients in a hospital, residents in a nursing home, or students in a school, for example) and what these guests need. Operational concerns are important; however, what the consumer does—and does not—desire becomes a parameter within which operating issues must be addressed.

Information in this book is organized to make it useful to read from cover to cover (such as students in a classroom setting might do) and, as well, to read on a by-topic basis (as, for example, a busy manager with a specific problem might do). We have included illustrations of some actual menus but have chosen to emphasize specific sections of other menus used in many types of food and beverage operations. Each has been selected for a specific purpose such as to illustrate how a specific principle might be incorporated into menu planning, design, or evaluation.

It is exciting to design a menu for a food and beverage operation that is just opening its doors. However, the menu-development process is never truly completed. The guests' preferences change, and management's ability to more effectively and consistently deliver what the guests desire should evolve as well. While an operation must plan a menu for its initial operation only once, it will continually improve its menus for as long as it is open for business. The principles to plan, design, and evaluate a menu are the same (or, at least, very similar) regardless of whether it is the first version or the hundredth version in an evolving chain of menu improvements. This book is about the principles used to help assure that the menu is the very best it can be.

## CHAPTER 1

# It All Starts With The Menu

## CHAPTER OUTLINE

## MENU TERMS USED IN THIS CHAPTER

À la carte menu
Advertising
Back-of-the-house
Banquet
Bin lists
Call brand
Cash cafeteria operation
Catering
Commercial operations
Contract food management company

Contribution margin
Convenience food
Cost control
Cross-selling
Cyclical menu
Du jour menu
Front-of-the-house
High check average
Just-in-Time (JIT)
Liaison
Make-or-buy analysis

Menu
Noncommercial operations
Operating costs
Point-of-sale
Revenue
Sales
Suggestive selling
Table d'hôte menu
Table tents

## CHAPTER OVERVIEW

You are about to begin an exciting journey to study the single most important element in the success or failure of any type of foodservice operation: the menu. Success can be measured in many ways, including assessing whether guests are pleased, whether financial goals are met, and the extent to which the operation is being operated without too many problems. The menu directly and immediately impacts all three of these measures.

This chapter provides an overview of our study of menu management. Its primary purpose is to show that the menu is of critical importance to all foodservice operations regardless of the type of menu or the guest to whom it is offered.

In this chapter we will explain how the menu is used for marketing and advertising. We will note how it helps to assure that revenues and guest counts are sufficient to meet profit or budgeted deficit goals and how it can help facilitate preparation and service, or make these tasks stressful.

We will note several common types of menus and explain the best use for each type. As well, we will discuss the concept of a menu-writing team; menus are too important to be planned and designed by one person (or even by only a very few persons). Rather, a team is necessary—with all members working, cooperating, and bringing their individual knowledge, skills, and experiences to the menu-writing task.

All foodservice operations have the same basic resources available, which are, unfortunately, in limited supply. The chapter discusses several common resources, including food, labor, products (food and beverages), equipment (machinery), money, time, energy, space, and operating procedures. We will provide examples to show the direct impact that the menu has on each of these resources to underline the chapter's premise that the menu is absolutely critical.

The menu impacts the nutritional content of the food that it offers. As well, it should influence the design and décor of the foodservice establishment. An effective menu can facilitate dealing with cost control concerns, including monitoring revenue, expenses, and profit goals. Finally, and most important, is that the menu will impact the long-term survival of the foodservice operation.

Our chapter begins by remembering an old saying in the foodservice industry, "*It all starts with the menu.*" After you finish studying this chapter, you'll appreciate another adage, "Foodservice comprises a large number of closely related subsystems; as one subsystem is changed, all other subsystems are affected." The menu is the common denominator that affects all parts (subsystems) of the foodservice operation. This chapter will discuss the very important role that the menu plays in all marketing, financial, and operating aspects of the food and beverage operation.

## A BRIEF HISTORY OF QUANTITY FOODSERVICE AND MENUS

The history of people eating together in large groups can be traced back at least 12,000 years, to well before agriculture and the domestication of animals, which began about 10,000 years ago. There is evidence that food was sold in public marketplaces 7,000 years ago, and historical accounts describing the banquets and feasts enjoyed 2,500 years ago by the ancient Greeks and Romans are well

known. Thus, the concept of food served in quantity is, indeed, very old. The oldest written recipes discovered so far date from the fourth century B.C. They were collected and published in the oldest known cookbook, written by Apicius. This means that the earliest recorded cuisine is that of the ancient Romans.

By the 1500's, public dining had largely become unpopular. Quantity food was produced primarily in religious institutions, and wealthy persons employed chefs who, in their own ways, advanced the culinary profession. France, with its *haute cuisine* (high food preparation), became a leader in fine dining by improving on many food preparation and service techniques that had been developed earlier in Italy, Russia, and Spain, among other European countries.

Before the 1600's there were some (but very few) inns available for travelers. The first travelers did so for trade and religious purposes, and there was little, if any, "pleasure" travel. In fact, the word "travel" comes from "travail" (which means hard labor; to toil). Sometimes, persons living along popular routes (the first hospitality entrepreneurs!) provided travelers who could afford it with a sleeping room and a meal ("bed and board"). There was no "menu" of food choices offered; these travelers ate whatever the family itself would be eating, and one presumes there was no medium other than the command "Sit and eat" used to deliver the message about what food was available and when it would be served.

Religious facilities such as monasteries also opened their doors to travelers. In this context, the Catholic Church might be considered the world's first multiunit hospitality organization. In addition, those who were wealthy enough sometimes traveled with servants who prepared meals during their journey.

Separate eating places, such as coffee houses, began to appear in the largest European cities. These establishments offered coffee and alcoholic beverages and served some food. In the mid-1700's, a Frenchman named Boulanger began selling soups that he represented to be health restorers. He called his eating place a *restauer* (French for "to restore"), and the restaurant was born. Soon after, "eating out" became a way of life; it is estimated that by about 1800 there were more than five hundred restaurants in Paris alone. In addition, the Industrial Revolution in the late 1700's created a new social class

of entrepreneurs, industrialists, and others, who began to demand higher food standards. Private clubs and more public venues evolved to meet the demands of these persons.[1]

The first menus were used by the chefs and cooks who prepared banquet meals—not by their guests who consumed these meals. Early menus were lists of food items to be prepared. These items were listed in the order in which they were served and represented, in part, "shopping lists" of ingredients required to prepare the meals being planned and the costs incurred for their purchase. Since some banquets offered many items (often over one hundred), it is obvious that the chefs would need this list in order to correctly prepare the food. On the other hand, because of the many items served at these events, it is easy to understand why menus were not provided to the tables, let alone to each guest seated at the table.

The word "**menu**," like so many others in the world of the culinary (such as *chef, sous chef, buffet, maitre d',* and *fricassee*), is French. Literally translated, it means "detailed list." Food and beverage managers and chefs think of this definition when, for example, they talk about what (the list of items) is available for service to guests. The term also takes on another meaning when, for example, the dining room receptionist or server provides a copy of a menu to guests when they are seated. In this context, the "menu" is both a list of what is available and the means by which the list is presented.

---

*Glossary Terms*
**Menu.** A French term meaning "detailed list"; in common usage it refers to a listing of the foodservice establishment's available food and beverage products and to the way this list is provided to the guest.

---

[1] An excellent summary of the history of the foodservice industry can be found in Lendal Kotschevar, *Management by Menu,* second edition. Boston: William. C. Brown Publishers, 1987.

Traditional French menus during the 1800's had up to thirteen separate courses, excluding beverages. A meal in a restaurant or hotel was, itself, an occasion. Figure 1-1 lists the categories of items a guest in a French hotel or restaurant during the 1800's may have consumed. It is easy to see why such a complicated collection of courses is almost never seen today. Courses within this classical structure do, however, still drive basic meal patterns typically seen in modern menus. For

example, formal restaurants offering a table d'hôte (fixed price) menu may offer the following six courses:

- appetizer (hot or cold)
- soup
- fish
- sorbet
- main course with vegetable accompaniments
- dessert

Figure 1-1. **Classic Menu for French Cuisine**

| Course Number | Name of Course | |
|---|---|---|
| | **French** | **English** |
| 1 | Hors-d'oeuvres froid | Cold appetizer |
| 2 | Potage | Soup |
| 3 | Hors-d'oeuvres chaud | Hot appetizer |
| 4 | Poisson | Fish |
| 5 | Relevé/Grosse piece | Main course |
| 6 | Entrée | Intermediate course |
| 7 | Sorbet | Sorbet |
| 8 | Roti salade | Roast with salad |
| 9 | Roti froid | Cold roast |
| 10 | Legume | Vegetable |
| 11 | Entremets | Sweet |
| 12 | Savoury | Savory |
| 13 | Dessert | Dessert |

À la carte restaurants (those offering individual items for specified prices) often divide menu offerings into categories that also roughly follow the sequence of courses in the classical French cuisine:

- appetizer
- soup or salad
- entrée with vegetables
- desserts

You can see, then, that a menu pattern established in Europe over two hundred years ago is still a consideration of many menu planners today.

The first menus for public use were what we today call "table d'hôte" or "prix fixe." These meals, representing the "table of the host," were complete meals at a set price. As we have noted, before the sixteenth century, guests of inns were not given a choice of menu items; instead, they ate and drank whatever the innkeeper provided. Some English taverns in the mid-sixteenth century continued this tradition. They served a daily "ordinary"—a mid-day or evening meal at a common table for a fixed price.

The French originally called the bill of fare the *escriteaux* (meaning announcements; written out). Menus for individual guests became popular in great restaurants in Paris during the 1800's. As public menus became more commonplace, many restaurants began to display posters at their entrance that informed potential guests about the items being offered. This practice of posting menus at or near the doors of restaurants is still relatively common throughout Europe today, and is also seen at the entrance to many hotel restaurants in the United States and elsewhere.

The first guests receiving menus at tableside likely read information handwritten on small, plain cardboard cards. Over time, the worth of menus for marketing, sales, "image," and other purposes has led to the great variety of creatively planned and designed materials presented to today's diners.

---

### THE WORLD OF THE CULINARY: A BRIEF HISTORY OF SOME FAMOUS CHEFS AND THEIR CONTRIBUTIONS*

**Bortolomeo Scappi**—His cookbook, written in the mid-1500's, was the most authoritative work until the mid-1700's. In addition to creative recipes, the book contained his illustration of an ideal kitchen layout. It shows a hood over the cooking fire, a bale of straw to hold knives (which are speared into it for safe keeping), and bread stored on high shelves to keep it safe from animals.

**La Varenne**—Considered the founder of French classical cooking, his cookbook was published in 1651, with thirty editions printed over seventy-five years. His contributions included adapting Italian cuisine to the basics of French cooking and the advancement of a new cuisine focusing on sauces, food temperatures, garnishing, and the order of foodservice.

**Amelia Simmons**—Her cookbook, published in the late 1700's, was the first written by an American for Americans. It was basically a personal collection of recipes handed down through several generations. Unlike the extravagant recipes in French, Italian, and English cookbooks, her recipes were more basic and included those for Johnny Cake, Indian pudding, and simple fish and meat items.

**Antonin Caremé**—Caremé is frequently mentioned as the greatest cook of all times. He analyzed and simplified cooking methods and menus to help define what is today known as "haute cuisine." His early work was as a pastry chef. His work and travels throughout Europe during the early 1800's provided the background for several very important cookbooks that followed. His most important work includes several hundred versions of soups and numerous variations of sauces. He is equally well known for his aspics, pastries, and ices.

**Auguste Escoffiér**—"The King of Chefs and the Chef of Kings," Escoffiér was the best known and most respected culinarian during the late 1800's and the early 1900's. Earlier great chefs worked primarily as employees of influential and wealthy families. Escoffiér, by contrast, practiced his art in restaurants and hotels. He teamed with Cesar Ritz, the great hotelier, to offer those who could afford it the best in genteel hostmanship and the finest cuisine in hotels that were the best of their day. In1902 he published a monumental book with over five hundred classic recipes and garnishes. This book, written for the professional chef, starts with the basics and proceeds to the most challenging food preparation procedures and recipes. Escoffiér was very influential in revising the way menus were planned from a style hundreds of years old, in which many dishes were served at once, to today's style of serving courses consecutively. Among his other contributions were to improve the culinary profession by treating subordinates with respect and to revise the organization of the kitchen. He emphasized that kitchen sections must work together rather than independently in the preparation of meals.

---

*For an interesting expanded discussion of world-famous chefs and their contributions, see Anne Willan, *Great Cooks from Taillevent to Escoffiér*. New York: McGraw-Hill Book Company, 1977.

Today's menu planners offer a seemingly endless variety of menu items to an increasingly smaller niche of consumers, ranging from a few items at a low price to many menu items at high prices—and everything in between. Our study of the menu and its management principles is difficult because in order to present a comprehensive overview, there must be both great depth and breadth to the discussion.

If the original concept of the menu has evolved over the centuries, the way that menus are presented to consumers certainly has as well. "Yesterday" the guest in a hotel or restaurant may have learned about available items as the menu (list) was recited to them by the server. Alternatively, the food server may have offered a very simple written menu, or perhaps the menu was written on signage somewhere within the dining area. Consumers in schools, hospitals, and nursing homes learned about menu choices by looking at hard copy menu lists or, perhaps, by observing what was available as they passed through the cafeteria line or when seated at a dining room table.

Today menus are "delivered" to prospective guests in numerous creative ways, including by the Internet (check out the home page of your favorite restaurant!), by the hotel's guestroom television (where you can frequently order breakfast electronically), or by fax machine (used, for example, by guests of a local sandwich shop to place their orders). Guests in schools, healthcare facilities, and business and industrial locations may learn about menu offerings by way of closed-circuit televisions, broadcast fax, mass e-mailings, Intranet as well as Internet sites, and related electronic media.

As this brief history of menu planning has shown, the variety of menu items available to guests and the way in which guests learn about these items have changed dramatically over the years. One thing, however, has not changed—the phrase "It all starts with the menu" is just as true today as it was yesterday. Because the menu states what will be produced and served, it drives the planning and operating needs of any type of foodservice operation. As well, it impacts the ability of the foodservice operation to attain financial goals as much as or more than any other single factor.

## THE MENU'S POWER AS A PLANNING TOOL

While technology has changed forever the way food and beverage operators can inform consumers about their menu offerings, it has not changed one important fact: the menu is the single most important tool that most dramatically impacts profitability (in **commercial operations**) or cost minimization (in **noncommercial operations**) and directs the operation of the food and beverage operation each day. The menu, like no other management tool, directly affects the marketing, financial, and operating success of the food and beverage operation.

> *Glossary Terms*
> **Commercial operations.** A food and beverage operation (such as offered in a hotel or by a restaurant) that exists primarily to generate profits from the sale of food and beverages.
> **Noncommercial operations.** A food and beverage operation (such as in a school, hospital, or business or industry) in which food and beverage services must be provided incidental to the primary purpose of the organization. (For example, the school exists to educate, the hospital to cure illness, and the business and industry setting to make a product or offer a service.) Also commonly referred to as an "institutional foodservice operation."

## The Menu Is a Marketing Tool

Marketing has been defined as the business from the perspective of the guest, and the menu is what markets a foodservice establishment to customers. Therefore, whether the customer is the guest of a commercial foodservice operation or is a student, patient, resident, office worker, or other consumer in a noncommercial operation, the impact of marketing is the same.

Some persons erroneously believe that a properly developed and designed menu is important for commercial—but not noncommercial—operations. They reason, for example, that if a hotel or restaurant does not offer what guests want, the guests will go elsewhere. This is, of course, true. However, it is just as true in the noncommercial setting. At worse, undesirable menus in noncommercial operations yield high **operating costs,** leading to financial deficits. For example, high food cost items that are not selected by guests must be discarded. A wise menu planner

would select less expensive items that would be consumed. Also, consumer dissatisfaction (which can lead, in an extreme example, to prison riots!) and disruptions in consumers' work schedules and the amount of work they get done (when, for example, prospective consumers leave the workplace to dine elsewhere) are likely to occur. As well, families of nursing home residents may, at least in part, judge the quality of the care given to their family members by their experiences with the facility's dining services. Consider, also, employees in high-stress organizations such as hospitals who can (rightfully!) become distressed when they perceive that the food and beverage offerings in the on-site establishment are less than adequate.

Menus can also be used as **advertising** and **sales** tools. We have noted that a menu in any type of foodservice operation must offer items preferred by customers for the operation to be successful. In fact, a well-designed menu will influence readers to select items that the operation would most like to sell (usually those that are profitable). Menu-evaluation techniques (see Chapter 9) enable the menu planners to design menus that are effective in-house selling tools.

> *Glossary Terms*
> **Advertising.** The activities employed to bring menu item offerings to the attention of potential and current guests (consumers).
> **Operating costs.** Expenses incurred by a food and beverage operation in the course of generating revenues. For example, an operation must pay for the food (one type of operating cost) that must be prepared and served.
> **Sales.** The activities related directly to the delivery of menu offerings to potential and current guests (consumers).

Figure 1-2 illustrates the concept of the menu as an important sales tool. Note the many ways a hotel can promote the use of its restaurant to its guests. Creative menu planners in all foodservice segments can find many ways to use information from their menus to promote their offerings. A properly designed menu communicates information (such as hours and days of operation, telephone and facsimile numbers, and e-mail addresses) and

advertises special features (for example, messages about upcoming events, popular offerings such as Friday night seafood buffets, or the property's excellent reputation for private parties).

Figure 1-2.  **Foodservice Cross-Selling in a Hotel**

| Menu Location | Menu Information |
|---|---|
| Front desk | Restaurant signage, daily specials |
| Room key envelope | Restaurant hours, locations |
| Hotel lobby | Stand-up signs, pictures |
| Hotel elevator | Pictures, sample menus |
| Guestroom (table top) | Daily, weekly, monthly "Specials" menu, room-service menu |
| In-room guest directory | Room-service and actual restaurant menus and hours of delivery |
| In-room door hangers | Room-service, breakfast menus |
| In-hotel television channel | Lounge, restaurant menus |
| Lounge cocktail napkins | Restaurant hours, location |
| Lounge matches | Restaurant hours, location |

An example of the menu as an advertising tool is shown in Figure 1-3. There, a private club advertises the menu for an upcoming gourmet wine dinner. Guests (club members) are invited to make reservations for the event and, as well, they are shown other food-related events planned for the club. This is an example of internal **cross-selling.** You will find many examples of cross-selling throughout this book.

While Chapter 2 will focus on the customers in greater detail, you should now understand that the menu is, in fact, the single most significant marketing tool available to any food and beverage operation, whether commercial or noncommercial.

*Glossary Terms*
**Cross-selling.** Tactics used by the menu designers to advertise other products and services offered by the food and beverage operation in addition to those offered on a

specific menu. For example, a dinner menu may alert readers about the property's Sunday buffet; a college menu planner may use signage in the cafeteria to alert students that they can order pizzas for delivery to the residence hall rooms.

## The Menu Is a Financial Tool

Commercial food and beverage operations want to make a profit from the sale of food and beverage products to customers. These profits will, hopefully, be equal to or greater than any alternative investment opportunities available to the business's owners and investors. A menu that offers what the guests want at a price they are willing to pay is essential to this objective. Chapter 5 will discuss in more detail menu-pricing tactics that focus on the property's financial goals.

Noncommercial foodservice operations also have financial goals. But while there may not be a profit goal, most if not all are concerned about minimizing expenses. Budgets dictate

Figure 1-3. **The Menu as an Advertising Tool**

Used with permission of the University Club, Michigan State University, Lansing, Michigan.

this "breakeven" goal. (*Note:* Some noncommercial operations have budget deficits, which must be defined to determine the extent to which organizational funds will be contributed to offset foodservice-related costs.)

Many noncommercial foodservice programs offer a **cash cafeteria operation**. The menu affects the **revenue** levels generated in these operations, which in turn influence the number of meals prepared (production volumes). Thus, the menu also has a significant impact on the extent to which the financial goals of noncommercial foodservice operations are realized.

---

*Glossary Terms*

**Cash cafeteria operation.** Foodservices in noncommercial operations in which some or all of the food and beverage products are sold for cash. For example, a college cafeteria may accept meal tickets with debit balances from students and cash for purchases by faculty members in the same cafeteria line. Alternatively, the cafeteria in a business and industry setting may accept cash only in a specific dining area even though all consumers must be employees of the organization.

**Revenue.** The amount of money generated from the sale of food and beverage products and other services offered by the food and beverage operation. (*Note:* The term "revenue" should not be confused with another term, "sales," which refers to the number of units of a product sold to guests. For example, a restaurant will have revenues of $25 if it sells five sandwiches at a selling price of $5 each.)

---

## The Menu Is an Operating Control Tool

Much of the rest of this chapter focuses on the numerous ways in which a menu impacts the day-to-day operations of a food and beverage operation. From purchasing items (for example, food ingredients dictated by the menu) to cleaning up (for example, discarding unconsumed food and beverage products), the menu plays an integral role in every aspect of the **front-of-the-house** and **back-of-the-house** operations of the food and beverage organization.

---

*Glossary Terms*

**Back-of-the-house.** The kitchen, storage areas, and other traditionally nonpublic spaces within a food and beverage operation; also referred to as "heart-of-the-house."

**Front-of-the-house.** The dining room, public rest areas, guest waiting area, and all other areas of the food and beverage operation that can be accessed by the establishment's customers.

---

We have briefly discussed marketing aspects of menu planning and design and will do so in great detail in Chapter 2. But it is important to emphasize again here that careful consideration must be given to marketing issues because significant operating problems arise when the menu planners make errors. The food and beverage ingredients and products *thought* to be desired by customers, but which really are not, must still be purchased, received, stored, issued, pre-prepped, prepped, and held for serving. Unfortunately, unless these unpopular items are made to order, they may be discarded or will likely deteriorate in quality if unused portions are held for service at a later time, becoming even less desirable!

Some, especially commercial, food and beverage operations offer menus that appear to be planned without any thought to customer preferences. Menus that offer hundreds (or more!) of choices might be interesting for the readers to look at. ("Boy, how can they make all of these things?") But in fact they may also suggest that the menu planners did not know guest preferences and felt a need to "offer something for everyone" so as not to displease their customers (whose needs were never defined!). Menu planners must carefully study past selection preferences because they will likely show patterns of food choices that could help focus menu-planning efforts. In the process, this would reduce operating problems and associated costs that arise when time, money, and effort arc unwisely spent.

Similar problems occur in some bar or lounge operations where the variety of **call brands** offered greatly exceeds those most frequently requested. Does a beverage operation need twenty or thirty brands of Scotch whiskey, for example? An analysis of what is sold to guests (and what has been purchased by the operation!) will reveal the most popular brands and those that might be omitted from the back bar selection.

> *Glossary Terms*
> **Call brand.** A high-quality (and, therefore, more expensive) brand of liquor that, in many operations, is sold only when the specific brand name is requested. In addition to the house brand (sometimes called the speed rail, pour, or well brand), some properties offer a third tier—premium—of still higher quality (and cost) brands for their more discriminating guests.

## TYPES OF MENUS

When some people think about types of menus, they think about meal periods (breakfast menu, lunch menu, and dinner menu, for example) or types of food items (appetizer menu or wine menu, for example). Others might think of where the food and beverage products are offered (dining room menu, room-service menu, or bar menu, for example). These are all acceptable ways to organize and to think more specifically about the domain of menu planning discussed in this book.

Another way to think about the menu is to consider how items are priced and the frequency with which thcy are offered. Four examples are **à la carte**, **table d'hôte**, **cyclical**, and **du jour**.

> *Glossary Terms*
> **À la carte menu.** A meal chosen item by item; each item is priced separately.
> **Table d'hôte menu.** A meal composed of menu items offered at a fixed price.
> **Cyclical menu.** A menu in which items are offered on a repeating (cyclical) basis.
> **Du jour menu.** A menu featuring items that change daily.

### À la Carte Menu

The term "à la carte" is a French term that refers to a meal in which guests select the individual items. Items are prepared to order and are priced individually. For example, a guest in a hotel restaurant that offers an à la carte dinner menu typically orders and may be charged separately for an appetizer, entrée (with salad and potato or vegetable), and dessert. A customer in a cash cafeteria operation in a school would self-serve and pay for each desired item separately.

### Table d'Hôte Menu

The French term "table d'hôte" refers to a meal composed of menu items offered at a fixed price. In this case, the guest of the hotel restaurant would pay a set price for all the items ordered if the hotel offered a table d'hôte menu. The consumer in the school cash cafeteria operation might likewise select a "dinner special" composed of an entrée, one or more accompaniments, and, perhaps, dessert and a beverage for a fixed price.

### Cyclical Menu

The term "cyclical" refers to the cycle or frequency with which a specific menu is repeated.

Cyclical menus are often used in noncommercial foodservice organizations where, for example, college students may be consuming all or most of their meals on site. To reduce boredom while, at the same time, reducing the need for menu planners to plan new menus daily, a cyclical (or cycle) menu might be used. For example, at Michigan State University there are two residence hall cycle menus (a "Green" menu and a "White" menu—the university's colors) that are repeated every five weeks. A student may choose between the "Green" menu in his or her own residence hall or may go to another residence hall that offers the "White" menu. During holiday periods, for residence hall special occasions, and for other special events, the normal cycle menu might be replaced by food offerings appropriate for the occasion.

## Du Jour Menu

The French term "du jour" means of the day. In other words, a du jour menu changes daily. Some operations, especially **high check average** commercial operations, may offer only several items daily, which change based on the quality of the ingredients that the proprietor or chef can procure at the market that day. Numerous foodservice operations offer "daily specials" such as soup du jour, seafood du jour, or coffee du jour.

***

*Glossary Terms*
**High check average**. Relates to the average price a guest pays for a meal; a guest consuming a meal in a high check average restaurant (such as a hotel's roof-top dining room) pays more, on average, than a guest in that hotel's coffee shop.

***

These four menu types are not exclusive. Food and beverage operations frequently offer combinations of more than one type. Consider, for example, the restaurant with an à la carte menu that has a du jour (special-of-the-day) salad, soup, and entrée, and the restaurant with a table d'hôte menu that changes daily (du jour). As already noted, a noncommercial facility can offer a cyclical menu but charge (on an à la carte basis) cash for some consumers who use the service.

## A CLOSE LOOK AT THE MENU-WRITING TEAM[2]

Who writes the menu? The best "answer" is "it depends!" Many factors affect the answer. Different foodservice establishments have different methods of assigning this responsibility, so the persons involved may vary among them. The first principle in effective menu writing, however, is the same: No one person writes the menus; it should be a team. (Generally, no single person has sufficient knowledge of all the needed facts about an operation; therefore, a team is needed.)

In a large hotel with a substantial food and beverage volume, the menu-writing team will include the food and beverage director (manager), the executive chef, the food and beverage controller, the purchasing agent, and the dining room manager. The **banquet** manager and the head of the **catering** department would also be members.

***

*Glossary Terms*
**Banquet**. Relating to setting the room for a group function and for preparing and serving the food required for the event.
**Catering**. Relating to selling a banquet event. In small operations, catering is a function of the marketing and sales department. In a large property, catering may be organized as a separate department.

***

[2] Adapted from Richard Hug and M. C. Warfel, *Menu Planning and Merchandising*, second edition. Richmond, Calif.: McCutchan Publishing Corporation, 1987, pages 67-75.

By contrast, in a small hotel, the menu-writing team will likely include the hotel's general manager, the food and beverage manager, the chef, the food and beverage controller, the purchaser, and the dining room manager (or receptionist/host/hostess). In a free-standing restaurant, while the employees' titles may differ from those used in a small hotel ("accountant" rather than "food and beverage controller," for example), the menu-writing team will likely involve the same individuals needed to plan the menu in the small hotel.

In a hospital, the team will likely include members of the dietary department (food-service director, dietitian, and foodservice manager) along with others (for example, the purchaser and business manager). Non-commercial facilities using a **contract food management company** often employ a **liaison,** who will review and approve menus planned by the management company's corporate staff and modified, perhaps, by the on-site management team.

> *Glossary Terms*
> **Contract food management company.** A for-profit foodservice organization retained by some noncommercial facilities to operate their foodservice program.
> **Liaison.** An employee of a noncommercial organization (often with commercial foodservice training and experience) who represents the organization in interactions with a contract food management company.

## The Food and Beverage Manager and the Chef

The food and beverage manager and chef must be involved in the menu- writing process for obvious reasons—these individuals should have a great deal of expertise in the process and are responsible for the success of the food and beverage operation (which, as already noted, is impacted by the menu).

## The Purchasing Agent

One of the principal duties of the purchasing department is to research market conditions and prices. The results of this research can be vital to the menu-writing process. Much of the operation's cost efficiency will depend on the accuracy of market research.

Hotels and restaurants with banquet business can use market information from the purchasing agent to great advantage, since banquet menus may be tentatively priced at the time the guest requests the banquet services. Banquet managers can also help guests make economical choices of foods if they know the current market prices and availability of items. The purchasing agent can advise about foods that are in short supply, out of season, of poor quality, or overpriced.

## The Food and Beverage Controller

The sales histories of menu items are vital to the menu-writing team. These histories are gathered in a variety of ways. In most operations today, electronic data machines provide this information. Regardless of the method used, the food and beverage controller must collect and provide this information when needed. In the menu-writing process, sales history information is necessary to help balance the items needed to properly distribute the workload among the cooking stations. The food and beverage controller's primary responsibility and principal contribution is to supply the cost information on individual items being considered for inclusion in the menu. The food purchaser supplies the raw costs, but the food and beverage controller must supply the portion costs.

## The Dining Room Manager

This staff member has direct contact with the customers—the all-important group for whom the menu is being created. The dining room manager can funnel customer feedback to the menu-writing team. What does the customer say about the menu selections?

Format? Pricing? Color? This feedback is crucial, especially at menu-revision sessions.

### The Banquet Manager

The menu-writing team for banquets should include the banquet manager and possibly one or more catering salespersons. In large hotels, the banquet manager should be on the menu-planning team when preset banquet menus are being prepared or revised. Also, banquet menus are in many instances developed item-by-item in a dialogue between the banquet manager and the guest. Even then, a review of a "draft" of this proposed menu by others on the team can help to identify and reduce operating problems that may arise as the menu is being produced and served.

## A CLOSE LOOK AT OPERATING CONCERNS

We have been emphasizing throughout this chapter that, in fact, the marketing, financial, and operational success of any type of food and beverage operation begins with the menu. In this section, we will discuss exactly how the menu impacts the management of resources in a foodservice operation's day-to-day activities. These resources are:

- labor (personnel)
- products (food and beverages)
- equipment (machinery)
- money
- time
- energy
- space
- operating procedures (methodology)

All foodservice organizations have access to some amount of the above resources. However, no menu-planning team has all of the above resources available in unlimited supply. The menu planner, then, must consider how to best use these limited resources in efforts to attain the marketing, financial, and operational goals. Let's look at how the menu impacts these resources.

### Labor

Food and beverage operations face a severe labor shortage in almost all areas of the country. It is often very difficult to find the required number of people to fill unskilled, entry-level positions. As the knowledge, skill, and experience requirements of personnel increase, the task of finding workers becomes even more challenging.

The menu directly impacts both the number and type of employees needed. Consider, for example, the need for a knowledgeable, skilled, and experienced chef to prepare delicate entrée sauces in some restaurants and for service staff trained in tableside food preparation in other operations. Contrast this with the lower level of knowledge, skills, and experience required for a cook and a cashier in quick-service restaurants.

The need for skilled and experienced personnel to produce the menu items is directly related to the type of products that are purchased. (Food and beverage products are discussed in the next section.) Assume, for example, that the menu planners believe that those being served would enjoy cheesecake as a dessert. A **make-or-buy analysis** should be undertaken to determine whether an acceptable-quality product is available as a **convenience food** or if an acceptable-quality cheesecake can be made only on site. If an acceptable-quality product can be purchased and if skilled staff (and the necessary equipment) are also available on site, the manager can begin to look at cost alternatives. However, if an acceptable-quality product cannot be purchased, it will have to be prepared on site if it is to be offered. Alternatively, if present food production staff do not have the necessary skills (or if equipment is not available), the product will need to be purchased if it is to be offered. (*Note*: Detailed information about convenience foods and make-or-buy analysis is presented in Chapter 3.)

---

*Glossary Terms*

**Convenience food.** A food item that has some or all of the labor built into it that otherwise would need to be provided on site.

**Make-or-buy analysis.** The process of objectively evaluating the quality and cost differences to the options of preparing a menu item on site, purchasing it in a convenience food form, or finishing it on site.

---

You can see, then, that the menu dictates the food items available to customers. If convenience-food alternatives are not available, these items will need to be produced by the operation's chefs, cooks, and other food-preparation employees or they cannot be offered.

An example from a restaurant's alcoholic beverage menu also illustrates this point. Consider, for example, restaurant and lounge operations that feature **point-of-sale** advertisements such as **table tents** or that request service staff to use **suggestive selling** techniques for specialty drinks. These specialty drinks can provide a restaurant operator with significant **contribution margins**, but they can become very disruptive to the operation.

Consider, for example, a beverage operation on a very busy night with many drinks being prepared for lounge and restaurant guests. What is the impact of this fast pace of production and service when an increased number of very labor-intensive drinks requiring use of a blender or layering of liqueurs of varying density must be produced? If these beverages are to be advertised on a beverage menu, the beverage menu planners must think about how they will be produced to the required quality standards without disrupting workflow. As well, bartenders will need to be trained in how to consistently produce these items to quality standards. The beverage menu does, in fact, impact labor in the beverage operation.

---

*Glossary Terms*

**Contribution margin.** The difference between the menu item selling price and the menu item food cost; the amount of revenue that remains after product costs are subtracted from the product's selling price. For example, a sandwich selling for $5 with a product cost of $1 will yield a contribution margin of $4.

**Point-of-sale.** Any on-site effort to influence the customer's purchase decision. This includes the use of table tents and suggestive selling.

**Suggestive selling.** Efforts made by a food and beverage server to increase sales of suggested items by offering these items to customers when orders are taken.

**Table tents.** Advertising messages typically folded to stand on the tables (sometimes they are inserted in transparent plastic sleeves) to promote sales of specified products or services to a guest while seated at a dining table.

---

## Products (Food and Beverages)

If a menu requires a food item (or the ingredients needed to prepare it), the item must be purchased and available on site. Conversely, if the menu does not offer a specific item (or the ingredients needed to prepare it), the product should not be purchased and will not be available on site. Details about product purchases are presented in Chapter 4 on purchase specifications.

## Equipment (Machinery)

The food-preparation methods suggested by the menu drive the need for the equipment the operation needs to produce and serve offered items. A menu offering deep-fried items, for example, requires a deep fryer on site; a menu indicating tableside food preparation requires that a wide variety of specialized (and expensive) equipment be purchased to deliver what the menu has promised.

Fortunately, much food-preparation equipment is multiuse. Ovens, griddles, grill tops, and steam equipment such as kettles and compartment steamer units can prepare a wide variety of foods. It is often unnecessary to purchase equipment for only one purpose.

Menus featuring a wide variety of fresh salads, soups, entrées, and other items made "from scratch" will likely require more on-site refrigeration, vegetable preparation, and food-handling work surfaces than will menus that do not offer these items. Likewise, when market forms of convenience foods are used for some or all of these items, less equipment is needed.

The issue of whether the menu drives equipment needs or the reverse (that is, the available equipment limits the food choices a menus offers) is a very serious consideration. At the time a kitchen is first designed it will likely have available all the equipment and associated workspaces required to produce the items required by the first menu, because the kitchen will be "designed around" the menu. However, over the years, the menu will likely change numerous times. The foodservice establishment incurs a significant expense when equipment is purchased or leased in order to prepare new food items. Often, it is difficult to find additional space to accommodate the equipment and, as well, there can be significant expenses for installation, ventilation, and related concerns that could easily be equal to or greater than the original equipment costs. For these reasons, menu planners frequently do not add menu items that require new equipment. (It is, instead, more likely that the operation will stop using a single-use piece of equipment if the current menu does not require its use.) We will discuss the menu's impact on layout and equipment in great detail in Chapter 3 on restaurant design.

## Money

A commercial foodservice operation must generate revenues equal to its allocated costs, with additional funds left over to satisfy the owners' and stockholders' investment requirements. Increasingly, noncommercial foodservice operations also have "bottom-line" goals to reduce subsidies that might otherwise be required by the parent facility for renovation, equipment purchases, and related foodservice operating and capital costs. Effectively planned and designed menus maximize revenue (in commercial operations) and participation (in many noncommercial facilities). At the same time, well-planned menus help the operation to minimize the expenses associated with purchasing and using the resources required to generate revenues. Therefore, the menu is again the key to success—whether one thinks of "money" as the revenue flowing into the operation, the costs associated with expending resources to generate the revenue, or ultimately the "bottom line."

## Time

Time, as we all know, is a very precious and limited resource. Menus have a significant influence on the amount of time required for food preparation. For example, some menu items might be cooked in large batches to save time; others must be cooked in small quantities to order for maximum quality. A significant amount of preparation time might be saved by buying some required menu items in a convenience food form. Other menu items might need to be made "from scratch."

Foodservice operations offering breakfast, lunch, and dinner menus have traditionally offered three completely different menus. In the "old days" eggs were for breakfast, sandwiches were for lunch, and heartier entrées were most popular for the evening meal. Today, for numerous reasons, customer preferences are changing, and this traditional "definition" of which items are appropriate for different meal periods is much less rigid. In fact, some operations feature a "California-style" menu in which the same items are offered for the entire time that the property is open (and some operate twenty-four hours daily!). To the extent that a wide variety of unique items is not required for each meal period, preparation labor can be reduced.

Menus also impact how managers use their work time. Menus offering large numbers of unpopular or unprofitable items cause management staff to invest time—better spent elsewhere—in purchasing, receiving, storing, and issuing these unnecessary items. As well, managers must spend unproductive time in developing reports and, sometimes, in taking corrective actions to increase customer acceptance of unpopular and unprofitable items.

### Energy

The cost of utilities needed for food preparation is of serious concern to all food and beverage managers in their efforts to reduce costs wherever possible without sacrificing their organization's quality standards. Make-or-buy analysis (noted above and discussed at length in Chapter 3) will address these and related costs in objective efforts to determine the very best way to produce and deliver items required by the menu.

### Space

We have already noted that the menu determines the need for equipment (which occupies space). Storage space is likewise affected. High check average properties offering extensive wine lists, for example, will require carefully designed and controlled (and expensive!) storage spaces to house all of the wines suggested by their "**bin lists**." While **just-in-time (JIT)** and related purchasing and receiving systems are becoming more commonplace, it is still relatively true that the more extensive the menu, the greater the storage needs.

*Glossary Terms*
**Bin lists.** A storage system for wine in which wines of a specific brand and type are stored in a specific place. Frequently, wine lists indicate the "bin number" in which the wine is located.
**Just-in-time (JIT).** A relatively recent food purchasing and receiving system in which products are ordered for receipt on the day of preparation and service to maximize product freshness, to reduce on-site storage space, and to reduce inventory carrying costs. These systems require an effective communication system between the purchaser and supplier and relatively large volumes of products for which purchase commitments are made in order for them to be considered cost-effective for either the purchaser or food supplier.

A popular menu encourages more guests to enjoy the operation's products and services. The space required for the dining room and food preparation and service areas, among others, is directly impacted by the volume of meals that are served and produced. Consider, for example, a mid-price steak house serving several hundred meals daily. If the menu were to change (for example, to seafood), it might be that, at least initially, guest counts would decrease significantly. The amount of required dining space would be much less, and this space, unfortunately, cannot be easily used for another purpose.

Service space is also affected by the menu. Dining rooms that offer "help-yourself" salad bars, for example, require space for the salad bar units. Dining rooms featuring tableside food preparation require wider aisles for server efficiency and guest safety.

### Operating Procedures (Methodology)

Procedures used to operate the food and beverage services are obviously affected by the menu—as demonstrated by our examples involving food preparation (make or buy; the use of convenience foods) and dining room service styles. The impact of the menu is far-ranging. Consider the uniforms of service personnel (tuxedos in a high check average property; much less formal attire in a quick-service operation). Training procedures provide another example: receiving staff must be trained to recognize the quality requirements of all incoming ingredients, and production staff must be trained to produce items required by the menu. As a final example, safety procedures are a much greater concern in kitchens with the potentially more dangerous food preparation equipment required by some menus. Consider, for example, a kitchen where steaks are being grilled over an open flame as compared to another facility where deli sandwiches are made with presliced meats and cheeses in a food preparation area containing no heat-producing equipment.

## Other Operating Concerns

The menu's impact on the resources available to the food and beverage operation has just been explored. Additional operating concerns, however, are significantly influenced by the menu. We will discuss four of these concerns next.

*Nutrition.* Historically, commercial foodservice operations have not been very concerned about nutrition. Managers have rationalized that their guests could select the items desired with a concern about nutrition only if the issue was of significant importance to the guest. By contrast, many noncommercial foodservice operators have always been concerned about nutrition. In some instances (such as correctional facilities, nursing homes, and some military installations), all (or almost all) of a consumer's meals are provided by the foodservice operator. The nutritional content of these meals is of obvious concern.

Today, many commercial foodservice managers recognize that serving nutritional food can give them a competitive edge. Nutritious menu items are increasingly found on the menus of commercial operations. Menus must be carefully planned to deliver nutritious meals to the guests desiring them (in commercial operations) and to the consumers needing them (in many noncommercial facilities). This topic will be discussed in greater detail in Chapter 6.

*Design and Décor.* Would a guest like to consume an Italian meal in a mock-up of a spaceship? How about a Western-themed meal in a monastery setting? While these are absurd questions with "no" as the obvious answer, some food and beverage managers have not appropriately addressed the consistency between their menu, food, and theme and the actual design and décor of the dining areas. Replacing pictures of Italian wines with pictures of cowboys and buffaloes when the theme changes from "Italian" to "Western" is not likely to satisfy today's guests who are looking for a dining "experience" rather than just a meal. The menu should, in fact, impact the design and décor of the restaurant and all of its front-of-the-house public areas. Guests want to consume their meals in an environment that is conducive to the enjoyment of the food and beverage products offered by the menu.

For many persons, the stereotype of a dining room in a noncommercial facility is that of a clean but drab facility. Out of necessity, common areas in these facilities may need to be multipurpose; they may be used for dining services during meal periods but be needed by staff members for other uses at other times. For example, in a public school the lunch period dining space may be used for recess in the morning and afternoon, for parent-teacher, scout, and community meetings in the evening, and even as a site to vote for candidates during elections. Operators of these facilities should recognize the importance of the foodservice experience to those whom they serve, and strive to make the dining area a pleasant place to eat.

*Cost Control.* **Cost control** efforts are impacted by the menu in many ways, as noted in the previous sections. Menus that minimize the number of ingredients to be purchased help the manager to control food costs; those that focus on a close set of labor skills for production and service help to control labor costs. Often, when "costs get out of hand," the problem can be traced to a menu with overwhelming choices, which does little to guarantee a successful food and beverage operation.

---

*Glossary Terms*

**Cost control.** A management responsibility that involves determining what costs should be, what they are, when they are excessive, and how to reduce them to planned levels without sacrificing quality standards.

---

*Long-Term Viability (Survival).* The unfortunate failure rate of many commercial food and beverage operations is well known. Also unfortunate is the number of other operations that remain open—but barely so. In the world of noncommercial foodservices, many previously self-operated programs have succumbed to operation by contract-man-agement companies. (*Note:* The decision about the use, if any, of contract-management companies is complicated and is well beyond the scope of this discussion. The authors' point is that while a noncommercial facility such as a hospital or college must remain open, there are alternatives to the management of its foodservice operation. In fact, a self-operated noncommercial foodservice unit can "go out of business" just like its counterpart in the commercial segment can.) Likewise, noncommercial facilities using one contract-management company may opt to switch to a competitive contract-management company. Thus, there is no segment of the vast foodservice industry where success is guaranteed.

Commercial food and beverage enterprises wish to generate income to achieve a profit sufficient to repay owners' and stockholders' investment in the business plus compensate them for the significant risk associated with the investment. Noncommercial facilities wish to assure that all goals of its foodservice program are, in fact, attained. No type of food and beverage operation can be successful unless the menu is successful—*It all starts with the menu.*

## THE MENU DEFINES YOUR OPERATION

Effectively planned and implemented, a menu can help to define the foodservice operation. What the menu tells the reader should be consistent with what the reader expects, not only about the food but also about the service, level of cleanliness, and general quality of the dining experience.

Menu planners can ask the following basic questions when reviewing the menu. Try asking these questions when you look at the menus in this text and the menus of restaurants you visit.

- What type of person is this menu trying to attract?

- How effective is the operation at communicating with the reader?
- Is the operation effective at "selling" itself? (Why should a person wish to dine at the property? What products does it want to sell?)
- What must be done for the foodservice operation to meet (or to exceed) the wants, needs, and desires of its customers)?
- Would you want to dine in this foodservice operation? Why or why not?
- What are the strengths of the foodservice operation?
- What are the weaknesses of the foodservice operation?

Any reader and, certainly, any experienced foodservice manager could ask many additional questions when evaluating a menu. The important point is, however, that menus do "speak" to those who read them. The message should be positive, making the reader want to experience all that the food and beverage operation has to offer.

Figure 1-4 shows the pivotal role of the menu in relation to other aspects of the foodservice operation. First, the menu must address the concerns of the customers. Customer demographics (age, gender, social class, income, and ethnicity, for example) must be addressed as the menu is planned. As well, menu planners must thoroughly understand the customers' wants and needs, concerns about pricing and value, and the purpose of the visit (if applicable). Nutritional concerns have long been important for

menus planned for consumers in noncommercial facilities and are becoming increasingly important to menu planners in commercial operations.

Second, several operating concerns directly impact the foodservice manager and staff. As noted in Figure 1-4 and the text, these factors include labor, product purchases, equipment, space (layout), time, energy, operating procedures, facility design and décor, sanitation, and cost control.

Finally, Figure 1-4 highlights the impact of the menu on the organization's financial success. Commercial operations desiring to make a profit and noncommercial operations desiring to minimize costs must achieve financial goals to have long-term viability. Financial success can come only as a result of a well-planned menu that changes to meet the changing needs of those being served.

## IN REVIEW: IT ALL STARTS WITH THE MENU

This chapter has explained that the success (or failure) of any foodservice operation can be traced to a successful (or an unsuccessful) menu. This chapter began by emphasizing *"It all starts with the menu,"* and it is very appropriate to end with the same observation.

Figure 1-5 presents a graphic summary of this chapter. As shown here, the menu helps to assure that both customers' standards and the foodservice operation's product and service quality standards are, in fact, consistently

met. Meeting these standards helps assure the marketing, financial, and operational success of the operation. The process is, in fact, cyclical; to better assure continued marketing, financial, and operational success, the menu planners will need to revisit and, probably, revise the menu in efforts to assure that it "keeps up" with the changing preferences and demands of the customers for whom it is planned.

Figure 1 4.   **The Menu Addresses Guest, Operating, and Financial Concerns**

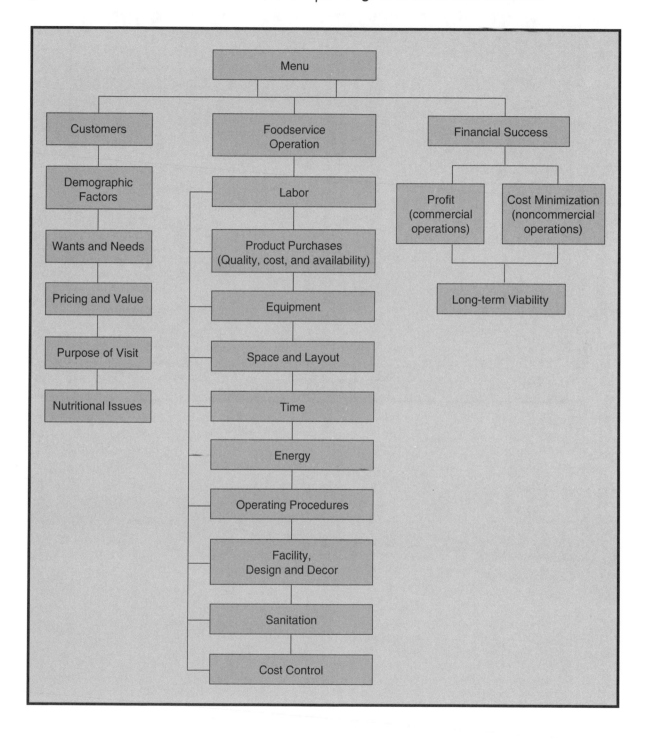

Figure 1-5.   **It All Starts with the Menu**

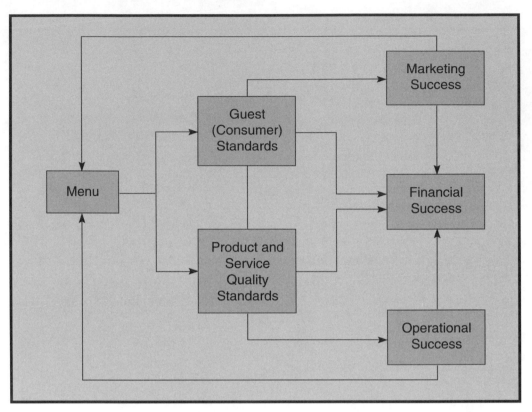

[*Note:* At the end of each chapter of this text, we will learn about the process of developing "Sigee's Menu" to illustrate concepts present in each chapter.]

## SIGEE'S MENU: A CASE STUDY

"This will really be a challenge," thought David Berger. As a graduate of the Hospitality Management Program at State University and a restaurateur for over ten years, David was not new to the menu-planning process. Now the newly hired food and beverage director of a mid-priced, 350-room, full-service hotel, he knew his skills would really be put to the test. He had been asked during his job interview if he could evaluate the hotel's current menu o¬erings and realign them with the goals of the hotel's new owners and general manager. David had assured the interviewer that he could do so. He knew he was up to the task, he was excited, but he also knew there was much work to be done.

Step one was to meet with Peggy Sill, the hotel's new general manager (GM), as well as the hotel's new owners, to get a complete understanding of what was expected. During that meeting, the GM was especially emphatic about the direction that should be taken by "Sigee's," the hotel's full-service restaurant. "What we want to do," said Peggy, "is completely re-evaluate all of our menu offerings." She went on to say that she wanted the hotel to be known for "Excellent food at traveler-friendly prices."

"And it's important," she continued "that we deliver on that promise. David, I want you to look at everything we are doing now, and recommend new menus that reflect this new direction. And I'd like you to start right away!"

As they continued to talk, David began to better understand the vision the general manager had for the hotel's food and beverage department. "Our weekly business traveler," said Peggy, "is an important segment of our business, but the couples and families traveling on the weekends are important too. I want a menu that is appealing to both." For the rest of the two-hour meeting, David and the GM discussed her views about how the food and beverage department could help the hotel's sales and marketing department better sell the property's products and services, expand the hotel's image in the local community, and, of course, contribute to the hotel's bottom line. "This menu revision is important, David," concluded Peggy, "and I'm counting on you to do it right!"

Back in his office in the kitchen, David picked up a copy of the dinner menu currently in use. It was large, and attractively printed. He carefully read the descriptions of two items.

*Chicken Nantaise* :   10 ounce lightly seasoned chicken breast stuffed with spinach and dill puree and finished with shallot butter sauce

$23.95

*Sirloin Saute:*   Extra thick and juicy, this 16 ounce New York Strip steak requires a little more broiling time than our regular steaks, but its worth the wait. Served with choice of potato.

$28.95

"Excellent food at traveler friendly prices?" he asked himself.  David was not sure.  He knew that the hotel's restaurant, while it was often busy when the hotel was full, had not, unfortunately, been an extremely popular dining spot even for the people living within a few miles of the hotel. David wondered why. He was, however, sure of one thing—the restaurant's menus would need to be re-evaluated, and perhaps changed dramatically, in light of the GM's new vision for the hotel's foodservice. And it was his responsibility to do the job right.

## CHAPTER 2

# The Marketing Aspects of Menu Planning and Design

## CHAPTER OUTLINE

## MENU TERMS USED IN THIS CHAPTER

Benchmark
Bidding
Continuous quality improvement (CQI)
Demographics
Direct competitors
Electronic point-of-sale (POS) system
Franchise

Indirect competitors
Market research
Penny profit
Psychographics
Shoppers' service
Signature items

## CHAPTER OVERVIEW

In Chapter 1 we showed that the menu is an important marketing tool. In this chapter we will explain that menu planners must keep *marketing* (defined in Chapter 1 as "the business from the perspective of guests") in mind as they develop the menu. Once developed, the menu remains an important marketing tool because it represents (or "positions") the foodservice operation to the guests.

Who is the guest? This chapter begins by

explaining that it is difficult to define the guests whom a new restaurant intends to serve or those whom an existing foodservice operation is already serving. However, defining exactly who the guests are and exactly what they want is extremely important in the menu-planning process. A wide range of demographic factors (i.e., personal characteristics) and psychographic factors (i.e., beliefs, opinions, and interests) can be used to describe the potential or the current guest market. This information must be collected and analyzed so that menu planners will have the best available information when planning the menu. In addition to carefully defining the target market, pricing strategies and location analysis are very useful components of the market research that must be done before the menu is developed.

Most foodservice operations face numerous indirect and, typically, at least several direct competitors. Who they are, where they are, and their weaknesses and strengths are important information to menu planners. Menu planners can use this information to design menus and the operating procedures to implement the menus so as to overcome the strengths and to emphasize the weaknesses of their competitors.

Several business philosophies can impact menu planning and the subsequent success or failure of the foodservice operation. These philosophies include attitudes and perceptions about the need for market research and analysis (the emphasis of this chapter) and about several other areas (including quality, financing, innovation, and pricing structure). While each of these other business views has some distinct advantages, they have more disadvantages. The chapter's intent is, then, to reaffirm the need to closely focus on the wants and needs of those in potential guest markets and to consistently deliver what these guests desire.

Another section in this chapter addresses the concept of menu evolution; the menu is never designed as the final answer to the question, "What do guests want?" Rather, the menu is evolutionary and will need revision as the marketplace changes and as the operation's resources that meet these wants and needs change.

Finally, this chapter focuses on special menu-marketing concerns. It begins by looking at how very large foodservice organizations manage their menus. It also addresses ways to monitor changes in guest preferences (which drive menu revisions) and the role that the menu plays on long- and short-term strategies for "managing" the competition.

## WHO IS THE GUEST?

Defined most simply, guests are those who purchase the products and services offered by the food and beverage operation. This definition, however, is often too simplistic. Consider, for example, a busy restaurant serving the following guests at the same time:

- Several businesspeople, each on a tight schedule, negotiating a contract
- A retired person enjoying a meal during what is normally one of the most pleasurable times of his or her day
- A family with young children

- A college-aged couple on a date
- A planning committee for a local community civic service group discussing ideas over a meal
- A married couple celebrating a special occasion

While all of these people are restaurant guests, the reasons for their visit—and what it will take to please them—are different and involve much more than a physiological need for food. While a well-planned commercial menu cannot offer "something for everybody," it must offer a range of products and services that will appeal to a large enough number of guests to assure the continued success of the operation.

Commercial menu planners have a marketing dilemma to consider—when they plan a new menu for a new operation should they plan a menu that attempts to attract a certain group of people not currently being served or should they try to attract a group of people who may not be satisfied with the available competitive alternatives (in this case the menu planners would consider products and services to attract these guests away from the competitors)? This dilemma is easily solved: Commercial menu planners do not "plan a menu and wait for the guests to come"; rather, **market research** should be done to determine who prospective guests might be—and what they prefer in food and beverage products and services. Then, the menu is designed to address these wants and needs, and, as stated throughout Chapter 1, most other planning and operating concerns will be driven by these menu decisions.

Menu planners in noncommercial foodservice operations typically must work with the reverse situation: A group of individuals with food and beverage product and service needs is already affiliated with the facility. This group is, initially, more narrowly defined. For example, potential guests are the faculty, staff, and students in an educational facility; physicians, staff, visitors, and others in a cash-cafeteria operation in a hospital; and enlisted personnel and officers in a military club. In these and related instances, the consumer group to be served is defined. However, *exactly* what the group desires as a whole is not known, and the preferences of individuals within the group may be very dissimilar. Therefore, menu planning in the noncommercial sector still requires market research. (*Note*: Market research will be discussed in detail in a later section of this chapter.) Even in noncommercial operations, careful market research is necessary because in most of

these facilities prospective diners are not captive—they may choose other foodservice alternatives.

---

*Glossary term*
**Market research.** The process of identifying ways to improve the food and beverage operation to more consistently deliver products and services that meet (or exceed) the organization's standards.

---

Even when menu planners know the types of guests the operation will serve, their work is difficult. For example, a restaurant may cater to residents of the "local neighborhood" or to affluent travelers (for example, in a high-check-average restaurant in a tourist destination). Diversity among the neighborhood residents and among the travelers visiting the area means that further study regarding the needs of the potential market of diners (those living in the neighborhood and those traveling to the area) will still be necessary.

The issue of diversity within a market also affects the noncommercial menu planner. The "market" may be students or nursing home residents, but significant differences among the members of these different populations still provide opportunities and challenges for the menu planners. For example, the group of students may include a large number of international students with different cultural backgrounds (which, in turn, influence dietary preferences). Similarly, the group of nursing home residents will likely include persons of different ages, of different ethnic backgrounds, and with different medical conditions that require special dietary attention.

Figure 2-1 reviews this flow of menu-planning concerns from one broad base of a potential market to a more focused set of specific guests most likely to use the products and services of the food and beverage operation. While reviewing Figure 2-1, assume that commercial menu planners think that the restaurant should meet the needs of two types of travelers—those traveling on business and those visiting the area for leisure or other personal reasons.

The needs of the business traveler are likely to differ from those of the leisure traveler. For example, business travelers may be less concerned about costs because the meal may be a business expense. Business travelers may come from all over the country (or world) and, therefore, they will likely have very diverse preferences for menu items and cooking methods. They may enjoy fine wine with their meals and may enjoy appetizers and "gourmet" desserts.

By contrast, the leisure traveler, spending personal funds and perhaps traveling with children, may be very concerned about costs, may be from the local region (because automobile travel is less expensive), and may be less interested in fine wines, appetizers, and gourmet desserts.

In this example, planning a menu that will appeal to generic "travelers" is not a sound strategy. It is critical to determine more specifically *who* is traveling to the community, *what* food and beverage experiences they prefer, and *how much* they are willing to pay for that experience.

Figure 2-1.    **Example of Marketing Challenges for the Menu Planner**

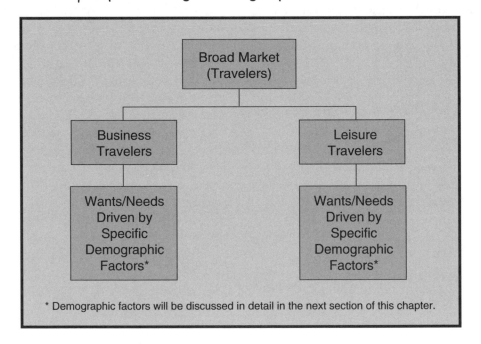

MARKET RESEARCH AND MENU DEVELOPMENT _____

The first step in determining what should be served on the menu is to identify who will be served. It makes little sense, for example, to plan a menu containing only the dishes the chef, owner, or manager likes if the guests who will be served do not also prefer those items. It is guest preference then, *not* opera-

tor preference, that must drive the menu-planning process. Even in noncommercial segments of the foodservice industry, including education and healthcare, the likes, the dislikes, and the needs of those being served must be considered before menus are planned.

For a new restaurant, the question of what guests prefer on the menu is difficult to answer because there are no current guests to question about likes and dislikes. Then it becomes even more important that the menu planners know about the demographics of their potential guests. Demographic information can be obtained by thoroughly researching the local market.

In addition to identifying the guests to be served, menu planners must also identify those competitors who seek to attract and serve the same guests. The restaurant business is very competitive. Those guests who enjoy existing restaurants may "experiment" by visiting a new one. (In fact, in many communities new properties are initially overwhelmed with guests who want to be among the first served. Unfortunately, the inability to handle large guest counts because staff are new and because procedures are yet to be learned can cause guests to leave with negative impressions.)

Frequent diners will not consistently consider different dining alternatives without good reason. A well-executed, creative, original menu served in an appropriate setting can provide such a reason. It is up to the menu planners, however, to know what competitors are offering and what could make guests select the menu offerings of a new restaurant over those already operating. Once the potential guests have been identified and the restaurants currently serving them have been analyzed, it is possible to make good decisions about what items to offer on the menu.

As we have mentioned before, a single menu should not attempt to be "all things to all people." Some diners want a French-style, table-service dining experience, while others prefer a carryout pizza—and one restaurant should not try to provide both. Instead, the menu planners must narrow the focus of who should be served at their establishment and concentrate on serving them well. The best menus are those where the menu planners have considered all variables; these menus feature items that the operator can consistently produce to quality standards and that appeal to the majority of guests.

## Identifying the Target Market

The best menus are written by people who know their market. Menu planners must therefore consider guest **demographics** and **psychographics,** which will affect the items sold and the prices at which they sell. In days gone by (and even today in some smaller communities), the restaurant operator personally knew many of his or her guests. In small restaurants, the owner can greet and seat the guests, and supervise the production of their food. In large, corporate-owned restaurants, however, the menu directly communicates the personality of the restaurant. In these cases, however, the menu must still reflect the desires of the guests. It is important then, that the target market for the menu be clearly identified before it is written.

---

*Glossary Terms*
**Demographics**. Characteristics of a population (such as a restaurant's potential guests), which, if known, can help the menu planners to better meet that market's wants and needs.
**Psychographics**. A system to measure the beliefs, opinions, and interests of consumers.

---

*Description of the Target Market*. It is fairly easy to understand that the food preferences of a ten-year-old boy are likely very different from those of a male senior citizen. It may be less easy to understand, but just as true, that the menu preferences of individuals within the group of "male senior citizens" also vary. Therefore, menu planners who want to attract male senior citizens to their restaurants have just begun the target-market definition needed to construct a successful menu.

Male senior citizens, just as all individuals, come from a variety of ethnic backgrounds and have a wide range of income levels. Their religious backgrounds differ, and they live in geographically diverse regions of the country. The foods they grew up with vary, as do their food preferences. They are single, married, divorced, or widowed. Some have children; some do not. They enjoy casual or formal dining experiences. Clearly, menu planners who seek to serve male senior citizens must know more than just the ages of their potential guests before they can develop a menu that attracts the guests.

A variety of demographic characteristics can help to identify different guest types. Among the most important of these characteristics to the menu planner are the following:

- *Age.* The ages of the potential guests.
- *Average household income.* The combined income of all persons in the household fifteen years of age and older, whether or not they are related to one another.
- *Average household size.* Calculated by dividing the number of persons living in households in the target region by the number of households.
- *Ethnic background.* The specific ethnic origin of a person. The main groups are Caucasians, Blacks, Asian/Pacific Islanders, and Spanish or Hispanic. (*Note:* Persons of Hispanic origin may be of any race. Ethnicity can be viewed as the ancestry, nationality group, lineage, or country of birth of the person or the person's parents.)
- *Gender.* Male or female.
- *Lifestyle.* Individual characteristics such as married or unmarried, with or without children in the household, and a variety of other personal preference characteristics that influence dining behavior.
- *Personal income.* An individual's annual wages, salaries, and other sources of money.
- *Race.* Determined by an individual's self-classification as the race with which he or she most closely identifies.

People can be classified in any number of ways in order to determine those to whom the menu should appeal. Consider, for example, a restaurant located across the street from a major shopping mall. The guests who will be visiting the restaurant are likely to come from a wide variety of backgrounds; they will consist of many demographic types and represent various ethnicities. Many of these otherwise diverse guests may, however, share the characteristic of seeking a moderately priced dining out experience that they could enjoy while dressed in the clothes they wear shopping. It is the job of the menu planners to identify the common characteristics of future guests.

The best target market research also considers psychographic information. Psychographics is a system for measuring a person's beliefs, opinions, and interests. It is similar to demographics; however, instead of identifying characteristics such as age, gender, and race, it identifies people based on psychological information such as opinions about politics, religious beliefs, music tastes, personality traits, and other items. Common areas of psychographic identification include the following:

- *Activities*
    work
    hobbies
    social events
    vacations
    club memberships
    community
    shopping
    sports
- *Interests*
    family
    home
    job
    recreation
    fashion
    food
    achievements
- *Opinions*
    politics
    business
    economics
    education
    future
    culture

A target market must be large enough to support the planned restaurant. Fortunately, in most cities, the local chamber of commerce will provide demographic and psychographic data about the area to new business ventures as part of their member services. (To find the address of the chamber of commerce that serves your area, go to http://www.chamber ofcommerce.com/.) The U.S. Census Bureau and the business departments of some local colleges and universities also provide market information, including the size of various demographic components.

In addition to identifying demographic and psychographic information about the potential markets to which the menu should be directed, a description of the target market should always indicate the size of that market. There may, for example, be people in the community who would enjoy the offerings of a sushi bar, but the menu planners must determine if there are enough of these individuals to financially sustain the menu concept. Once a guest base has been identified and defined and after it has been determined that this base is large enough to support a food and beverage operation, the menu planners must next consider the pricing strategy that will be used.

***Pricing Strategy.*** Menu prices are affected by many factors, including the cost of ingredients and labor, the prices charged by competitors, and the desire to achieve a predetermined profit or to stay within a budget. A menu communicates not only the item's prices but also a pricing strategy consistent with the entire restaurant concept. This strategy will attract a target guest.

For example, consider a quick-service, take-out establishment that serves burgers and fries at prices charged in a table-service restaurant. The restaurant concept is inconsistent with the pricing strategy. Potential guests will not only be confused but might perceive a lack of value. ("Why," they are likely to think, "should I eat there and pay the same price as

at a nice restaurant, but receive no service?") Unless the menu planners can convince the target guest that the quick-service restaurant offers something special to justify charging table-service restaurant prices, this "same price" strategy will not work.

When items are properly priced, guests will be better able to equate the prices charged with the quality of products and environment they receive. As a result, they are more likely to perceive that they have received a fair value for their dining dollar. An important part of identifying the target market is to firmly establish the pricing strategy.

For the purpose of establishing pricing strategy, commercial foodservice menus can be divided into four distinct groups:

- Value-priced menus
- Family-priced menus
- Moderate-priced menus
- Upscale-priced menus

Value-priced menus attract a guest who seeks speedy service, consistent food quality, and accurately filled food and beverage orders. Of course, these guests also seek the very low prices offered by these value menus. Many quick-service restaurants with counter and drive-through (window) services feature this pricing structure. They appeal to those on a limited budget and those in a hurry, such as families who want to minimize eating-out expenses. But even here, good food quality is important—successful restaurant chains have created excellent, low-priced menus that consistently attract and retain their target market.

Family-priced menus attract guests who seek clean dining or service areas, unique foods, fast service, consistently good quality, and high perceived value. These guests may or may not have low incomes. This menu segment is one of the most popular among all diners because, while many guests may choose to dine at these clean, comfortable table-service restaurants, increasing numbers of patrons are buying carryout food from these restaurants to eat at home. This market purchases carryout food frequently, recognizes quality, and will become loyal guests if the menu consistently provides the value promised.

Moderate-priced menus attract guests who seek timely service, an attractive setting, and a "dining experience" in addition to the food purchased. Consider, for example, a common menu item—the hamburger. This menu item is popular in a wide variety of restaurants and at a variety of prices. Value-priced menu diners enjoy the item because of its cost. Family-priced menu guests also like the quality they receive when purchasing burgers. Moderate-priced menu guests also like the burger but would expect it to be made with fresh ingredients, served in a creative setting by knowledgeable and efficient servers, presented attractively, and prepared in a manner that justifies its higher price. While all restaurants should provide quality service, moderate-priced restaurants must especially ensure that good service and friendly staff are a mainstay of their establishments. A dining experience includes more than just food, so moderate-priced restaurants must have the good service and inviting atmosphere that will reinforce the perceptions of the restaurant's patrons that they are receiving a high-value dining experience.

Upscale-priced menus attract a market that seeks exceptional food quality, unique settings, and far-above-average service levels. Not just the wealthy and those dining on expense accounts visit these restaurants. Diners at all income levels visit upscale restaurants for special occasions such as birthdays, anniversaries, and other celebrations. While many individuals enjoy upscale food dishes, it is important to recall that upscale-priced restaurants must also appeal to the emotional needs of their clientele. This means that restaurant operators must consider this market's desires for "the best" in food quality and service and attention to detail. As well, the purpose of the guests' visit must be recognized.

Knowledge of the potential guests' income levels and what they want to pay is critical to a restaurant's success. There must be a sufficient number of guests available to support the restaurant. This is especially true with moderate- and upscale-priced restaurants. Identification of the target market includes a recognition of the impact that pricing strategy will have on the size of the target market.

*Location Analysis.* Experts have long debated the importance of location to the success of a restaurant. On the one hand are those who say that the three most critical factors in a restaurant's success are "location, location, location." Alternatively, nearly everyone knows of an "out-of-the-way place" that serves great food and, because it does, guests drive miles to visit it.

Despite the debate, the fact remains that physical location is an important consideration when menu planners begin to identify their target markets. In some cases, the location decision is made for the food and beverage manager. For example, a country club manager planning a menu knows the location of the intended service. However, decisions must still need to be made about indoor and outdoor venues, formal dining rooms, family and golf-access dining, snack bar service, and, often, numerous other food and beverage alternatives. For the menu planners responsible for choosing a new business site, the location decision is much more complex and includes considerations such as automobile or foot traffic patterns, population density levels, visibility, and convenient entrances and exits.

The impact of location on determining the target market can best be viewed from both macro- and microperspectives. From a macroperspective, experienced menu planners know that the food preferences of target guests are determined in part by where those guests live. In the United States, for example, the Pacific Northwest and the Coastal South are the largest centers of fish consumption. By contrast, the Midwest and Southwest consume more beef and chicken per capita. Pizza restaurants, while popular everywhere in the United States, are strongest in the Northeast (home to a large southern and eastern European immigrant population where this menu item originated). It is not surprising to learn that Mexican-style food, while popular throughout the United States, is most liked in the West and Southwest. These examples simply illustrate that the geographic location of a restaurant helps determine the menu: The location will draw business from a group of guests who have pre-established food preferences, while it may also attract travelers to the area.

It is critical that the target market be identified prior to the development of the menu. The characteristics of potential guests, the menu price levels to which they will best respond, and the physical location of the restaurant must all be considered prior to writing the menu. After menu planners review their target guests, they must then identify their competition.

## Identifying Competitors

Some foodservice operators feel that anyone who serves food should be considered a competitor. This is not the case. Many establishments serve food and, therefore, could be considered indirect competitors. To say, however, that a grocery store's carryout deli counter competes with an upscale fine-dining establishment is to misunderstand the needs of the marketplace. The individual who purchases carryout food from a grocery deli or quick-service restaurant is seeking speed of service and ease of food preparation. The diner at an upscale restaurant is seeking the best in quality food, service, and, perhaps most important, recognition. For the menu planners, the critical element to consider is the number of **direct competitors,** not the number of **indirect competitors**.

*Glossary Terms*
**Direct competitors.** Those foodservice operations that offer similar menu items, at similar prices, and in similar settings to guests with similar needs.
**Indirect competitors.** Those operations that offer any type of food and beverage products and services.

As our glossary definition states, direct competitors are restaurants that "offer similar menu items, at similar prices, in similar settings to guests with similar needs." Consider, for example, a restaurant that seeks to offer high-quality, take-out pizza. Its direct competitors are other high-quality, take-out pizza restaurants in the area. However, other direct competitors would include take-out restaurants that offer different but similarly priced and equally popular items such as Oriental food, burgers, and deli sandwiches—because these restaurants may appeal to the same guest markets.

***Characteristics and Location of Competitors.*** It is important for menu planners to recognize which foodservice providers will compete directly with their menu. These competitors will have specific characteristics that can be identified. (For example, they may offer a similar cuisine.) Or, they may offer a similar dining experience. (For example, a mid-priced family-style restaurant may feature mainly fish items, but compete directly with a mid-priced family-style restaurant across the street that predominately features steak.)

The best way to identify direct competitors is, first, to list the characteristics of the foodservice operation for which the new menu is being planned. For example, the owner of a new restaurant in the downtown area of a mid-sized city might list the following attributes of the restaurant:

• Cuisine
• Product quality levels
• Service quality levels

- Menu-pricing strategy
- Number of seats
- Meals served (breakfast, lunch, dinner)
- Hours of operation
- Management quality
- Special features (live entertainment, bar, etc.)

Then, the same process should be used to define the restaurant's location. Significant location characteristics may include:

- Proximity to population centers
- Ease of access
- Parking
- Allowed signage
- Street visibility
- Exterior building appearance
- Interior and entrance appearance

The next step in the process of identifying competitors is to analyze the strengths and weaknesses of your restaurant compared with those of its competitors.

*Analyzing the Weaknesses and Strengths of Competitors.* Most restaurants will have direct competitors—some of these competitors will compete very well and others less so because of poor management, food quality, or service. To truly understand a restaurant's best competitors, it is necessary to analyze them. This process begins by identifying operations that are direct competitors and continues with evaluating their weaknesses and strengths. Applying a ranking to each competitor's identifying characteristics is one way to effectively evaluate the competition.

Figure 2-2 is an example of a ranking scale that can be used to assign point values to each important characteristic identified by the evaluator. Figure 2-3 is an example of how this scale can be used to rank competitors by selected characteristics. The menu planners must select which characteristics to rank. In this example, menu planners are evaluating three competitors to a seafood restaurant being planned. If the menu planners honestly and objectively assign evaluation scores, critical information about each competitor's weaknesses and strengths will be obtained.

Figure 2-2.  **Strength and Weakness Scale**

```
5= Extremely strong
4= Strong
3= Average
2= Weak
1= Extremely weak
```

In Figure 2-3, the sample analysis shows that each competitor has weaknesses and strengths. Richardson's is clearly the strongest competitor to the proposed new restaurant; however, while strong in many categories, it is below average in seating capacity. Thus, providing more seating may give a competitive advantage to the proposed restaurant. Alternatively, Farley's Place, while weak in food quality and service, scores best of all the restaurants on ease of access and special features (perhaps because it offers music or some other form of regular entertainment). By analyzing the competitor's weaknesses and strengths, menu planners can gain valuable information about how the proposed menu can be developed to maximize operational effectiveness.

Figure 2-3. **Competitive Analysis Worksheet**

| Name of Operation | Richardson's | The Wharf | Farley's Place |
|---|---|---|---|
| **Operational Features** | | | |
| Product quality levels | 5 | 3 | 2 |
| Service quality levels | 5 | 3 | 1 |
| Price competitiveness | 4 | 3 | 3 |
| Seating capacity | 2 | 4 | 4 |
| Management quality | 4 | 4 | 1 |
| Special features | 1 | 1 | 5 |
| | | | |
| **Location Features** | | | |
| Proximity to population centers | 3 | 2 | 2 |
| Ease of access | 4 | 3 | 5 |
| Parking | 5 | 5 | 2 |
| Allowed signage | 5 | 4 | 3 |
| Street visibility | 5 | 2 | 2 |
| Exterior building appearance | 5 | 5 | 1 |
| Interior entrance appearance | 5 | 2 | 1 |
| | | | |
| Total Competitiveness Score | 53 | 41 | 32 |

A realistic competitive analysis is as important a part of the menu-planning process as is the process of identifying the target market. With a solid understanding of the target market and a thorough review of the competition, menu planners should be ready to use this market analysis data to develop the menu.

## Business Philosophies Impact Menu Planning

This section discusses five relatively common business philosophies that can shape organizations and, in the process, the menus that they will offer.

*Market Research and Analysis Philosophy.* Using a marketing research and analysis approach to help plan the menu is part of an overall management philosophy. This philosophy considers a thorough understanding of the wants and needs of the guests as the most critical key to success in business. Essentially, those who subscribe to this philosophy believe that a focus on the markets being served is the best foundation for making management decisions, including that of menu planning. While the wisdom of this philosophy may seem self-evident, it is not, in fact, a philosophy shared by all business professionals. There are other, competing philosophies that are shared by some managers within the food-service industry, including these four: quality philosophy, financing philosophy, innovator philosophy, and lowest-price philosophy.

*Quality Philosophy.* In this view of business, the quality of the product (including food, service, and décor) takes center stage. For example, proponents of this philosophy believe that focusing on the specific manner in which menu items are prepared and served is the key to the success of the restaurant. Interestingly, chefs, professional cooks, and those who are self-trained in the culinary arts often advocate the quality approach.

Recently, this approach to management has reached new levels of popularity. In fact, the investigation of quality has become a management topic in itself. The study of quality includes the definition of quality, how to attain and maintain it, how to improve it, and how to encourage employees and managers to strive for it.

While there is no question that quality food and beverage products are desirable, it is also important to remember that in the food business—unlike some other businesses—quality is directly related to price. Few would argue, for example, that guests would perceive that a hamburger steak (at a cost to the restaurant of $2.00 per pound) is of the same quality as a New York strip steak (at $8.00 per pound). This is not to suggest that the hamburger steak should not be prepared in a way to best ensure that it reaches the diner at the peak of its quality. Rather, the manager must recognize that quality is directly related to the ingredients purchased, to how those ingredients are handled, and to the selling prices that can ultimately be charged.

Quality is important, of course, and all experienced foodservice managers can think of a restaurant where the food or service was top quality. Serving quality food and beverage products should be the goal of every foodservice manager. However, even if the quality level sought by a manager who ascribes to the quality philosophy is consistently attained, that achievement must be effectively marketed to the guests who really care about the accomplishment.

In addition, these guests must be willing to pay for the quality levels produced, because in the restaurant business attention to details in food production and service comes with a price tag that not all diners are willing to pay. Of course, the success of chains such as Starbucks Coffee demonstrates that many guests are willing to pay higher prices for outstanding quality. If there are insufficient numbers of these guests or if guests are unaware of a restaurant's quality achievements,

the restaurant will not be successful regardless of its the menu.

***Financing Philosophy.*** Some foodservice managers believe that the key to success is how the restaurant is financed. Not surprisingly, this philosophy is often held by those with limited experience in the restaurant business but with extensive experience in investment, banking, or other financial areas. In addition, many who are financially successful in nonfoodservice businesses sometimes seek additional success in the restaurant business. Initial investor-related successes, however, often lead to business decisions that do not contribute to the long-term health of the venture.

Those familiar with the Planet Hollywood restaurant chain, a movie-themed restaurant group that entered Chapter 11 bankruptcy protection in 1999, will recognize this philosophy. Planet Hollywood offered upscale, higher-priced hamburgers (hamburgers are the single most popular menu item in the United States), sandwiches, and merchandise to diners, in a restaurant where the walls were covered with movie memorabilia. With their highly publicized openings, the concept first appeared wildly successful. However, guests seldom returned, and food quality was often not "upscale." Excited guests, after one or two visits, felt they had "seen" the concept (much like you would "see" a movie), and did not return. As a result, despite financial backing from many well-known actors, the restaurant chain did not enjoy the success of The Hard Rock Café, its chief competitor.

The original Boston Chicken franchise (now Boston Market), purchased in 2000 by a subsidiary of McDonald's Corporation for $173.5 million in cash and debt as it emerged from its 1998 bankruptcy filing, is another example of a poor business model that resulted in significant investor losses. Aggressive expansion and a high-quality but restricted menu resulted in weak sales that led to a cash shortage. This forced Boston Chicken to write off hundreds of millions of dollars in loans to franchisees who had borrowed to expand the chain.

There is no doubt that sound financing along with maximizing financial resources are critical to a successful restaurant business plan. It would be unwise, however, to believe that investors' money alone will replace a thorough knowledge of what diners seek on their first and (management hopes) many subsequent visits to a restaurant. Investors' money can disappear through operating losses or through withdrawals by the investors. Experience shows that loyal guests, however, will continue to frequent a foodservice operation that offers popular menu items at reasonable prices.

***Innovator Philosophy.*** Some managers believe that success in the restaurant business results from being viewed as the most innovative. Innovation (that is, to introduce something new) is an interesting concept that menu planners must carefully consider. Certainly some innovations, such as drive-through windows in quick-service restaurants and the use of touch screen electronic data machines to place orders in high-volume restaurants, have made a big impact on the foodservice industry. In addition, restaurants offering cuisines such as Cajun, Middle Eastern, and Thai—which have not traditionally been a large part of the American dining scene—can achieve great success among guests who want to experience these different offerings.

It is important to remember, however, that innovative foodservice operations that do not capture the loyalty of guests quickly fade from the scene. This may be because the innovation lacks staying power or because too many of these operations are built. An example is the rapid rise (and just as rapid demise) of many cookie-only restaurants, bagel stores, and, more recently, gourmet bread shops. While the best of these may flourish, it is important to remember that changes in food preferences, somewhat like changes in clothing fashions, occur rapidly.

Being the first in an area to offer a menu item or a complete restaurant concept may lead to success. However, the absence in the market of either of these possibilities may indicate that foodservice operators had considered the menu item or restaurant concept earlier but had determined that there was insufficient demand to support it. Guests may try new things easily, but unless the menu offers reasons to return regularly, the restaurant will not enjoy long-term success. The innovation philosophy should be carefully considered, and new ideas should be implemented when practical. However, it is clearly not a substitute for a thorough understanding of consumer behavior when the menu is planned.

***Lowest-Price Philosophy.*** One of the most common (and least understood!) operational philosophies is the lowest-price philosophy. Managers with this perspective believe that operators who can offer diners the lowest cost menu items will be most successful. Those who think about food as a commodity (like steel, paper, or plastic) often hold this operational viewpoint. Their reasoning is that guests, faced with the choice of two exactly equal food items (such as two different gallons of milk) will naturally select the less-expensive item. As a result, the focus of these operators is to reduce prices and to communicate the "low cost" of their items to guests.

In fact, this approach will appeal to a definable, but often rather small, market segment. This is true because, in reality, most people are sophisticated enough to realize that there is only a rare occasion when two food items are exactly equal. Many factors (not merely price alone) affect a guest's perception of value. Would McDonald's sell more hamburgers, even at a price higher than their competitors, if their bathrooms were impeccably clean? Yes, they would. Numerous factors in addition to price, then, affect guests' dining decision. Most guests intuitively know that menu prices are not merely what they pay for food and beverages; prices also reflect what they will receive from the entire dining experience.

Certainly foodservice managers must keep their costs under control. Guests should not be charged higher prices simply to subsidize managerial inefficiencies. Lowest price alone, however, is not the most important factor most persons consider when making critical decisions about which doctor to use, which automobile to buy, or where to take a vacation. Wise advocates of the lowest-price philosophy realize that the price paid for an item is, among other things important to guests, a powerful status symbol, an affirmer of self-worth, and an indicator of success. The inability of some managers to recognize these psychological aspects of price has caused many otherwise sound foodservice operations to fail.

Identifying a menu's proposed markets, discovering the needs and wants of those in the markets, and analyzing the competitors that the guests in these markets currently patronize form the core of market research and analysis. The process can be as complex as that faced by a professional in franchise real estate who must analyze mountains of statistical data or as straightforward as the experience of a college foodservice director talking to students in the dining room about their food preferences. All foodservice guests have basic likes and dislikes. Simply put, effective managers must identify these likes and dislikes and consider them carefully while developing their menu.

## THE MENU MUST EVOLVE

The menu is not written and then left unchanged. It is, in fact, an evolving resource that must change to keep up with the changing wants and needs of guests. Updating the menu is too important to do only "when the menu planners have time." Systems to collect and analyze market research information must be in place and must be consistently used to keep menus current.

Menu changes are typically small and made gradually over time rather than extensive and done all at once with long time intervals between revisions. Menu planners should practice the art and science of **continuous quality improvement (CQI)**. This concept suggests

that even if one menu item is changed to meet guest desires, the menu has been improved. The process of menu evaluation (described in Chapter 9) will provide additional details about how to evaluate menus to improve them.

---

*Glossary Terms*
**Continuous quality improvement (CQI).**
The process of determining ways to improve the foodservice operation to more consistently deliver products and services that meet (or exceed) the organization's standards (which, in turn, are driven by what the guests want and need).

---

## SPECIAL MENU-MARKETING CONCERNS

Since the menu is of critical importance to all foodservice operations, constant attention must be given to ways to improve it. While those owning relatively small commercial foodservice operations can change menus at will (they are, after all, the owners!), it is more difficult to make changes in other types of

operations. In this section, we will review the process of managing menu changes in large foodservice organizations and, as well, we will present ideas about the need to monitor changing guest preferences and to review the impact of the competition on menu planning.

## Menu Changes in Large Foodservice Organizations[1]

Chain restaurant organizations such as those in the quick-service and midscale dining segments typically have standardized menus. This consistency is a major advantage of these organizations ("the best surprise is no surprise"). Guests can visit any unit in the chain with the expectation that the menu will be the same or similar and what they order will meet their expectations with no surprises.

Menu planners in these organizations have an awesome responsibility. How can they plan menus that will be competitive with other dining alternatives when there are so many units over perhaps vast geographic areas? How are menus revised at the corporate level and what, if any, discretion does an individual unit owner or manager have to make menu changes? We will discuss these and related issues in this section.

Let's think about a very large quick-service ("fast food") organization with several thousand (or more) units, some of which may be company-owned but the vast majority of which are **franchise** units. How are menu items for this organization planned? A major concern is that menu items must have mass-market appeal to attract lots of people from all demographic groups. These items are usually neutral to the palate—that is, they must not be too spicy, too sweet, too sour, or otherwise strongly flavored.

---

*Glossary Terms*

**Franchise**. An agreement between an organization that originally developed the business (franchiser) and a company that operates under the agreement (the franchisee). The franchise agreement specifies that the operating company can use the franchiser's brand name in return for complying with contractual requirements (many of which are related to helping assure consistency between units) and paying agreed-upon fees.

---

Another concern is "purchase repetition"; that is most menus offer items that guests will purchase repeatedly. Consider, for example, a restaurant that plans to serve hamburgers and barbecued ribs. Hamburgers will be consistently popular over the long run because they are a staple in the diets of many people. Ribs may be very popular in the short term, but many guests will become disinterested in them after several purchases because they are not a commonly consumed item for many people. The solution: Manage the hamburger so it is a mainstay, priority item on the menu. Offer the barbecue rib for a short promotional period; then remove it from the menu and, perhaps, reintroduce it later (even many months later!).

How a large, international, multiunit organization plans a special food promotion is interesting. Corporate officers may begin planning a promotion one year or longer before it is offered. In the case of barbecued ribs, for example, pork farmers, buyers, and others in the supply chain must be made aware of the upcoming promotion to prepare for it. They must know, for example, that the promotion will last for a specified number of weeks and will be offered in a specified number of restaurants in specified locations throughout the country.

One aspect of menu planning relatively unique to the quick-serve market involves the use of packaging. This resource is expensive (sometimes, in the case of salads, for example, the price of packaging may exceed the product cost!). Also important is the space required for packaging in the storage area and, even more important, in the preparation, guest order, and counter areas. Significant problems occur as new items are introduced on a menu. On the one hand, packaging must be different so that both the guests and the employees will be able to recognize it. On

---

[1]This section was developed with the assistance of Theda Rudd, The School of Hospitality Business, Michigan State University.

the other hand, finding space for additional packaging is an ever-present operating problem.

Pricing concerns are another marketing-related issue that large organizations must consider in unique ways. For example, management staff in corporate offices may recommend a price, but they cannot set menu prices for franchisees because of laws against the establishment of monopolies. Many organizations will establish a temporary promotional price for menu products to judge guest acceptance. The goal here is that sales of these items will add incremental revenue and will not decrease revenues generated from the sale of other products during the promotional period. Over time, however, the pricing challenge for large organizations is the same as that for their smaller counterparts; planners must consider what the products cost relative to the revenues they can receive from the sale of these products.

The availability of the same or similar items across large geographic areas is both an advantage and a disadvantage. If, as suggested above, items have a large and wide market appeal, they should, by definition, be popular everywhere. However, what about operators in specific areas whose market enjoys other items (and who are willing to go to a competitor for them!)? Large organizations recognize this problem and address it in at least two different ways. First, many offer their franchises an "approved list" of menu items that contains many more products than are traditionally on a menu. Individual operators can offer these items for special events or can feature them on the menu indefinitely. Examples include cherry pie or mint-green milk shakes. These might be offered for holiday celebrations (George Washington's birthday and St. Patrick's Day, respectively) or as a regular menu item. Second, managers and staff members in some units might "discover" a new product. This item could be tested in corporate offices and then be tested in several stores before being "rolled out" on a larger scale. More commonly, however, ideas

for new menu items result from ongoing study by a team of product-development personnel in corporate offices.

The concept of "**penny profit**" is very relevant to all financial decision-making in the quick-service market. Menu planners must consider the profit potential in the context of the narrowest of margins (the penny profit) in this market segment, just as menu planners are concerned about profitability in all market segments.

---

*Glossary terms*
**Penny profit.** An item's selling price less the combined food costs and paper costs; it is, then, a variation of the term "contribution margin" (selling price less food costs) that is used by commercial operators other than those in the quick-service segment.

---

How menu items should be dispensed (a marketing-related decision, in part) presents other marketing challenges. Consider, for example, salad bars. Many guests like them; however, it is difficult to control costs, and sanitation concerns sometimes arise. The solution: It depends on the organization. Some offer them, others do not, and still others allow them as an option for individual franchisees. A second example involves the dispensing of soft drinks. Should they be dispensed by the order taker or by the guests themselves after they receive a cup from the order taker? Again, because the cost calculations are sometimes controversial (or, at least, arbitrary), it is difficult to accurately determine the labor and related costs of these alternatives.

What are special concerns about the menus presented to guests? In many quick-service restaurants, the listing of available menu items is presented on a menu board in the guest order area (the counter indoors or the drive-up area outdoors). Research done at the corporate offices about item placement on menu boards is provided to individual units. These suggestions are generally accepted, which lends to consistency among the franchises. This helps guests visiting different properties find desired items.)

Large organizations conduct extensive research to help plan menu board designs. Traditionally, food groups (salad and dessert, for example) were listed in separate areas of the menu board. Today, items from different groups (such as sandwich, French fry, and beverage) are packaged together. Like their table-service counterparts, quick-service properties attempt to locate their best-selling items in the highest profile areas of the menu board.

Point-of-sale advertising is done in relatively unique ways at a quick-service property. For example, many use "register toppers" (similar to table tents but placed on top of electronic registers in the guest order areas). These are used to suggestively sell items such as add-on desserts. Table tents in dining areas can also be useful. Guests might see a special (two pies for a specified price or an ice cream special, for example) and return to the counter to order these items after they have completed their meal. Order takers are also taught to suggestively sell preferred menu items in some quick-service operations. These tactics are most effective when employee incentives for sales of preferred items are part of the promotional efforts.

As can be seen, then, small and independent foodservice operations have more discretion in making menu changes than do their chain-affiliated and larger restaurant counterparts. Small independent operators view this as an advantage; they can make quick changes in response to changing guest preferences. However, it is always necessary to evaluate the need for and impact of proposed menu changes before these changes are made. An objective and deliberate (not subjective and quick) process is needed to assure that there are "no surprises" as new menus or menu items are made available for the guests.

## Monitoring Changes in Guest Preferences

Many successful foodservice operations seldom, if ever, make menu changes. Change for the sake of change is seldom justified. These establishments may, for example, offer numerous **signature items** that attract guests and encourage repeat business. Visitors to New Orleans are attracted to the community, in part, because of its unique, world-famous cuisine. They, along with local citizens, enjoy Cajun and Creole meals. Commercial operations that cater to the tourist market must continue to offer these regional specialties to draw tourists to their properties. More typically, however, foodservice managers find marketing and profitability benefits to purposeful menu change.

---

*Glossary terms*
**Signature items.** Food items that are unique to or are associated with a specific foodservice operation. Guests are attracted to the operation because of these items and frequently request them. Guests may associate a restaurant, for example, with a "one-pound pork chop," a "mile-high pie," or a "shrimp boat" (a loaf of French bread hollowed out and filled with deep-fried shrimp).

---

How can changes in guest preferences be noted? First, commercial and noncommercial foodservice operations should maintain sales history information about the items that have been served. With today's **electronic point-of-sale (POS) systems,** this is relatively easy to do. Most of the POS systems sold today can produce sales history data (number of items sold in a given accounting period month) in graphic form such as that displayed in Figure 2-4. Using attached printers, POS systems can graphically represent data in ways that are meaningful to those analyzing menu-item popularity. Alternatively, the same data can be presented in a more traditional format

that simply lists, for a given accounting period, the number of times a menu item has
sold, its sales revenue, and its popularity (sales
as a percentage of total sales). An example
is shown in Figure 2-5.

Figure 2-4.  **Graphic Sales History**

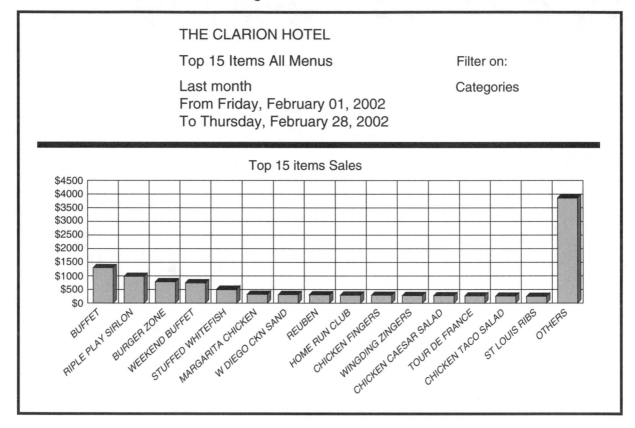

Figure 2-5.  **Traditional Sales History**

| Quantity | Description | Sales | Percent |
|---|---|---|---|
| 237 | BUFFET | $1,410.15 | 11.11% |
| 97 | TRIPLE PLAY SIRLOIN | $1,156.24 | 9.11% |
| 143 | BURGER ZONE | $850.85 | 6.70% |
| 118 | WEEKEND BUFFET | $820.10 | 6.46% |
| 58 | STUFFED WHITEFISH | $633.36 | 4.99% |
| 48 | MARGARITA CHICKEN | $444.96 | 3.51% |
| 75 | SAN DIEGO CKN SAND | $444.00 | 3.50% |
| 72 | REUBEN | $426.24 | 3.36% |
| 69 | HOME RUN CLUB | $408.48 | 3.22% |
| 65 | CHICKEN FINGERS | $384.80 | 3.03% |
| 62 | WINGDING ZINGERS | $367.04 | 2.89% |
| 55 | CHICKEN CAESAR SALAD | $353.65 | 2.79% |
| 59 | TOUR DE FRANCE | $349.28 | 2.75% |

Modern POS systems can also sort data by item popularity (sales), day part (breakfast, lunch, or dinner), hour of the day, day of the week, specific server, item profitability, or a variety of other sales characteristics unique to a specific menu. Sales history information along with findings from the menu-evaluation process (see Chapter 9) can be very helpful in managing changes in guest preferences.

If analysis of sales histories can help indicate items that guests do—and do not—prefer on an existing menu, how do the menu planners determine what, if any, new menu items should be added? An easy response is, "Just ask your guests!" While this idea may seem oversimplified, some guests, especially frequent ones, would be very happy to provide suggestions (and, in fact, many guests probably provide unsolicited advice frequently!).

Getting input from guests can be done in several ways. A genuine request for information by the manager who goes from table to table "meeting and greeting" diners is a good start. (Too often, managers who "manage by walking around" overlook this opportunity to question their regular guests about items they would like to see, for example, as menu specials.) Other ideas are to ask for menu suggestions on guest comment cards and to provide samples of proposed new menu items to guests as a complimentary, value-added offering during their visits. (Some managers think about and plan their marketing expenses to include only those funds used to purchase advertising, to provide contributions to community groups, and to purchase exterior signage, for example. These are examples of advertising expenses. However, funds specifically allocated for complimentary food and beverage tastings within the restaurant can also be allocated toward the operation's marketing expense account.) Marketing experts agree that it is easier and less expensive to keep your current guests rather than to find new ones. Spending advertising money on existing guests, then, makes excellent economic sense!

Managers who know their clientele will likely have ideas about changing guest preferences and the impact that these changes may have on menu revisions. As well, numerous professional associations and trade magazines run frequent articles describing, in great detail, the changing preferences of guests who have specific demographic characteristics. For example, if menu planners know the trends relating to the nutritional concerns of persons in specified age groups or geographic locations, they might match these demographics with their own guest base to improve the menu.

Does the concept of changing menus apply in noncommercial operations? Yes, it does, in the majority of outlets where the consumer has dining choices. However, the process of menu change is more difficult and time-consuming in many noncommercial operations because of nutritional constraints. Menus in cash cafeteria operations for employees and public can often be changed as desired. However, changes in menus offered to patients or residents in hospitals and nursing homes must be analyzed to assure that minimum daily nutritional requirements are met. In large noncommercial operations there can be formalized structures for input from consumers in a process that leads to menu changes. This data can be collected through focus groups; "menu committees"; numerous oral, hard copy, and electronic surveys; and menu-item tasting panels.

## Competition and Menu Planning

There is little question that the menus of commercial and noncommercial foodservice operations are affected by the competition. A strong menu should evolve to consistently help attain the organization's marketing, financial, and other objectives. Therefore, the foodservice operation remains viable and can withstand competitive threats. The need for a competitive menu is clear in commercial foodservice operations where, it seems, restaurants and food and beverage operations—both those that are freestanding, and those in hotels—come and go with rapid frequency.

Noncommercial operations also need a strong, competitive menu; ineffective menus are likely to yield dissatisfied administrators and consumers. The facility's management might then consider using a contract foodservice management company. In effect, then, a self-operated foodservice management team continually competes with an alternative: operation of the foodservices by a contract management company.

Assume that a contract foodservice management company is retained and that it also uses ineffective menus. Consumer dissatisfaction may then prompt facility administrators to let the foodservice contract out for **bidding**. In effect, then, contract management companies also compete with each other. The bidding process will, hopefully, result in the facility contracting with a contract management company that offers a menu that will enable the facility to better attain its economic and marketing goals.

---

*Glossary Terms*
**Bidding**. The process by which foodservice contract management companies develop proposals that meet a noncommercial facility' requirements for its foodservices. These proposals are then analyzed, and a contract is negotiated with the company offering the best proposal.

---

*Long-Term Implications.* The menu of a single competitor can have a long-term effect on an operation's menu offerings. In some cases, if a new and very popular menu item is developed by one restaurant, other restaurants may duplicate that item. For example, after the dipping sauce used by Outback Steakhouses for their deep-fried onion appetizer was introduced, it quickly gained wide guest acceptance. Today, several other restaurant chains as well as individual restaurants use a variation of this sauce with their fried-onion products. Competitors saw the wisdom of offering this new, and popular, item.

Menu planners must be careful, however, not to change the entire menu concept simply because a competitor is enjoying success. For example, if the menu planner at an Italian restaurant found that a new, Mexican-style restaurant was enjoying great popularity, it is not a signal that all or part of the Italian menu should be changed to include Mexican-style dishes. It may be, however, that the menu planner at the Italian-style restaurant can learn from the newly introduced Mexican-style restaurant. Are the new restaurant's prices very competitive? Are its cleanliness, service, and speed of service outstanding? These are restaurant features that appeal to guests. Rather than change menu items to duplicate the offerings of the new restaurant, it would be better to monitor new competitors as a way of continually evaluating changing guest preferences. Menu-item popularity will change over time, and wise menu planners monitor these changes and look for those that will have an impact on their own operations.

*Short-Term Implications.* It is more difficult to consider the short-term impact of a menu on competition. Recall, first, that a guest does not make a decision to visit a commercial foodservice operation on the strength of the menu alone. Issues such as the location, the object of the visit, the quality of the service, the extent of cleanliness, and the overall dining "experience" are normally considered in addition to the specific food and beverage products offered. Likewise, the relationship between the menu and competitive threats to a noncommercial foodservice operation over the short term are difficult to quantify. Again, numerous factors including food quality, portion size, and hours of foodservice availability, along with the items offered on the menu, all impact the short-term success of the foodservice operation.

How should a foodservice operator consider the impact of short-term competitive threats on the menu? One tactic applicable to both commercial and noncommercial foodservice operations is to **benchmark** the competition. One way to do this involves management and other staff visiting competitive dining alternatives. A review of the menu itself along with tasting the food and beverage items offered would be done during this visit.

> *Glossary Terms*
> **Benchmark.** The process of comparing the practices and methods of one's organization against those of others who are considered "world-class performers" and who compete for the same market of potential guests.

Another way to obtain useful information that could be used to make improvements is to use a **shopper's service** to point out weaknesses in and to make suggestions about a property's own menu and other aspects of the operation. Figure 2-6 identifies the wide range of menu-related and other items that can be addressed in a shopper's visit. To the extent that a shopper fits the demographics of the guest market served by the foodservice operation, a shopper's input can help to determine the potential for menu improvement in the foodservice operation.

> *Glossary terms*
> **Shopper's service.** Assistance provided by trained foodservice professionals or by others employed by a foodservice operation who pose as guests and evaluate all front-of-the-house procedures (such as menu offerings, service techniques, products, and quality) offered by the foodservice operation.

It is important, then, that menu planners in all types of food and beverage operations seek ways to continually improve their menus. Input from all sources, including competitive analysis, can be helpful.

Figure 2-6.　**Components of a Shopper's Report Applicable to Food and Beverage Products**

**Part A**

| Menu | Acceptable | Unacceptable | Comments |
|---|---|---|---|
| 1. The menu was clean and free from spots. | ❑ | ❑ | |
| 2. The menu fit the theme of the dining room. | ❑ | ❑ | |
| 3. The menu was well organized and its size was physically manageable. | ❑ | ❑ | |
| 4. The menu was clearly written and the number of items was appropriate. | ❑ | ❑ | |
| 5. The menu was easily read and descriptions were appetizing. | ❑ | ❑ | |
| 6. The menu was a marketing tool. | ❑ | ❑ | |
| 7. Specials were available. | ❑ | ❑ | |
| 8. Vegetarian and children portions were available. | ❑ | ❑ | |
| COMMENTS: | | | |

| Beverages | Acceptable | Unacceptable | Comments |
|---|---|---|---|
| 1. Looked refreshing. | ❑ | ❑ | |
| 2. Were fresh and served at correct temperature. | ❑ | ❑ | |
| 3. Were served correctly and presented tastefully. | ❑ | ❑ | |
| 4. Had excellent flavor. | ❑ | ❑ | |
| COMMENTS: | | | |

**Part B**

| Food | Strongly Agree | Agree | Disagree | Strongly Disagree |
|---|:---:|:---:|:---:|:---:|
| 1. The food items corresponded with their menu descriptions and your perceived value. | ❑ | ❑ | ❑ | ❑ |
| 2. All items ordered were available. | ❑ | ❑ | ❑ | ❑ |
| 3. Hot items were served hot. | ❑ | ❑ | ❑ | ❑ |
| 4. Cold items were served cold. | ❑ | ❑ | ❑ | ❑ |
| 5. Appetizer: _____<br>  a. looked appealing<br>  b. was fresh<br>  c. had excellent color<br>  d. had excellent flavor<br>  e. was well-seasoned<br>  f. was tastefully presented | <br>❑<br>❑<br>❑<br>❑<br>❑<br>❑ | <br>❑<br>❑<br>❑<br>❑<br>❑<br>❑ | <br>❑<br>❑<br>❑<br>❑<br>❑<br>❑ | <br>❑<br>❑<br>❑<br>❑<br>❑<br>❑ |
| 6. Soup: _____<br>  a. looked appealing<br>  b. was fresh<br>  c. had excellent color<br>  d. had excellent flavor<br>  e. was well-seasoned<br>  f. was tastefully presented | <br>❑<br>❑<br>❑<br>❑<br>❑<br>❑ | <br>❑<br>❑<br>❑<br>❑<br>❑<br>❑ | <br>❑<br>❑<br>❑<br>❑<br>❑<br>❑ | <br>❑<br>❑<br>❑<br>❑<br>❑<br>❑ |
| 7. Bread: _____<br>  a. looked appealing<br>  b. was fresh<br>  c. had excellent color<br>  d. had excellent flavor<br>  e. was tastefully presented | <br>❑<br>❑<br>❑<br>❑<br>❑ | <br>❑<br>❑<br>❑<br>❑<br>❑ | <br>❑<br>❑<br>❑<br>❑<br>❑ | <br>❑<br>❑<br>❑<br>❑<br>❑ |
| 8. Salad: _____<br>  a. looked appetizing<br>  b. was fresh<br>  c. had excellent color<br>  d. had excellent flavor<br>  e. was well-seasoned<br>  f. was tastefully presented<br>  g. had excellent dressing | <br>❑<br>❑<br>❑<br>❑<br>❑<br>❑<br>❑ | <br>❑<br>❑<br>❑<br>❑<br>❑<br>❑<br>❑ | <br>❑<br>❑<br>❑<br>❑<br>❑<br>❑<br>❑ | <br>❑<br>❑<br>❑<br>❑<br>❑<br>❑<br>❑ |
| 9. Entrée: _____<br>  a. looked appetizing<br>  b. was fresh<br>  c. had excellent color<br>  d. had excellent flavor<br>  e. was well-seasoned<br>  f. was neatly plated and tastefully presented<br>  g. was appropriately portioned<br>  h. was of excellent quality | <br>❑<br>❑<br>❑<br>❑<br>❑<br>❑<br>❑<br>❑ | <br>❑<br>❑<br>❑<br>❑<br>❑<br>❑<br>❑<br>❑ | <br>❑<br>❑<br>❑<br>❑<br>❑<br>❑<br>❑<br>❑ | <br>❑<br>❑<br>❑<br>❑<br>❑<br>❑<br>❑<br>❑ |

| | | | | |
|---|---|---|---|---|
| **10. Vegetable Name:** | | | | |
| a. looked appetizing | ❏ | ❏ | ❏ | ❏ |
| b. was fresh | ❏ | ❏ | ❏ | ❏ |
| c. had excellent color | ❏ | ❏ | ❏ | ❏ |
| d. had excellent flavor | ❏ | ❏ | ❏ | ❏ |
| e. was tastefully presented | ❏ | ❏ | ❏ | ❏ |
| **11. Starch Name:** | | | | |
| a. looked appetizing | ❏ | ❏ | ❏ | ❏ |
| b. was fresh | ❏ | ❏ | ❏ | ❏ |
| c. had excellent color | ❏ | ❏ | ❏ | ❏ |
| d. had excellent flavor | ❏ | ❏ | ❏ | ❏ |
| e. was tastefully presented | ❏ | ❏ | ❏ | ❏ |
| **12. Dessert Name:** | | | | |
| a. looked appetizing | ❏ | ❏ | ❏ | ❏ |
| b. was fresh | ❏ | ❏ | ❏ | ❏ |
| c. had excellent color | ❏ | ❏ | ❏ | ❏ |
| d. had excellent flavor | ❏ | ❏ | ❏ | ❏ |
| e. was tastefully presented | ❏ | ❏ | ❏ | ❏ |
| 13. Each of the food items corresponded with the menu description. | ❏ | ❏ | ❏ | ❏ |

COMMENTS:

OVERALL VISIT COMMENTS:

## SIGEE'S MENU: A CASE STUDY

"How was everything"? asked David Berger as he approached a table in his hotel dining room. David had just left his office in the kitchen, having finished reviewing Sigee's sales data from the previous week. The number of items sold and their relative popularity had been tabulated by his POS system. He knew it was important to monitor the popularity of his menu items, but he also knew the importance of face-to-face guest contact and feedback.

The couple, Mr. and Mrs. Stanley, had just completed their meal. As he talked to them, David discovered that they were celebrating their thirtieth wedding anniversary. They lived just two miles from the hotel and ate at Sigee's at least once a month. They came, stated Mrs. Stanley, "because the room is so beautiful, and we like the view!"

David moved on to the next booth where he introduced himself and met Ms. Schwartz. Ms. Schwartz, David discovered, was a businesswoman involved in systems analysis for a large software company. She had never been to the hotel before, she stated, but did mention to David that "My meal would have been perfect if you would have had a fat-free raspberry vinaigrette for the salad". They chatted for a few more moments; David made a mental note of the salad dressing comment and then approached the next table.

Here he met Mrs. Sharpe and her daughter Julia. David could see that they had not yet ordered. As they talked, David learned that they were attending a gymnastics competition at the local university. Julia was quite talented, and she and her mother frequently spent weekends at events such as the one bringing them to the hotel.

"Is there a coffee shop in the hotel?" asked Mrs. Sharpe. "No", replied David, "just Sigee's. Why do you ask?" "Well," replied Mrs. Sharpe hesitantly, "we were looking for something a little lighter than these menu items." David thought about his menu. He had been in the restaurant business for a long time, and he knew instinctively that it was his menu prices, and not the menu items themselves, that had made Mrs. Sharpe uncomfortable. He was aware that the least expensive entrée item on the dinner menu was $19.00. He also knew that a table service chain restaurant just one-half mile from the hotel offered moderately priced dinner entrées ranging from $6.00 to $15.00.

"Our operating costs are higher," thought David, but he wondered if guests like Mrs. Sharpe understood or even cared about that.

David visited briefly with several other guests, including a retired couple who had come to the city to visit their grandchildren, a trainer who was in the hotel to conduct a sales seminar the next day, and a married couple with two younger children who had arrived that day to attend a wedding of a close friend.

As he left the dining room and returned to his office he was somewhat perplexed. "So many different guest types," he thought, "and so many different tastes." "I don't think I can write one menu that will satisfy everyone. However, I do need to write a menu that appeals to my current guests and to those that I want to attract. It will be a challenge to build a menu that pleases both groups."

## CHAPTER 3

# The Menu and Facility Layout, Equipment, and Design

## CHAPTER OUTLINE

**The Menu and New Facilities**
**The Menu in Existing Facilities**
**The Impact of the Menu on Workstation Spaces**
  Office Space
  Back-of-the House Workstations
    Receiving
    Storing
    Issuing
    Pre-Preparing
    Preparing
    Holding
    Serving
    Service
    Clean Up
  Front-of-the-House Workstations
**Evaluation of Menu Changes**
**The Menu Influences Facility Layout**
**The Menu, Convenience Foods, and Facility Design**

A Look at Convenience Foods
Make-or-Buy Analysis
**The Menu and Facility Design and Décor**
  The Dining Room Is Part of the Dining Experience
  Ten Principles for Changing a Dining Room's Theme
  Serviceware Is Important
**The Bar Menu Influences the Bar Layout and Design**
  Bar Design and Layout Principles
  Space Requirements for Beverage and Storage Areas
  Glassware Control
  The Bar Menu Affects Bar Sales
    Concerns of Bar Guests
    A Close Look at Bar Menus
    The Menu Affects the Bar's Atmosphere
    Specialty Menus and the Bar Layout
**Sigee's Menu: A Case Study**

## MENU TERMS USED IN THIS CHAPTER

Bottleneck
Check average
Cocktail
Cost effective
Décor
Design
Finishing
From scratch
Highballs
Ingredient room
Make-or-buy analysis
Portion control

Potentially hazardous foods
Reconstitute
Server station
Service
Service bar
Serviceware
Serving
Temperature danger zone
Workflow
Workstation
Wow factor

## CHAPTER OVERVIEW

Our study of the importance of the menu and the role it plays in almost every aspect of the food and beverage operation continues as we study how the menu affects a facility's layout, equipment, and design. Some readers may be surprised to learn about the extent to which the layout of space, the equipment housed within that space, and the design of "back-of-the-house" and "front-of-the house" areas are influenced by the menu.

The chapter begins by studying what appears to be a relatively easy job for menu planners before their food and beverage operation is built: design the new facility around the new menu. By contrast, the menu planners who "inherit" an existing facility face significant limitations that will likely influence their decision making. Over time, though, all menu planners will face these same limitations as their menus evolve through the life of the facility—a facility is only "new" when the initial menu is planned.

There are many workstations in a food and beverage operation: from purchasing to receiving, storing, and issuing; to pre-preparing, preparing, and holding; to serving and service and clean up. The menu directly impacts each workstation in every area of the food and beverage operation, and affects the square footage needed and the equipment that must be housed within it. After workstations are designed, they must be arranged to facilitate workflow. Since individual workstations should be designed with the menu in mind, the layout of the entire facility is, therefore, influenced by the menu.

Not every menu item is made on site. Today, the numerous market forms of convenience foods provide alternatives to the menu planners. The extent to which convenience foods are used has an impact on menu planning. Either alternative (to use a convenience product or to prepare the item on site) can be evaluated first according to quality requirements and then according to price considerations. It then becomes possible to make decisions about whether and which items are to be included on the menu and whether and which items should be prepared (all or in part) on site.

The menu also impacts the design and décor of the facility because many guests desire an "experience" as they dine; that is, the food, beverages, and service they receive are important but, increasingly, so is the dining environment. There must be some consistency between the food products the establishment orders and serves and its environment. We will explore this relationship in this chapter.

Finally, we will focus on ways in which the menu impacts the layout and design of the bar area. We outline basic facility design principles relevant to menu planning and discuss how the menu affects the bar's atmosphere and the ways in which specialty drinks required by the menu impact the bar layout.

The theme *"It all starts with the menu"* runs throughout this book, including this chapter. Space considerations, specifically the layout and the design of the facility and the equipment within it, are also driven by the menu and the food items that must be produced for it.

## THE MENU AND NEW FACILITIES

Suppose you are the manager or owner of a new restaurant venture. Land has been purchased, and you are working with architects, kitchen designers, and others on blueprints that detail the design and layout of the new property. How much space should be allocated for product receiving, storing, pre-preparation, and preparation? How about for dining space and for the dish- and pot-washing workstations? What about the office space needed for you and other managers and for the sales and accounting staff?

When a new foodservice operation is being planned "from the ground up," it is possible and preferable to allow the menu to drive answers to many of the above and related questions. For example, if the menu will feature relatively low-cost, quick-serve (fast food) items, plans will probably require a large-volume operation with specialized food production equipment (such as a broiler and deep-fry units).

Alternatively, let's assume the menu for your new operation will offer on-site-produced bakery products (breads, buns, and desserts) and will feature these items for both on-site and take-out consumption. The bakery operation will likely require a large dry storage space for the flour, sugar, and other bakery ingredients, unless frequent delivery of these and related items is expected. Also, bakeshops require preparation equipment (mixer and ovens), preparation space (to include, for example, wooden-top baker tables and carts, and the space to roll them) for proofing bread, and also space for holding the baked products. An operation with the same menu but which purchases bakery items will not require such extensive dry-goods storage space or the specialized baking equipment.

If the menu you are planning for the new facility includes char-broiled, grilled, or deep-fried entrées, then special equipment, and the space to house it, will be required. As well, most cooking equipment must be ventilated according to strict municipal safety codes. Ventilation equipment is expensive; the square footage under the venting system must be minimized because of the high cost. Therefore, the menu helps determine the type and amount of equipment that will be required, which in turn affects the equipment budget. Clearly, the menu greatly influences a new facility's layout, equipment, and design.

## THE MENU IN EXISTING FACILITIES

In many cases, the owner or manager planning a new operation will be using an existing building with an existing kitchen. As well, existing operations will likely require new menus (or, at least, new menu items) in efforts to keep up with changing guest preferences. While the equipment necessary to produce new menu items can often be added, it is likely that the menu planners will at least consider limiting menu items to those that can be produced with the existing equipment, layout, and space in the kitchen in order to minimize the costs associated with making changes.

Let's consider the frozen storage areas, for example. Assume the facility has several small reach-in or chest-type freezers but no larger-size walk-in freezer. If the menu planners are considering a revised menu that will offer a wide variety of items to be purchased in frozen form, the frozen storage space may be inadequate unless daily deliveries are made. Additional frozen storage will be required unless these proposed menu changes are reconsidered. Where can a walk-in freezer be located? The menu planners might find that without significant and costly renovations, the facility lacks sufficient square footage for this freezer.

As a second example, let's assume the menu planners want to feature a large variety of deep-fried items. Unfortunately, the facility has inadequate deep-fryer equipment. Now, they are confronted with the same space and ventilation problems noted earlier, but additional problems are also encountered. First, will local fire and safety codes require specialized fire extinguishing systems in areas where deep fryers are located? Second, what is the type and location of worktable space required as items are removed from the deep fryer? Will fryer baskets that are swiveled across a work aisle to a nearby worktable with oil and fat dripping create a slippery-floor work hazard? Third, is there room under the venting system (which we've noted to be expensive space!) to house a worktable? The concept of **workflow** is important; it is impacted by the menu and affects the productivity of preparation employees and the speed of service to guests. These examples illustrate that in existing facilities the layout, equipment, and design of the available workspace directly drives or at least significantly influences the menu.

In these examples, the costs to purchase space or to renovate existing space and to purchase additional equipment will be significant, creating limitations for almost every menu planner. Space and equipment is required to store, prepare, and serve all items required by the menu. In both new and ex-

isting facilities, a serious effort is required to assure that menu-planning decisions are **cost effective**.

---

*Glossary Terms*

**Cost effective.** Something that is worth more than it costs. For example, if menu planners introduce an item that requires expensive specialty production equipment but will generate relatively low revenue levels, then they are probably not making a cost-effective decision.

**Workflow.** The movement of a product from receiving to storage, to pre-preparation and preparation areas, and on to service personnel. Ideally, there is a straight-line flow with little back-tracking. This enables processing to be done most efficiently and effectively.

---

## THE IMPACT OF THE MENU ON WORKSTATION SPACES

Figure 3-1 focuses on three categories of work areas: office, back-of-the-house, and front-of-the-house. **Workstations** for each area must be coordinated into the design and layout of a food and beverage operation.

Figure 3-1. **The Menu's Influence on Workstations**

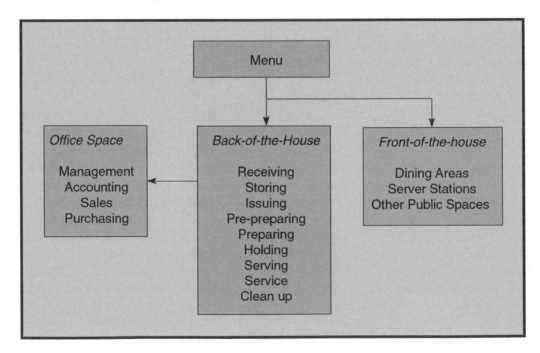

> *Glossary of Menu Terms*
> **Workstation.** The space needed (including necessary equipment) to do work of a certain type. For example, the food and beverage manager needs space with a desk, computer, telephone, and other office equipment; a fry cook may need space for a refrigerator to store items to be prepared during the shift, a deep-fryer, space to bread or otherwise make ready items for deep-frying, space to hold the plates, pans, or other serviceware to serve or hold finished products, and space for numerous small equipment items.

## Office Space

Office space is required for management, accounting, sales, and purchasing activities. Large foodservice operations will require space for human resources personnel. These administrative functions are done regardless of the type of menu offered, and the menu does not directly affect space for these activities. For example, space might be allocated to accommodate all these functions in one general area ("the office") or, alternatively, these functions can be separated into different smaller areas not critical to workflow or service concerns. (*Note*: Sometimes office spaces are in ideal locations. In many facilities, management offices are close to food production space, and may even contain windows overlooking the kitchen. Sales offices will allow convenient access for prospective clients, and purchasing functions are best situated close to the loading dock, receiving, and storage areas. Accounting space may be located between the manager's and purchasing agent's office spaces.)

## Back-of-the-House Workstations

The menu directly affects back-of-the-house workstation spaces. We'll next look at how the menu affects each back-of-the-house function.

*Receiving.* If the menu requires meat, poultry, fish products, or other of the many items

that are purchased by weight, a scale of adequate size will be required in the receiving area. These food items are expensive, and receiving personnel must be able to weigh incoming products to assure that the invoices specifying purchase costs (cost per pound times the number of pounds purchased) are correct. If large volumes of fresh produce are required, dollies, skids, and other transport and storage equipment will likely be needed. If the menu being planned is for a high-volume operation, space for quantities of incoming shipments to be spread out for proper inspection before moving into storage areas will be important.

*Storing.* Adequate refrigerated, frozen, and dry storage areas will be required to hold all items required by the menu before pre-preparation and preparation activities begin. If the operation will be offering alcoholic beverages, additional and special lockable storage areas for these products will be needed. Wines to be chilled before service will need to be properly and securely stored in, perhaps, a centralized storage area when received and in another storage area closer to the dining area before service. Operations offering buffets will need space to store buffet serviceware. Facilities that will offer tableside food preparation will need space to store these types of small equipment items. As a final example, properties that offer carryout products and quick-service operations that require extensive quantities of disposable products (including wrapping papers, plates, cups, and flatware) will need significant storage space for these items.

*Issuing.* Noncommercial facilities are sometimes planned with **ingredient rooms**. If, for example, the menu requires fresh-baked bread, already weighed and measured ingredients for these items may be issued to the bakeshop or other production areas. Space to perform these tasks is required.

Properties that sell alcoholic beverages may

issue full bottles to bar areas when they return empty bottles to the storage area. Space to hold these empty containers until disposal (some local laws require breakage) is required.

---

*Glossary Terms*

**Ingredient room.** A space (ideally located between the storage and the preparation areas) used to weigh and measure ingredients required for recipes to be produced in preparation areas.

---

*Pre-preparing.* Food and beverage operations that offer numerous items made on site (**from scratch**) will need space to pre-prepare items prior to final preparation. Examples of pre-preparation tasks include washing and chopping salad greens; thawing, peeling, deveining, and butterflying frozen shrimp; portioning ground beef into hamburger patties and butchering meat and poultry products. A large amount of well-planned space to accommodate sinks, work surfaces, pot and pan washing and storage and for the cooks to perform these tasks will be required.

---

*Glossary Terms*

**From scratch.** The use of raw ingredients to prepare items on site; for example, a stew made from scratch would require the purchase of beef (which would need to be cubed), celery, potatoes, carrots, and other ingredients that must be processed and cooked in the property's kitchen.

---

*Preparing.* The impact of the menu on the preparation workstation is clear. We have noted, for example, the need for equipment to prepare items required by the menu to the desired quality standards. Consider the oven overload that could occur when many people are served a banquet menu that consists of a baked appetizer, fresh-baked bread, a baked entrée, and a baked dessert. The **bottleneck** created when a menu requires production that taxes (or exceeds!) the

facility's resource capabilities causes great difficulty for everyone, including the guests. The worst-case scenario in this example is when oven capacity is exceeded and, at the same time, one oven (or more) is out of service for routine maintenance or for repair. The stress created for production personnel and the disappointment to guests of a long wait or cold food make this a situation that no manager or menu-planning team wants to confront.

---

*Glossary Terms*

**Bottleneck.** One or more places in the production system where workflow is interrupted. Causes include too little or the wrong type of equipment and a production step such as breading or filleting that slows production output.

---

The menu has a dramatic impact on a kitchen's equipment, space, and design and layout requirements. Assume, for example, that a restaurant features sandwiches and related items made with numerous types of loaf breads and buns; an on-site bake shop is required to consistently provide the quality of baked products that are the signature items of the restaurant. Figure 3-2 shows equipment placement that influences the workflow and helps with the efficient production of these items. A pre-preparation table (labeled 1 in the figure) with a sink allows bread ingredients to be easily weighed, measured, and assembled before being combined in a mixer (6). The pre-prep table has been properly designed—it is open beneath the tabletop to house mobile bins that hold the flour and sugar. When the dough is proofed (risen), dough can be portioned and then divided and rounded automatically (2). Dough can then be placed in pans on the bake table (3) and, if necessary, proofed again on bun pans placed in available pan racks (4) before being placed in the oven (5). After baking, the products can be cooled and held until service or transported to the service

Figure 3-2. **Sketch of Bakery Workstation\***

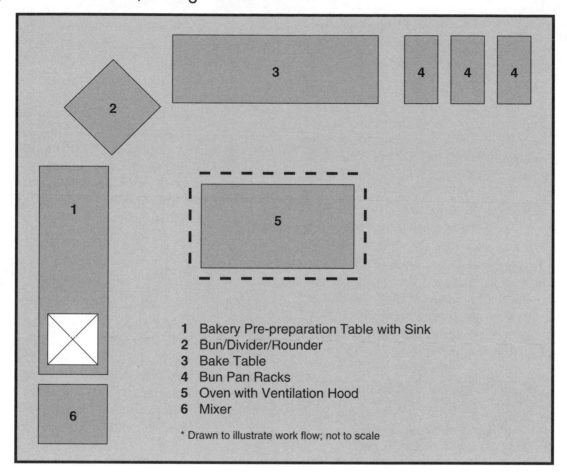

1 Bakery Pre-preparation Table with Sink
2 Bun/Divider/Rounder
3 Bake Table
4 Bun Pan Racks
5 Oven with Ventilation Hood
6 Mixer

\* Drawn to illustrate work flow; not to scale

counter on the bun pan carts (4).

Some menu items to be served hot might be prepared ahead of time and then **reconstituted** as they are ordered. Equipment such as refrigeration (to hold items until ordered) and a convection oven (to heat, or reconstitute, the item when it is ordered) will be needed. Since some preparation space is used only for preparing food (and not for holding or serving it), this type of kitchen space is often purposefully very small. Expensive to build, and often designed to be out of the way of meal service areas, the size and location of preparation space will greatly impact the menu that can be produced from it.

When the preparation space is used to ac-

tually cook food to order, the limitations on the menu can be even greater. In a restaurant that features many types of pancakes, for example, a disproportionately large area of the preparation space would consist of griddle tops and the ovens required to produce specialty pancakes. Items such as bacon and sausage that could also be cooked on a griddle top or oven would "fit" this menu, but space limitations may be such that a broiler, which could be used to cook ham steaks that would accompany the pancakes, would not fit. In this situation, the ham steaks would, by necessity, be cooked on the existing equipment or be removed from the menu.

> **Glossary Terms**
> ***Reconstitute.*** To convert a food item from a nonedible to an edible form. Reconstituting occurs, for example, when water is added to a dry product or when heat is applied to a chilled product.

*Holding.* Some menus require stews, casserole dishes, sauces, and other items that must be prepared ahead in either small or large quantities because they cannot be prepared to order. In these cases, space and equipment is needed to hold these items at proper temperatures until service. Special sanitation concerns are important here: **potentially hazardous foods** must be kept at hot temperatures (above 140° F) or cold temperatures (below 40° F). The time that food is held within the **temperature danger zone** (40° F to 140° F) must be minimized. Special equipment is required to do this.

> **Glossary Terms**
> ***Potentially hazardous foods.*** Generally, foods of animal origin or those that contain large amounts of foods of animal origin, which are most prone to contamination by microorganisms that might cause food-borne illness.
> ***Temperature danger zone.*** The temperature range of 40° F to 140° F, within which microorganisms responsible for most food-borne illnesses best grow and reproduce.

Hotels, resorts, and other properties face special challenges when holding foods offered on roomservice menus. Two important considerations when planning a roomservice menu are (1) the time between portioning in the kitchen to delivery in the guestroom and (2) the transport containers that are used, which have a significant impact on food quality. Consider, for example, the guests' disappointment when crisp French fries and fluffy omelets prepared in the kitchen arrive soggy and cold after transport to guestrooms.

Another instance where holding affects food quality is in facilities that transport meals from a central kitchen to remote "satellite" serving centers such as schools. Items such as canned vegetables can become either cold or overcooked because of improper holding temperature or equipment during transport.

Buffets, salad bars, and "help yourself" dessert stations pose additional holding problems that should be considered by menu planners. As well, labor costs are affected by buffet menus when staff must be available to carve meats or prepare made-to-order omelets and other items during the entire time that the buffet is available for guest service.

*Serving.* **Serving** is the process of moving food and beverages products from production to service staff. In restaurants, serving is traditionally performed in nonpublic (back-of-the-house) areas between the kitchen and the dining room. Complicated menus that offer many food items make this task more difficult, can delay service, and can cause cooks, service staff, and guests to become frustrated. Inadequate space for the pick up of menu items can cause problems in the kitchen and in the **service bar** areas.

> **Glossary Terms**
> ***Serving.*** The process of moving products (food and beverages) from production (cook or bartender) to service staff.
> ***Service bar.*** A bar used to produce beverages ordered by servers who subsequently provide the beverages to guests; guests do not, themselves, order drinks at service bars. Guests may order and directly receive beverages from public bars.

To illustrate how the menu affects the serving area, let's consider an extensive menu offered by a foodservice operation that guests self-serve on a buffet serving line. Several thousand guests are expected. In this instance, the banquet menu certainly impacts the design of the buffet serving area and, as well, the required serving equipment. Figure 3-3 provides an excellent example of this type of banquet.

When reviewing Figure 3-3, note that Part A specifies the menu for a "Pacific Rim" buffet theme and Part B illustrates the placement of buffet serving tables and shows the extensive amount of labor, equipment, utensils, paper, and linen needs required to "deliver" the Pacific Rim menu.

*Service.* Let's begin by examining the affect of **service** on service areas in traditional restaurants. Service is the process of moving products from service staff directly to the guests. Salad or dessert bars are obvious examples of the impact of the menu on service space and equipment. Another example is the relatively wider aisles required when the menu offers tableside food preparation or dessert carts.

---

*Glossary Terms*
**Service.** The process of moving products (food and beverages) from service staff to the guests.

---

For cafeteria service, more space is normally required for "scramble-type" cafeteria lines than for more traditional "straight-line" serving lines. The menu influences which serving line configuration to select. For example, a menu featuring made-to-order sandwiches probably cannot be implemented in a traditional cafeteria serving line configuration in which all consumers follow each other through the line in succession, because service bottlenecks will occur.

Commercial operations featuring take-out or drive-up service must be concerned about

Figure 3-3. **The Menu Affects Buffet Layout**

---

**Part A: The Menu**

PACIFIC RIM
(3 stations) (6 Chinese Chefs)
Char Sui Salad Station
(dressing on the side)
Chinese Barbecue Pork Lomien Noodles
(6 sets)
(1/2-pint to-go containers and paper chopsticks)

Dim Sum Station
Pork Buns, Shomai, Shrimp Dumplings & Potstickers
(Hot Mustard and Chinese Soy Sauce)
(1/2-pint to-go containers and red paper chopsticks)

Sushi Action Station
(6 Sushi Chef and 6 Kimono Ladies)
Tuna, Shrimp, Salmon and Whitefish Nigiri, California, Spicy Tuna and Cucumber
Maki, Negi-Hamachi with Wasabi and Pickled Ginger
(Japanese Soy Sauce)
(black trays and chopsticks)

Figure 3-3.  **(continued)**

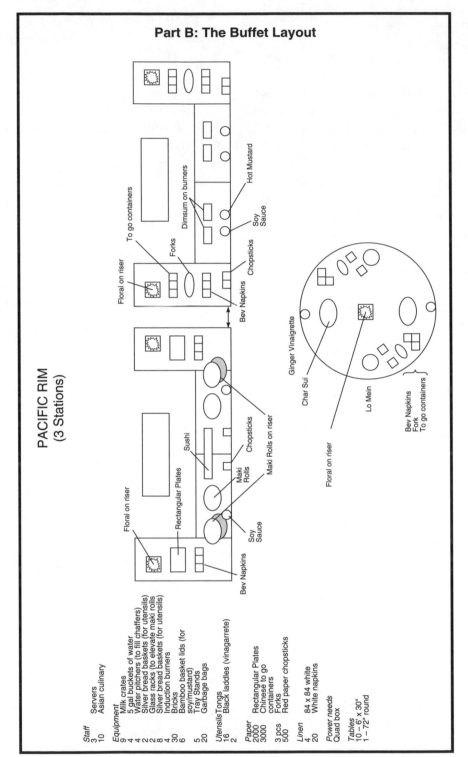

the space and equipment required for these activities, which may impact the design of the building's exterior spaces. In addition, municipal zoning, landscaping, and a wide range of other requirements and limitations may dictate what the menu planners can—and cannot—do. How, for example, are traffic lanes planned to help prevent automobile and pedestrian accidents in parking lots? What about the need, if any, for separate parking areas and entrances, and how do fire safety codes affect these areas and thus guests who desire pick-up service? So, while it is very easy for menu planners to state something on a menu, it is very often another thing to be able to consistently deliver the menu's promises according to the property's quality product and service standards for these items.

*Clean Up.* Menus featuring made-to-order items and those prepared in small batches will create more clean up of small kitchen wares than will menus that include items that can be produced in large batches. Menus offering food items that must be served on a variety of serviceware of different sizes and shapes and with numerous types of utensils require more dishwashing labor. Menus that offer "fast food" items served in disposable containers and available for carry out pose another clean-up problem: to be a good business neighbor, employees may need to clean carry-out debris from the parking lot and even from the streets and sidewalks for some distance from the building.

## EVALUATION OF MENU CHANGES

Many of our examples to this point have addressed how a new menu in either a new or an existing facility affects that facility's layout, equipment, and design. However, the menu can have a very dramatic impact on these resources even when only "minor" changes are made. Let's consider three examples:

## Front-of-the-House Workstations

We have discussed some of the ways that the menu impacts the space and equipment needs in back-of-the-house areas. Similarly, the menu impacts the layout of the front-of-the-house, or public, areas.

**Server stations** in public areas are also affected by the menu. For example, in restaurants featuring ice cream desserts, dispensers or storage areas for ice cream may be in server stations. Entrées and sandwiches often require service staff to bring condiments such as catsup, mustard, and tartar sauce to guests' tables. Space is needed to conveniently store these items in server stations.

---

*Glossary Terms*
**Server station.** A work area often located in front-of-the-house areas, sometimes separated from a dining area by a screen or other room divider, that is used by service staff to store serviceware, condiments, table linens and other products and supply items needed for guest service.

---

Other public spaces found in many food and beverage operations are foyers and other waiting areas, carry-out and pick-up counters, and bar and lounge areas. Menus impact these areas when, for example, they indicate the availability of carry-out and pick-up services and when the menu's popularity creates a waiting line for available tables. Front-of-the-house waiting areas provide an opportunity for point-of-sale advertising (see Chapter 2), which might influence what items guests will order.

- *Example One:* A pizza operation has traditionally offered a single-crust pizza. It uses a straight-line workflow system, illustrated in Figure 3-4. In this workflow scheme, you will note that the pizza dough is first shaped and panned, then toppings are added, and finally the product is baked. Assume the menu planners decide to add a two-crust

Figure 3-4. **Workflow for Pizza Production**

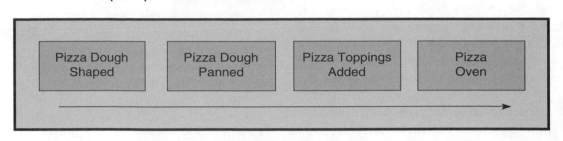

pizza. As before, pizza dough must be shaped and placed on the pizza pan, but for this new product, it must also be added to the top of the pizza after the pizza toppings are added and before it is baked. How must the workstation be revised? Will space be available immediately before placing pizzas in the oven to store the additional pizza dough and also to shape the dough and work with the pizza as the topping is added? Or will the pizza be returned to the beginning preparation station where dough is shaped? The seemingly small change ("Let's add a two-crust pizza") can create serious production problems in the workstation.

- *Example Two:* Menu planners in a quick-service restaurant decide to add a "large" salad to the present offering of a "regular" salad. What kind of new disposable container is needed? Where will it be placed in the guest order workstation? How will space be allocated on the menu board to advertise this item? Again, a seemingly small addition of a second portion size of an item already available creates serious production and service considerations that need to be addressed before the menu item is introduced.

- *Example Three:* Menu planners decide to feature a "nightly special ice cream drink" in the patio bar during the summer. Since it is a seasonal operation, the bar is a small, portable unit that can barely handle the present production and service of traditional alcoholic beverages along with the

dispensing of beers and wines served by the glass. The ice cream drink will require the need for ice cream storage, blender placement, containers for garnishes, and specialty drink glassware that cannot be used for the **highballs** and **cocktails** currently being served. Where will these items be placed? What disruptions in workflow are likely?

---

*Glossary Terms*
**Highballs.** Alcoholic beverages made with one liquor to which water, juice, soft drink, or other nonalcoholic beverage is added.
**Cocktails.** Alcoholic beverages such as a martini or Manhattan that contain the liquor as the primary ingredient.

---

These examples show that what appear to be "minor" changes in an existing menu can cause dramatic operational challenges. The time to address these potential problems is, of course, as the menu item change is considered—not after it is implemented. This point helps to justify the discussion in Chapter 1 that the menu should be planned with input from a number of affected staff members. Production staff members (who are most affected by the proposed menu changes) may be able to identify potential problems and suggest solutions as decisions about menu modifications are made.

## THE MENU INFLUENCES FACILITY LAYOUT

Figure 3-5 illustrates how the individual workstations discussed previously might be put together to form a layout for the food and beverage operation. As we have seen, the menu impacts each workstation. It also impacts the flow of work within and between workstations. Menu planners must consider how required items are to be handled at each step in the process, from the flow of specific ingredients into and out of storage areas to the final service of menu items to guests.

Notice in Figure 3-5 that the kitchen designer has attempted, where possible, to use a straight-line workflow. Food items (ingredients and ready-serve products) are moved from the loading dock to the receiving area; dry, refrigerated, and freezer storage areas are conveniently located in this area. After issuing (also done in this area), ingredients and products move sequentially through pre-preparation, preparation, and holding and serving workstations. After serving, items can be transported for service in the à la carte dining room or in the banquet dining room. The clean-up area is also located near à la carte and banquet dining rooms and close to the holding and serving areas (so that washed dishes and flatware can be transported for reuse).

## THE MENU, CONVENIENCE FOODS, AND FACILITY DESIGN

Items required by the menu can be totally prepared either on site or off site. As well, they can be prepared partially off site, with **finishing** done at the facility. The use of convenience foods can have a dramatic impact on the layout of back-of-the-house storage and preparation areas.

> *Glossary Terms*
> **Finishing.** The task of providing additional ingredients or labor to a convenience food product before service. For example, shrimp can be purchased in a peeled and deveined market form, with additional on-site labor used to butterfly the product before breading and deep-frying.

### A Look at Convenience Foods

Menu planners should consider the several advantages and disadvantages to using convenience food products. Advantages include the following:

- A reduced need for space and equipment.
- The need for fewer skilled pre-preparation and preparation personnel.
- Opportunities for increased menu variety without the need for additional on-site labor, space, and equipment.
- If **portion control** items are purchased, the weight and cost of food items served can be effectively managed.

> *Glossary Terms*
> **Portion control.** Any activity to help assure that the size (by weight or volume) of a menu item is consistent. Examples include the use of a scoop or ladle to serve foods prepared in batches or larger quantities and the use of a preportioned item (such as a 6-ounce hamburger patty) for items cooked to order.

The potential disadvantages to the use of convenience food products include the following:

- A reliance on external suppliers. (For example, there are probably more suppliers

Figure 3-5.  **Schematic of the Menu's Influence on Facility Layout**

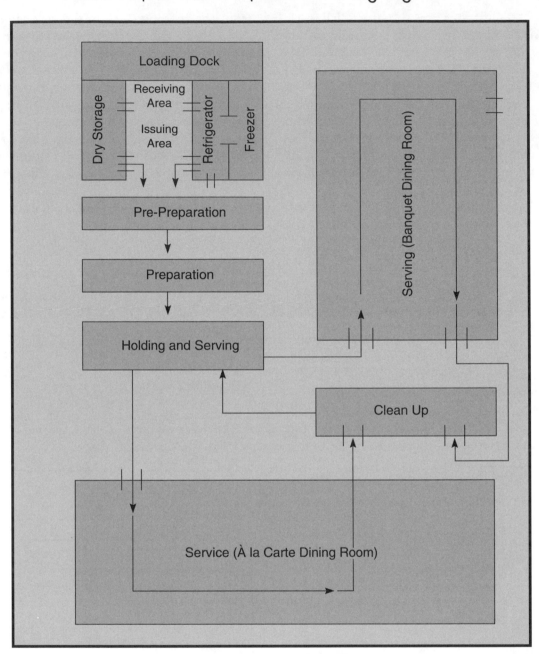

who can provide the fresh produce needed to prepare beef stew on site than there are suppliers who can provide the required quality of prepared beef stew.)

• Public acceptance concerns may arise. In some operations in some markets, the concept of "fresh is best" is very real. As selling

prices increase, guests typically expect items to be prepared on site. Likewise, guests would not normally want to consume the same menu item at alternative restaurants if, for example, the same product is purchased by both properties from the same supplier. (Finishing a convenience food product with additional ingredients and using an on-site prepared sauce and a special garnish, for example, are alternative ways to address this concern.)

- Employee resentment. Production personnel who take pride in their creativity and culinary skills may resent the use of convenience food products. If convenience food items are used extensively, there could be a concern that positions would be eliminated.

Note that two very critical factors must be considered when evaluating whether to use convenience food alternatives: quality and cost. It is not possible to generalize that quality is always better and cost is always lower when an item either is prepared on site or is purchased as a convenience food alternative. The level of food preparation skill and equipment available in foodservice operations varies greatly as does the quality of available convenience food alternatives. Therefore, when menu planners consider whether a proposed menu item should be made entirely on site, purchased as a convenience food, or purchased partially prepared and finished on site, they must carefully analyze what is best for their own operation. We describe this "make-or-buy" analysis in the next section.

## Make-or-Buy Analysis

As mentioned, whether to use convenience foods is not an "all or nothing" decision. Figure 3-6 illustrates the opportunities for decision making as product specifications are developed. While this example considers only one product (shrimp), there can be several alternatives for many of the menu items. This figure shows the many available market forms of shrimp. Shrimp can be purchased fresh (with head on or headless), which is less expensive but requires more on-site labor for processing. Alternatively, frozen shrimp is available processed to different extents, each requiring successively less on-site pre-preparation, as shown in the figure. In addi-

tion, each increasingly processed market form of frozen product will have a greater food purchase cost.

If menu planners want to offer several items containing shrimp, they should evaluate the purchase of the same size shrimp for use in several items (shrimp bisque, seafood platter, shrimp platter, and shrimp sandwich, for example), and then conduct a **make-or-buy analysis** to determine which type of product (fresh or a frozen alternative) to buy. The menu planners must first assess the quality of alternatives. There is no need to determine cost differences between options if the quality of the alternatives to be evaluated is not acceptable. For example, let's assume that in response to many requests from guests, the menu planners want to add a cheesecake with a choice of fruit toppings to the dessert menu. Can the desired quality product be made on site or can it be purchased? The manager and chef will likely have access to numerous recipes for cheesecake. These recipes can be tested, with special attention given to required equipment, necessary skills, and the labor time required for preparation. Cheesecake that is prepared according to the recipes should be evaluated by the property's management and preparation and service staff (as well as a sample of guests, if practical). At the same time, product samples can be obtained from applicable vendors for quality evaluation. Ideally, the products prepared on site according to several recipes that yielded an acceptable product in a first test can be compared with one or more convenience food products that received an acceptable evaluation.

> *Glossary Terms*
> **Make-or-buy analysis.** The process of objectively evaluating the quality and cost differences to the options of preparing a menu item on site, purchasing it in a convenience food form, or finishing it on site.

Figure 3-6. **Range of Convenience Food Alternatives for Shrimp**

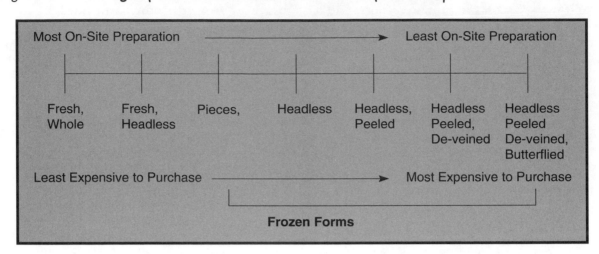

After evaluating the quality of alternative products, the menu planners can begin to make decisions. If, for example, cheesecake of acceptable quality cannot be purchased, it must be prepared on site if it is to be offered. Alternatively, if cheesecake of acceptable quality cannot be produced on site, it must be purchased if it is to be offered. If cheesecake of acceptable quality cannot be prepared or purchased, it is obvious that the cheesecake dessert cannot be offered. On the other hand, if acceptable-quality products can be prepared on site and also purchased, the second step in the make-or-buy analysis—cost considerations—becomes important.

To the extent practical, all costs unique to the alternative under consideration should be assessed. For example, if the cheesecake can be made on site, the costs of ingredients and labor for preparation should be evaluated. If the product is to be purchased, this cost along with any associated on-site labor (for example, the preparation of the fruit sauce) should be considered. It is not necessary, however, to consider costs the alternatives share. Examples here include the cost of portioning, serving, and washing the serving plates and flatware for the desserts.

Figure 3-7 illustrates several points applicable to cost considerations of food prepared on site and convenience food. Note that for on-site food preparation, food costs are normally less and labor costs normally more than for the convenience food alternative. It follows that food costs are more and labor costs less when a convenience food alternative is selected. What becomes important to the menu planners is *not* the specific food or labor costs for each menu item, but, rather, the total of both food and labor costs for each item. In short, quality and price—the two most important considerations in whether to purchase a convenience food—must be assessed specifically for the product under consideration. It is not possible to generalize that one alternative typically has a quality or cost advantage over its counterpart. Figure 3-8 provides another illustration of the concerns involved in and procedures required when undertaking a make-or-buy analysis.

Figure 3-7. **The "Real" Cost of Convenience Foods**

| Cost | On Site | Convenience Form | Total |
|------|---------|------------------|-------|
| Food | Less | More | ? |
| On-site labor | More | Less | ? |

Figure 3-8. **Make-or-Buy Analysis**

The food and beverage director and the chef of the Leilani Hotel are revising the banquet menu. In the past, several clients have requested petit fours (sweet, highly decorated "finger food" cakes). While not on the menu, the purchasing department can procure acceptable convenience food frozen products that only need to be thawed before service. The menu planners thought there was potential in offering these items on preplanned banquet menus to guests. They were also interested in the product because it could have multiple uses; in addition to being included on the banquet menu, the petit fours could be used as garnishes on the dessert trays in the à la carte dining room (and could be sold as an "assorted petit four" dessert plate). They could also be used on coffee break menus, on the Sunday brunch dessert bar and even as a garnish with ice cream and other desserts. Should they make the product, purchase it, or not offer it at all?

**Option 1:**   **Buy the 500 petit fours ready made.**

Purchase cost   =   $0.24 per piece (500 pieces per carton)
              =   0.24  x  500   =   $120.00

**Option 2:**   **Make the 500 petit fours on site.**

Labor:   Baker 1:   4 hours @ $12.50   =   $50.00

(Assemble ingredients, baking utensils; prepare recipe; decorate pieces)

Baker 2:   2.5 hours @ $10.00   =   $25.00

(Assist Baker 1 with preparation and decoration tasks; clean up utensils, equipment, and work areas)

| | |
|---|---|
| Total direct labor cost | $ 75.00 |
| Add 20 percent fringe benefits | $ 15.00 |
| Total labor cost | $ 90.00 |

Ingredients cost:
(Flour, sugar, fat, and other items
needed for cake and frosting)   $ 22.00

Total On-Site Preparation Cost   $112.00

Savings with On-Site Preparation   $  8.00

The menu planners believe that 500 petite fours could be sold weekly; therefore, annual savings with on-site preparation will be **$416.00** ($8.00 per week times 52 weeks). What should the menu planners do?

## THE MENU AND FACILITY DESIGN AND DÉCOR

You have learned that the food, service, and environment in any type of commercial food and beverage operation make up the guests' impression of their dining experience. Successful foodservice operators believe that the value of these three factors is worth their cost and important in encouraging repeat business. In many noncommercial foodservice operations consumers evaluate the same factors—the total dining experience is also the sum of the food and service provided and the environment within which the meal is consumed.

### The Dining Room Is Part of the Dining Experience

Commercial food and beverage operators should attempt to offer a dining environment that is consistent with the menu. First, cleanliness is important in every foodservice establishment. All areas must be clean, including, but not limited to, those in public view. Beyond that, the **design** and **décor** of the dining area are important.

> *Glossary Terms*
> **Design.** The manner in which space and dining areas are used. Typically, dining room furniture, bars, reception, and server areas are considered part of the design.
> **Décor.** Decorations including window treatments, wall and floor coverings, and tablecloths within the dining area.

It is easy to suggest that dining areas must complement the menu in order to offer guests a total and consistent experience. In practice, however, having the menu complement the decor is difficult to implement because it is costly. Consider, for example, the restaurant or hotel dining outlet that opened initially with a steakhouse theme (the menu featured steaks, and the dining room was designed and decorated in an "Old West" theme). The menu may change several times over the life of the dining room. Is it possible to replace the rustic dining room furniture, the plank floors, and the "corral" design woodwork on the walls if the menu changes to a different theme? Yes it is, but only at great expense (and time for the conversion will need to be scheduled).

Memorable dining rooms, as well as the design features they contain, add greatly to the guests' overall dining experience, in both commercial and noncommercial foodservice operations. As mentioned, altering a dining room's theme when a menu is changed significantly can be expensive. But if menu planners understand the following design principles, they can help reduce costs related to facility design changes that result from the revision of a menu's main theme.

### Ten Principles for Changing a Dining Room's Theme[1]

1. Remember that room color is one of the most important features in defining a theme. As a result, paintable surfaces, including walls, door trim, and accent areas, are an inexpensive way to demonstrate a theme "change," especially when an establishment seeks to draw its previous clientele to the new menu.
2. Carpets and floor coverings (as well as expensive wall vinyl and window treatments) should be kept as neutral as possible. Avoid using these elements for theme definition because they are expensive to change and cannot, by themselves, establish a complete theme. Entry mats and appropriate area rugs can help add accent to floors and add significantly to the new theme's development, as can accents around window areas.

---

[1] These principles were suggested by Peggy Hayes, President of Designs from the Heart, and hospitality industry foodservice consultant. Reprinted by permission, Designs from the Heart, copyright 2002.

3. Table coverings and napkins are significant. Tablecloths can add elegance (as in white tablecloth and white napkin restaurants), or they can be used to add a casual flair (as in checkered Italian-style cloths). The material the table covering is made from (such as cotton, vinyl, or paper) adds to theme development, as does the type of napkin used. Select paper for casual, cloth for more formal, and appropriate colors that complement and enhance the selected theme.

4. Significant theme-related elements are needed to "greet" the guests immediately as they enter the dining area. Place these items where guests will quickly notice them.

5. Remember that in addition to carpets, chairs, tables, and wall hangings, there are many design elements, including dishes, flatware, table-top arrangements and organizers, glassware, and, of course, the appearance of the menu itself. Consider all of these and their effect on efforts to establish the new design theme. Dishes and flatware generally do not need to change to establish a new theme. Glassware changes, however, can be an effective, although somewhat expensive, design enhancer.

6. Music is an excellent tool for creating an identifiable theme. Properly selected and played at an appropriate volume, music can be a tremendous help in establishing a unique dining setting.

7. Recessed and ambient lighting are more flexible lighting features when redesigning a room than are ornate or unusual lighting fixtures that hang from ceilings or walls. Lighting levels also influence design. In addition, the color of the lights can be used to enhance design themes.

8. Several larger, significant items (rather than many small ones) can determine an entire room's theme. It is not necessary to "theme" every design element in the room to achieve the desired result if the guests' attention is clearly drawn to a memorable focal point.

9. Employee uniforms are an effective and inexpensive way to help establish a definable theme. Employees as well as guests welcome creative and attractive uniforms.

10. The dining room's accessories (wall hangings, artifacts, signs, plants and other visual accents) are the most noticeable features a designer uses in creating the impressions that guests will remember. Guests will view these items while going to their tables and also during their meal. These accessories, more than any other design element, must "fit" and help establish the restaurant's overall feel. Fortunately, these items need not be expensive and, when selected by a professional with design experience or by a manager with an excellent eye for design, can do much to help create a desired theme.

Operators of noncommercial foodservice operations often have a unique problem: the dining room may need to be used for numerous purposes besides dining. For example, in an elementary school, the dining room may be a multipurpose room used for recess, for schoolwide student gatherings, and even as a public polling place. Dining rooms in post-secondary schools may be used for study halls and evening entertainment. Dining areas in business and industry settings may be used for small group meetings and for eating vending machine items when the cafeteria is closed. In these and related examples of multipurpose rooms, facility administrators would do well to design an attractive facility. For example, it could be bright, uncluttered, and, perhaps, broken into modularized areas (as compared to the "barracks style" of open dining in a large and unattractive dining area).

## Serviceware Is Important

How will food and beverage products be served? **Serviceware** is another concern of the menu planner. Certain serviceware choices are obvious: Menu planners do not serve a high-**check-average** dinner on disposable serviceware; quick-service or elementary school menu planners will not use expensive, washable items.

Beyond these extremes, however, serviceware should still be an important consideration. Historically, plates and bowls have been of neutral color (perhaps with a colored rim or other slight decorative design) so as to not distract from the food presentation. Today, however, many commercial operations combine an eclectic fusion of foods, garnishes, serviceware, and décor, among other elements, for an unusual presentation that creates a "**wow factor**" for guests. "Yesterday" the compartment trays in public schools, the flat trays in post-secondary schools and in many healthcare facilities, and the bulky, heavy, and unattractive serviceware used in other noncommercial operations did little to create a positive dining experience. Today, interesting serviceware with interesting colors, shapes, and materials create a much more positive dining experience in noncommercial operations.

---

*Glossary Terms*

**Check average.** Food revenue divided by the number of guests served; the average amount spent by guests in the food and beverage operation.

**Serviceware.** The plates, bowls, dishes, and flatware (knives, forks, spoons, and other eating utensils) for serving food, along with the cups and glassware used to serve beverages.

**"Wow factor."** Something unexpected and designed to increase a guest's interest in the dining experience.

---

## THE BAR MENU INFLUENCES THE BAR LAYOUT AND DESIGN

The bar menu impacts the design and layout of the bar, which, in turn, affects the efficiency of the operation. The bar menu also determines the bar's theme, style, color scheme, furnishings, and lighting. Whether a bar is sleek and modern, old world or decorated according to a theme (such as nautical, Polynesian, or 1920's), the design establishes the mood. Guests desire more from a bar than just drinks. They want to relax, socialize, and escape their everyday routines. The bar's menu and design sets the scene to help meet these needs.

Most bars offer a range of drinks; many offer low-priced (house), higher-priced (call), and even higher-priced (premium) brands of liquors. The menu planners must consider which brands to offer to best reflect the desires of the guests. Space behind the bar must be sufficient to hold all the alcoholic beverages required by the bar menu. In addition to considering which drinks to serve (which, in turn, dictates which liquors and other drink ingredients are required), the menu planners must specify the garnish and glassware. As well, a wide range of specialty drinks (which should be creatively advertised within the bar or restaurant) may be specified by the bar menu.

Designing a bar and beverage facility is complex and challenging. Menu planners should do extensive research to learn about the demographics of the guests and what products they will order and what services they desire. Planners must evaluate the entire operation in which the bar will be located and assure that the bar will complement the rest of the operation, both aesthetically and functionally.

Should the mood of the bar be intimate, with low lighting, small tables, and soft colors? Or, is the goal to have a meeting place with bright lighting, room to walk about and socialize, and a theme that motivates people to talk? In short, design and layout decisions are made early in the planning stages of any operation and are constantly monitored to assess how well they are working. Design involves more than surface décor and the mood it sets. Design is the end result of many details, including décor and layout; it creates an efficient workflow and coordinates the work operation with guest satisfaction. The key to good design is to keep all the components in balance.

## Bar Design and Layout Principles

Following are the two basic principles important in the design of the beverage operation.

1. *A marketing perspective is important.* A marketing viewpoint affects more than just the front of the house. Wise menu planners know that public areas (the space within the guests' normal view) must be designed with the guests in mind. Designers know that guests purchase more than beverages. They buy a "total experience," including products (drinks and possibly snacks), service, atmosphere, and cleanliness. Public areas should be designed to please the guests. These decisions should be based on demographic research in order to produce a market-oriented facility. After identifying who the guests will be, plans to please them (which begins with the menu) must be developed and implemented.
2. *The entire facility must be designed at the same time.* Although the need for simultaneous bar and restaurant design is obvious, it is sometimes ignored. Menu planners must consider the beverage operation at the same time they plan the foodservice aspects of the business. It is not effective to allocate the needed space for foodservice and let the beverage operation have the remainder; both revenue sources (food and beverage) must be planned together.

## Space Requirements for Beverage and Storage Areas

Behind-bar storage must be adequate to store all the liquors, wines, draft beer, and soft drink dispensing equipment required by the menu. Since behind-bar space is often at a premium, refrigerated storage for beer and soft drink storage can be at a remote site with dispensing lines, pumping equipment, and other related items housed in nonpublic spaces. (If the menu specifies a wide variety of draft beers, additional refrigerated storage areas for these items must be considered.)

Less storage space is needed when automated systems with remote liquor racks for some or all liquor types are used. From a control perspective, behind-bar storage areas must be adequate in size, easily locked, and close to (if not within) the bartenders' work center, so that bartenders do not need to waste time getting additional supplies when they are busy serving guests.

In addition to alcoholic beverages, a sufficient quantity of other items, including disposable products such as straws, napkins, and stir sticks, must be stored in the immediate bar area. Drink mixes, juices, garnishes, and similar products also need space for preparation and storage room. There must be an adequate supply of all necessary glassware and sufficient space to handle soiled and drying glassware. Refrigerated storage may be necessary for cream, drink mixes (such as Bloody Mary mix and mixes for exotic drinks made with fruit juices if a specialty drink menu is offered), vegetables for garnishes, and fruits for drinks such as daiquiris. Ice cream and other frozen mixes require specialized storage space; counter space for mixers, register equipment, and a wide range of other equipment and supply items is generally necessary.

## Glassware Control

Some glassware breakage is inevitable, but excessive breakage can undermine the finances of an otherwise successful bar operation, which points out the necessity for glassware control. Menu planners should limit the number of different types of glassware needed for the available drinks. Since space behind the bar is generally limited, the proper supply of glassware must be ready for immediate use before the shift begins. In addition, adequate equipment is necessary to wash glasses safely and to sanitize them. Even when plans call for most glasses to be washed elsewhere, some arrangements for behind-bar glass washing are generally necessary.

Space must be planned to accommodate clean up and storage of glassware. Racks to hang glasses suspended from the ceiling are popular, since they can be incorporated into the facility's décor. Shelving and countertops may also be used. In some operations, glasses needed for lounge service are given to bartenders by beverage servers at the time beverage orders are placed. This reduces glass storage needs behind the bar (but increases storage needs elsewhere). The beverage facility planners must make sure that there is room to store soiled, clean, and drying glassware.

## The Bar Menu Affects Bar Sales

Even bar operations that have a "regular" clientele may need to constantly attract new guests if they are to thrive; to increase sales and profits often requires an ever-expanding guest base. Effective managers realize the importance of obtaining and retaining a guest base sufficient to continue the life of the business. Everything that is done must ultimately contribute to this goal.

The key in any business to keeping current guests and attracting new ones is to focus on sales. This goal consists of several steps:

- Step 1: Let guests know what products and services you provide.
- Step 2: Demonstrate that the prices you charge represent value.
- Step 3: Encourage the sale.

- Step 4: Deliver the products and services as promised.
- Step 5: Resolve discrepancies between promised performance and actual performance.

The bar menu is the primary tool for accomplishing Step 1.

*Concerns of Bar Guests.* It is easy to believe that many guests value price above all else. One of the first questions many buyers ask is "How much?" It is important, however, not to think that the answer to that question determines whether the buyer forms a long-term (or even short-term!) relationship with the seller. Guests today, as in the past, value and pay for one of four product characteristics. In order of importance, they are

- quality,
- service,
- cleanliness, and
- price.

Guests expect a certain level of quality and service when they make a purchase decision. When their expectations are exceeded, they perceive high levels of quality. When their expectations are not met, they perceive low levels of quality. Consider, for example, two guests. One buys a beer for $0.75; the other pays $3.00. In the first case, the guest, after a twenty-minute wait, receives a warm, flat 12-ounce beer in a dirty glass. In the second case, the guest promptly receives a beautiful 12-ounce frosty mug of sparkling fresh beer, delivered by a smiling server in a pleasant, clean environment. The first guest received no value for the expenditure; the second received a great value and will likely return.

*A Close Look at Bar Menus.* Bar menus are effective tools that managers can use to communicate with their guests. Many facilities create separate menus for food products and for beverage products. Other operators find it more appropriate to have menus that combine food and beverage offerings. Regardless of the choice the operator makes, the menu is an excellent opportunity to build impulse sales or to communicate special sales and services offered by the property. With the increased use of computers and inexpensive on-site color printing, bar menus can be created at a very low cost and can be changed frequently. In addition, menu "clip-ons," which are smaller menu segments clipped to more permanent menus, can prove very effective in influencing impulse buying.

Bar menus should be clean and not worn. They should be free of writing or doodles by customers and from food and beverage spills, because menus indicate to the guests the overall quality of the operation. Colorful, interesting menus help build strong bonds between the guests and the property. Menu design and menu pricing are very important to the overall profitability of the beverage facility. Chapters 6 and 7 provide more information about, respectively, menu planning and menu design; much of that discussion is applicable to bar menus.

Some managers believe that bar menus are unnecessary for their operation. This may not be the case. While complete menus citing all drinks served are not appropriate (nor even possible to provide!), guests do want to know what special products may be offered and the prices they will be paying for these products. Failure to provide a menu is to ignore an extremely effective tool for building the business. Operators can get ideas for effective menus from other operators and from their beverage vendors; or, they can use their own creativity. They should recognize that a beverage menu is an excellent tool that can be very useful to them.

***The Menu Affects the Bar's Atmosphere.*** The bar's general décor and the products the guests see are extremely important merchandising strategies. Menus and displays should "show off" the operation's products and let guests know what is available. Bottle labels on the back bar should always face outward, and bottles should be kept organized and neat. Some operations categorize inventory by price and keep the more expensive brands on the right of the bar, since the eye normally travels in that direction.

If wines are sold, wine lists should be available, interesting, and appealing to the guests (see Chapter 6). The types of guests who patronize an establishment will also impact the atmosphere or image of the operation. For example, a quiet, darkly lit, romantic facility will attract different guests than will a bright, airy establishment. Naturally, all facilities (including restrooms) should be clean, well lit, and comfortable.

***Specialty Menus and the Bar Layout.*** Beverage operations that offer specialty drinks must consider bar space, design, and equipment. Consider, for example, the specialty drink made of several liquors and crushed ice. First, space must be available to store the specialty glassware, if any, used only for these drinks. As well, a blender to crush ice cubes (or a specialty machine to dispense crushed ice) is required. Space for specialty liquors (Chartreuse, Drambuie, Galliano, and Blue Curacao, for example) are needed as is space for extra fruit or other specialty garnishes. Typically, space behind bars is limited, and it can be a challenge to find adequate storage and preparation space to produce specialty drinks. As noted earlier in this chapter, some menu planners implement specialty drink menus with little thought given to anything besides point-of-sale table tents or other advertising media. The result—production bottlenecks causing service delays and bartender and server stress because of inability to do the work as efficiently as desired—could be avoided with proper planning.

## SIGEE'S MENU: A CASE STUDY

"Well, I have what I have," reflected David Berger as he considered the physical layout of Sigee's kitchen, dining room, and lounge. The hotel for which he was the food and beverage director had been built about thirty years ago. At that time, more storage space was devoted to dry and refrigerated items than to frozen food items. As a result, the amount of freezer space in the kitchen was adequate, but not generous. David wondered how many of the new menu's items would be affected by this limitation.

The equipment that had been originally installed on the cooks' line also reflected an era that contained no microwaves (although one of excellent size and speed had been installed in the past two years) and emphasized sautéed items cooked on a gas range top.

"I want to remember my equipment limitations when I set this new menu," thought David. Samuel Ludwig, David's executive chef, had been very helpful in reviewing with David the bottlenecks and difficulties involved with the current menu. "We currently operate a pretty traditional hotel-style restaurant menu here," stated Samuel. "To produce the very best dishes, and with such a heavy emphasis on sauces, the entrée items must be made at the same time the sauces are finished. Of course, I can have the stocks and brown sauces made ahead of time, but the reductions and finished sauces take time. This can really slow us down when it gets busy."

David considered the chef's comments. Samuel was an excellent chef, but David knew that the restaurant itself contributed less than 25 percent of the hotel's total food and beverage revenues. The remaining sales came from the hotel's catering and banquet efforts. It seemed, however, that the complexity of the restaurant's menu resulted in Samuel spending much more than 25 percent of his time attending to its operation. The quality of the food produced by Samuel and his team was truly outstanding. David wondered, however, how many items on the restaurant menu should be made on site and how many could be purchased from the hotel's food suppliers without any loss in quality. He was fairly certain the chef would take the position that any item that could be purchased from a food supplier could be better made from scratch, but he also knew the chef carefully controlled his labor costs and because of that, always kept an eye out for quality pre-prepared ingredient items that could help reduce labor costs.

Deep in thought, David walked out of the kitchen and into Sigee's dining room. "It's a great dining room," reflected David. It had undergone one major remodeling since it had been built. It had large windows overlooking an outside patio area. Also, wooden beams added a rich feel to the area (but were light enough in color that they did not make the room appear overly dark). David noticed that the brightly colored hanging lamps were often dimmed.

The bar area, visible from much of the dining room, was similar in décor to the dining room. It consisted of small cocktail-type tables and chairs and muted lighting, but the area was very open. Obviously, the same designer had done both the Sigee's restaurant and lounge areas. Any new menu would have to take into account the limitations of the kitchen area as well as the dining area and lounge. It was a lot to think about, but David was convinced he and his menu-planning team could do it right. "We will alter the things we can," he thought, "and then plan a great menu around the items that we can't change. I know our guests will be pleased when we're done!"

## CHAPTER 4

# Standard Recipes and Purchase Specifications Deliver the Menu

## MENU TERMS USED IN THIS CHAPTER

"A" ingredients
Blind testing
Chained recipe
Dram shop liability
Precosting
Purchase specification

Purchase unit
Quality
Standard recipe
Supply chain
Value

## CHAPTER OVERVIEW

For a foodservice operation to succeed, not only must menu planners carefully plan a menu designed to meet the wants and needs of those being served, but each menu item must be consistently delivered according to the quality and quantity requirements established for the food and beverage operation. Several planning tools must be in place for this purpose; the two most important are standard recipes and standard purchase specifications.

Standard recipes provide the "roadmap" for preparing each of the food and beverage products offered by the operation. If, for example,

menu planners put beef stew and cherry pie on the menu, they have an idea of what these products should be like. Each time the item is prepared, it should look and taste the same and cost the same to make. This consistency creates marketing and financial advantages that benefit the guests and the foodservice operation.

Standard recipes are critical for any type of foodservice operation of any size in both the commercial and noncommercial segments of the industry regardless of their location. Menu planners, working with a team of management, production, and service personnel (and sometimes even the guests themselves), should assure that these important control tools are developed and then consistently used.

Standard purchase specifications are a second tool needed to deliver the menu. Let's assume the menu offers a variety of seafood platters, many containing shrimp. What size shrimp should be on these seafood platters? Relatively small shrimp (36 to 42 per pound, for example) cost considerably less than larger-size shrimp (16 to 20 per pound, for example). In addition, the market form (fresh or frozen, for example) may affect the quality of shrimp.

Menu planners are concerned about consistency from the perspectives of both the diners and the foodservice operation. Consistency can be assured only when purchase specifications for at least the most expensive menu ingredients are developed and used. (By "used" we mean the activities of communicating the specifications to suppliers and requiring the suppliers to consider these specifications when quoting prices and selecting products for delivery.)

A successful foodservice operation consists of many key ingredients. An effectively designed menu and the standard tools (including recipes and purchase specifications) to "deliver" the menu are at the top of the list of these key ingredients. This chapter will focus on standard recipes and purchase specifications. Application of this information will help assure that the benefits of an effectively planned and designed menu will be realized.

## STANDARD RECIPES DELIVER THE MENU

Throughout this book we have, when necessary, made distinctions between commercial and noncommercial food and beverage operations. These distinctions are not important in this chapter, however, because, without exception, all foodservice operations regardless of type, size, location, or type of guest need **standard recipes**.

---

*Glossary Terms*
**Standard recipe**. Information required to prepare a food or beverage item to consistently meet a foodservice operation's required quality and quantity standards. A standard recipe should indicate the type and quantity of each required ingredient, pre-preparation and preparation procedures including required large and small equipment, yield (number of portions and portion size), garnishes, and any other information needed to produce and serve the menu item.

---

### Objectives for Standards

A primary goal of all menu planners is to plan and offer menu items that guests will enjoy. The many factors that must be considered as the menu is planned are discussed throughout this book. But, as mentioned, the items on a well-developed menu designed to please the guests must all be consistently delivered according to the quality and quantity standards that menu planners have specified.

A standard recipe helps to assure consistency for both the guests and the foodservice operation. Consistency for the guests means that each time they order a menu item it will taste, look, smell, and be the same menu item. This will, in turn, help ensure that guests perceive consistent value—that is, the guest will pay the same amount each time an item is offered and will receive the same quality and quantity of the item each time it is served. Consider, for example, the guest who visits a restaurant and enjoys the seafood platter so much that he or she returns with friends and encourages them to try this entrée. If the product consistency is the same, all guests will have experienced the meal as the initial guest described it. By contrast, if the entrée is different (fewer, different, or differently prepared seafood items, for example) the guest and his or her associates may be disappointed, and the opportunity to encourage them to return has been lost.

Consistency for the foodservice operation means that the selling price of the menu item (see Chapter 5) should be based, in part, on the cost of menu item ingredients. Since the same type and quantity of ingredients will be used each time a standard recipe is followed and since the yield (number of portions and portion size) will be the same, there will be a consistent cost. A food and beverage operation can better meet financial goals when costs that impact revenues and operating budgets are consistent. Cost control can be assured only when an essential cost tool—the standard recipe—is used.

An advantage to the use of standard recipes in addition to the two objectives just described—consistency from the perspectives of both the guests and the foodservice operation—is that the recipe becomes a "road map" for the preparation of a menu item. Properly developed, a standard recipe will indicate the following:

- Each necessary ingredient, including the quantity (weight or volume) needed.
- The types of small utensils (measuring spoons, pots, pans, and mixing bowls, for example) needed to prepare the item.
- Large equipment needed for production, such as a slicer or convection oven, along with operating instructions.
- Exact pre-preparation and preparation procedures.
- Yield (number of portions) and portion size along with portion-control tools, if applicable.
- Special instructions of numerous types, including work-simplification suggestions (for example, "Gather all small utensils required before beginning Step 1") and sanitation and food safety concerns (for example, "If leftovers are to be reused, they must be quickly cooled: place in the refrigerator immediately in a shallow pan. Place the pan in an ice water bath and stir frequently.")

If the menu drives the plans for the food and beverage operation (which it should), then product-related concerns are implemented by the use of standard recipes.

## Sample Standard Recipes

Standard recipes should be used for all food and beverage products. Figure 4-1 shows a standard recipe used in a manual system. Note that it includes the elements just mentioned. If the recipe is followed, it will assure that the correct quality and quantity of food and beverage menu items are always produced.

Figure 4-2 shows three standard recipes used to produce one menu item. Each is computer-generated, and two are **chained recipes**. Note that the entrée recipe (enchiladas de jocoque) contains two ingredients (enchilada sauce and pico, a Mexican topping) that require recipes for preparation.

---

*Glossary Terms*
**Chained recipe.** A recipe that yields an ingredient in another recipe.

---

Some advantages of properly developed computer-generated recipes are the ability to quickly adjust the amount of ingredients required for varying yields (portion quantities or portion sizes; this topic is discussed next) and to more accurately calculate these adjustments.

Figure 4-3 shows a sample standard recipe for an alcoholic beverage. It is just as important to assure that the quality and quantity of beverages are consistent when served as it is for the operation's food.

Once developed, standard recipes should be consistently used each time a food or beverage item is produced. Note that "used" does not necessarily mean that recipes (either hard copies on a workstation table or electronic copies on a computer monitor) must be physically available when items are produced. Rather, "used" means they must be followed. For example, after a cook prepares a food item or after a bartender prepares a drink several times, these production personnel are likely to know all procedures and will be able to follow them

Figure 4-1. **Sample Standard Food Recipe**

| **Recipe Name:** Walnut Encrusted Salmon Fillets | **Yield:** 28 lbs. (56 servings) |
|---|---|
| **Category:** Entrée | **Portion Size:** 8 oz. |
| **Portion Utensil:** Spatula | **Cooking Temperature:** 425°F |

**Utensils/Supplies:** Cutting board, knife, sheet trays, spatula, plastic gloves, clean foodservice cloths, measuring spoons, and cups

| | |
|---|---|
| **Cooking Time:** 10-12 minutes | **Holding Temperature:** 140°F |
| **Holding Time:** n/a | **Estimated Prep Time:** 1 hour |
| **Holding Equipment:** Hot box | |

| Ingredients | Quantity | Procedure |
|---|---|---|
| Chopped walnuts | 5 lbs. + 5 oz. | 1. Combine the walnuts, bread crumbs, butter, parsley, salt and pepper in a bowl. |
| Bread crumbs | 3 qts. + 1 cup | 2. Season salmon fillets with salt and pepper and set aside (skinned side down) on oiled baking sheet. |
| Butter | 2.5 (2½) cups | |
| Parsley | 2.5 (2½) cups | 3. Spread a teaspoon of mayonnaise on top of each fillet. |
| Salmon | 28 lbs. | |
| Mayonnaise | 1.5 (1½) cups | 4. Top with walnut mixture (press mixture into fish). |
| Salt | To Taste | 5. Bake salmon 10-12 minutes until done. |
| Pepper | To Taste | |

SPECIAL INSTRUCTIONS:

Courtesy of Chef Robert Nelson, The School of Hospitality Business, Michigan State University, East Lansing, Michigan.

without needing to review the physical recipe. The ability to "use" standard recipes by memory rather than by reading a recipe is obvious, for example, during peak production times at a bar. It would be very time-consuming if bartenders needed to find a recipe before preparing each drink. Experienced bartenders and well-trained but less-experienced bartenders will have memorized the recipes for most of the drinks guests order.

### Evaluating Standard Recipes

The food and beverage manager or chef will likely be able to find new standard recipes for any new items offered on the menu. As well, menus with "daily specials" and buffets featuring several unspecified items provide opportunities to broaden the range of menu offerings (and perhaps increase guest interest in the foodservice operation).

Figure 4-2. **Sample Computerized Standard Recipe**

```
REPORT#: 90     * * * CBORD FOODSERVICE MANAGEMENT SYSTEMS * * *        PAGE:    1
OPTION : 3.5.8.          MENU MANAGEMENT SYSTEM - V6.30                  MAR 05 02
USER#  : 77         MSU Residence Halls Spring -LCode 2                  1054 HOURS
                 PRODUCTION RECIPE

FUNCTION NAME:
       UNIT:
       DATE: TUESDAY   03/05/02
==================================================================================
1154  ENCHILADAS DE JOCOQUE - MSU
                                             YIELD    :    0.67 SCP

PORTIONS :      8.00      8.00 OZ   COOKING TIME :
PORTION DESC : 2 ENCHILADAS        COOKING TEMP :
PREP TIME:                         COOKING EQUIP:
                                   SERVING PAN  :
PREPARE MAIN BATCH  1 TIME(S)      SERVING UTEN :

     INGREDIENT        ------- MAIN BATCH -------- ------ PARTIAL BATCH ------
                                 QUANTITY                  QUANTITY

CORN TORTILLA 6 INCH                  16     EACH
SOUR  CREAM                   1 LBS    1     OZS
FEA MILD SHREDDED CHEDDAR             12     OZS
GREEN ONIONS CHOPPED FINE              4     OZS
GROUND CUMIN SEED                    1/4     OZS
SAUCE, ENCHILADA REC 1362          2 1/4     CUP

     -----------GARNISH----------------------------------------------------
FEA MILD SHREDDED CHEDDAR              6     OZS
MONTEREY JACK CHEESE                  5     OZS
PICO TOPPING SUBR 1798              1/2     CUP

     NOTE:
          ** STEPS 1-4 MAY BE DONE 1 DAY IN ADVANCE.
     1. FRY (DREDGE) CORN TORTILLAS AT 250F FOR 2 SECONDS WITH A PAIR
        OF TONGS, AND PLACE IN PERFORATED PAN.  USE PAPRE TOWELS TO
        ABSORB EXCESS OIL.
     2. MIX TOGETHER SOUR CREAM, SHREDDED CHEDDAR CHEESE, GREEN ONIONS
        AND CUMIN.
     3. PLACE #24 SCOOP OF FILLING ON EACH TORTILLA AND ROLL UP, LEAVING
        ENDS OPEN.  REMEMBER PRODUCTION LINE SETUP (MIS EN PLACE).
     4. PLACE 2 ROWS OF 12 EACH IN A SCP SPRAYED WITH VEGELENE.
     5. MAKE ENCHILADA SAUCE ACCORDING TO RECIPE 1362.
     6. BAKE COVERED WITH FOIL 8-10 MINUTES AT 350F.
     7. SPREAD 3 CUPS HOT ENCHILADA  SAUCE OVER BAKED PRODUCT.
     8. SPRINKLE 9 OZ. SHREDDED CHEDDAR CHEESE OVER ENCHILADAS,
        COVERING EACH PORTION.
     9. SPRINKLE 5 OZ. SHREDDED MONTEREY JACK JUST DOWN THE MIDDLE OF
        EACH PORTION.
    10. ADD .5 OZ OF PICO DOWN THE MIDDLE OF EACH PORTION.
    11. SERVE 2 ENCHILADAS PER SERVING.

    NOTE: ***
    **   BATCH COOKING OF THIS PRODUCT IS IMPORTANT.  AVOID LONG
         HOLDING TIMES.
    COPYRIGHT 1990 MICHIGAN STATE UNIVERSITY BOARD OF TRUSTEES
    1990 - DIVISION OF HOUSING AND FOOD SERVICES
```

Courtesy of Michigan State University Division of Housing and Foodservices, Michigan State University, East Lansing, Michigan. Steps 5 and 10 are chained recipes.

Figure 4-2 (continued)

```
REPORT#: 90    * * * CBORD FOODSERVICE MANAGEMENT SYSTEMS * * *      PAGE:    2
OPTION : 3.5.8.            MENU MANAGEMENT SYSTEM - V6.30            MAR 05 02
USER#  : 77            MSU Residence Halls Spring -LCode 2          1054 HOURS
                  PRODUCTION RECIPE

FUNCTION NAME:
        UNIT:
        DATE: TUESDAY   03/05/02
===================================================================================
1362   SAUCE ENCHILADA
                                                  YIELD    :    0.53 QT

PORTIONS :        8.53    2.00 OZ    COOKING TIME :
PORTION DESC :                       COOKING TEMP :
PREP TIME: 25 MIN                    COOKING EQUIP:
                                     SERVING PAN  :
PREPARE MAIN BATCH  1 TIME(S)        SERVING UTEN :

     INGREDIENT            ------- MAIN BATCH -------- ------ PARTIAL BATCH ------
                                   QUANTITY                  QUANTITY

     REVISED 2.04.94

FLOUR                         1 TBSP         1/4 TSP
MARGARINE                                    1/2 OZS

WATER                                        1 3/4 CUP
VEGETARIAN CHICKEN BASE                      1 1/4 TSP
GROUND CHILI POWDER           2 TBSP         1/2 TSP
TOMATO PASTE                  3 TBSP         1/2 TSP

    1. MAKE ROUX IN STEAM KETTLE.   COOK 5 MINUTES.
    2. ADD WATER, VEGETARIAN CHICKEN BASE, AND CHILI POWDER.
    3. COOK UNTIL SLIGHTLY THICKENED.
    4. ADD TOMATO PASTE AND SIMMER 15-30 MINUTES.
       DO NOT SIMMER LONGER OR FLAVOR WILL BECOME MUCH STRONGER.
```

```
REPORT#: 90    * * * CBORD FOODSERVICE MANAGEMENT SYSTEMS * * *      PAGE:    3
OPTION : 3.5.8.            MENU MANAGEMENT SYSTEM - V6.30            MAR 05 02
USER#  : 77            MSU Residence Halls Spring -LCode 2          1054 HOURS
                  PRODUCTION RECIPE

FUNCTION NAME:
        UNIT:
        DATE: TUESDAY   03/05/02
===================================================================================
1798   PICO (MEXICAN TOPPING)
                                                  YIELD    :    0.12 QTS

PORTIONS :        7.97    0.50 OZ    COOKING TIME : 3 MIN
PORTION DESC :                       COOKING TEMP :
PREP TIME:                           COOKING EQUIP:
                                     SERVING PAN  : HALF DEEP COUNTER PAN
PREPARE MAIN BATCH  1 TIME(S)        SERVING UTEN : SERVING SPOON

     INGREDIENT            ------- MAIN BATCH -------- ------ PARTIAL BATCH ------
                                   QUANTITY                  QUANTITY

FRESH RED PEPPERS                 1      OZS
FRESH GREEN PEPPERS               1      OZS
RED ONIONS                        1      OZS
FRESH TOMATOES                    1      OZS

    1. MEDIUM DICE PEPPERS, ONIONS, AND TOMATOES.
    2. MIX TOGETHER.
    3. USE IN 1/2 OZ. PORTIONS TO GARNISH.

    NOTE: GARNISH FOR ENCHILADAS.
```

Figure 4-3. **Sample Beverage Recipe**

| Item Name: Whiskey Manhattan | | | | | | | | | Recipe #: 102 | |
|---|---|---|---|---|---|---|---|---|---|---|

| | | | Date: _____ | | Date: _____ | | Date: _____ | |
|---|---|---|---|---|---|---|---|---|
| Ingredient | Purchase Unit Size | Amount | Cost For | | Cost For | | Cost For | |
| | | | Unit | Portion | Unit | Portion | Unit | Portion |
| B. Whiskey | 32 oz. | 2 oz. | 5.35 | .33 | | | | |
| S. Vermouth | 32 oz. | 1 oz. | 2.35 | .07 | | | | |
| Bitters | 16 oz. | Dash | 3.25 | .01 | | | | |
| Garnish | | | | | | | | |
| M. Cherry | Gal. (240) | 1 | 10.60 | .04 | | | | |
| B. Pick | | 1 | | | | | | |
| S. Stick | | 1 | | .01 | | | | |
| | | | | .46 | | | | |

Mixing Procedure:

*Iced*: Pack old-fashioned glass with ice; measure ingredients with jigger. Add dash of bitters. Garnish; serve with cherry and bar pick. Insert swizzle stick.

*"Up"*: Portion ingredients into shaker glass, add ice; stir to chill. Strain into cocktail glass. Garnish; serve with cherry and bar pick.

Glassware:
Iced:   7 oz. old fashion
"Up":   4½  oz. cocktail

A formal system to evaluate standard recipes can help assure that the very best recipes are used. This, in turn, will help assure that the menu-planning objectives for including the item on the revised menu are attained. Figure 4-4 illustrates a form that might be used to evaluate standard recipes. Note that in the left column selected recipe evaluation factors are listed. Raters are then asked to indicate their perceptions of each factor on a scale from "dislike very much" to "like very much." Space is provided for comments on each factor.

Who should be asked to evaluate standard recipes? The best answer is "as many persons as possible in each affected constituency," including facility managers (this group would include the hotel and restaurant foodservice manager) and administrators in noncommercial foodservices facilities, food and beverage managers, food preparation and service personnel, and the guests themselves. Many noncommercial foodservice operations use the services of "advisory committees," whose members have a broad range of responsibilities, including those of menu-item evaluation.

While recipe evaluation is important when adding new items to the menu, the evaluation process can also be used for existing recipes. Consider, for example, changes in guests' preferences. (For example, a specific market may, over time, enjoy either more or less spicy food items.) Consider also the availability of new or revised ingredients. (For example, menu planners may find new turkey and ostrich products that will be useful in an existing stew or casserole recipe.) **Blind testing** can be a useful process to evaluate preferences for alternative recipes that address potential menu additions.

*Glossary Terms*
**Blind testing.** The process of evaluating items produced from standard recipes in such a way that the evaluators know neither the recipe nor its ingredients before or during evaluation. This method helps reduce biases that are formed when raters know they are assessing favorite or unpopular recipes and when they have formed perceptions (favorable or unfavorable) about recipe ingredients.

The menu planners should carefully compile and study the information from the recipe-evaluation forms. This data can be very helpful in guiding changes to improve the menu. The data should be provided to production personnel who can address suggestions in efforts to assure that all recipes do, in fact, deliver the quality and quantity requirements that guests desire.

## "Arithmetic" of Standard Recipes

We have established that all items required by menu planners must be prepared according to standard recipes. Sometimes, recipes can be found that yield the exact number of desired

Figure 4-4. **Recipe-Evaluation Form**

| Recipe-Evaluation Factor | Your Evaluation 1 = Dislike Very Much; 5 = Like Very Much | Comments |
|---|---|---|
| Portion size | 1  2  3  4  5 | |
| Color | 1  2  3  4  5 | |
| Texture | 1  2  3  4  5 | |
| Taste | 1  2  3  4  5 | |
| Aroma | 1  2  3  4  5 | |
| General appearance | 1  2  3  4  5 | |
| Ingredients | 1  2  3  4  5 | |
| Compatibility with other menu items | 1  2  3  4  5 | |
| Garnish | 1  2  3  4  5 | |
| Other: _____ | 1  2  3  4  5 | |
| Other: _____ | 1  2  3  4  5 | |
| Other: _____ | 1  2  3  4  5 | |

Recipe Name: _____     Recipe No.: _____
Test Date(s): _____     Evaluated by: _____

Instructions:  Please circle the number that best represents your perception of each factor using the following scale:  1 = Dislike Very Much; 5 = Like Very Much.

Should this recipe be used in our operation?     ❏ Yes     ❏ No
Explain:

portions in the correct portion size. Often, however, the food and beverage operation must adjust recipes to its specific needs. The three basic types of recipe adjustments are (1) those that change the number of portions, (2) those that change the number of portion sizes, and (3) those that do both.

***Adjustment for the Number of Portions.*** Sometimes, menu planners may desire to use a recipe with a specified portion size, but need to change the number of portions the recipe yields. Figure 4-5 shows how to do this. When reviewing this figure, note that two steps are required to determine the quantity of ingredients needed for a recipe when only the number of portions (not portion size) differs between the two recipes. First, an adjustment factor is calculated by dividing the desired number of portions by the number of portions in the original recipe. Second, the adjustment factor is multiplied by the quantity of ingredients in the original recipe to determine the quantity of ingredients for the new recipe.

Note that experienced chefs do not use this process to initially determine the quantities of herbs, spices, and other seasonings needed for a revised recipe. Typically, these flavor ingredients are adjusted only gradually after the quantity of other ingredients has been determined, with a careful note made of the amount of seasonings added to the revised recipe. One "rule of thumb" suggests that the amount of an herb or spice be initially determined as follows: the original amount multiplied by the adjustment factor, divided by two, with appropriate additional amounts added "to-taste" thereafter.

***Adjustment for Portion Sizes.*** Sometimes, the menu planners desire to use a standard recipe yielding the same number of portions, but they wish to change the portion size. The process to do this is explained in Figure 4-6. When reviewing this figure, note that the process to determine the recipe adjustment involves, first, determining the quantity of yield in both the original and desired recipes. In the example, you will note that 18.8 cups of product were yielded by the original recipe; 56.25 cups are desired. After dividing the desired yield by the original yield, the resulting adjustment factor

Figure 4-5. **Recipe Adjustment for Number of Portions**

Assume the original recipe yields 75 portions (½ cup each); the restaurant wants to make 50 portions (½ cup each).

**Step 1:** Calculate the adjustment factor.

$$\text{Adjustment factor} = \frac{\text{Number of desired portions}}{\text{Number of original portions}}$$

$$= \frac{50}{75}$$

$$= 0.67$$

**Step 2:** Multiply the adjustment factor by the quantity of ingredients in the original recipe to determine the amount of ingredients in the new recipe.

Example: Assume ½ pound (8 ounces) of butter is required in the original recipe.

| 8 ounces | x | 0.67 | = | 5.4 ounces (rounded) |
|----------|---|------|---|----------------------|
| (original amount) | | (adjustment factor) | | (desired amount) |

Figure 4-6. **Recipe Adjustment for Portion Size**

Assume the recipe yields 75 portions (¼ cup each); 75 portions (¾ cup each) are desired.

**Step 1:** Calculate the adjustment factor.

$$\text{Adjustment factor} = \frac{\text{Desired portions} \times \text{Portion size}}{\text{Original portions} \times \text{Portion size}}$$

$$= \frac{75 \times \text{¾ cup}}{75 \times \text{¼ cup}}$$

$$= \frac{56.25 \text{ cups}}{18.80 \text{ cups}}$$

$$= 3.0 \text{ (rounded)}$$

**Step 2:** Multiply the adjustment factor by the amount of ingredients in the original recipe to determine the amount of ingredients in the desired recipe.

Assume ½ pound (8 ounces) of butter in the original recipe.

| 8 ounces | x | 3.0 | = | 24 ounces (1½ pounds) |
|:---:|:---:|:---:|:---:|:---:|
| (original amount) | | (adjustment factor) | | (desired amount) |

(3.0) is used in Step 2 in the same manner the adjustment was used when only the quantity (not portion size) was changed (see Figure 4-5). When the adjustment factor of 3.0 is multiplied by the amount of butter (8 ounces) in the original recipe, the amount of this ingredient required for the desired recipe (1½ pounds) can easily be determined.

*Adjustment for the Number of Portions and Portion Size.* A third example of recipe adjustment involves changing both the number of portions and portion sizes. This process is illustrated in Figure 4-7. Note that the process shown in this figure is very similar to that explained in Figure 4-6. The first step involves calculating the quantity of yield in both recipes and dividing the desired yield by the original yield. The second step involves multiplying the resulting adjustment factor by the quantity of each ingredient in the original recipe. The 8 ounces of butter in the original recipe is multiplied by the adjustment factor of 2.0 to yield the necessary amount of butter for the revised recipe (16 ounces).

**Precosting Recipes**

We noted earlier in this chapter that two of the menu planners' most important goals are more consistently met when standard recipes are used. First, there will be consistent product quality, which is desired by the guests. The process of recipe adjustments (see the previous section) helps to assure that the same proportion of each ingredient is used whenever the recipe is used, even if the number of portions or the size of the portion changes. Second, information about product costs is better attained through use of standard recipes. To determine the cost of menu items, a process called **precosting** is used.

Figure 4-8 shows a worksheet that can be used to determine the total cost and per-portion cost to produce the Walnut Encrusted Salmon shown in the standard recipe in Figure 4-1. While reviewing Figure 4-8, note that for each major ingredient the amount, **purchase unit**, cost per purchase unit, number of units used, and total cost is listed. The amount (in purchase units) of each ingredient needed is multiplied by the cost per purchase unit to

Figure 4-7. **Recipe Adjustment for the Number of Portions and Portion Size**

Assume the original recipe yields 75 portions (¼ cup each); 50 portions (¾ cup each) are desired.

**Step 1:** Calculate the adjustment factor.

$$\text{Adjustment factor} = \frac{\text{Desired portions x Portion size}}{\text{Original portions x Portion size}}$$

$$= \frac{50 \times \text{¾ cup}}{75 \times \text{¼ cup}}$$

$$= \frac{37.5 \text{ cups}}{18.8 \text{ cups}}$$

$$= 2.0 \text{ (rounded)}$$

**Step 2:** Multiply the adjustment factor by the amount of ingredients in the original recipe to determine the amount of ingredients in the desired recipe.

Assume ½ pound (8 ounces) of butter in the original recipe.

| 8 ounces | x | 2.7 | = | 16 ounces (pound) |
|---|---|---|---|---|
| (original amount) | | (adjustment factor) | | (desired amount) |

determine the total cost of that ingredient in the recipe. For example, 2.5 cups of butter are needed; butter is purchased by the pound (the purchase unit). Since there are two cups of butter per pound, 1.25 purchase units are needed (2.5 cups divided by 2 cups equals 1.25 pounds). Since one pound of butter costs $2.55, the cost of butter needed in the recipe is $3.19 (1.25 pounds times $2.55 per pound). As this process is repeated for each ingredient, it becomes possible to calculate both the total recipe cost (the cost to produce the total number of portions yielded by the recipe) and the cost to produce one portion.

*Glossary Terms*
**Precosting.** The process of determining the cost to produce all portions and a single portion of a menu item when a standard recipe is accurately followed.
**Purchase unit.** The measurement unit normally used to purchase food products. For example, fluid whole milk may be purchased by the gallon; flour is purchased by the pound.

Increasingly, precosting is done by computer. This makes it easy, for example, to make adjustments in recipe costs for all recipes containing a major ingredient each time that the ingredient cost changes. However, the point of this discussion is that the menu planners must know the cost to produce one portion of a standard recipe yield when that portion is produced according to the exact procedures required by the standard recipe.

If the food and beverage operation has only an à la carte menu, the per-portion cost can provide information for menu pricing (see Chapter 5) and for menu evaluation (see Chapter 9). Often, however, the menu provides several items at a specified cost. For example, the selling price of an entrée may include the choice of potato, a salad with choice of dressing, and bread and butter. In some operations, other items (a second vegetable and dessert, for example) may be provided. In these instances, the cost to produce one portion of a specified food item must be combined with the cost of other food items to determine the base cost for the meal served to the guest.

Figure 4-8.  **Precosting a Standard Recipe**

| Recipe: | Walnut Encrusted Salmon | | | | |
|---|---|---|---|---|---|
| Yield: | 56 | | Portion Size: | 8 ounces | |
| | *(number of portions)* | | | | |

| INGREDIENT | | | COST | | |
|---|---|---|---|---|---|
| **Name** | **Amount** | **Purchase Unit** | **Cost Per Purchase Unit** | **No. of Units** | **Total Cost** |
| Walnuts | 5 lbs. + 5 oz. | Pound | $ 4.25 | 5.31 | $ 22.57 |
| Bread crumbs | 3 qts. + 1 cup | Pound | 1.10 | 3.50 | 3.85 |
| Butter | 2.5 cups | Pound | 2.55 | 1.25 | 3.19 |
| Parsley | 2.5 cups | Bunch | 0.69 | 2.00 | 1.38 |
| Salmon | 28 lbs. | Pound | 12.40 | 28.00 | 347.20 |
| Mayonnaise | 1½ cups | Gallon | 17.50 | 0.09 | 1.58 |
| Salt | To Taste* | — | — | — | — |
| Pepper | To Taste* | — | — | — | — |

**Total Recipe Cost**  $379.77

$$\frac{\$379.77}{\text{Total Recipe Cost}} \div \frac{56}{\text{Number of Portions}} = \frac{\$6.78}{\text{Per-Portion Cost}}$$

*Amount used is impractical to calculate.

## Calculating Menu Costs

Figure 4-9 shows a worksheet that can be used to determine the per-portion cost for all the food items provided as part of a specific meal. Note that it lists the per-portion cost of the salmon entrée ($6.78) that was costed in Figure 4-8 and illustrated in the standard recipe in Figure 4-1. In the restaurant where this precosting is done, other items are included with the selling price of the entrée. For example, guests have a choice of a potato, vegetable, and salad with dressing. The cost of the plate garnish, bread and butter, and condiments served with the entrée are also costed. If all the items that the meal "Walnut Encrusted Salmon" comprises are prepared, portioned, and served exactly according to the applicable standard recipes, the total per-portion (that

is, meal) cost will be $8.30. It is this cost that will be used for menu pricing (see Chapter 5) and for menu evaluation (see Chapter 9).

Note in Figure 4-9 that guests have a choice of potato, vegetable, and salad with dressing with the entrée. It is likely that the product cost for each choice will vary depending on which alternative the guests select. How should these choices be costed? There are several ways to handle this challenge. Perhaps the most practical way is to calculate the cost of the highest-rated choice in each category and to use it when the meal is costed. For example, assume that a serving of mashed potatoes has a per-portion cost of 0.22 and a serving of twice-baked potatoes has a per-portion cost of 0.33. A conservative menu planner would, then, cost the potato choice at 0.33. (This is the tactic

Figure 4-9. **Precosting an À la Carte Menu Item**

| Meal: | Walnut Encrusted Salmon | |
|---|---|---|

| Category | Item | Per-Portion Cost |
|---|---|---|
| Entrée | Walnut Encrusted Salmon | $ 6.78 |
| Potato choice | Mashed, Twice Baked | 0.33 |
| Vegetable choice | Du Jour | 0.43 |
| Salad choice | Tossed Green, Caesar's | 0.35 |
| Dressing choice | 5 Choices | 0.20 |
| Garnish | Lemon Slice | 0.03 |
| Bread | Choices | 0.12 |
| Butter | Butter, Margarine | 0.04 |
| Condiment(s) | | 0.02 |
| | **Total Per-Portion (Meal) Cost** | $8.30 |

Figure 4-10. **Costing Sheet for a Salad Bar: Number of Portions and Cost**

| Salad Bar Item | Beginning Quantity | Add During Meal Period | | | Total Portions | Less Left-overs | Total Portions Served | Per-Portion Cost | Total Item Cost |
|---|---|---|---|---|---|---|---|---|---|
| (1) | (2) | (3) | (4) | (5) | (6) | (7) | (8) | (9) | (10) |
| Potato Salad | 50 | 50 | 25 | 25 | 150 | 20 | 130 | 0.20 | $26.00 |
| | | | | | | | | | |
| | | | | | | | | | |
| | | | | | | | | | |

$437.85*

Total Item Cost (column 10) ÷ Number of Guests = Total Per-Portion Salad Bar Cost
$437.85 ÷ 210 = $2.09

*total cost for all salad bar items.

used in Figure 4-9.) This approach assures the menu planners that the calculated total meal cost is as high as it will be if all standard recipes are consistently used.

## Calculating Buffet and Salad Bar Costs

It is relatively easy to cost menu items when one serving is pre-portioned by production or service staff. However, how should items be cost when guests serve themselves on a "help yourself" buffet or on a self-service salad or dessert bar? Figure 4-10 illustrates a worksheet that can be used for this purpose.

When reviewing Figure 4-10, note that one item on the salad bar is potato salad (see column 1). It is prepared according to a standard recipe to yield 50 portions, which are all placed on the salad bar at the beginning of the meal period (column 2). During the meal period, 100 additional portions of potato salad are transferred to the salad bar (see columns 3 to 5). The total number of portions brought to the salad bar (150) is shown in column 6. At the end of the meal period 20 portions of potato salad remain (column 7). Therefore, 130 portions (150 available portions minus 20 portions left over) were served (see column 8). Each portion costs $0.20 (column 9); therefore, the total cost for all potato salad used during the meal period was $26.00 (130 portions times $0.20 per portion; see column 10). The process used for potato salad would be repeated for each item served on the salad bar during the meal period.

The total item cost (column 10) for all portions of all items on the salad bar is then summed. This total item cost (column 10) divided by the number of guests served represents the per-guest cost for the salad bar. For example, in Figure 4-10 the total item cost was $437.85; the total number of guests served was 210. Therefore, the total per-guest salad bar cost was $2.09 ($437.85 divided by 210). The total item cost (column 10) is the cost, then, that would be used in the salad choice in Figure 4-9 if the restaurant offered a salad bar.

Note that the detailed process to estimate per-portion self-service costs, illustrated in Figure 4-10, does not need to be ongoing. Rather, the menu planners might use this worksheet for several (or more) meal periods when implementing a new buffet or salad bar or when first implementing a precosting plan for an existing buffet or salad bar. The results would be an average per-guest (portion) cost that would then be used for subsequent precosting requirements. As product costs change over time and as the variety of buffet and salad bar items changes, the costing process could be replicated.

Many menu planners are concerned about the inability to control product costs when guests help themselves. Are there tactics to control costs without interfering with the guests' opportunities to serve themselves? Several guidelines can be helpful[1]:

### Guideline One: Proper Management Philosophy Is Important

- Recognize that guests desire acceptable quality at a price that represents value.
- Understand that food waste reduces profits. The more waste, the higher the food costs. If managers don't care (or just assume that this is a historical problem with no solution), how can they expect their guests to become waste-conscious consumers?
- "Learn from your garbage can." How bad is the plate waste problem? Often the dishwasher can better answer this question than can the manager! Managers cannot address a problem until, first, they are aware of it. Statistics such as perceived high food cost percentage may be verified by a look at the garbage can and an on-going conversation with those who empty it. Is the volume of plate waste large? Are there some items that are most frequently wasted? Assure that you

[1] The remainder of this section is from Simon Liu and Jack Ninemeier, "Managing Food Costs: Guidelines to Reduce Waste," *The Michigan Restaurateur*, July/August 1999.

really understand guest preferences. This is important for managers in all types of operations. It makes no sense to offer items that guests do not like in a self-serve operation in order to reduce food cost. It makes no difference whether waste is off the plate or out of serving containers at the end of the shift. Both types of waste end up as garbage. Higher food costs result, and the diners do not receive value for the dining dollars they spend.

***Guideline Two: Assure that Menu Analysis Is Continuous***

- Keep constant track of the variety and volume of items that are produced, transported to self-service stations, and left over. Review these production and leftover records when developing production forecasts and when considering menu changes.
- Assure that your menu is flexible. Perhaps some items should not be offered, for example, if market prices increase dramatically (either seasonally or during times of temporary shortages).
- Sometimes leftovers can be reused. (Sanitation and quality issues are a critical concern as these decisions are made!) The ability to use leftovers is another of many planning considerations that confront the manager as self-service items are considered.

***Guideline Three: Carefully Manage Food Preparation and Service***

- Use standard recipes. Standard recipes provide consistency for both the guests and the property. Nothing is gained, for example, when a restaurant guest enjoyed an item during a previous visit, returns and selects the item again, and becomes disappointed (and does not eat what is placed on the plate) when the item is different. As well, recipes containing the same amount and type of items are easier to manage from a cost perspective.

- Portion control is often possible even in self-service operations. For example, can items be portioned onto casserole dishes or plates of a specified size? Can chicken be cut into quarters rather than halves? Separate food visibly (for example, salmon steaks or pork chops) to prevent items from sticking together. (For example, sometimes a diner desiring one breaded pork chop cannot separate two that are stuck together. Both are selected—even though only one may be desired.) Sometimes, perhaps, the portion size can be bigger than that which might be used in an à la carte alternate. Consider, for example, a "big" cookie, which is relatively inexpensive compared to other desserts. Selection of the cookie can reduce food costs!
- Replenish self-service stations with less food more frequently. There are at least two reasons for this suggestion. First, many people perceive that food being brought from the kitchen is fresher than that which is already on the serving line. In fact, quality will likely be better if food is not held on the serving line for long time periods. Food that is not presented in an attractive fashion will not be selected or is less likely to be consumed. Either way, food waste results. A second reason to suggest more frequent replenishment is that diners who see a large volume of food may subconsciously equate this with "limitless" amounts—and may help themselves accordingly.
- Assure that food presentations are attractive. Visual effect is an important first impression for many self-service diners. Self-service stations often need almost constant attention to keep them clean and attractive. When practical, serving pan or tray garnishes are a nice touch as are decorations in or on the serving stations themselves. These and related tactics suggest that the manager cares about the food and the guests. This may, in a subtle way, help some guests place a greater value on the food as well.

*Guideline Four: Keep Thinking About Portion Control*

- Use the right serving utensils at the right places. Utensils help determine the size of the portions taken. A ladle that is too large for a sauce, a salad dressing, a beef stew, or a shrimp creole, for example, makes it easy for someone to take too much and hard for someone to take a smaller portion if they would like to.
- Use the correct size serviceware. For example, plates and bowls that are larger than necessary can confuse guests. How much food am I supposed to take? How much food must I take to attain value? (Does the manager plan selling prices based on the large volume of food suggested by the oversized serving plates?) Managers cannot be psychologists, but they can think about guest perspectives as they make their many decisions about what to serve themselves. The manager's goal should be to use serviceware of the appropriate size: large soup bowls or large salad plates, for example, may be best for relatively inexpensive items. By contrast, smaller plates for entrées can be useful—especially when signage indicates that guests can return to the service line for additional portions. As another example, a large cup might be avail-

able for soft drinks. Even if the diner fills the cup completely, the amount of soft drink served is likely to be less than if people fill two smaller cups to satisfy their thirst.

- Consider the portion size of self-service items compared to their counterparts in an à la carte operation. Frequently, portion sizes are smaller in the self-service operation. This is compensated for by providing a larger variety and by diners' having the option to select more food or a desired type. Managers determine the proper portion size by considering the type of food and its cost and the methods of food presentation, among other factors. Staff manning the service stations must be taught the correct portion size to initially offer. Foodservice managers must be concerned about food costs along with the many other resources they manage. The foodservice operation can use several strategies to reduce food costs that are within the control of the foodservice operation. These must be addressed. However, it is incorrect to think that there are no practical ways to manage these costs in self-service operations. Managers of these facilities are challenged to manage food costs. Their success is in the best interests of the property, those being served, and the community in general.

## SPECIAL CONCERNS WHEN USING STANDARD RECIPES _____

This chapter has emphasized the need for consistent use of standard recipes to help deliver the menu. Menu planners must assure that standard recipes are used. To do this, it is obviously necessary that required ingredients always be available for each recipe in required amounts. Operating difficulties occur, diners are displeased, and cost concerns arise when production personnel must be "creative" and substitute ingredients when the items needed for a recipe are unavailable.

Also, tools specified by recipes must be available. For example, it does little good to specify

that a 6-ounce portion of sliced ham steak be served if, in fact, the preparation area does not have a working calibrated scale. Likewise, it does not make sense to specify use of a number 12 scoop (12 level servings per quart) or a 4-ounce ladle to portion a menu item if these tools are not available. Many problems relating to the misuse of a standard recipe can be traced to management's failure to provide the required resources for compliance with recipes.

We have noted earlier that standard recipes should be used for alcoholic beverage items as well as for food products. In addition to quality and cost issues, there is one additional reason why standard recipes are needed in bar operations. Today's **dram shop liability** laws allocate blame for injuries and accidents resulting from the consumption of alcoholic beverages in hotels, restaurants, and other establishments. Operators who use standard recipes and portion tools such as shot glasses or metered dispensing systems have a greater defense in identifying the exact quantity of alcohol served (the number of drinks times the amount of alcoholic beverage per drink) than do their counterparts who do not use standard recipes and portion-control tools.

Finally, the role of standard recipes in cost control should be noted. Product costs have an impact on the ability of a foodservice operation to achieve financial goals. Menu planners are concerned about these goals as well as guest acceptance goals when menus are planned. Both of these concerns relate directly to planned product costs that assure standard recipes are used. We will explore these issues more in depth in chapters on menu pricing (Chapter 5) and menu-evaluation strategies (Chapter 9).

---

*Glossary Terms*
**Dram shop liability.** A legal concept that allocates responsibility to third parties such as commercial food and beverage operations for accidents and injuries caused by persons who consume alcoholic beverages in an operation. (By law, the "first party" is the person injured or harmed; the "second party" is the person causing the injury; the "third party" is anyone else contributing to the injury.)

---

## PURCHASE SPECIFICATIONS DELIVER THE MENU

When menu planners develop the menu, they have in mind a certain quality for the menu items. They develop standard recipes to help assure that these quality standards are attained. When they price standard recipes, they assume that the proper quality of ingredients has been purchased, received, and used in preparation.

Let's assume that menu planners design a great menu section on salads, and, because of the low cost and popularity of these items among frequent guests, let's further assume that the planners want to feature several salads as signature items. One salad, "The Chef's Special Salad with Tangy Remoulade Sauce," features several colossal olives as part of a garnish made, in part, of shaved fresh carrots and lemon and lime peels.

The olive is an integral part of this garnish. If there is no specification for the olives, what should the purchaser order ("The biggest you've got," "Some big ones," or another phrase to suggest colossal-size)? In fact, there is an olive size specification for a super colossal olive: not to exceed approximately thirty-two olives or less per pound of drained olives. The purchaser can specify this size by name, and on a routine but random basis can count the olives received to assure that the **purchase specification** for olive size is attained. This simple example shows why purchase specifications are important to help deliver the menu.

---

*Glossary Terms*
**Purchase specification.** A definition of required quality that must be met by products purchased by the foodservice operation.

---

### Purchase Specifications and Quality

Food purchasers must focus on achieving several goals for effective purchasing:

- Obtaining the *right* product
- Procuring the *right* **quality**
- Receiving at the *right* time
- Obtaining the *right* price
- Using the *right* supplier

Developing Purchase Specifications

How is "quality" described? For some items, the proper quality is a brand name. For example, this is very common in the purchase of alcoholic beverages. Purchasers may buy a lower quality (and lower cost) "house" brand of gin, a higher quality (and higher priced) "call" brand of gin, and, perhaps, a still higher (and still higher priced) "super premium" brand of gin.

Food distributors sometimes carry more than one quality of, for example, canned green beans. Perhaps they offer a "red label" brand of good quality and a "blue label" brand of a higher quality. In these examples of gin and green beans, the purchase specification can be the brand. For many products purchased, however, there is no brand. Most food products are generically grown, processed, or manufactured and are distributed through the **supply chain** without an attached brand name. Since it is not possible to purchase the vast majority of all products required by the foodservice operation with a brand name, the purchaser must then rely on a purchase specification.

*Glossary Terms*
**Quality.** Suitable for intended use; the more suited that a product is for its use, the more appropriate the quality is for the product. A "quality" product, then, requires that it do what it is supposed to do better than any other product.

The use of purchase specifications focuses on the first two goals—the *right* product is one that meets the property's *quality* requirements.

The definition of quality makes the purchaser think about the use for the product when determining the purchase specification. The olive garnish example illustrates this. Other examples include whether expensive skinless whole canned tomatoes must be purchased if the product is going to be finely chopped for a casserole dish. Or, is it acceptable to purchase chicken breasts with skin tears if the product is going to be battered and deep-fried? (This is probably acceptable.) The concept of "most suitable for intended use" requires the purchaser to first think about how the product will be used and then to consider the purchase specification for it. Specifications should be developed for, at least, the **"A" ingredients** that are purchased.

*Glossary Terms*
**"A" ingredients.** The relatively few ingredients that make up 75 percent or more of the total purchase dollars; in other words, most purchase dollars are spent to purchase the relatively few "A" ingredients.

Purchase specifications are important for "A" ingredients, whether they are specific ingredients in a recipe (such as tenderloin tips in a stew) or whether they are entire menu items (such as a lasagna purchased in a ready-to-serve convenience food form). Quality requirements must be determined before these products are processed.

*Glossary Terms*
**Supply chain.** The channel of distribution through which products move from the initial grower, processor, or manufacturer through wholesalers, distributors, and brokers to the final user (the foodservice operation).
**Value:** The relationship between price and quality. Guests desire value: the greatest quality of products, services, and environment for the least amount of money that they must pay for the dining experience.

When purchasers think about quality, they must also think about price. The concept of **"value"** refers to the relationship between quality and price. When we in our personal lives seek to purchase clothing, an automobile, or almost any other commodity or service, we think about value. Purchase decisions typically involve "getting the most for the money," and people usually must make fairly subjective decisions about what is "the most."

When foodservice purchasers make purchase decisions, they must have the same concerns about value as we do when we make purchase decisions for ourselves. For example:

- If quality is constant and the price increases, then value decreases.
- If quality is constant and the price decreases, then value increases.
- If quality increases and the price decreases, then value increases.
- If quality decreases and the price increases, then value decreases.

Managers who use purchase specifications first define quality requirements and then search for the "best" prices for the desired quality.

## The "Mechanics" of Purchase Specifications

Who develops the purchase specifications? Several groups can play a part in the process:

- *The foodservice manager, chef, and production employees*—These staff members define the need for the product (only ingredients required by the menu should be purchased; these staff members plan the menu). As well, they can provide technical expertise as the specification is developed, can suggest potential suppliers who might supply the product, and can evaluate and test alternative products. These staff members should make the final decision about specifications.
- *Purchasing personnel*—These advisory experts can question suppliers about products judged most appropriate to meet quality requirements. They can arrange for samples or trial orders, obtain information, give advice, and check in-coming products for quality issues.

Purchasing personnel provide assistance but do not make final decisions about purchase specifications.

- *Supplier personnel*—Suppliers can provide information about available products, advise about what other foodservice operations use, and provide counsel about new products to be introduced. They can also objectively evaluate drafts of the proposed specifications. Supplier personnel have no responsibility in the development of purchase specifications but can provide technical assistance.

How are purchase specifications developed? If the menu planners desire to develop a specification for a menu item already on the menu, several steps are taken:

- Select a sample that is of the proper quality.
- Ask the supplier who normally provides the product to describe it (size, grade, and the like).
- Write a draft of a purchase specification.
- Ask other eligible suppliers to objectively evaluate the specification draft and to make suggestions for revision.
- Modify the purchase specification as necessary.
- Use the specification.

Menu planners who want to develop a purchase specification for a product that is not currently on the menu but will be added to it must undertake several steps before they can use the above procedures:

- Provide an oral description of product needs to reputable suppliers; stress product use.
- Analyze any samples that are provided.
- Select the product judged to be the proper quality.

After these three steps are completed, the menu planner can follow the procedures described for developing specifications for products currently used.

Figure 4.11. **Format for Standard Purchase Specification**

Date: _____

Name of Property (Facility): _____
1. Name of "A" ingredient (or product): _____
2. Purpose (use) of ingredient (or product): _____

_____

_____

3. General quality description: _____

_____

4. Other quality information: _____

_____

_____

5. Process to test for quality standards: _____

Earlier in this chapter, we noted the need to *use* standard recipes after they are developed. The same concern is important to stress in our discussion of purchase specifications—*they must be used*. It does little good to commit the time and effort required to develop standard recipes and standard purchase specifications unless they will be used. Purchase specifications are used when they are provided to eligible suppliers with the requirement that quoted prices and the delivered products must meet the quality requirements indicated in the purchase specification.

Figure 4-11 lists some of the information that should be provided as a specification for "A" items. Note that in point 2, the purpose of the ingredient should be specified. This relates directly to our earlier definition of quality, which focuses on the intended use of the product.

Note also that the standard purchase specification format allows the menu planners to provide some general and other quality information to describe the product. Finally, the purchase specification format suggests that the menu planners think about the process

that will be used to test for quality standards. This is an important component of the purchase specification. It does little good to detail quality requirements for necessary product purchase specifications unless there is a practical way to assure that these quality requirements will be met. As a rule of thumb, menu planners can assume that they will *pay* for the quality of products ordered; there is less assurance that this quality will be *received* unless it can be verified. Recall our previous example of super colossal olives—menu planners will pay for this high-quality product but should routinely (but at random intervals) count the number of olives in a pound to assure that the minimum size requirements are met.

## Purchase Specifications and Standardization

The purchase specification yields a standard quality definition and helps assure that the same quality of product will be purchased each time regardless of the source. Its use is, then, perhaps the best way to assure that purchased products consistently meet quality requirements.

Minimum requirements must be addressed by purchase specifications to help assure that standardization goals are met:

- They must accurately describe the required quality.
- They must focus on observable features.
- They must be realistic so that acceptable products can be found.
- They must be clearly written without excessive detail.
- They must permit the purchase of readily available products.
- They must permit supply from more than one vendor.
- They must allow for some flexibility for both the buyer and the seller.

Some general information is required for all product orders that are placed; this information should *not* be included in purchase specifications:

- Delivery instructions.
- Personnel authorized to purchase and receive products.
- General bidding and order procedures.
- Qualifications for eligible suppliers.
- Quantity needed.
- Agreed-on price.
- Purchase unit size.

Menu planners recognize several advantages of specifications when "A" products are purchased:

- Clearer understanding of required products.
- Smaller variety of required products.
- Reduced cost for the correct quality of product.
- Increased competition for the menu planner's purchase dollar.
- Help in product receiving.
- A better assurance that the required quality of products will be consistently purchased.

It does take some time and effort to develop purchase specifications. As well, there will be increased duties for purchasing personnel. Expertise about products is required, and purchase specifications, like menus, will likely need to be revised over time. However, concerns about developing purchase specifications are easily countered by the many advantages we have discussed here.

Can purchase specifications be used by small food and beverage operations without access to full- or part-time purchasing specialists? The answer is "Yes." First, menu planners in small operations can write brief statements to describe the most important quality factors in "A" items. Then, they can receive help from suppliers to develop practical purchase specifications. By concentrating first on the most expensive "A" items, it will be possible to, over time, develop purchase specifications that can help assure that quality requirements are consistently met. As this occurs, the menu planners will have better assurance that the quality of product desired for the guests will be consistently delivered.

## SIGEE'S MENU: A CASE STUDY

"It's Ocean Perch. Take it back," said Samuel Ludwig, the hotel's executive chef to the man making a food delivery at the kitchen's receiving dock. "I'll just have to see if I can get what I need from another supplier before tonight!"

"O.K.," said the deliveryman, "Whatever you say. I'll take it back." With that, the driver for National Foods removed the top box from a stack of boxes he had unloaded, and placed the rejected box back on his truck.

As David Berger, the hotel's food and beverage director, approached the executive chef, he could see that Samuel was upset. "What's the problem Samuel?" asked David. "The problem," replied Samuel, "is National Foods and Lake Perch."

"What do you mean?" asked David. "Well," said Samuel, "today is Friday, and you know how popular our 'Friday Fish Fry' special has been." "Yes," replied David. "It's going great." David knew that Samuel had developed an "All You Can Eat" Friday Night Fish dinner special that was very popular with the area's local residents. It had been promoted highly, and Lake Perch fillets were the featured item. The hotel's supplier of the perch, as well as many other meat and seafood items, was National Foods.

"National Foods claims they are out of Lake Perch. I've got to get on the telephone and find some. I'm not sure what we will have to pay for it," said Samuel as he hurried away, "but dinner starts in four hours."

David went to his telephone also. He called Toshia Lawrence, his sales representative at National Foods. "Toshia," began David, "you can't be out of Lake Perch! We have over 100 people coming to dinner tonight and at least half of them will want our Fried Fish Special!" "I'm sorry David," replied Toshia, "but it's like I told Samuel when we first bid on your purchase specification, and he placed the order with us. Lake Perch is a tough one. Its availability depends on the catch, and that varies weekly. That's also why the cost varies so much from week to week. Remember, Samuel said he wanted fresh, not frozen, fillets, and trust me, . . . if I have them, I can ship them to you. If I don't. . . well, all I can do is try to make the best substitution possible. But I know Samuel doesn't like it!"

David again considered his menu. Samuel was simply trying to maintain the quality standards established for the Fish Fry Special. He knew that this particular menu item was extremely popular, but he could not help feeling that it had been selected poorly. The fresh Perch fillets were very tasty, but the volatility of their supply had caused problems before. He wondered if there were other seafood items that could be just as popular but could be procured at a more consistent cost and without the supply problems they were currently experiencing. He decided right then to explore his alternatives.

"Toshia," said David, "you know the seafood market, as well as the tastes of our local clientele. What item would you recommend if we were considering a permanent replacement for the Lake Perch?"

# Menu-Pricing Tactics

## CHAPTER OUTLINE

## MENU TERMS USED IN THIS CHAPTER

Base selling price
Break-even analysis
Contribution margin
Excessive price spread
Income
Incremental sales

Niche marketing
Operating budget
Price cost
Revenue
Subjective pricing methods
Value

## CHAPTER OVERVIEW

Menu pricing is one of the most important aspects of menu management. It is also one of the least understood and most incorrectly managed aspects of menu planning. Careful attention to menu selling prices is absolutely necessary—first, to please the guests (who are concerned about the cost of their food and beverage purchases) and, second, to attain the operation's financial objectives. In this chapter we will explore the basics of menu pricing. You will discover that objec-

tive systems based, in part, on product costs are at the heart of successful pricing systems.

Some menu planners seem unaware that selling prices impact the financial success of the foodservice operation. They use subjective menu pricing methods that have little, if any, relationship to their revenue or cost plans. Rather, they make a "wild guess," attempt to identify what they believe guests will perceive to be a good value, or charge "what the market will bear." When these and related methods do not work, they simply change the selling price until they believe the selling price is "fair" for both the guests and the foodservice operation (or, at least, until they cannot charge more without sales declining).

Fortunately, there are methods that do help menu planners objectively translate financial goals to selling prices. In this chapter we discuss three simple mark-up methods (which establish base selling prices by using budgeted food costs) and three additional methods in which menu planners take information from the operating budget: contribution margin pricing, ratio pricing, and simple prime cost pricing. None of these methods dictates what the menu selling prices should be. Each, however, helps the menu planners to establish a foundation from which to consider other factors.

All commercial food and beverage operations sell products to the public. Many noncommercial foodservice operations have opportunities to generate revenues from cash, credit card, or other selling alternatives. The principles of establishing the menu selling prices are the same regardless of the type of guests to which the food and beverage operation is marketed.

The chapter also presents information about other pricing issues. For example, menu planners can use break-even analysis to consider the impact of selected factors, including how selling prices affect guest counts. Tactics to manage daily specials and price increases, when necessary, are also presented. The chapter concludes with a discussion about psychological pricing factors, which consider how guests evaluate selling prices as they make purchase decisions.

## THE IMPORTANCE OF EFFECTIVE MENU PRICING _____

What selling price should the hotel food and beverage operation or restaurant set for its steak dinner? How much extra, if any, should be charged for "unlimited" trips to the salad bar (and how much should be included in a "complete dinner" price for the first trip)? A high school cafeteria offers complete lunches for a specified price and à la carte pricing for other items. What should these prices be? In a business corporation's dining room, how should items be priced for the employees who choose to eat there? Menu planners should pay significant attention to these and related questions as an integral aspect of the menu planning and design process. This emphasis should be obvious; however, as shown in the next section of this chapter, menu planners often use very subjective systems that focus on a myriad of issues not directly related to the operation's financial structure.

Among the many reasons why menu pricing is important to all foodservice operations are the following:

- *Marketing-related concerns.* Guests in all types of foodservice operations are looking for **value** when they make purchase decisions. They want to be assured that what they receive (products, service, and environment) for what they pay is worthwhile. If customers perceive that menu items are overpriced, they might feel resentment, which will cause decreased spending on their initial visit and on their subsequent visits, if they return at all.

- *Financial concerns.* The amount of **revenues** generated by the foodservice operation is directly related to the financial success of the operation. If effective pricing is in place, increased revenues will yield increased **contribution margins,** which are the key to the operation's financial success.

- *Other concerns.* Some menu-pricing concerns relate to both marketing and financial issues. Consider, for example, competition. Guests in all commercial and many noncommercial foodservice operations have dining alternatives. Customers consider selling price, at least in part, when they decide where to dine. In other words, they assess the perceived value they will receive from alternative dining options. Menu planners who want to achieve marketing and financial goals must, then, consider the competitions' selling prices when making their own pricing decisions.

---

*Glossary Terms*
**Contribution margin.** Menu item selling price less menu item food cost; the amount of revenue that remains after product costs are subtracted from the product's selling price. For example, a sandwich selling for

---

$5 with a product cost of $1 will yield a contribution margin of $4.

**Revenue.** The amount of money generated from the sale of food and beverage products and other services offered by the food and beverage operation. Note that the term "revenue" should not be confused with another term, "sales," which refers to the number of units of product sold to guests. For example, a restaurant will have revenues of $25 if it sells five sandwiches at a selling price of $5 each.

**Value.** The relationship between price and quality. Guests desire value: the greatest quality of products, services, and environment for the least amount of money that they must pay for the dining experience.

---

## SUBJECTIVE MENU PRICING METHODS

Pricing methods that do not consider the foodservice operation's financial structure and requirements are called **subjective pricing methods**. Unfortunately, many menu planners have traditionally used subjective pricing methods and, in the process, have been unable to maximize the marketing and financial benefits of the menus being planned.

---

*Glossary Terms*
**Subjective pricing methods.** Procedures to establish menu selling prices that do not consider, at least in part, the financial structure and requirements of the foodservice operation or the product costs of the menu items being priced.

---

While there are variations on subjective pricing methods, the following are some of the most frequently used:

- *The "wild guess" method.* Menu planners who use this pricing tactic basically "pick a number" to set selling prices.
- *The "perceived value" method.* This tactic requires the menu planners to put themselves in the place of guests and answer the

question, "What would I pay for this item if I were a guest in my food and beverage operation?"

- *The "keep trying" method.* This tactic is basically a trial-and-error approach to menu pricing. The menu planners, in effect, believe that selling price is the primary determinant of product sales. Therefore, if an item is popular, its selling price should be increased. The reverse is also true: As the product sales decrease, the selling price should be decreased accordingly.
- *The "what the market will bear" method.* This method requires the menu planners to consider the highest price a guest will pay for a menu item. Using this estimate, the menu planners establish the selling price.
- *The "blanket pricing" method.* When this method is used, the menu planners rationalize that diners are willing to pay a specified price for a meal. The task becomes, then, one of determining menu items that can be sold at that price while generating the desired income.
- *The "get them in" method.* With this pricing plan, the menu planners establish a very low price for some menu items to attract

diners to the food and beverage operation. Then, losses from the sale of these low-priced items can be recovered through the sale of other items. A common example is the tactic of selling low-priced meal specials (perhaps sold for below product costs!) with the plan to recover these losses and generate additional revenues from the sale of other items such as beverages and desserts. This pricing strategy *may* be effective in *some* circumstances. However, it must be a well-thought-out tactic in an organized marketing campaign that is, in turn, based on knowledge of the operation's financial structure as marketing tactics and selling prices are developed.

- *The "lower than the competition" method.* Managers who use this method set product selling prices lower than those of their competitors. The focus here is the product name on the competitor's menu without regard to how, if at all, the two products may differ.

For example, portion size, ingredient quality, décor, entertainment, and numerous other factors may justify price differences for the "same" product because, in the eyes of the diner, the products are different, and value is received when different prices are paid.

These subjective menu pricing methods do have advantages: They are easy to use, and they take little time to implement or to revise. A critical disadvantage to these methods, however, more than offsets justification for their use: They do not incorporate concerns about the foodservice operation's financial structure and goals. If these methods are sometimes effective, it is probably more by chance alone than by purposeful planning. Wise menu planners make an effort to use objective pricing methods to minimize the impact of faulty assumptions on the operation's financial success.

## OBJECTIVE MENU PRICING METHODS

As we mentioned before, menu planners who use objective pricing methods must consider the following three elements:

- *Financial structure.* The financial structure of a foodservice operation is normally expressed in its **operating budget**; this planning tool outlines plans for revenues, expenses, and **income** (profits).
- *Financial goals.* The amount of income that remains after all expenses associated with and allocated to the foodservice operation are deducted from revenues.
- *Product costs.* The cost to produce one serving of each item on the menu when each

menu item is produced according to the standard recipe.

---

*Glossary Terms*
**Income.** Also called "profit" (in a commercial operation) and sometimes "operating surplus" (in a noncommercial operation), income is the "bottom line"; it is the amount of money remaining after all expenses associated with or allocated to the foodservice operation are deducted from its revenue.
***Operating budget.*** A financial plan that estimates planned revenue, expenses, and income for a specific period. Budgets are usually planned for a twelve-month period on a bimonthly basis.

---

## A Word About Profits

Commercial foodservice operations exist to generate an income ("profit"). Likewise, noncommercial foodservice operations generally have financial goals such as breaking even (expenses must equal revenues, if any, plus subsidies, if any, from the sponsoring institution). In either case, there are two ways to view profits:

1. Revenue − Expenses = Profit
2. Revenue − Profit = Expenses

While these two formulae are arithmetically equal, they are—from the viewpoint of management—worlds apart. The first equation suggests that the menu planners are satisfied with "what's left" after expenses are subtracted from revenue. The plan is to "pay everyone else first" and, then, to use the leftover revenue to meet the owner's and investors' needs or to improve the operation (in the case of a noncommercial facility).

The second equation means that the menu planners "pay" themselves first after revenue is generated; what's left represents allowable expenses. The approach of assuring that the amount of revenue remaining after profit is deducted will be sufficient to cover required expenses without sacrificing quality requirements is done through the budget-development process.[1]

Objective menu pricing methods are, then, "profit pricing" models because they recognize the need to generate the amount of profit expected as the current operating budget is developed. In fact, all of the numbers that drive objective pricing methods are derived from a current and well-planned operating budget.

## Requirements for Objective Pricing

Objective menu pricing methods require that three basic control tools be consistently used:

- *Standard recipes.* Standard recipes will assure that ingredients of a specified type and quantity are used, and that portions of a specific size are served. This is critical because objective pricing methods are based on product costs, which are driven by the consistent use of standard recipes.
- *Precosting with accurate costs.* Each standard recipe for each component of the menu item being sold must be precosted, with costs reflecting the current market prices for all ingredients used in standard recipes. (*Note:* Standard recipes and precosting procedures are discussed in Chapter 4.)
- *Accurate operating budget data.* Basic assumptions underlie objective pricing methods. Menu planners' assumptions when developing the operating budget suggest reasonable expectations of revenues and applicable expenses for the fiscal period. It is important, then, that both the menu prices and the operating budget be established for the same time period.

## Objective Pricing Methods

Let's review objective menu pricing methods by using the data in Figure 5-1. To simplify the calculations, we will assume the property is open for dinner only.

---

[1] Activities involved in budget development are beyond the scope of this discussion. For more information, see, for example, Raymond Schmidgall et al., *Restaurant Financial Basics.* New York: John Wiley and Sons, Inc., 2002.

Figure 5-1.  **Operating Budget Data for the Leilani Restaurant**

Assume:
- Estimated number of guests:            85,000
- Guest check average:                   $15.00
- Food cost:                             35 % of revenues
- Labor cost:                            $375,000
- Other nonfood costs (excluding labor): $293,250

Therefore:
| | | |
|---|---|---|
| (A) Total revenue | = 85,000 guests x $15.00 | = $1,275,000 |
| (B) Food cost ($) | = $1,275,000 x 35 percent | = $  446,250 |
| (C) Labor cost (%) | = $375,000 ÷ $1,275,000 | = 29.4 % |
| (D) Other nonfood costs (%) | = $293,250 ÷ $1,275,000 | = 23.0 % |
| (E) Income (profit) | = Revenue – [Food cost + Labor cost + Other nonfood costs] | |

= $1,275,000 – [$446,250 + $375,000 + $293,250]

= $1,275,000 – $1,114,500

= $160,500 (12.6 % of revenue, rounded)

We will first develop an abbreviated operating budget that can be used for several objective menu pricing methods. When reviewing Figure 5-1, note that the amount of revenue is not given but must be calculated. As shown in "A" in the figure: 85,000 guests spend approximately $15 each (the guest check average) for revenue of $1,275,000. Notice also that food cost is stated as a percentage (35 percent of revenues), not in dollars. The dollars of food cost are calculated in "B" by multiplying the food cost percentage (35 percent of estimated revenue) by the revenue:

$1,275,000 (revenue) x 0.35 (percent of revenue) = $446,250 (food cost)

Labor cost is shown in dollars, but procedures in "C" to calculate the labor cost percentage are provided:

$375,000 (labor) ÷ $1,275,000 (revenue) = 29.4 percent labor costs.

Other nonfood costs (those excluding labor, which was separately calculated) are calculated by dividing their value ($293,250) by the estimated revenue:

$293,250 ÷ $1,275,000 = 23 percent.

Finally, to complete the operating budget, income (profit) must be determined.  As shown in "E":

Income (Profit) = Revenue – All costs (Food costs + Labor costs + Other Nonfood costs).

The budgeted profit is, then, $160,500 (12.6 percent of revenues).

A simplified operating budget can be developed using these calculations. Figure 5-2 shows a completed operating budget for the Leilani Restaurant. When reviewing Figure 5-2, note that estimated revenues are $1,275,000 and that food, labor, and other nonfood costs are $446,250, $375,000, and $293,250, respectively. Income (profit) is estimated to be $160,500. Percentages for each category of cost and income (profit) are also reported.

Next we will explain how the information in Figures 5-1 and 5-2 can be used to establish an objective **base selling price** for some menu items.

> *Glossary Terms*
> **Base selling price.** The selling price of a menu item derived from the use of an objective pricing method. The base selling price is not necessarily the price advertised on the menu. Rather, it is a foundation selling price based on operating budget data. This price may be modified after menu planners consider factors including marketing issues, the competition, and psychological pricing.

Figure 5-2.  **Completed Operating Budget for the Leilani Restaurant**

| | Dollars | | Percentage | |
|---|---|---|---|---|
| Revenue | | $1,275,000 | | 100.0% |
| Food cost | ($ 446,250) | | (35.0%) | |
| Labor cost | ($ 375,000) | | (29.4%) | |
| Other nonfood cost | ($ 293,250) | | (23.0%) | |
| Income (profit) | | $ 160,500 | | 12.6% |

***Simple Mark-Up Pricing Methods.*** The most simple objective pricing methods use a multiplier on food costs to establish base selling prices. Three examples follow.

1. *Simple Mark-Up Method.* The simple mark-up method uses a mark-up factor developed by dividing 100 percent (the total amount of revenue) by the budgeted food cost percentage (which is the amount of revenue, as a percentage, required to pay the food cost). In the Leilani Restaurant, for example, the budgeted food cost is 35 percent of revenue (see Figure 5-2). Therefore, the mark-up factor is 2.86 (100 percent divided by 35 percent equals 2.86, rounded). Once the markup is determined, the menu planners multiply the menu item's food cost by the markup. Assume, for example, that the food cost for a chicken dinner is $5.70. (This includes the ingredient cost for all items that make up the "chicken dinner" when a standard recipe precosted with current purchase prices is used. Let's assume also that a "chicken dinner" means the chicken

entrée with sauce, salad, vegetable accompaniment, and dinner roll with butter.)

To calculate the base selling price using the simple mark-up method, menu planners multiply the total cost of ingredients ($5.70) by the markup (2.86) to yield a base selling price of $16.30 (rounded).

2. *Entrée Mark-Up Method.* The entrée mark-up method is similar to the simple mark-up method just discussed, but uses the cost of only the entrée. In pricing the chicken dinner previously discussed, let's assume that the entrée (chicken with sauce) represents $3.25 of the total $5.70 product cost. Before a base selling price can be determined, the mark-up multiplier must be determined.

To calculate the markup for using the entrée mark-up method, menu planners must consider the estimated cost of all entrées to be purchased during a budget period. Assume, for example, that 65 percent of the $446,250 in total food costs (see Figure 5-1) will be used to purchase entrées. (*Note:* Analysis of invoices for entrée purchases during a past budget period indicated that the total entrée cost was 65 percent of the total food cost. The assumption is that the percentage of food purchases represented by entrées will remain constant for the new budget period.) With this information, a markup for the entrée mark-up method can be calculated:

Total revenues ($1,275,000) ÷ ($446,250 x 65 percent) = Entrée markup
$1,275,000 ÷ $290,063 = 4.40 (rounded)

The base selling price for the chicken dinner can now be calculated:

Cost of entrée ($3.25) x markup (4.40) = Base selling price ($14.30).

Why would menu planners want to use the entrée mark-up method? An advantage is that one need know only the entrée cost (for example, chicken with sauce) rather than the additional recipe costs for other components of the menu item (salad, vegetable accompaniment, and dinner roll with butter). This facilitates calculation of a base selling price. One disadvantage, however, is that time must be spent to determine the amount of total food costs represented by entrées. In some instances this may be relatively easy (as, for example, when most entrées are purchased from specific suppliers such as a meat and poultry vendor who sells few or no other items to the food and beverage operation). It becomes more difficult when numerous suppliers are used and when invoices from these suppliers must be sorted by entrée and nonentrée.

3. *Markup with Entrée and Accompaniment Cost.* Accompaniment costs include all product costs that are not part of the entrée. (In our example, the accompaniments are the salad, vegetable accompaniment, and dinner roll with butter.) A four-step process can be used to calculate a base selling price when the markup with entrée and accompaniment cost method is used.

*Step 1:*   Calculate per-guest accompaniment costs.

| | |
|---|---|
| Total food costs: | $446,250 (see Figure 5-2) |
| Total entrée costs: | $290,063 (see our discussion about the entrée mark-up method) |
| Total accompaniment costs: | $156,187 ($446,250 – $290,063) |
| Total number of guests: | 85,000 (see Figure 5-1) |

$156,187                 ÷   85,000          =   $1.84 (rounded)
(total accompaniment          (number of              (per-guest accompaniment
costs)                        guests)                  cost)

*Step 2:*   Calculate total menu item food cost.

| | |
|---|---|
| Entrée cost: | $3.25 |
| Accompaniment cost: | + $1.84 |
| Total menu item food cost: | = $5.09 |

*Step 3:* Calculate markup.

$$\frac{100 \text{ percent}}{\text{Budgeted food cost percentage}} = \frac{100 \text{ percent}}{35 \text{ percent}} = 2.86 \text{ (rounded)}$$

Note: The markup (35 percent) is the same as that used with the simple mark-up method, since the food cost ($5.09) represents the menu item's total food cost (which was also the case when we used the simple mark-up method).

*Step 4:* Calculate base selling price.

| $5.09 | x | 2.86 | = | $14.56 |
|---|---|---|---|---|
| Total menu item food cost (Step 2) | | Markup (Step 3) | | Base selling price |

In short, the entrée and accompaniment mark-up cost method requires four steps. First, the per-guest accompaniment cost must be calculated ($1.84 in Step 1 above). Then, the total menu item's food cost is calculated by adding the entrée cost to the accompaniment cost (Step 2). The markup is determined in the same way that the markup was calculated using the simple mark-up method; a budgeted food cost percentage is divided into 100 percent (Step 3). Finally, the base selling price is determined by multiplying the total menu item's food cost by the markup.

Mark-up methods are relatively simple to use; all information is readily available if precosted standard recipes and data from the current operating budget are used. Two important disadvantages, however, must also be noted. First, simple mark-up methods do not reflect the fact that more (or less) labor may be used to produce some menu items. As well, it is important that current and accurate total food cost data be available. This typically involves calculating (and deducting) food costs applicable to employee meals, marketing expenses, and transfers to the beverage operation. As well, transfers to and from the beverage operation to the food department must also be calculated.

Other menu-pricing methods are more sophisticated than these simple mark-up methods because they focus on unique aspects of the relationship between product costs and other variables. Three of these methods are contribution margin pricing, ratio pricing, and simple prime cost pricing.

***Contribution Margin Pricing Method.*** As discussed earlier, the concept of "contribution margin" relates to the difference between a menu item's selling price and its food cost:

Contribution margin = Selling price – Food costs.

The contribution margin represents, then, the amount of money generated from the sale of a menu item that can be used to pay for all nonfood costs and to make a contribution to the income (profit) requirements of the foodservice operation.

A two-step method is used to establish base selling prices using the contribution margin pricing method. First, it is necessary for the menu planners to determine the average contribution margin per guest:

(Nonfood costs + Profit) ÷ Number of expected guests = Average contribution margin per guest

Second, the base selling price must be determined by adding the average contribution margin per guest to the menu item's standard food cost. Let's use information in Figures 5-1 and 5-2 to illustrate the contribution margin pricing method.

*Step 1:*   Determine the per-guest contribution margin.

$$\frac{\text{Labor cost} + \text{Other nonfood costs} + \text{Profit}}{\text{Number of guests}}$$

$$\frac{\$375,000 + \$293,250 + \$160,500}{85,000 \text{ guests}}$$

$$\frac{\$828,750}{85,000} =$$

$$\$9.75$$

*Step 2:*   Add the per-guest contribution margin to the menu item's food cost.

| | |
|---|---|
| Food cost (chicken dinner) | $ 5.70 |
| Per-guest contribution margin (from Step 1) | + $ 9.75 |
| Base selling price | = $15.45 |

Once the per-guest contribution margin is known, the menu planners know, on average, the amount of nonfood costs that must be generated by the selling price ($9.75 in Step 1). The nonfood cost (contribution margin) that is derived from the sale of the menu item will be used to pay for all nonfood costs (including labor) and to contribute to the property's profit requirements. All that remains, then, is to add the food cost ($5.70 for the chicken dinner in Step 2) to arrive at a base selling price of $15.45.

When the contribution margin pricing method is used, menu planners need to calculate the per-guest contribution margin only once. In effect, this becomes a "seat tax"; every guest, regardless of what menu item is purchased, is expected to pay his or her "fair share" (contribution margin) to support the property's nonfood cost and profit requirements.

***Ratio Pricing Method.*** The ratio pricing method considers the relationship between product costs and all other costs plus profit to develop a base selling price. There are three steps involved when the ratio pricing method is used. Information in Figures 5-1 and 5-2 provide the data needed for the calculation:

*Step 1:*   Determine the ratio of food costs to the contribution margin.

$$\frac{\text{Contribution margin (Labor costs} + \text{Other nonfood costs} + \text{Profit)}}{\text{Food costs}}$$

$$\frac{\$375,000 + \$293,250 + \$160,500}{\$446,250} =$$

$$1.86 \text{ (rounded)}$$

The ratio of 1.86 does not refer to dollars or to percentages. It simply means that, for each $1.00 of food costs, an additional $1.86 is required to pay for the contribution margin (labor, other nonfood costs, and profit).

*Step 2:* <u>Determine the total amount of labor, nonfood costs, and profit (contribution margin) applicable to the menu item by multiplying the food cost for the menu item by the ratio:</u>

| | |
|---|---|
| Food cost (chicken dinner): | $ 5.70 |
| Ratio | x  1.86 |
| | $10.60 |

This calculation indicates that $10.60 is required from the sale of the chicken dinner to pay for the item's "fair share" of labor, nonfood costs, and profit.

*Step 3:* <u>Add the menu item's food cost to its calculated labor, nonfood costs, and profit.</u>

| | |
|---|---|
| Food cost (chicken dinner): | $ 5.70 |
| Labor, nonfood costs, and profit (Step 2 above): | $10.60 |
| | $16.30 |

As Step 1 shows, a ratio (1.86) is calculated to indicate the number of dollars of nonfood cost and profit that must be generated for each $1 in food costs. The ratio is multiplied (in Step 2) by the food costs for the applicable menu item to determine the amount of the item's selling price required to meet labor, nonfood costs, and profit requirements. Then, (in Step 3) the total amount of nonfood costs and profit is added to the food cost to establish the item's base selling price.

***Simple Prime Cost Pricing Method.*** The term "**prime cost**" refers to the sum of product (food and beverage) and labor costs incurred by the foodservice operation. As its name suggests, then, the prime cost pricing method requires the menu planners to assess the labor costs and factor these into the pricing equation. Three steps are required to use the simple prime cost pricing method. Data in Figures 5-1 and 5-2 provide all the necessary information.

> *Glossary Terms*
> **Prime cost.** The sum of product (food and beverage) and labor costs. Prime costs can be calculated for a menu item or for the total of these costs (for example, in an operating budget). They can be expressed in dollars or as a percentage of total costs.

*Step 1:* <u>Calculate the labor costs per guest.</u>

$$\frac{\$375,000}{85,000 \text{ guests}} = \$4.41$$

*Step 2:* <u>Calculate the prime costs per guest.</u>

| $4.41 | + | $5.70 | = | $10.11 |
|---|---|---|---|---|
| Labor cost per guest | | Food cost for new item | | Prime cost per guest |

*Step 3:*   Divide the prime cost per guest by the prime cost percentage.

$$\frac{\text{Prime cost per guest}}{\text{Prime cost percentage}}$$

$$\frac{\$10.11 \text{ (Step 2)}}{35.0 \text{ percent (budgeted food cost percentage)} \ + \ 29.4 \text{ percent (budgeted labor cost percentage)}}$$

$$\frac{\$10.11}{64.4 \text{ percent}}$$

$$= \underline{\$15.70} \text{ (rounded)}$$

The first step in using the simple prime cost method is to calculate the labor cost per guest (Step 1). This cost is then added to the menu item's food cost (Step 2). At this point, the menu planners know the prime cost (the food cost + labor cost) for the menu item being priced. Then, in Step 3 the prime cost per guest (Step 2) is divided by the budgeted prime cost (budgeted food cost percentage + budgeted labor cost percentage). In our example, the prime cost per guest (food and labor totaling \$10.11) equals 64.4 percent of the total amount of revenue required from sale of the item. One need only to divide the prime cost per menu item (\$10.11) by the prime cost percentage (64.4 percent) to yield the base selling price for the menu item when the simple prime cost method is used.

### Which Objective Pricing Method Should Be Used?

In this section we have discussed three simple mark-up and three other menu-pricing models that allow menu planners to incorporate objective operating budget data along with the item's food cost into the pricing deci-

sion. None of these methods yields an "absolute price" that must be stated on the menu. Rather, as noted in our introduction to this section, each model uses its own specific factors to suggest a base selling price that has been objectively derived. This base selling price can then be adjusted by other (perhaps less objective) factors considered important by the menu planners.

Which method should be used? All are relatively simple because they make use of operating budget information that must already be available for other purposes. It is not possible to state with 100 percent confidence which method should be used. Rather, some menu planners use several methods and consider the impact of each on their overall pricing structure. Others may use several methods and establish a selling price based on the average of the prices suggested by alternative methods. Regardless of the model used, however, menu planners are more able to meet marketing and financial management goals when objective—not subjective—menu-pricing methods are used.

### OTHER PRICING ISSUES

Menu planners should use objective, budget-driven information to establish base selling prices for their menu items. In addition to establishing base selling prices, menu planners must set prices for special events and

for daily menu "specials." There may also be an occasional need to manage price increases on existing menus. These price issues and the psychological aspects of menu pricing are discussed in this final section of the chapter.

## Break-Even Analysis

**Break-even analysis** (also called cost-volume-profit analysis) is a useful tool that menu planners can use when making some menu-pricing decisions. Break-even analysis can be used to help with certain types of pricing decisions such as:

- How many more guests must be served on our Sunday buffet to break even if we add a steamship round of beef and a carver but do not increase the buffet's selling price? What if the buffet's selling price were increased by $1.50?
- How many additional guests must be served on Wednesday night to break even if an entertainer is hired for $300? What would the cover charge need to be to pay the entertainment costs?

> *Glossary Terms*
> **Break-even analysis.** Also called cost-volume-profit (CVP) analysis, this process can be used to study the relationships between revenues, variable costs, fixed costs and profit. Its use includes, but is not limited to, menu-pricing decisions.

A wide range of other issues can be addressed with break-even analysis such as those relating to extending dining room hours, the number of guests needed to be served to yield a specified net income (profit) level, and so on. However, in this section we will address break-even analysis specifically as it focuses on menu-pricing considerations. The break-even analysis model defines the break-even point:

Break-even point = Total revenue − (Total variable costs + Total fixed costs)

Variations of this basic equation can be used to address the two questions raised above. Let's assume the following:

- The number of guests served on an average Sunday buffet is 200.
- The selling price of the Sunday buffet is $12.95.
- The per-guest variable cost (food, labor, and supplies for buffet) is $6.25.
- The total buffet fixed cost is $4.20 per guest. To simplify, assume that the restaurant is open seven days weekly, but the buffet is served on Sundays only; therefore, one-seventh of all fixed costs are applicable to the Sunday buffet. The per-guest fixed cost can then be calculated:

Total annual fixed cost ÷ Total annual buffet guests = Per-guest fixed cost

*Question 1:* How many more guests must be served on our Sunday buffet to break even if we add a steamship round of beef and a carver and leave the selling price of the buffet the same? (Assume that there will be no change in variable costs but that the per-portion cost of beef [not served on the existing buffet] will be $1.10, and the carver will be paid $50 in wages and benefits for work done on the buffet.)

*Answer:*

$$\text{Additional guests to break even} = \frac{\text{Total new fixed costs}}{\text{Guest check average} - \text{Per-guest variable costs}}$$

$$= \frac{(\$1.10 \ \times \ 200) \ + \$50}{\$12.95 - \$6.25}$$

$$= \frac{\$220 + \$50}{\$6.70}$$

$$= \frac{\$270}{\$6.70}$$

$$= 40 \text{ guests (rounded)}$$

When reviewing the break-even analysis above, note that menu planners need only to divide the total new fixed costs by the check average minus the per-guest variable costs. In effect, total fixed costs are divided by "what's left" from the average guest check to pay fixed costs (because guest-check average minus per-guest variable costs equals per-guest fixed cost).

The "new" fixed costs are the per-portion cost for beef ($1.10) and the beef carver's wages ($50). Note that we will assume that the total beef cost is fixed because the product is purchased for the buffet only. (Leftovers, if any, will be minimal and may run out on Monday or may be used for employee meals.)

The result of the break-even analysis (in our example, 40 guests) provides great information to the menu planners: They will need to serve 40 more guests to break even if a steamship round of beef and a carver are added to the buffet if they wish to keep the buffet selling price at $12.95 per guest. Assuming the purpose of this menu addition is to increase the guest count, this will be a formidable task because the count will need to increase by 20 percent to just break even. In this case, the foodservice operation will benefit from the addition of this item only if the count exceeds 40 additional guests for each buffet.

*Question 2:* How many additional guests must be served on the Sunday buffet to break even with the addition of a steamship round of beef and a carver if the buffet's selling price is increased by $1.50? (Assume that the per-portion cost of beef and the carver's wages and benefits do not change.)

*Answer:*

$$\text{Additional guests to break even} = \frac{\text{Total fixed costs}}{\text{Guest check average} - \text{Per-guest variable costs}}$$

$$= \frac{[\$1.10 \times 200] + \$50.00}{\$12.95 + \$1.50 - \$6.25}$$

$$= \frac{\$220 + \$50}{\$8.20}$$

$$= \frac{\$270}{\$8.20}$$

$$= 33 \text{ guests (rounded)}$$

When reviewing the above analysis, note that the only component that has changed is the amount of the guest check average minus the per-guest variable cost, which resulted from increasing the selling price by $1.50. This amount increased from $6.70 in question 1 to $8.20 in question 2. Therefore, if the buffet selling price did increase by $1.50, an additional 33 guests would be required to break even. This would be 17 percent (rounded) more guests than the number of guests currently being served.

While menu planners can calculate the impact of buffet selling price increases on the number of additional guests required to break even, they will at some point see a decrease in guest count because of the increased price. Menu planners should, therefore, also consider ways to reduce the fixed costs of the new item. (For example, serving presliced beef will eliminate most of the beef carver's wages. The carver would slice the beef in the kitchen in a relatively few minutes rather than needing to carve for several hours during the buffet serving period.) It may also be possible to reduce variable costs (by, for example, replacing a current buffet item with the beef). At any rate, all the information resulting from the menu planners' break-even analysis will help in the buffet planning and pricing process.

*Question 3:* How many additional guests must be served on Wednesday night to break even if an entertainer is hired? (Assume the cost of the entertainer will be $300 and a newspaper advertisement costing $125 is used to publicize the event.) Note that the weeknight guest check average is $15.95, 250 guests are normally served, and the per-guest variable cost (exclusive of buffet variable costs) is $10.40.

*Answer:*

$$\text{Additional guests to break even} = \frac{\text{Total new fixed costs}}{\text{Guest check average} - \text{Per-guest variable costs}}$$

$$= \frac{\$300 + \$125}{\$15.95 - \$10.40}$$

$$= \frac{\$425}{\$5.55}$$

$$= 77 \text{ guests (rounded)}$$

In this situation, the menu planners incur two new fixed costs: $300 for entertainment and $125 for the newspaper ad. This total ($425) is divided by $5.55 (which represents the amount remaining from the guest check average after all variable costs are removed to pay for these new fixed costs). The result—77 guests—provides a benchmark for the menu planners: 77 new guests will be required just to break even on offering entertainment. Many new guests are needed to gain a financial benefit. Is supplying entertainment reasonable? Now let's see what happens if additional revenue is generated on Wednesday nights.

*Question 4:* How many additional guests must be served on Wednesday nights to break even if the selling price of meals is increased by $2.00 during hours of entertainment or if a cover charge is added?

*Answer:*

$$\text{Additional guests to break even} = \frac{\text{Total new fixed costs}}{\text{New guest check average} - \text{Per-guest variable costs}}$$

$$= \frac{\$300 + \$125}{(\$15.95 + \$2.00) - \$10.40}$$

$$= \frac{\$425.00}{\$7.55}$$

$$= 56 \text{ guests (rounded)}$$

Note that the above calculations are the same as in the previous examples except that an additional $2 has been added to the guest check average. By doing this, the guest check average minus the per-guest variable costs (that remaining from the selling price to recover the new fixed costs) has increased to $7.55 (from $5.55). This calculation indicates that 56 new guests will be required to recover the new fixed entertainment costs if an additional $2 price increase (or cover charge) is included. Menu planners can consider this variable (the addition of a $2 charge) in their assessments about the impact of entertainment. In this instance, alternatives may be limited to decreasing the cost of entertainment by paying less for the entertainer or the advertisement.

These examples of break-even analyses related to decisions about menu selling prices illustrate how menu planners can use objective information to help make pricing and financial decisions. Even with these calculations, however, subjective assessments about, for example, the impact of price increases on guest counts and guests' potential interest for something different (a beef carving station on the buffet and entertainment on Wednesday nights, for example) must still be made.

## Managing Daily Specials

Many foodservice operations offer special prices to entice guests to visit the property and to spend more while they are there. Restaurants may, for example, offer an "early bird" or a "senior citizen" special. They may also offer special menu items not on the menu or discounted prices for menu items to all diners at times when business is normally slow. Noncommercial foodservice facilities may practice similar marketing tactics as when, for example, they combine a menu item, vegetable accompaniment, and dessert for a special price.

There are some situations in which special pricing for selected menu offerings may make good sense for the menu planners. All of these situations essentially offer the guests some price reduction in exchange for increased total revenues for the restaurant. Common discounting (specials) pricing methods include the following:

- *Two for Ones.* In effect, this offer is for one-half off the normal menu price. This tactic is effective when the restaurant seeks to increase total guest counts and has the seating capacity to do so. The rational for this pricing strategy is that the guests purchasing the "Two for One" item (for example;

entrées) will, while they are at the restaurant, purchase additional items such as drinks or desserts that may generate additional restaurant profits. This approach is also known as "Buy One Get One Free."

- *Bundling.* Here specific "go together" menu items are put together as a group and are assigned one special price. As a result, the menu price of the group of items is lower than if the items in the group were purchased separately. For example, many quick-service restaurants bundle, for a special price, a sandwich, French fries, and a drink. This approach encourages the guests to buy more because the best "value" exists if they buy the entire bundled offering. It is important, however, that the guests can easily recognize, by the price of the bundled items, that there is true value offered.

- *Inclusive.* Similar to bundling, the inclusive price discount approach consists of offering the guest "one price for everything." Consider, for example, the restaurateur who wishes to promote a New Year's Eve dinner special. In this case, the menu planners may suggest that a single price be established to cover the cost of a predinner reception, cocktails, dinner, champagne, and after-dinner coffees. By establishing one lower price for the event than for each item purchased separately, the restaurant, of course, seeks to attract more guests.

- *Discounting.* Traditional discounting simply refers to offering a menu item at a reduced price. This is often done, for example, on a specific day of the week (such as a Monday Night Special), at a certain time of the day (from 4:00 P.M. to 6:00 P.M.), or even seasonally (Summer Special). Of course, if the discount is offered at all times, it will not be viewed by guests as a discount at all, but rather as a simple price decrease.

The "arithmetic" of daily specials typically works against the concept in ways that many menu planners may not realize. Figure 5-3 provides an example.

When reviewing Figure 5-3, note that the impact of a price reduction for a daily special can have significant consequences. We learn that the contribution margin generated from a typical night's sale of 75 spaghetti dinners is $483.75. When the selling price is reduced by $3.00 for the daily special, it is necessary to sell 140 dinners (almost a 100 percent increase) to generate the same contribution margin. Can this be done? Will the incremental number of additional diners purchase other food and beverage products to offset the potential loss in contribution margin? These and related questions can be answered by only the menu planners. The point is, however, that simple price reductions do not automatically generate the additional business necessary to offset the losses in contribution margin.

This example refutes the commonsense perception shared by some menu planners: "You can't lose money if the restaurant is busy." As this example shows, it is the dollars of contribution margin, *not* the number of guests being served, that correlates most closely with financial success. Another marketing-related issue must be considered: Will some diners who would normally pay the regular menu selling price become accustomed to paying only the markdown selling price? In other words, will they wait for a daily special to visit the operation or become dissatisfied (and not return) if they must pay the regular price?

Figure 5-3. **The "Arithmetic" of Daily Specials**

Assume:
- A spaghetti dinner has a food cost of $3.50 and a selling price of $9.95.
- The spaghetti dinner, then, has a contribution margin (selling price minus food cost) of $6.45 ($9.95 – $3.50).
- The menu planners offer a daily special: Spaghetti dinner for $6.95 (a $3.00 mark down from its original selling price of $9.95).

The impact:
How many spaghetti dinner specials must be sold in one night to provide the same profit as from the average nightly sale of 75 regularly priced spaghetti dinners?

The answer:
*Contribution margin (typical evening):*
  75 dinners @ $6.45 (contribution margin) = $483.75

*Contribution margin (daily special):*
  $6.95 (Selling price)
– $3.50 (Food cost)
  $3.45 (Daily special contribution margin)

*Number of spaghetti dinner specials needed to be sold:*
$$\frac{\$483.75 \text{ (Contribution margin on typical evening)}}{\$3.45 \text{ (Daily special contribution margin)}} = 140 \text{ (rounded)}$$

Other variations of the daily special model are the use of "dining clubs" and participation in "community menu books." By joining menu clubs, diners may, for example, receive one free meal valued at a specific price after they buy a specified number of full-price meals. With community menu books, a food and beverage operation participates in a community-wide promotion in which buyers of discount books receive discounts for specified purchases at specific community businesses. In these and related instances, the menu planners must consider financial objectives and remember that filling seats with diners does not necessarily help meet marketing or financial objectives. Careful attention to these "opportunities" is necessary.

Menu planners are sometimes confronted with other issues related to markdowns on food and beverage sales. Examples include the seemingly innumerable requests for donations (free or reduced-price meals, for example) to the community's civic service, educational, religious and, other groups. Solicitors may suggest that their group's members patronize participating businesses who comply with these requests. While these and related issues do impact selling prices, they are concerned more with marketing, advertising, promotion, and "good will" issues than they are to menu pricing, which always has subsequent marketing and financial impacts. These issues are not, then, included as part of this discussion.[2]

## Managing Price Increases

Traditionally, the first tactic used by food-service operators confronted with cost increases or challenges in meeting financial goals has been to increase selling prices. Today, however, with guests insisting that they receive greater value for their dollars and with the competitive pressures from this consumer attitude, raising selling prices should gener-

ally be one of the last tactics implemented. Interim steps can involve efforts to generate **incremental sales** and to reduce operating costs without sacrificing required quality standards. Several tactics can be used to reduce food costs and to increase revenues. (Many of these will be discussed in Chapter 9).

---

*Glossary Terms*

**Incremental sales.** Additional revenue generated by marketing efforts that yield more guests visiting the property, by suggestive selling, or by other techniques that increase the amount of revenue spent by guests.

---

Sometimes, unfortunately, increasing selling prices is necessary. This should occur relatively infrequently (not more often than annually or when new or revised menus are introduced) and be well thought out. Suggestions for managing selling price increases include the following:

- Consider adding a value-added component. For example, a price increase of $2.00 for an entrée with a "complimentary" dessert selling for $3.50 with a food cost of $0.75 still yields an increased contribution margin of $1.25.
- Consider passing on only cost of goods sold increases to guests. Consider the following example:

| | |
|---|---|
| Menu item food cost | $6.00 |
| Food purchase cost increases | $1.25 |
| Total new menu item food cost | $7.25 |

Assume that the new menu item is priced to yield a 35 percent food cost:

---

[2] Readers interested in more information about marketing aspects of food and beverage operations are referred to Bill Marvin, *Guest-Based Marketing: How to Increase Restaurant Sales Without Breaking Your Budget.* New York: John Wiley and Sons Inc., 1997.

*Old selling price for menu item:* $\dfrac{100 \text{ percent}}{35 \text{ percent}} \times \$6.00 = \$17.15$

*New selling price for menu item:* $\dfrac{100 \text{ percent}}{35 \text{ percent}} \times \$7.25 = \$20.70$ (rounded)

Let's look at what happened in this very typical situation: The food costs for a menu item were $6.00. Menu planners using a simple markup with a 35 percent food cost had a base selling price of $17.15 (100 percent ÷ 35 percent = 2.86; 2.86 x $6.00 = $17.15).

There was a food cost increase of $1.25, which resulted in a new total menu item food cost of $7.25. The new selling price was also calculated with a 35 percent food cost (100 percent ÷ 35 percent = 2.86; 2.86 x 7.25 = $20.70). While the food cost increased by $1.25, the selling price increased by $3.55 ($20.70 – $17.15). The menu planners may do well to consider just adding the food cost increase of $1.25 to the existing base selling price of $17.15. With this plan, then, the new selling price would be $18.40, which is $2.30 less than the base selling price that would otherwise be charged. To the extent that there would be customer resistance to paying the higher selling price ($20.70), this tactic can be very useful.

- Reduce the contribution margin to reduce selling price increases. Assume that a menu item sells for $9.95 and that this selling price includes a garnish that costs $0.25 and a twice-baked potato that costs $1.50. Assume also that the cost of the twice-baked potato is about $0.75 more than the cost of any other potato choice included in the entrée's selling price. If a garnish costing $0.10 was used and, if the twice-baked potato was eliminated as a choice with the entrée, the contribution margin would increase by $0.90 without increasing the selling price. As well, incremental sales might be generated from à la carte pricing of the twice-baked potato at, for example, $1.50 (which is $0.75 above its product cost).

- Examine the price spread of existing menu items. Recall that a guest dining in a food and beverage operation receives the same service, cleanliness, atmosphere, and other nonfood aspects of the experience as do all other diners. For example, what does a guest paying $20 for a steak receive that a guest paying $5 for a hamburger does not receive? The answer is, of course, a different menu item. However, both guests may dine at the same table and receive the same quality of service and enjoy the same dining environment for a very different amount of money. The concept of "**excessive price spread**" considers this issue. Menu planners should review the range of selling prices. As the difference between the lowest and highest selling prices of menu items competing for the guests' attention increases, a lower guest check average may result.

> *Glossary Terms*
> **Excessive price spread.** The observation that guest check averages may be skewed downward when there is a significant range of menu item selling prices. Guests may select lower-priced items because they still receive many aspects of the total dining experience at a reduced cost.

There may, in fact, be increased business generated by a menu offering "something for everyone." (Consider the steak and the hamburger in the above example.) Today, however, with **niche marketing** tactics in use, many managers consider the demographics of the primary markets of diners whom they are trying to reach when they plan menus. As they do this they can keep the range of prices lower and, in the process, keep the check averages higher.

## Psychological Pricing Factors

In our earlier discussion of objective menu pricing methods we noted that the result of the calculations was a base selling price that menu planners may—or may not—use as the final selling price printed on the menu. Additional factors to consider when setting final menu prices are psychological pricing considerations, which anticipate how guests will perceive menu selling prices. Here are some examples:

- *Pricing at odd cents.* Odd-cents pricing may create a perception of a discount. For example, will a guest perceive a better value if a menu item is priced at $6.50 or at $6.49?
- *Distance between price points (dollar units).* Some menu planners believe that a guest will perceive the difference between $2.89 and $2.99 to be less than the difference between $2.99 and $3.09 even though, in both instances, there is only a $.10 difference.
- *Number of digits in the selling price.* Some guests may perceive that menu selling prices are increased more when, for example, the price moves between $9.99 to $10.25 (a $.26 price increase) than when it moves from $19.25 to $19.75 (a $.50 price increase).
- *Consider rounding prices.* Some menu planners believe that consumers only perceive

$0.25 price increments on menu items priced below $5.00; on menu items priced over $5.00, they recognize only $.50 and $.95 increments. For example, if the base selling price of a new menu item is under $5, the selling price might be rounded up to the next $.25 price point (for example, a sandwich selling for $3.60 might be rounded up to sell at $3.75). An entrée with a base selling price of $7.55 might be rounded up to a price point of $7.95.

Other tactics that may be helpful to manage selling prices on menus include the following:

- *Placement on item list.* Some menu planners believe that guests are more likely to order items placed first or last on a list (for example, lists of sandwiches or of desserts); they suggest that items the property desires to sell be placed in these positions.
- *Help menu readers to focus on the product, not on the price.* Consider eliminating the dollar sign that precedes the price (for example, 10 not $10.00). To further de-emphasize the price, place it at the end of the menu description with the same typeface and in the same type density (boldness).
- *Do not isolate prices on a right margin list.* Help guests to focus on the menu item and its description—not on its selling price.
- *Do not use "leader dots"* (dotted lines that connect the product description to the selling price). Guests are more likely to select menu items because they like them rather than because of their cost if menus emphasize product descriptions rather than cost.

Figure 5-4 illustrates these tactics. How, if at all, would you react differently if you were a guest viewing this menu item?

Figure 5-4. **The Placement of Selling Prices on Menu Item Descriptions**

**Basket O' Fries** - A heaping bounty of our seasoned shoe-strings ... ...................................$1.92

**Basket O' Fries** - A heaping bounty of our seasoned shoe-strings.......................................1.92

**Basket O' Fries** - A heaping bounty of our seasoned shoe-strings                    $1.92

**Basket O' Fries** - A heaping bounty of our seasoned shoe-strings        $1.92

**Basket O' Fries** - A heaping bounty of our seasoned shoe-strings        1.92

Menu planners should realize, however, that guests generally have a sense of the restaurant's price structure before they ever receive a menu. That is, the restaurant's appearance, its implied service levels, and its interior ambiance are all factors that influence the guests' perceptions of price. Therefore, pricing strategies developed for the physical menu can influence a guest's buying behavior, but only after that guest is seated inside the restaurant or is reviewing the menu board.

## SIGEE'S MENU:  A CASE STUDY

"I think we should always end the prices in a 'nine.' People think things are less expensive that way.  I read about it in an article once," said Gerlindy Hoffman, the dining room supervisor. She, as well as Samuel Ludwig (the executive chef), Reesie Davis (the restaurant manager), and David Berger (the food and beverage director) were meeting to discuss the menu prices to be established for the new Sigee's menu.

"End in a 'nine'?" asked Reesie. "What do you mean?" "Well," replied Gerlindy, "If you sell an item for $5.99 it sounds like it's less than $6.00."

"That's because it is less than $6.00!" said Samuel impatiently. "I mean it sounds like it's a lot less than $6.00," retorted Gerlindy as she raised her voice slightly toward Samuel.

This entire meeting, thought David Berger, had been somewhat tense. Everyone seemed to have different ideas about how to price the new menu that was, at this point, beginning to take shape. He too had an idea of what he thought he wanted, but he always tried to get the input of everyone involved before he made an important decision, and that was why he had called this meeting.

"The way you set menu prices is to find out the food cost percentage you want and then make sure all the items you price are at that percentage . . . or lower" said Samuel. "No way, Sam," said Reesie. "If that were true, we would have 25 cent sodas. They only cost 5 or 10 cents.  Do we really want to reduce our prices on the inexpensive items and raise them sky high on others?"

"Okay," said Samuel, "what do you suggest?"

"I'm not sure," said Reesie, "and I don't know what our best approach is. I do know that guests only complain that prices are too high—never that they are too low! And I can tell you that having so many different prices is confusing for everyone. It's too bad we can't just set one price for everything!" The group laughed in agreement as David began to speak.

"Reesie, I think you are on to something, and it fits with an idea I have," he began. "I think we should keep our price variation to a minimum also. I know if we monitor our sales and costs, we can set prices that ensure we get the food cost percentage Samuel wants and the total contribution margin we need. I think the most important thing to remember is that our prices will either complement or conflict with our basic theme. Since the new theme is casual, upbeat, and fun, I think a price structure that gets guests asking, "Why are your prices like that?" would be really fun also. We will let our guests know that they can relax at Sigee's, and that we are a hotel restaurant that takes food quality and service seriously, but doesn't take itself too seriously." For the next ten minutes, David discussed his idea for menu pricing.

"I like it," said Gerlindy, "it will be different!"

"Just like our new menu," added Reesie.

"I don't know," said Samuel, as David finished, "it sounds a little far out there to me. What do you think the G.M. will say?" David wasn't sure what the G.M. would say initially, but he knew that the idea would be fun, and a bit irreverent, but most of all traveler friendly. He was sure Peggy Sill, the hotel's G.M., would love it—at least he hoped she would!

# CHAPTER 6

# Principles and Procedures of Menu Writing

## CHAPTER SIX OUTLINE

**Overview of the Menu-Planning Process**
Remember Menu-Planning Priorities
Select Menu Categories
Consider Items for Each Category
Select Menu Items for Each Category
Establish Standards for Each Menu Item
Write Menu Descriptions
**Accuracy in Menus**
**Other Menu-Planning Concerns**
Revising Existing Menus
Healthy Foods on the Menu

**Menu Planning for Banquets**
Ten Questions to Ask for a Unique Banquet Menu
**Developing the Wine List**
Characteristics of an Effective Wine List
Order of Wine Listings
Wine and Food Pairing
Wine List Pricing
**Checklist for Menu Planning**
**Menu-Planning Resources**
**Sigee's Menu: A Case Study**

## MENU TERMS USED IN THIS CHAPTER

As purchased
Center of the plate
Competitive edge
Cuisine
Food fads
Food trends
Line-ups

Menu rationalization
Signature items
Standard of identity
Trade puffing
Truth-in-menu
Wine list

## CHAPTER OVERVIEW

As you have learned in the previous chapters of this book, much planning and decision making is required before the menu planners determine what items to offer on a menu. In this chapter we will review details about the menu-planning process itself. First, readers will be reminded about the menu-planning priorities—a focus on the guests, product quality, operating resources, and financial goals—that

must always be considered as the menu is planned.

Then, we will describe steps that must be followed in sequence during menu planning. The first step is to select menu categories (such as appetizers, salads and soups, entrées, and desserts). Second, menu planners evaluate items for each category and then select the actual menu items in each category. After these decisions are made, standards are established for each menu item, and menu item descriptions are written. When these tasks are completed, the menu can finally be designed. (Menu design is discussed in Chapter 7.)

As menu planners develop their menus, it is essential that the menu item descriptions be accurate. Yes, menu planners want to effectively merchandise their items to sell them. At the same time, it is important to be truthful in menu descriptions; guests should not be misled by incorrect statements or inaccurate photographs.

This chapter also explores two other menu-planning concerns. First, existing menus, regardless of how effective they were at the time they were developed, must be revised. As well, we address the increased guest interest in healthy foods offered on the menu with a discussion about nutritional menu choices.

Banquet menus are also discussed in this chapter. These menus provide unique challenges depending, in part, on their purpose. For example, banquet menus can provide food and beverage products and services to guests for meals (breakfast, lunch, and dinner) and, as well, for coffee breaks, on-site catering opportunities, and other venues.

A final major section of the chapter focuses on the wine list, which is the equivalent of the "food list" (the menu) in the food operation. A good wine list has many important characteristics. Several of these focus on the relationship between the food being the served and the available wines. Traditionally, specific wines have been "recommended" for specific types of food items. Wine list developers should be aware of these pairings but, as well, they should also recognize that the "best" wine for a food item is the one the guest prefers. This section includes information on the order in which wines are listed. The chapter discusses several common alternatives because no specific method is automatically the best.

There are different opinions about how wine should be priced. While the chapter provides no firm answers to this issue (because there are none!), it does provide detailed information that will help readers when they price wine lists in the future.

We then provide a checklist for menu planners. After a final draft of the menu is designed, it is wise to review it one last time against a checklist of potential concerns. The chapter concludes with a list of menu-planning resources to which readers may refer for additional information.

## OVERVIEW OF THE MENU-PLANNING PROCESS

As you begin this chapter, you may wonder why you have studied over half of a book on menu planning, design, and evaluation before reaching a chapter focusing on menu planning! In fact, you have seen that a great deal of pre-planning is required before the actual menu can be planned. We have considered the necessary prerequisites to menu planning during our discussions of its importance, marketing aspects, design of the physical facility, and the equipment within the facility. Likewise, we emphasized the quality aspects of developing and delivering items that will be required by the menu as we talked about the need for standard recipes and purchase specifications, and in the previous chapter we discussed the basics of menu pricing and the use of objective operating budget data to establish base selling prices for the items to be offered. We are now ready to discuss the physical task of menu planning.

Figure 6-1 outlines each step that menu planners should use in both commercial and noncommercial foodservice operations to plan a menu. The figure provides a "road map" for the organization of this chapter. Note, however, that Step 7, "design the menu," will be discussed fully in Chapter 7.

### Remember Menu-Planning Priorities

Earlier chapters have emphasized that menu planners must simultaneously consider four priorities as they plan the menu:

Figure 6.1. **Overview of the Menu-Planning Process**

| | |
|---|---|
| **Step 1:** | Remember menu-planning priorities: guests, product quality, operating resources, and financial goals |
| **Step 2:** | Select menu categories |
| **Step 3:** | Consider items for each menu category |
| **Step 4:** | Select menu items |
| **Step 5:** | Establish standards for each menu item |
| **Step 6:** | Write menu descriptions |
| **Step 7:** | Design the menu |

- *Guests.* Marketing issues related to guest demographics (gender, age, socioeconomic status, and occupation, for example) along with their wants and needs and their reasons for dining out are very important. (For example, business meetings or pleasure trips may influence guest visits to commercial operations; nourishment may be a primary objective for some consumers in some noncommercial foodservice operations.)
- *Product quality.* Any food or beverage item to be produced must meet the property's quality requirements related to factors such as flavor; consistency; texture, form, and shape; nutritional content; visual and aromatic appeal; and temperature.
- *Operating resources.* Many factors limit the ability of most food and beverage operations to produce an unlimited variety of food and beverage products, including the knowledge and skill of the staff, ingredient availability, peak volume production and operating concerns, layout and equipment limitations, sanitation factors, and the level of operating costs (which, in turn, drive selling prices and guest acceptance).
- *Financial goals.* There is great wisdom in the observations of experienced food and beverage managers who suggest that if you "Take care of guests and meet their quality requirements, then the finances will take care of themselves." However, it is also true that wise menu planners consider their operating budget, which specifies estimated income (profit and operating surplus or break-even

level) when their menu is developed. It is simply not possible for a quick-service restaurant to offer $25 entrées or for gourmet restaurants to offer $1.89 entrées. Guests would not be happy in either instance, and this would translate into a failure to meet the property's financial goals. Knowing the price the guest is willing to pay helps the menu planners to determine product costs when objective pricing methods are used (see Chapter 5). Therefore, product costs considered at the time the menu is planned directly affect the financial success of the operation.

## Select Menu Categories

Most menu items are organized into logical categories on the menu. These groupings allow readers to consider choices among reasonably equivalent alternatives. As a general rule of thumb, food and beverage operations with higher guest check averages tend to offer more menu categories. For example, a high-check-average, gourmet restaurant may offer numerous appetizers, soups, salads, hot and cold entrées, vegetables, other accompaniments, desserts, and beverages along with a wine list. By contrast, a quick-service property may offer fewer categories with fewer items within each category: sandwiches, soups, salads, side dishes, desserts, and beverages.

Let's look at alternative menu item categories more closely:

- *Entrées*. Menu planners, like many of us as we make our own choices in a restaurant, plan entrées first and then select other items that go with the selected entrée. Popular entrées are made of beef, pork, poultry, fish, and lamb. Entrée salads and vegetarian entrée items are becoming more popular. Many guests think of entrées as hot items, and many are. Others, such as a chef salad, may be cold. Still others may be hot and cold such as a cold Caesar salad topped with a hot grilled chicken or salmon fillet. Casseroles—another type of entrée—are popular in both commercial and noncommercial operations. Examples include combinations of meat and pasta (including Italian dishes such as lasagna, ravioli, and spaghetti with sauce), seafood and pasta, tuna casserole, and cheese and pasta (such as baked macaroni and cheese).

- *Appetizers*. These items, served before the meal to "tempt" one's appetite, are often (but not always!) small, bite-sized items. They may be hot (such as stuffed mushrooms and escargot) or cold (such as shrimp cocktail or cheese and fruit). Some properties offer fruit or vegetable juices as appetizer items.

- *Soups*. Some food and beverage operations list soups as a separate category on the menu; others include them as part of the appetizers or with the salads. With either option, most soups are served hot. A soup can be clear and made of a consommé or broth with or without additional items such as vegetables or meats. It can also be thick such as a chowder or cream soup that can be served with numerous types of meats, seafood, poultry, and fruits and vegetables. Soups can also be cold; vichyssoise is an example of a cold cream and chicken stock soup made primarily from potatoes, onions, and leaks.

- *Salads*. Menu planners may offer two types of salads: entrée salads (see above) and accompaniment salads. These side salads include those made from lettuce and other greens and other vegetables (cole slaw and potato salad, for example). Salads can also be made of fruits, including oranges, melons, pears, apples, and pineapples.

- *Vegetables and accompaniments.* Vegetables such as potatoes, asparagus, broccoli, peas, carrots, and onions of many different types and preparation styles are offered on many menus. Other side dishes such as small portions of seasoned or white rice, corn, beans of all types and preparation methods, pastas, dumplings, and noodles are sometimes offered as an accompaniment on the menu. The specific dish offered is often dictated by the cuisine. For example, in Southwestern and Mexican cooking, the accompaniments are likely to be rice and beans. In an Italian restaurant, pasta would be more common.

- *Desserts*. These after-dinner sweets are often included on the menu with other items. Increasingly, however, a separate menu is used to feature these items. Sometimes, the dessert menu is a cart or tray brought to the table with samples of the available desserts.

- *Beverages*. Menu planners have an increasingly large variety of beverages that can be offered to guests. Traditional items such as coffees, teas, and soft drinks may be listed on the menu. Sometimes, the brands of soft drinks are listed. (Some distributors may partially reimburse the property for the cost of menu design and printing, for example, if their brand is cited. The volume of beverage product sold by the restaurateur is likely to influence the distributor's decision to assist in the cost of menu production. Even menu planners for small-volume restaurants should, however, approach these distributors to inquire about any financial assistance the distributor is offering to help offset the cost of menu development.)

Sometimes, separate coffee menus with a wide variety of cappuccinos, lattés, and coffees of seemingly innumerable flavors are available. Some restaurant menus feature suggestions about traditional cocktails made of distilled spirits. In addition, many restaurants feature (often with separate menus!) specialty drinks and a wide variety of domestic and imported beers along with their counterparts from "boutique breweries." Today's large variety of bottled waters may even call for a separate beverage category—if not a separate menu!

- *Specialty categories.* Some restaurants offer additional categories of food, sometimes as **"signature" items**. Examples of specialty categories include selections of cheeses or mushrooms; on-site-prepared ice creams; entrées of all types, sizes, and preparation methods; and unique delivery styles such as a "Basket of Fries" (in a real basket), "Buckets of Beer" (in real buckets), or flamed desserts. The point to remember is that virtually any item that is creative, well prepared, and appealing to diners can become a signature item.

---

*Glossary Terms*
**Signature items.** Food items that are unique to or are associated with a specific foodservice operation. Guests are attracted to the operation because of these items and frequently request them. Guests may associate a restaurant with, for example, a "one-pound pork chop," a "mile-high pie," or a "shrimp boat" (a loaf of French bread hollowed out and filled with deep-fried shrimp).

---

How many categories should be on the menu? There is no rule; the answer to this question relates to the menu planners' marketing concerns, which address other questions such as these:

- How many categories are needed to encompass all of the menu items the diners will likely desire?
- Is there a category or categories for which a large number of items or unique items can be listed that will help provide a "**competitive edge**"?
- How closely have menu planners defined the market of those to be served by the food and beverage operation? (Must the restaurant "be all things for all persons" and, therefore, require more categories of menu items?

Alternatively, has the market been defined with a very clear focus, which, in turn, can help reduce the number of menu categories and items that must be available?) In a noncommercial foodservice operation, perhaps the emphasis should be on a "traditional" meal pattern (such as, for example, a salad, entrée, vegetable, bread with butter, and dessert in an extended care nursing facility). In post-secondary school settings, menu categories and patterns may be anything but traditional. For example, "categories" may need to include, for every meal, numerous types of dry cereal and soft-serve ice creams.

- Are there time restrictions on the guests? For those tableservice restaurants that hope to serve luncheon guests within an hour, a four-course menu is not a good choice. That is, guests are unlikely to be able to be served and consume appetizer, salad, entrée, and dessert courses in a one-hour period. Of course, these same guests may well have time to do so in a restaurant that serves dinner.
- How many categories are required to make the menu easy to read and re-read as diners select their choices? Too few categories mean excessively long lists. Too many categories can be just as confusing.

---

*Glossary Terms*
**Competitive edge.** Any tactic, process, or procedure used by a food and beverage operation and desired by diners that is not offered by competitors (or is not offered as well by them).

---

As is often the case, the menu planners should keep in mind that the menu should not only list the items available for sale but also help diners to easily make their selections. An appropriate number of categories offered by a well-conceived menu will help in this process.

## Consider Items for Each Category

After the menu planners have a basic structure in place (that is, they know the categories of menu items), the items to be included in each category must be assessed. A first step is to consider the wide variety of possibilities and to then use an elimination process to select which items to offer. Several menu-planning tools will be helpful at this point, including the following:

- *Copies of old menus.* If the food and beverage operation is not new, existing (and previous) menus can help menu planners subjectively consider items that have—or have not—been popular, profitable, or operationally efficient to produce and serve.
- *Copies of menus from competitors.* Knowledge of what the competition does—and does not—offer may be useful in determining "signature" items to be placed on the menu.
- *Menu evaluation data.* Objective information about the popularity and profitability of items on existing menus can be extremely helpful. (Menu evaluation will be discussed in Chapter 9.)
- *Standard recipes.* Standard recipes formulated for use in quantity food production operations are readily available in trade magazines, cookbooks, and textbooks, and from product and equipment manufacturers and suppliers, among numerous other sources.
- *Product, inventory, and ingredient availability information.* Knowledge about the availability of products and ingredients (which impact the costs) and the ability to secure these items in inventory without quality deterioration (a variable in supplier selection and procurement procedures) is helpful to assure that menu items can be cost-effectively offered during the life of the menu.
- *Input from management, employees, and diners (if applicable) or evaluation teams.* It should be obvious that input from all possible sources including management, employees, and guests of the food and beverage operation should be solicited. Don't forget to ask servers (who typically have more contact with guests than anyone else!) and the dishwashers (who, unfortunately, know from what they discard while washing dishes what guests do not like).

Typically, menu items in the entrée category are considered (Step 3 in Figure 6-1) and are then selected (Step 4 in Figure 6-1) before items in other categories are considered. There are, however, exceptions; a foodservice operation known for its wide range of fresh baked desserts, for example, may consider this category (desserts) as important as its entrée category. However, guest decisions about *where* to go (in commercial operations) and *if* to go (in some noncommercial operations) are often based on entrée selections, which helps to justify as an initial priority the selection of items for the operation's entrée category. As well, restaurants that offer dining themes (ethnic restaurants and those offering specific dining atmospheres, for example) need specific types of entrées to enhance the marketing of their theme or dining experience. By contrast, different types of restaurants can offer many of the same soups, side dishes and accompaniments, beverages, and desserts.

After entrées are selected, many menu planners then consider, in sequence:

- appetizers
- potatoes, rice, and other vegetable accompaniments
- soups
- salads
- desserts
- breads
- beverages

What factors should be considered as the menu planners evaluate potential items for each category? Important concerns typically include:

- *Range (variety).* Normally there should be a range of temperature, preparation methods, texture, shape, and color in the items composing a menu item category.
- *Temperature.* There is typically an expectation that some items will be served hot (meat, poultry, lamb, and veal entrées and potatoes, for example) and that other items will be served chilled (cold), including chef's and

side salads and fruit and cheeses, for example. When applicable, items to be served both hot and cold can be offered within a menu item category to increase its range (see above).

- *Preparation method.* Meats can be cooked using a moist-heat method (steaming, boiling, or poaching) or a dry-heat method (such as roasting, baking, broiling, grilling, sautéing, or pan frying). Preparation methods incorporating both moist heat and dry heat, including braising and stewing, are other possibilities. Likewise, vegetables can be boiled, baked, braised, fried, or sautéed, and desserts can be served fresh, chilled, cooked, or baked. Diners enjoy considering these alternatives. Some items such as seafood might be offered as prepared to order, depending on the guest's preference (deep-fried, pan fried, grilled, or baked, for example).
- *Texture.* Alternative menu items can be soft, firm, or crunchy. They can be liquid or solid, dull or shiny, or wet or dry. Texture adds to the food's presentation and should be considered as items for each menu category are selected.
- *Shape and sizes.* Menu items can be round, square, or long and can be presented in a tall or flat portion. Different shapes and sizes of alternative menu items on the same plate have a dramatic impact on presentation. Wise menu planners assure that this impact is positive—not negative.
- *Flavor.* While menu planners have traditionally thought of flavor in terms of the basics (sweet, sour, salty, bitter, and so on), today's menu planners include additional flavors such as various degrees of hot (buffalo wings), spicy (Thai and Cajun dishes), and smoked (barbecue meats and poultry). While the concept of "taste" is very complex and involves more than flavor, the diner's perceptions about "what the food will taste like" is very important. Plan a variety of flavors, when applicable, in each menu item category.
- *Color.* Color is an integral part of the eye appeal of a menu item. Multiple colors are more appealing (but too many colors can be confusing). The preparation method may affect color (one normally expects the coating of fried chicken to be darker than the surface of a baked chicken), and color is also related to the specific food item. For example, expect broccoli to be a shiny, medium-dark green and green beans to be a duller, more olive green. In addition, wise menu planners recognize that the use of garnishes can help to assure that the color is "right" on the plate.
- *Composition and balance.* These factors relate to the overall impact of the menu items as presented to the diner. Some menu planners have no control over how the items relate to each other on the plate or tray. Consider, for example, guests passing through the serving line in a commercial buffet or a noncommercial cafeteria operation. These guests determine the plate (tray) presentation based on what they select. Menu planners in operations with self-selection can do little more than to generally consider the variety, temperature, preparation method, shape, size, color, and other features of the menu items that guests select in the serving lines. However, when items are proportioned and predished (such as in a commercial à la carte operation), the menu planners do have more control over these factors. Then, the composition and balance of the "overall" plate should be considered. For example, in many foodservice operations today the **"center of the plate"** concept is used to create an aesthetically pleasing "picture" as the diner views the food presentation on the plate.

---

*Glossary Terms*
**Center of the plate.** The tactic of positioning different portions of food on a plate by working from the center of the plate toward its rim while slightly overlapping each menu item. There is, then, no space in the center (eating) area of the plate exposed to the guest.

## Select Menu Items for Each Category

To this point, the menu planners have considered many items that might be included in each menu category. How, from this list, are the items to be included on the menu actually selected?

Recall that Figure 6-1 identified the menu-planning priorities to focus on: (a) guests—and what they want and need, (b) product quality (and the ability to consistently produce and deliver products meeting or exceeding these standards), (c) limitations imposed by the operation's resources, and (d) the operation's financial goals. Menu planners should have considered each of these priorities when developing the tentative list of possible items for each menu category.

Next, menu planners must focus once again on these priorities and consider how each menu item in each category fits with the following:

- The theme or style of the food and beverage operation
- The **cuisine** of the operation
- A focused look at the prospective guests and what they are most likely to want and will be willing to pay
- Careful analysis of the costs (in all types of operations) and profitability (in commercial operations)
- The opportunity to use **menu rationalization**. If, for example, an ingredient such as shrimp of a specific size can be used for several (or more) menu items such as a seafood platter, seafood stew, and shrimp platter, it becomes possible to produce these different items with fewer operational difficulties than when three items made of three distinct main ingredients must be purchased.

It is also necessary for menu planners to consider the "mix" of items being considered. For example, it is obvious that an oven must be available to prepare the baked items required by the menu. However, is sufficient oven space available to prepare a large number of baked appetizers, entrées, side dishes and accompa-niments, desserts, and bread if these are required by the menu? If not, either additional oven space must be acquired or the number of items requiring baked preparation must be reduced.

*Glossary Terms*
**Cuisine**. The style and range of menu items to be offered by the foodservice operation.
**Menu rationalization**. The use of a primary recipe ingredient such as shrimp or chicken for several (or more) different menu items to reduce the operational difficulties that arise when many different items for different recipes must be purchased.

The ability of production staff to produce a wide range of "made-from-scratch" items is another variable that needs to be reviewed as the items suggested for each menu category are considered and as the process of eliminating menu items evolves. A "make-or-buy analysis" (see Chapter 3) may be required to determine whether existing staff and equipment can produce a larger number and wider variety of menu items.

As the menu-planning team reviews alternative items in each category, an effort should be made to eliminate items that are judged less likely to meet the menu-planning priorities. In practice, this effort becomes one of "trial and error." Few, if any, commercial or non-commercial foodservice operations open with a specific menu and never change it. Rather, over time menus are revised to continue the effort to better meet the menu-planning priorities. Menu evaluation (see Chapter 9) is as an integral aspect of this evolution in selecting menu items as are other steps useful in revising menus, which will be discussed later in this chapter.

## Establish Standards for Each Menu Item

After menu planners have determined the menu items to offer in each category, they must next establish standards for each menu item, which must be consistently attained each time the item is produced and served. The two most important tools to do this are standard recipes and purchase specifications.

Standard recipes were discussed previously in Chapter 4. We have also noted that standard recipes are helpful resources when the menu planners begin considering menu items for each category (see Step 3 in Figure 6-1). After menu items are selected, it is important to review the applicable standard recipes to assure that all production and service personnel understand the exact ingredients, preparation methods, and serving sizes needed. As well, there must be agreement about the serviceware to be used and, at least for food products, standard recipes must be precosted with current market costs. Finally, there must be agreement among all concerned personnel that the standard recipe will be closely followed *every time* the food or beverage product is produced.

The use of purchase specifications was also discussed in Chapter 4. Once menu planners develop these standard control tools, they should provide them to suppliers and require from the suppliers that the quality of product defined in the purchase specification will, in fact, be (a) the product quality for which a price is quoted and (b) delivered to the property.

Other important standards include the portion size and appearance of the product. It is critical that all personnel use the correct portion size and serviceware. To ensure this, photographs of plated items can be used in foodservice stations where food is being portioned by production staff. Photographs can also be used for initial training of service staff and for coaching activities done during preshift **line-ups**.

Another tactic to help ensure consistent quality is to use effective resources for training production and service staff to attain standards. Management activities relating to the development and implementation of total quality management programs (which are beyond the scope of this discussion) can be helpful.[1]

After standards are established for each menu item in each category, Step 6 (write menu descriptions) follows.

## Write Menu Descriptions

Effective menus communicate with the guests. First, they explain what items are available, and second, they can influence the guests' choices. This section will review important tactics in writing menu descriptions; aspects of the menu, including descriptions, that apply to selling will be discussed in Chapter 7.

Menu item descriptions should address questions that a menu reader is likely to have. Let's take two examples of menu items: "seafood fettuccine" and "bouillabaisse." Many guests will likely know that fettuccine is pasta. (Fewer will know that to be called fettuccine, each noodle should be less than one-half inch wide and about the length of spaghetti.) No reader can know the type of seafood or the sauce that will be used for the seafood fettuccine unless this information is written in the menu.

In most areas of the country, few diners are likely to be familiar with bouillabaisse. Like many items in Cajun and Creole cuisine, there is no **"standard of identity"** that identifies specifically what must be included in this usually spicy seafood soup or stew. Therefore, it becomes important for menu planners to inform guests about this product in general (it is a "spicy stew," for example) and, more specifically, about the ingredients used to prepare it.

---

*Glossary Terms*
**Line-ups.** Brief training sessions conducted before the start of employee shifts to update staff members about the current situation (daily specials, items to be emphasized, number of leftover portions to be served, and special functions going on within the property, for example).

---

[1] For a discussion of total quality management in the hospitality industry, please see Robert Woods and Judy King, *Quality Leadership and Management in the Hospitality Industry*. East Lansing, Mich.: Educational Institute of the American Hotel & Lodging Association, 1996.

Would a menu reader have questions about a menu item called "walnut-crusted salmon"? Yes, of course! Is the salmon a fillet? What is its approximate **"as purchased"** weight? What is the preparation method? Is there a sauce? As a basic guideline, then, menu planners must answer the question, "What must a menu reader know about this menu item to make an informed purchase decision?" The answers to this question will help drive the writing of the menu description.

Here are some additional suggestions for writing menu descriptions:

- *Write plainly.* Unless the menu is for an ethnic-themed operation, use foreign terms sparingly. If the menu features "swordfish quenelles" it is probably better to use the term "dumplings" in the description rather than "quenelles." If an entrée is served with velouté sauce, the menu writer might be effectively communicating with the term "velouté" if, for example, the market is composed of persons with the background to know about this item. By contrast, it would be helpful to indicate that this item is served with a "thick, creamy sauce made from a veal stock" if guests are less likely to have knowledge about a velouté sauce. Indicating that a side salad is served "with the chef's own special salad dressing" is not an effective way

to communicate. The servers' time will be wasted as they must continually explain the dressing and its ingredients to inquiring guests who have no way of knowing what the "special" salad dressing is.

- *Tell the readers what they must know.* If an item is spicy or has a pronounced taste of garlic, anchovy, or curry, for example, indicate this on the menu. An effective menu provides a sufficient description of an item so that there will be "no surprises" when guests receive their orders.
- *Use suggestive selling descriptions carefully and correctly.* Not every item can be a "house specialty" and not every item can be "the best in the city." Details about menu accuracy will be discussed later in this chapter.
- *State item descriptions correctly.* Manhattan Clam Chowder (which contains tomatoes and has a red color) is not the same as New England Clam Chowder (which is white).
- *Spell words correctly.* Menu planners make numerous common spelling errors. They should know how to spell:
  - portobello (mushrooms)
  - béarnaise (sauce)
  - barbecue (sauce)
  - potato (vegetable)
  - welsh rarebit (cheese-flavored cream sauce)
  - vinaigrette (dressing)
  - escalloped (potatoes)
  - hors d' oeuvres (appetizers)
  - au jus (with juice)

  These are just a few of the many menu terms that should be carefully checked for spelling when writing menu descriptions. Menu planners can find a comprehensive list of menu terms at this website: www.cuisinenet.com/glossary/terms.html.

  In addition, many dictionaries are specifically dedicated to food terms. (Interested menu planners may go to www.amazon.com and enter the words "menu terms" into the "books" search field.)
- *Write clearly, punctuate properly, and capitalize consistently.* While most menu readers do not expect menu writers to have perfect grammar, obvious errors on menus will be discov-

ered (and pointed out!) by many diners. In addition, poor grammar may cause confusion. For example, in the following illustration only menu item number four properly describes a sirloin steak "smothered" with onions and accompanied by a baked potato.

1. Sirloin Steak, served with baked Potato smothered in onions.
2. Sirloin Steak, served with baked potato, and smothered in Onions.
3. Sirloin Steak, smothered in onions and baked Potato.
4. Sirloin Steak, smothered in onions, and served with Baked Potato.

Although descriptions 1 through 3 come close to accurately describing the item, the poor grammar and punctuation used make them confusing (or even comical!) to the menu reader.

- *Write and rewrite; edit and re-edit.* The task of developing a good menu is just as difficult as (or more difficult than!) the task of developing a good recipe. Significant time will be required as the menu evolves through the many required development and writing phases. Menu descriptions should be reviewed by the manager, production personnel, and, when practical, by interested others to help assure that the menu effectively explains the available items.

## ACCURACY IN MENUS

We have indicated that menus must effectively communicate with the reader. The accuracy of the information provided is an essential aspect of this communication. Unfortunately, menu planners sometimes exaggerate, if not actually misstate, menu information (often in efforts to merchandise the items to increase sales). Menu planners must truthfully represent the items being served, and they should be very concerned about accuracy-in-menu (also referred to as **truth-in-menu**") issues. Problems with menu accuracy can occur in several ways. These can be categorized as follows:[2]

---

*Glossary Terms*
**Truth-in-menu**. The requirement that menu descriptions accurately portray the quantity, quality, point of origin, and numerous other factors that help menu readers understand the items being described; also referred to as accuracy-in-menu.

---

- *Quantity.* A two-egg omelet should contain two eggs; an eight-ounce steak should weigh approximately eight ounces. (As noted above,

menu planners can note that the weight stated on the menu is "before cooking" to communicate that shrinkage and weight loss does occur during cooking. In other words, this notice will inform the reader that the actual weight of the item on the plate will be less than that stated on the menu.)

- *Quality.* The term "prime," when used to describe a steak, refers to a specific U.S. Department of Agriculture grading standard. U.S. Grade A or U.S. Fancy for vegetables and Grade AA for eggs and butter also indicate quality grade. Only the quality actually used should be indicated on the menu. If it is not possible to ensure that the intended quality grade will always be available, it is best not to list the quality designation on the menu.
- *Price.* If there are extra charges (for example, for call or premium-brand liquors) these prices should be identified. If there are service charges (for example, for groups larger than a specified size), these should be indicated.
- *Brand names.* If a specific product brand is specified (Coca Cola or Pepsi Cola, for example), this exact brand should be served.
- *Product identification.* For example, maple syrup and maple-flavored syrup are not the

---

[2] These categories were suggested by National Restaurant Association, "Accuracy in Menus." (Position paper). 1977.

same. Neither are orange juice and orange drink or mayonnaise and salad dressing.

- *Points of origin.* "Pacific" shrimp, for example, cannot be from the Indian Ocean; Idaho potatoes cannot be from Wisconsin; Lake Michigan whitefish should not be from Lake Erie.
- *Merchandising terms.* Guests recognize that "**trade puffing**" is different than misrepresentation.
- *Preservation.* For example, frozen apple juice should not be represented as fresh; canned green beans should not be referred to as "fresh."
- *Food preparation.* "Made on site" is not the same as a convenience food product made elsewhere; also, food should be prepared as stated on the menu—for example, a product sautéed in butter should not be sautéed with margarine.
- *Verbal and visual presentation.* A menu photograph depicting, for example, eight shrimp on a shrimp platter should accurately represent the number of shrimp served; a specialty

drink pictured in a fancy stemware glass with a unique garnish should be served in this manner. A food server who indicates that the deep-fried calamari is prepared from a fresh product should be telling the truth.

- *Dietary and nutritional claims.* If the menu indicates, for example, that "egg substitutes are available," they should be and must be served when this product is requested. Additional information about the nutritional aspects of menu planning is presented later in this chapter.

> *Glossary Terms*
> **Trade puffing.** Boasting about a product as an advertising tactic. For example, "Mile-High Pie" is obviously not one-mile tall; "best hamburger in the world" is probably more merchandising than it is a fact. However, "Our bread is baked on-site daily" and "Our seafood is flown in fresh daily from the Pacific Coast" do imply information that should be true.

## OTHER MENU-PLANNING CONCERNS

To this point we have been focusing on tactics used by menu planners to plan a new menu for a new foodservice operation. You have seen that this activity is difficult and time-consuming when done correctly. Fortunately, a new foodservice operation begins only once! After that, menu-revision activities become important. Fortunately as well, most of the procedures used to plan an initial menu are very useful when revising existing menus.

There is increasing concern today about offering nutritious and healthy food items. Special concerns are relevant as the menu planners address these issues. Menu items should appeal to and be healthy for the guests. As well, it must be practical for the operation to serve the items "as promised" by the menu.

These two topics—revising existing menus and planning for nutritional food choices—are the topics of this section.

### Revising Existing Menus

Can menu planners develop an initial menu for the foodservice operation to offer "forever" without change? In almost all cases, the answer is an emphatic "NO." At its best, menu planning is as much an art as it is a science. A great deal of subjective decision making is necessary even when guest focus groups, surveys of potential markets, analysis of consumption patterns (in multiunit organizations with outlets in the same general location), and other objective planning techniques have been used. Menu planners do make decisions based on the best available information; sometimes, however, this information is not optimal and, therefore, neither is the "final" menu.

Another important factor—changing guest preferences—also points to the need for menu revisions. Some guests in some markets enjoy trying the latest **food fads** and **food trends** when dining out. If blackened seafood is "in," if Asian-Pacific fusion cooking is making its way across the continent, and if steamed foods are replacing deep-fried foods in popularity, many diners will likely enjoy these alternatives.

---

*Glossary Terms*

**Food fads**. Food products, preparation methods, or cuisines that are extremely popular for a relatively short time period.
**Food trends**. Food products, preparation methods, or cuisines that, unlike a food fad, are ongoing, beginning slowly and more gradually increasing in popularity.

---

New equipment or attachments to equipment may become available that enable menu planners to offer items that could not be produced to desired quality standards previously. New management or food production and service staff brings new ideas to a foodservice operation. New convenience foods become available that may provide additional menu options. These and related factors might also lead to menu revisions.

In fact, menu planning is nearly always a "work in process." It is never finished, and menu planners are on an almost constant journey of improving the menu to better meet the needs of the diners and, at the same time, to meet the financial and other goals of the foodservice operation.

One excellent menu-revision technique that menu planners should use involves the process of menu evaluation. This process (see Chapter 9 for a complete discussion) allows menu planners to study historical sales, to assess each menu item's popularity and profitability, and to make menu-planning (items to offer or discontinue) and menu-design (placement of items on the menu) decisions. The effectiveness of a menu today—not when it was planned—affects guest satisfaction, the profitability of the foodservice operation, and the ultimate failure or success of the operation.

In addition to menu evaluation, techniques to consider for help in the menu-revision task include:

- Questioning guests about their likes and dislikes.
- Questioning food servers, bus persons, and dishwashers—who often know more than do their managers about guests' menu preferences!
- Focusing more specifically on an ethnic or experiential theme to better distinguish the foodservice operation from its competitors.
- Recognizing the seasonal availability of produce and other items at times when the highest quality is available at the best price.
- Making use of "daily specials" (and ensure that they do change daily!) to appeal to frequent diners. Careful study of the sales of these daily specials can be helpful, since they are a "proving ground" for potential menu additions.

Modern transportation and food-preservation systems have made it possible to have almost any product available at any time of the year. However, some properties market the fact that they feature fresh-grown (sometimes organic) produce or other food items. These are affected by the local weather and other conditions and point to the need for these operations to change menus or menu items more frequently.

In communities with wholesale or retail produce, seafood, or other markets, managers, purchasers, or chefs from some operations determine daily menu item specials by visiting these marketplaces and by making decisions about what's "best" for the day. Suggestive selling on menus (see Chapter 7) and by service staff can turn this tactic for selecting daily specials into increased sales.

Some food and beverage operations offer a constant menu (that is, most offerings do not change daily) with one or two daily specials. Other restaurants feature the fact that their entire menu changes daily. Still other properties are somewhere in the middle; they offer numerous "permanent" items but also emphasize a significant number of specials that change daily.

Menu planners must use their knowledge of the guests and what they desire to plan and provide menus to meet the guests' needs. Sometimes diners' needs are like a "moving target." Menu planners must, therefore, use all possible methods to assess what the diners want and to assure that these preferences are available on the menu.

Foodservice operations in areas with seasonal weather fluctuations typically change menus as the seasons change. Cold weather soups and stews can be replaced by lighter menu items as the warmer weather arrives. Some restaurants and many noncommercial foodservice operations offer a cyclical or du jour (of the day) menu with at least some items changing daily. Obvious advantages to a changing menu include less chance that the diners (who must consume the food) and the production personnel (who must prepare it) will become bored by eating or preparing the same food each day.

Other possibilities for variety include "soups of the hour" that change several times during the day or meal shift, or the foodservice operation might feature some of the same, most popular, desserts but also some different desserts daily.

### Healthy Foods on the Menu[3]

Many guests in commercial food and beverage operations enjoy opportunities to order healthy food. The same trend is true in noncommercial foodservice programs. In certain residential situations such as long-term nursing care, correctional facilities, and some military feeding operations (naval ships on long-term cruise operations, for example), the nutritional content of the meals offered is very important.

Menu items with a nutrition emphasis can be included on a menu in either of two basic ways:

[3] This section is adapted from "A Diner's Guide to Health and Nutrition Claims on Restaurant Menus," www.cspinet.org/report/dinersgu.html.

1. They can be integrated into the menu along with other items in the same category (for example, entrées prepared using a more healthy method can be listed with all other entrées).
2. They can be included in a special category of the menu (for example, a menu may contain a special section: "Here's to Your Health").

Each alternative has advantages and disadvantages. If the food and beverage operation offers only one or two such items, integration of the items into the normal menu listings becomes an advantage. This is countered, however, by a potential disadvantage that guests who desire this type of item may not easily find it. (Some menus use symbols such as a heart-shaped logo to help guests identify these items more easily.)

An advantage to a separate listing is that it provides a "message" that the food and beverage operation is concerned about the nutritional health of the guests, that many items are offered, and that the restaurant wishes to overtly market to guests who desire these items. A possible disadvantage is that since a greater amount of space on the menu will be required to display these items, menu planners must assure that these items are as popular as other menu items and contribute their "fair share" of the profit of the total menu items sold.

Regardless of where these items are listed, it is critical that they be carefully selected so as to not interfere with the ongoing production of items from the "regular" menu. Consider, for example, the operational problems that can arise when production staff must recall whether an item is to be prepared with butter or margarine. Worse yet is this scenario: A relatively large batch of a menu item must be prepared and then, because of insufficient popularity, is not sold and must be discarded.

Another approach to offering guests nutritious alternatives is to indicate that a variety of food-preparation methods is available. For example, if a menu features a seafood category, the guest could be informed that selected items can be prepared baked, sautéed, broiled, or deep-fried.

Fortunately for menu planners, commercial and noncommercial foodservice operations are not legally required to supply complete nutrition information to guests, as are manufacturers of processed foods. However, there should be some reasonable way to substantiate claims such as "low fat" or "heart-healthy" on the menus. Perhaps, for example, recipes that yield "nutritious" portions are from a reputable source such as a professional health or dietary association. As a second example, a recipe used for a more nutritious item might substitute margarine for butter or might use a smaller amount of butter.

Since May 1997, restaurants making claims such as "lite," "low fat," and "heart-healthy" must comply with definitions established by the U.S. Food and Drug Administration (FDA). If, for example, a restaurant claims its mashed potatoes are "low fat," the serving must contain no more than 3 grams of fat. The food and beverage operation must provide nutrition information to guests on request. (This information does not need to appear on the menu.) Nutrition data can be provided in writing (such as on a brochure or page from a notebook), or it may be provided verbally from a server or other staff member.

Restaurants must be prepared to provide only information pertaining to a specific claim. If, for example, a "low sodium" claim is made, it is necessary only to inform requesting guests about the amount of sodium (number of milligrams) in a typical serving as calculated from nutrient databases or a cookbook—it is not necessary to provide guests with information about calories, fat, or other nutrients, since no claim about these items was made.

Potential issues about nutritional claims were noted earlier in our discussion about accuracy in menus. The following definitions are useful to help assure that menus do not mislead guests:

- *Low fat.* As noted above, the FDA has established that items referred to as "low fat" have 3 grams of fat or less in a serving. However, if a restaurant serves a portion size larger than the FDA's standard portion, a "low-fat" food may contain a correspondingly larger amount of fat.
- *Lite.* This term can describe the taste, color, or texture of a food, or it may indicate that a food's calorie, fat, or sodium content is reduced. The menu must clearly indicate what "lite" means for the specific menu item.
- *Cholesterol-free.* Foods such as meat, poultry, and seafood naturally contain cholesterol. Therefore, they contain cholesterol even if they are prepared in "cholesterol-free" cooking oil. As well, menu planners should recognize that "cholesterol-free" does not mean the same as "fat free."
- *Sugar-free.* This term does not mean "calorie-free" or "fat-free."
- *Healthy.* Foods noted to be "healthy" should be low in total fat and saturated fat and should not be high in cholesterol or sodium. There are not, however, limits on the amount of sugar or calories that a "healthy" food may contain.
- *Heart.* Menu claims such as "heart-healthy" or "heart-smart," and heart symbols imply that a food may help reduce the risk of heart disease. Foods to which a heart-related claim has been made should be low in total fat, saturated fat, and cholesterol and should not be high in sodium.

Menu planners desire to please their guests. Plans might be in place to accommodate guests who make reasonable dietary requests. If these procedures can be implemented, there might be less need to introduce numerous healthy foods or to add a "healthy food" section to the menu. If possible, menu planners should allow guests to do the following:

- Order sauces and salad dressings separately; low-calorie dressings can be available for guests who request them.

- Request reduced-sized portions at a reduced price (or, at least, guests should be allowed to take unused portions of meals home with them).
- Request foods be prepared with olive or canola oil rather than with butter or shortening.
- Ask that food be broiled or grilled rather than deep-fried.
- Substitute skim or 1 percent milk for dairy products with a higher fat content.

- Select baked, broiled, or grilled poultry or seafood rather than red meat.
- Order leaner cuts of red meat such as sirloin steak or fillet mignon.
- Substitute a salad, vegetable, or baked potato for French fries.
- Request butter or sour cream on the side rather than on top of a baked potato.
- Request whole grain bread or rolls.
- Order a fresh fruit rather than a sugary, high-fat dessert.

## MENU PLANNING FOR BANQUETS

There are two basic types of banquet menus: (1) preset (standardized) and (2) customized for specific situations.

The preset banquet menu may provide several pages of options to help the prospective guests select appetizers, entrées, desserts, and so on. Also available are complete meal packages featuring a suggested appetizer, salad, entrée with accompaniment, and, perhaps, desserts.

The preset menu package is the primary sales tool for those in the catering department who sell banquets. A brochure containing the preset menus and, often, other components must be well thought out and appropriately designed. Concerns such as format, layout, colors, paper stock, graphics, copy, and related presentation factors are very important.

Customized menus are developed for the guest who prefers something unique. While menu planners must know what they can—and cannot—do, staff members in the catering department should be willing to work with prospective clients to develop a menu that is "best" for their function. The following list identifies ten questions that, when answered, will help menu planners design an appropriate customized menu.

### Ten Questions to Ask for a Unique Banquet Menu

1. **How many people do you expect?** This question helps the menu planners plan the equipment and production needs for the function. Some items (for example, roast beef) may be easy to make for a very small group of five or six diners, while other items (for example, cooked-to-order steaks) may be difficult, if not impossible, to prepare for a group of 1,000.

2. **What is the makeup of the group?** Women often prefer different foods in different portion sizes than do men. Older guests too are likely to have food preferences different from children. Knowledge of the demographics of the group to be served helps the menu planners select appropriate dishes with the proper portion size.

3. **Have you established a budget for the meal?** When menu planners know the spending range of potential guests, a menu that falls within that range can be planned. Difficulties and sometimes embarrassment arise if the menu planners suggest an exceptionally attractive menu only to find the guest's budget does not allow for such a menu.

4. **At what time will the meal be served?** Most often, luncheon menus will be different from dinner menus. Breakfast menus require a special set of menu items.

Menus must, to some degree, reflect the expectations of diners about the time of day at which the meal will be eaten.

5. **Will the meal be served (by wait staff) or will it be a self-service buffet?** This decision not only affects the type of menu items to be offered but also impacts the time that should be allotted for meal service. Single-course meals provided by wait staff can be served very quickly (probably much faster than if guests serve themselves on a buffet line). By contrast, self-served buffet meals usually are served faster than are multiple courses served by staff members. The amount of time available to begin and complete the meal often affects this decision. In addition, the menu planners must be aware that control over the number of entrées served in a buffet is often less than in a staff-served meal (as some guests may take two or more entrées). As a result, the cost of producing a buffet meal often exceeds the price of producing a staff-served meal.

6. **Will there be alcohol served with the meal?** The addition of alcohol (such as wine) to the menu assists the menu planners in determining the appetizers, entrées, and desserts. In addition, of course, the total price of the meal will be affected if alcoholic beverages are included.

7. **Do any of the guests have special dietary needs?** Guests who are allergic to specific foods, are vegetarians, have dietary restrictions, or who have intense likes or dislikes should be identified so that the menu either accommodates them or offers an alternative.

8. **What are the beverages (excluding alcohol) you wish to offer the guests?** Many special-function menus limit the number of beverages offered to speed service and reduce dining time. For example, a banquet for 1,000 will be served more quickly if guests may choose only between regular coffee and iced tea than if those same guests are allowed to choose between regular and

decaffeinated coffee, hot tea and iced tea, assorted carbonated sodas, lemonade, fruit juices, and sparkling waters.

9. **How many entrée choices will be offered?** When one entrée choice is offered, the menu planners must take care that the item will have wide appeal to the group to be served. For example, grilled liver and onions might be an excellent third entrée on a "Southern-Style" buffet menu that includes fried chicken and baked ham and is designed to serve 250 guests. It would, however, probably be a poor choice as a single entrée for a staff-served meal for the same group. Many diners would probably not enjoy the entrée, and as a result may be unhappy with the entire meal. The question of whether "the guest is always right" should be noted here. What, for example, should be done if a host or hostess does prefer liver and onions for 250 guests? Will the diners be dissatisfied with the host or hostess or with the property? Most observers would believe guests would be upset with the property; effective catering personnel must know how to encourage good menu choices, how to discourage poor choices, and how to say "no" when they would otherwise run the risk of serving many unhappy guests.

   When two or more entrées are to be served, they should complement each other but also provide contrast where possible. For example, a beef entrée would likely be complemented by and contrast nicely with a chicken item, while pork roast would not likely be a good companion item to pork chops.

10. **When will a final count be known?** Often, those who plan banquet events are unsure of the final count until a few weeks, days, or even hours before the event. As a result, menu items may need to be selected by the lead time available to production staff. A cold deli sandwich buffet may, for example, require only a few hours'

notice for a final count, while a cooked prime rib dinner may require days of lead time because the item must be purchased and roasted prior to service.

Each type of banquet function presents special challenges for the menu planners. In all cases, the objective of the event planners must be well understood to help assure that the appropriate menu is available. Let's look at special considerations for special banquet functions:

- *Breakfast functions.* Typically, speed of service is a concern for many breakfast banquets. If the meal is to be tableservice, a preset food plate followed by a plated egg (or other) entrée with a potato accompaniment may be appropriate. If the buffet is preferred, the menu may call for a choice of juices, eggs, breakfast meats, and other items. Add-on items such as juice cocktails, special coffees, fancy pastries, and tomato- or orange-based juices without alcoholic beverages may be appropriate.
- *Coffee breaks.* Refreshment breaks offered to guests attending lengthy meetings provide great opportunities for menu planners to be creative. These breaks, typically scheduled at mid-morning and mid-afternoon times, can offer hot and cold beverages, fruits and vegetables, and other items such as pastries (for morning breaks) and cookies (for afternoon breaks). Beverages for all breaks should typically include coffee (both regular and decaffeinated) and cold beverages including a diet-type soft drink and sparkling water or club soda.
- *Luncheons.* Sometimes, "working lunches" are ordered, and menu planners provide luncheon meats, cheeses, and other items that permit attendees to prepare their own sandwiches. Salads (or components for them) can also be provided. At other times, a preplated lunch featuring relatively smaller portions of chicken, beef, or other entrées than those served at an evening meal will be enjoyed.

In most cases, the number of courses offered on a luncheon buffet will be smaller than on a dinner buffet to reflect the shorter meal time typically allotted for lunch. Of course, if the luncheon buffet is to be eaten at a leisurely pace, as is the case with many Sunday or holiday brunches (Easter, Mother's Day, and Father's Day, for example), the number of menu offerings and courses may be quite extensive.

- *Receptions and stand-up events.* These types of functions will typically require bite-sized food items that make it easy for guests to balance plates of food and, perhaps, glasses of beverages while socializing. Items for stand-up receptions should be easy for guests to hold and to consume. Items should not be messy or greasy. Small plates are better than larger ones because they are easier to handle and will discourage waste, since a reduced amount of food can be placed on them. Menus for stand-up receptions can also include items that servers may pass in addition to items to which guests can help themselves on serving lines.
- *Evening meals.* These special functions allow catering personnel to offer menus that involve more courses, higher-priced meals, and wine (or other alcoholic beverage) service. When preplated events are offered, a salad might be preset on the table when guests arrive. Salads can be followed by a soup and the main course, which may be served preplated, prepared at tableside (if a relatively small number of guests are being served), offered on platters for serving to guests, or provided in large serving bowls or platters that guests can pass among themselves.
- *Off-site catering.* Some foodservice operations offer catering to off-site locations. This is a complex challenge, in part because of the unique and specialized equipment required for safe food handling. The range of alternatives for off-site catering range from a simple boxed lunch (sandwich, coleslaw or potato salad, and cookie, for example) to

elaborate meals requiring sophisticated equipment to hold and serve hot food.

Entire books have been written about catering banquet functions.[4] These resources provide much more information than can be provided here about menu planning and the delivery of meals for group functions.

## DEVELOPING THE WINE LIST

Wine, normally assumed to be a beverage made from grapes, is actually any fermented beverage made from grapes, fruits, or berries. The wine menu in a restaurant is commonly called the **wine list**. A quality wine list is just as important a sales tool for wine as the menu is for food.

> *Glossary Terms*
> **Wine list.** A menu indicating wines (often with explanations of them) and prices available for sale by the food and beverage operation.

Sometimes the wine list is a separate menu; at other times, it is incorporated into the regular food menu. The wine list, like the food menu, should reflect the personality of the restaurant and, when properly created, should include wines that complement and harmonize with the restaurant's food menu offerings. In all cases, however, it should be recognized that historically and in a large number of cultures, wine is the beverage of choice while dining. As a result, those restaurants that offer an appropriate and attractively presented selection of wines with their food items will likely enjoy increased check averages and greater guest satisfaction.

### Characteristics of an Effective Wine List

Many of the principles explained in this book that apply to creating a food menu also apply to creating a wine list. A wine list can be extensive or simple but should always include basic characteristics such as the following that will ensure the list is appropriate for the restaurant:

- *The wines selected should complement the food on the menu and the character of the restaurant.* The most important feature of a good wine list is that it consists of wines that go well with the food items served and that it is in keeping with the overall objectives of the restaurant. For example, if the wine list is created to complement a mid-priced Italian-style restaurant, the wines selected should reflect the style and atmosphere of the cuisine being served. Guests of this type of restaurant will have some expectations that can be met, in part, by the wine list. These expectations may include inexpensive house wines, some wines produced in Italy (or other European countries), and good quality domestic wines with which these guests are likely to be very familiar. Each wine should have a role to play on the wine list. That is, each should be selected for its ability to complement the food items served or to further the restaurant's character.
- *The wines selected should complement the pricing structure of the restaurant.* Some guests (but certainly not all) will want a high-quality and relatively expensive wine to complement their meal. Others will prefer a more modestly priced wine. The best wine lists offer something for both types of guests. In all cases, however, the price of the wines offered should be in keeping with the menu's entrée prices. If they are not, less wine will be sold. Extremely rare and expensive wines will not sell on a wine list that accompanies a menu designed for a mid-priced restaurant.

---

[4] See, for example, Joe Perdue et al., *A Club Manager's Guide to Private Parties and Club Functions.* New York: John Wiley and Sons, Inc., 1998.

- *The selection of a wine from the menu should be made easy for the diner.* Most (but not all) guests are less familiar with wines than are the wine list planners. Also, many of the best wines made and sold today are of foreign origin and have names that may be difficult to pronounce. A result is that it can sometimes be difficult or potentially embarrassing for diners to buy wines. When appropriate because of potential ordering difficulty for guests, the establishment should offer pronunciation assistance or use the common technique of assigning a "bin number" to each wine to ease the guests' task of selecting a wine.

- *The wine list includes "by the glass" offerings.* While wine has traditionally been perceived as the alcoholic beverage of moderation, the fact remains that diners are more cautious than ever about excessive alcohol consumption. More diners are limiting alcohol consumption during meals to one or two drinks. Sales of wine by the glass appeal to these diners because they can enjoy their preferred beverage with their meal and still moderate their total consumption of alcohol.

- *Descriptions of the wines are included whenever possible.* When space allows, it is always a good idea to provide as much information about the wines as is practical. Interesting information such as origin, flavor, and special characteristics make the wine list more appealing to the diners and will typically result in increased wine sales.

- *The list avoids repetition.* A smaller offering of quality wines is better than a larger offering of wines that are very similar. Wines that do not sell rapidly result in excessive inventory costs.

- *Wine information listed on the menu is accurate and spelled correctly.* This is a common error. Always obtain the spelling of the wine directly from the bottle's label. Accuracy in identifying vintage and region or vineyard is also important. Bottle sizes should also be properly identified where appropriate.

- *The wines listed on the wine menu are readily available.* It is never a good idea to list wines that cannot be held in inventory in good supply. Just as menu planners do not want to list items on the menu that cannot be served, wines that will not be stocked consistently should also not be listed.

- *The wine list is clean and attractive.* Whether the wine list is part of the main menu or is provided separately, it should be eye-catching, stain-free, and in good condition. Just as food menus must be kept immaculately clean, so too should the wine list.

- *The wine list is presented to every diner.* While this is an operational issue rather than one directly associated with the wine list itself, a wine list that is not readily seen by the guests cannot help to sell wine. If the wine list is not part of the regular food menu, it should always be presented to diners at the same time as the food menu.

Wine lists that incorporate each of the above characteristics will help the foodservice operation to sell more wine and, therefore, better satisfy its wine-drinking guests.

## Order of Wine Listings

There is no universally accepted standard for which wines should be listed first on the wine list. Traditionally, the decisions made on the listing order result in one of the following:

- *Option 1.* List wines in the order they are to be consumed; that is, appetizer wines first, followed by wines to be served with the main course, and then those wines normally consumed with dessert.

- *Option 2.* Group wines by type. That is, the wine list maker determines that all wines of a given characteristic be grouped together. Assume the characteristic is color; then, for example, all red wines will be listed together and all white wines will be categorized separately. Alternatively, the characteristic may be point of origin. In this case, all French wines will be listed as a group, all Italian wines will be listed as a second group, domestic wines will be separately listed, and so on.

Other characteristic types that can be used to create the list include viticultural area, grape-type used to make the wine, vintage, container (bottle, glass, and carafe, for example), or degree of sweetness. As long as the grouping makes sense to the guests and enables them to better understand the wines offered, this can be a very helpful and effective way to create the wine list.

• *Option 3.* List wines in the order of the most expensive to the least expensive. In this case, for example, Champagnes and very expensive wines are listed first. They are not only the most costly, but they are generally also the most glamorous. Many menu planners believe that guests perceive less-expensive wines to be an even better value when they compare their price to the expensive wines they read first.

Some wine list makers blend one or more of the above approaches. For example, within a color type the wines may be listed from most expensive to least. The main rule to remember is that the wine listings should make it easier, not harder, for the guests to select a wine that complements the food items they purchase.

## Wine and Food Pairing

Some wine lists include information on wine and food pairings. That is, they suggest that selected wines be "paired" or "matched" to certain menu items. Properly done, this can be helpful to some wine drinkers. However, if this is not done appropriately, the tactic can actually diminish the enjoyment of the guest because it may imply that their preferred wines are inappropriate.

Those planning wine lists must remember that wines are made to be enjoyed with food, and while there are traditional pairings that can be recommended, the objective of the wine list is to sell wines for the guests' enjoyment—not to intimidate wine drinkers. In addition, if too strong a case is made that a

certain wine "goes" with one type of menu item only, the wine list may diminish, not increase, wine sales.

Consider for example, a couple dining in a restaurant. The female wishes to order a beef dish; the male desires a chicken dish. If the wine menu suggests only one wine for each dish (for example a Cabernet Sauvignon for the beef and a Chardonnay for the chicken dish), it is probable that the couple will not order wine because it is unrealistic to assume that each will order a separate bottle. Wine by the glass may resolve this difficulty, but it is much better to suggest a wine that can be enjoyed with both dishes. (*Note:* Those who disagree with offering a wine to go with both dishes may be taking the selection of the "right" wine a bit too seriously. The couple in this example will appreciate the server who is sensitive to their dilemma and seeks to assist by suggesting a wine that will complement both dishes.)

Figure 6-2 lists some traditional wine and food pairings that can help make recommendations on the wine list if such suggestions are to be included. In some cases, the food menu itself will also list a suggested wine with each, or with selected, entrées.

## Wine List Pricing

The pricing of wine in restaurants has been hotly debated for years, and the debate continues. On one side of the argument are the wine producers and wine distributors who truly believe that restaurants hurt wine sales (and overall restaurant profitability) by marking up the price of wines excessively. These understandably self-interested parties point out that a guest who can buy a bottle of popular wine in a grocery store for $12.00 may hesitate at paying $30.00 for that same bottle of wine in a restaurant. To sell more wines, they contend, restaurateurs should reduce the markups on their wines to no more than two times the cost of the wine (and even less for very expensive wines).

Figure 6-2. **Wine and Food Pairings**

| With | Traditional Recommendation |
|------|----------------------------|
| Hors d'oeuvers | Champagne |
| Soups | Sherry |
| Fish and poultry | White wines |
| Pork and veal | White or rosé wines |
| Beef | Red wines |
| Cheeses | Port or white Zinfandel |
| Dessert | Champagne |
| All foods | The guest's preferred wines |

On the other side of the argument are the restaurant operators who have traditionally marked up the price of the raw food ingredients they purchase by a factor of two, three, or even four times the cost. (That is, a chicken breast purchased for $2.00 may be the main ingredient in a dish that sells for $4.00, $6.00, or $8.00 depending on the mark-up factor used.) For example, assume the restaurateur purchased a wine for $10.00. Using a three times markup, the wine would indeed sell for $30.00. Menu planners contend, with some justification, that if it is more profitable to sell alternative alcoholic beverages such a cocktails or beer (which can generate markups of three, four, or even five times their cost!), it is probably in the best interests of the restaurant to do so. Markups of only two times product cost, they maintain, would result in less, not more, profits.

Proponents on each side of this issue make valid points that thoughtful wine list developers should consider. Excessive markups on wine will result in decreased sales. Wine, however, must be a profitable item or restaurants will not sell it. Lost in the argument is the fact that meals are more elegant, more memorable, and more festive when wine is included. Total revenue is the result of guests spending money each time they come to the restaurant. When wines complement meals and when wines are sold at a fair price, repeat business results, and a restaurant's profits will increase.

Just as it is not possible to categorically state what a restaurateur should charge for a steak listed on the menu, we cannot state how much should be charged for a specific wine. A rational approach to wine pricing, however, will result in the wine list maker following some reasonable guidelines regarding markups and price:

- *Price wines in keeping with the overall price structure of the menu.* Guests who frequent moderately priced restaurants will expect moderately priced wines as well. If a restaurant is very elegant and higher priced, it makes sense for the wines offered to reflect that fact. Just as most food menus offer of a range of entrée prices (which defines how expensive the restaurant is), the same is true of the wine list. Assure that the prices of the wine list and of the food menu are in harmony.

- *Some inexpensive wines should be offered.* The additional costs incurred to serve wine to guests who are already dining in a restaurant are minimal. If the operation seeks to achieve a reputation as an establishment where wine is a natural part of the dining experience, some inexpensive wines should be offered to encourage even the most cost-conscious diners to try the wines.

- *Offer something for those who want very good quality.* All of the wines selected for the wine list should be good; however, just as many bars stock, in addition to well brands, premium and super premium products for those who desire them, wine drinkers who want the "best of the house" should be able to purchase it. This can, and should, be reflected in the wine's price.

- *Consider the guest's alternatives when pricing.* Wine is one of several choices guests have when electing to purchase drinks as part of their dining experience. Consider the couple that desires a very nice dining experience. Assume this couple will consume two drinks each during their visit. Their alternatives are many. They could, for example, order before-dinner cocktails and after-dinner drinks. The total cost to this couple of their alcoholic beverage choices will be the price of the four drinks. Alternatively, assume they elect to buy a 750-ml. bottle of wine that will yield four good-sized glasses. It makes sense that the price of the wine must have some relationship to the cost of these guests' other alternatives. If the wine is lower in cost than the four-drink alternative, it will sell better than if it is perceived as much more expensive than the four-drink alternative. The wine list makers must evaluate the prices charged for all alcoholic beverages in the restaurant and then price the wine list accordingly.

- *Evaluate contribution margin as well as cost percentage.* At the heart of the wine list pricing debate is the issue of the importance of contribution margin relative to the importance of low product cost percentages. In the case of wine pricing, the issue is less confusing than in other areas of restaurant pricing. Contribution margin (the wine's selling price minus its product cost), not its cost percentage (product cost divided by selling price) must dictate the wine-pricing decision. It is the profit per bottle that is important—not the wine's cost to its selling price ratio.

If, in fact, the restaurant insists on using mark-up factors to price wines, Figure 6-3 suggests mark-up factors to apply by wine type.

Figure 6-3.  **Mark-up Factors by Wine Type**

| Wine Type | Mark-Up Factor |
|---|---|
| Bulk wines, (box, carafes, house, for example) | 4-5 times |
| Inexpensive bottled wines | 3 times |
| Moderately expensive bottled wines | 2 times |
| Highest-priced bottled wines | Less than 2 times |

## CHECKLIST FOR MENU PLANNING

Earlier chapters in this book along with the material in this specific chapter have identified seemingly innumerable factors that impact the task of the menu planners. Figure 6-4 reviews some of these factors. Wise menu planners should assure that these and related concerns are addressed as menus are planned, implemented, and evaluated.

Figure 6-4.  Checklist for Menu Planning

**Personnel**
- ❏ The menu communicates strategies for meeting or exceeding guest expectations.
- ❏ The image of the menu is evaluated based on appearance, readability, clarity, and pricing strategies.
- ❏ The skill levels of production personnel are evaluated.
- ❏ The skill levels of service personnel are evaluated.
- ❏ Suppliers are asked for preparation and merchandising suggestions.
- ❏ Sanitation, quality, and cost-control standards are maintained.
- ❏ Servers know the meaning of terms used to describe menu items and their preparation.
- ❏ Servers are trained to know about quality concerns that guests may have.
- ❏ Service staff are asked about guests' likes and dislikes.

**Equipment**
- ❏ Equipment is selected based on initial costs, capacity, availability of energy sources, operating costs, maintenance costs, and skill levels of employees.
- ❏ Equipment is easy to clean and sanitize.
- ❏ Equipment design, layout, and installation facilitate both product and people movement in the kitchen and service areas.
- ❏ Special functions, banquets, and room service menus are planned realistically and are based on the operation's equipment resources.
- ❏ Accessible support service (back-up help from suppliers and in-house maintenance assistance, for example) has been identified.
- ❏ Equipment meets hygiene and safety standards.
- ❏ Staff are trained in proper equipment use.

**Inventory**
- ❏ The menu achieves the financial objectives of the operation.
- ❏ Records are maintained on the menu's sales mix and the popularity of every menu item.
- ❏ The effect on all control points is considered when the menu is planned.
- ❏ Menu items are rationalized, and ingredients are cross-utilized as much as possible.
- ❏ High-quality convenience foods are evaluated and used where appropriate.
- ❏ Menu offerings are based on the expectations of the target markets.

**Facilities**
- ❏ Traffic flow in the kitchen and dining room is evaluated, and the design and layout of the facilities are changed when necessary.
- ❏ The facilities' ambiance is appropriate to the menu and the expectations of the target markets.
- ❏ Special functions and banquets are booked with the limitations of the establishment's facilities in mind.
- ❏ The facilities are maintained in a clean and sanitary manner.

**Truth-in-Menu (deliver what you promise)**
- ❏ Accurate descriptions are used for raw ingredients and finished menu items.
- ❏ Quality or grade statements are factual.
- ❏ Sizes, weights, or counts advertised on the menu are correct.
- ❏ Frozen or canned items are never billed as fresh.
- ❏ Preparation techniques are accurately stated.
- ❏ Additional charges for extras are clearly stated on the menu.
- ❏ Pictures used on the menu correctly illustrate the product to be served.
- ❏ Oral descriptions by servers are factual.
- ❏ Dietary or nutritional claims are precise.
- ❏ Points of origin are accurate and not misleading.
- ❏ The correct method of preparation is stated on the menu.

**Other Menu-Planning Factors**
- ❏ Offer chef's specials of the day when appropriate.
- ❏ Offer variety of flavors, colors, and so on when planning menus.
- ❏ Be sure to create menus in all necessary languages.
- ❏ Be sure to serve appropriate serviceware (dishes and glasses, for example).
- ❏ Use guest surveys to learn about guests' needs.
- ❏ Highlight the chef's creations (signature items).
- ❏ Assure that items are easy to consistently portion to the correct size.
- ❏ Assure that desired items are in the prime estate portions of the menu.
- ❏ Take advantage of traditional cooking methods that minimize costs.
- ❏ Precosted standard recipes are used for all menu items.
- ❏ Menu-design factors are considered when menus are designed.
- ❏ Target markets are always considered when making menu decisions.

## MENU-PLANNING RESOURCES

Fortunately, a variety of resources are available to the foodservice professional responsible for menu planning. These resources consist of printed materials, web sites offering free and "for purchase" information, and menu-planning software programs designed exclusively for the hospitality industry. Some of the most widely used of these resources follow.

### Books

- John A. Drysdale and Jennifer Adams, *Profitable Menu Planning*. Third Edition. Upper Saddle River, N.J.: Prentice Hall.
- Paul J. McVety, Bradley J. Ware, and Claudette Levesque, *Fundamentals of Menu Planning*. Second Edition. New York: John Wiley.
- Jack W. Miller and David Pavesic, *Menu Pricing and Strategy*. New York: John Wiley.

For detailed information on any of these titles, go to www.amazon.com and enter the title or author name.

### Websites

- http://www.menucookbook.com. This site, while applicable for home use also, provides great menu-development information to the hospitality professional.

- http://hin.nhlbi.nih.gov/menuplanner/menu.cgi. This free site, sponsored by the National Heart, Lung, and Blood Institute, includes an interactive menu planner designed to guide daily food and meal choices based on one day's calorie allowance. It may also be used to add up total calories, as well as fat, and carbohydrates consumed in a specific menu.
- www.hospitalitylawyer.com. This site lists foodservice consultants in a variety of areas, including food and beverage management.

### Software Providers

- www.calcmenu.com. This European site offers free downloads of its menu-planning program.
- www.cbord.com. This site will introduce you to Cbord, one of the world's largest providers of software for a variety of hospitality tasks, including menu planning.
- www.computrition.com. This international company, based in California, provides menu management, inventory control, nutrition office management, HACCP guidelines, and nutrient analysis software.
- www.foodtrac.com. This software provides menu-planning information, inventory control features, and more.

---

### SIGEE'S MENU: A CASE STUDY

"How was everything?" asked the waitress to David Berger as she approached his table.

"Very nice . . . as always!" David replied to her.

"How was yours?" David asked Michelle Rodgers, his dinner companion for the evening and director of sales and marketing for the hotel at which David was food and beverage director of Sigee's, the hotel's restaurant. At least once a month David and Michelle found time to get together and talk about their hotel and how their two departments could work together more closely.

"It was really great. I ate too much!" replied Michelle. They were at Balatino's Italian Café and had just finished crisp antipasto salads followed by pasta with Alfredo sauce, topped with grilled vegetables and chicken.

"Did you save room for our 'Mile High Apple Pie' or 'Endless Ice Cream Bowl'?" asked the waitress. Michelle looked at David, "Not for me," she said.

"I guess not. Just two coffees please," said David, as the waitress smiled politely and walked away.

"You know," said David, "that happens at Sigee's most of the time also."

"What's that?" asked Michelle

"Well," said David, "we have excellent desserts at Sigee's, but they don't sell as well as I think they could. People don't seem to want to eat dessert anymore. Too health conscious I guess."

"That's not what I experience," replied Michelle, "when we sell banquets at the hotel people always want to talk about the desserts they will get! People may say they watch calories . . . but sweets sales are as high as ever."

"It's not that I don't like sweets," continued Michelle "it's that I really couldn't see just the two of us with a "Mile High" anything. Not after the heavy meals we had. I would have liked something light instead."

"Like what?" asked David.

Like an "Inch High anything," replied Michelle with a laugh. "I just can't see spending as much for a dessert as for an entrée . . . when I know I won't be able to eat most of it anyway. Why do you restaurant people do that?"

David considered her question. It made some sense. The desserts at Sigee's were huge, designed for their taste and showiness when taken into the dining room. They were tasty, and they were showy, but the reality was that most diners did not order them.

"Tell me Michele," began David, "how would you market desserts like the ones you would buy? And how would you make those real signature items on the Sigee's menu?"

"Well," began Michelle, "I don't think I am an expert in the restaurant business, but when I sell, I try to make a strong positive out of the main features I am selling. Here you would be selling two things. One is a smaller size, so emphasize that. Make a big deal about it. As a diner, let me know why a small "taste" is as good as an "Endless Bowl!"

"And then," she continued, "Just as strongly emphasize the lower price that comes with that smaller size. But let me ask you something else—Do you really want to sell more desserts if they are sold at a lower price?"

David thought about that. "That depends," he began, "on how successful this approach would be. But, if we sell significantly more desserts, even at a lower price, our check average, as well as guest satisfaction, will go up. And that is our goal."

"Michelle," continued David, "let me ask you, which approach, larger size and larger price, or smaller size and smaller price do you think would be considered more 'traveler friendly'? What do you think guests coming to the hotel would prefer?"

David leaned forward in his chair and listened intently as Michelle began to answer.

## CHAPTER 7

# Menu-Design Procedures[1]

## MENU TERMS USED IN THIS CHAPTER

Clip-ons
Cross-selling
Menu layout
Prime real estate
Seat turnover rate

## CHAPTER OVERVIEW

After the menu planners identify which items to offer, their next step is to inform their guests about them. To do so, they must develop a physical menu to give to each guest (in table-service operations) or to be read by guests (for example, on a wall-mounted menu board or on a sign located on the drive-through lane of a quick-service restaurant).

Food and beverage operations use physical menus to advertise their products and services to the guests. The design of the menu is critical to help assure that the items the menu planners wish to sell (those that are

---

[1] Parts of this chapter are adopted from Richard Hug and M.C. Warfel, *Menu Planning and Merchandising*. Second Edition. Richmond, Calif.: McCutchan Publishing Corporation, 1997. The authors also wish to acknowledge the assistance of Ms. Jill Daniels, Conrad Hilton College of Hotel and Restaurant Management, University of Houston, for her contribution to the chapter.

most profitable and popular) are, in fact, those sold.

The chapter begins by reviewing general types of menus. Most menus are of the conventional type presented to guests at table-service operations. They come in all shapes, sizes (dimensions), and number of pages. Fortunately, basic design principles can be used for each type, and the most important of these are discussed.

Nontraditional menus can provide alternative and creative ways to advertise products and services to guests. Some nontraditional menus are used in table-service settings. These can be rolling, hand-carried, or table-mounted; "menus" can even be oral messages recited by service staff! Other examples of nontraditional menus include menu boards in quick-service and cafeteria (serving line) operations that are used to advertise their products. Menus of all types have one thing in common: They must effectively communicate (advertise) and represent the food-service operation to those being served.

Our study of traditional menus begins by focusing on menu covers. We discuss materials, types of covers, and the information that should be placed on them. Other physical concerns involve the size of the menu and its cleanliness. We also present information about the materials from which menus are made and about menu copy, descriptions, and typography (type styles and sizes).

Menu-layout concerns focus on how menu items will be placed on the menu. Preferred locations for placement of the most popular and profitable items are discussed. Information about colors, decorative details, and clip-ons is included in our discussion about the "mechanics" of menu design. Menu planners must know about menu-shape alternatives and about printing considerations if menus are to be duplicated off site. These topics are also discussed. (*Note*: Increasingly, menus are printed on site with desktop publishing software. This topic is explained in detail in Chapter 8.)

We next focus on menu merchandising, presenting ideas about ways to direct readers' attention to those items the property wishes to sell during the very short time that most guests normally review menus.

Information about the use of professional menu designers is discussed. Readers will learn about the "dos and don'ts" of using their expertise on the menu-design team. When should they be used? This chapter helps to answer this question.

Procedures to plan a menu (see Chapter 6) helped to explain how to make decisions about what menu items should be available. In this chapter the emphasis will be on informing guests about which items are available. Our discussion will focus on the menu as an advertising tool, the purpose of which is to sell those items that menu planners desire to sell. At the same time, since the menu represents the foodservice operation, it must be designed so that it is attractive, informative, and in concert with the operation's general theme.

## MENU DESIGN IS EVOLVING

Before about 1930, the menu's principal function was to list the food selections and their prices. It was the waiters' job to "sell" the items and to balance the load in the kitchen. During the prosperous days immediately following World War I, the restaurant business experienced rapid growth, which led to a deficit of skilled waiters capable of perform-ing this important sales function. Enterprising restaurateurs met this crisis by introducing the element of communication into menus, which transformed them from dull, lifeless lists to interesting and eye-catching sales tools.

Today, many menu planners still design and produce all (or most) of their menus. Still others work with professional menu designers. (We will discuss this option later in this chapter.) Increasingly, however, menu planners use modern technologies such as desktop publishing to design menus. (This option will be discussed in Chapter 8.)

Until recently, menu writers had to be familiar with type sizes, paper stock, and other elements necessary to produce a menu. Since few people are experts in all these areas, it was necessary to find a reliable professional menu printer to provide counsel.

This brief discussion about the evolution of the menu underestimates the difficulties of achieving an effective menu design. Several specialized "arts-and-crafts" skills are needed to create this important merchandising tool. Knowledge of the culinary arts, an understanding of the printer's craft, and a feel for effective advertising are all required.

## GENERAL TYPES OF MENUS

Food and beverage operations can let their guests know about what items are offered in many ways. We will review common alternatives in this section.

### Conventional Menus

In most (but certainly not all!) table-service restaurants, guests are offered a menu when they are seated. These menus can be made of many different materials and come in several different shapes and sizes. Figure 7-1 illustrates some of the more common types:

- *A—Single-sheet vertical menus.* These menus feature information including menu item descriptions on one or both sides.
- *B—Two-sheet menus (folded).* These menus open like a book. They may feature the restaurant's name on the cover and then include menu items on the inside two pages and, perhaps, on the back as well.
- *C—Multi-sheet menus.* These menus are like the two-sheet menus except that they have additional inside sheets.
- *D—Two-sheet (three panel) menus.* These menus feature two half sheets that open to reveal a full sheet beneath. Writing can appear on all three panels on both sides of the menu.
- *E—Multi-sheet, die-cut menus.* These menus are expensive to produce, but allow the menu planners to write on pages of increasing size from top to bottom or from front to back.

- *F—Menu inserts.* These are similar to "A"; this single-sheet insert is placed inside a two-sheet folded menu (see B). It is removed by the viewer, and this special handling is a suggestive selling tactic.
- *G—Vertical die-cut menus.* These menus are similar to E. They are read top page to bottom page rather than left page to right page.

### Nontraditional Menus

Guests of table-service restaurants can be informed of the menu items in many ways besides the traditional, hand-held menu. Some creative examples include rolling or hand-carried chalkboards brought to each table, wall-mounted or ceiling-hung menu boards, and table-mounted "jukeboxes" containing menu pages. We have seen binoculars through which guests view three-dimensional photos of menu items, wine bottle "labels" that serve as menus, items listed on phonograph records, and meat cleavers (the cutting edges are ground flat!) with menu copy etched on the blades. Some properties feature no menus at all; service staff recite (or even sing!) menu offerings to the guests.

### Menu Boards

Quick-service restaurants and cafeterias in noncommercial foodservice operations are examples of dining outlets that often use menu boards to inform guests about their food and beverage items. Menu boards can be

Figure 7-1.  Different Menu Types

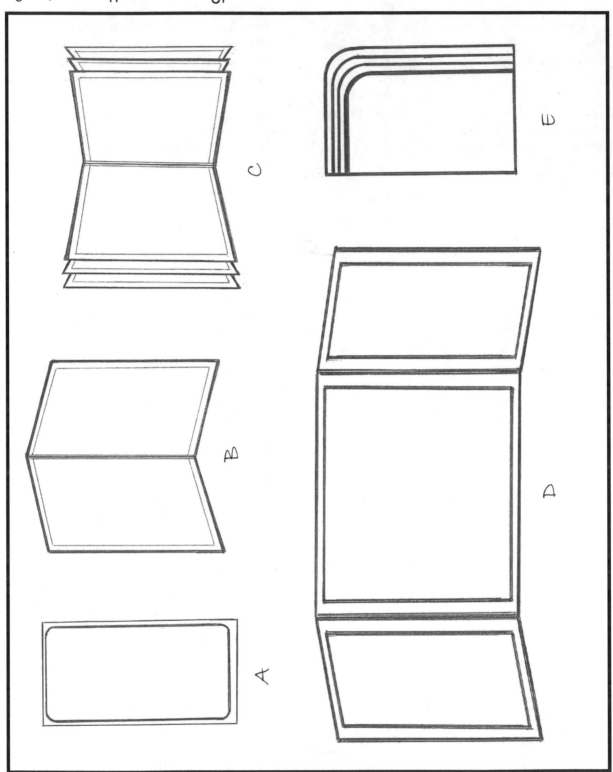

**Figure 7-1.** (continued)

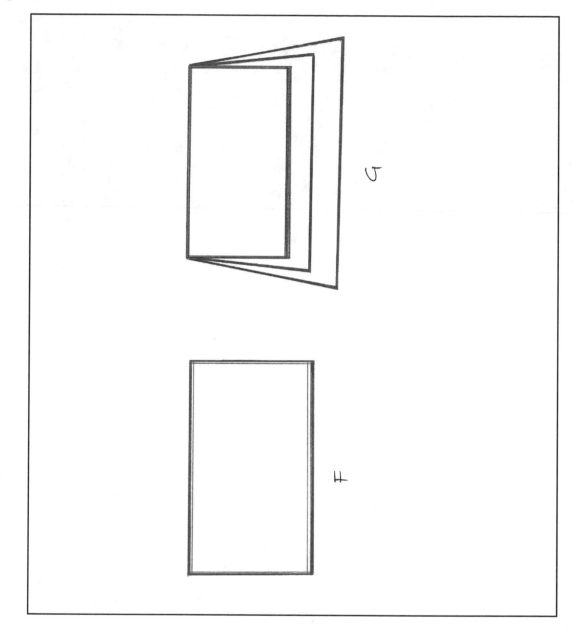

designed and constructed to meet any need. Graphics can be fitted onto back-lighted or front-lighted panels or can be attached by magnets to metal frames. Custom photographs can be used or, at a much lower cost, desired graphics can be selected from a library of previously developed resources. Figure 7-2 shows the components of a typical menu board. When designing a menu board, menu planners follow these four steps:

*Step 1.* Select the type of the menu boards desired. Construction, dimension, lighting, and other requirements are important considerations.

*Step 2.* Plan the number of panels in the boards.

*Step 3.* Determine the food and beverage categories for which graphics are needed.

*Step 4.* Select the specific graphics desired.

Figure 7-2. **Sample Menu Board**

Used with permission of International Patterns Incorporated, Bay Share, New York.

## A CLOSE LOOK AT CONVENTIONAL MENUS

Since most table-service properties use conventional menus, we will examine them most closely. Figure 7-3 reviews factors that menu designers must consider as they design the menu. It provides a framework for our discussion in this chapter.

### Menu Cover

When they visit a restaurant, guests should first be impressed by the restaurant's exterior and entrance areas. They should admire the coordination between the type of restaurant and its décor. Friendly receptionists and service staff along with the ambiance of the dining and other public areas all contribute to the guests' positive impression.

The menu, specifically the menu cover, also gives guests an early visual impression. Not only does the design of the menu cover further identify the type of restaurant, but an attractive cover is also evidence of a well-operated restaurant. The menu cover will invite guests to enjoy the forthcoming meal, so careful consideration of this component of the physical menu is very important.

What should appear on the front cover depends on the type of restaurant. The design must fit with the restaurant's décor and theme. For example, an operation with a nautical theme can build the cover design around a ship, a beach, seashells, or fish. An inexpensive source of art for such a cover can come from old prints or engravings, which are usually economical to purchase and easy to reproduce.

The design of a menu cover should not be so busy that it is hard for guests to read important information, including the name of the property, which is typically included on the menu's cover. However, copy describing credit cards accepted, the schedule of operating hours, and related information is usually better placed elsewhere on the menu. A history of the restaurant, including a discussion of its theme, can be used effectively in menus. This copy should generally appear either inside the front cover or on the exterior of the back cover.

Figure 7-3. **Factors to Consider in Menu Design**

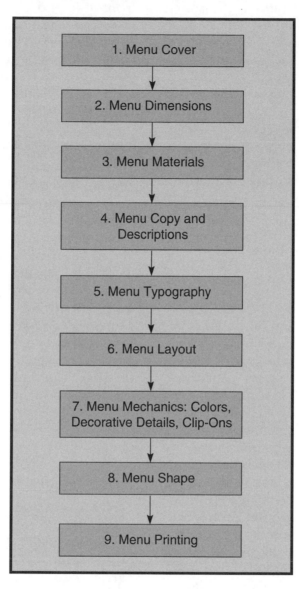

Very expensive padded menu covers and backs made from imitation (or even genuine!) leather, velvet, or other materials are available. These covers typically house removable and reusable page inserts. Since the menu covers are expensive, they are reused with each menu change. Other menu cover materials are wood, metal, plastic, or any other material that creative menu designers can imagine. Inexpensive paper covers that change daily (or more frequently!) are featured in some restaurants that use desktop publishing systems (see Chapter 8).

Less-expensive menu covers include those containing see-through "pockets" that may feature the cover on one side and a menu page on the back of the cover. (These may have additional pockets that allow panels to show through both sides of the pockets.) Paper menus laminated in a clear plastic coating are also popular. Plastic-laminated menus can be easily wiped off with a damp cloth and are popular in relatively low-check-average restaurants such as family-style establishments.

What type of menu cover, if any, should be used? The answer is the same as for every other phase of menu planning and design: it depends on the type of food and beverage operation, the price range of the menu items, and management's analysis of the cost-benefit relationship of the marketing and advertising "message." High-check-average food and beverage operations typically (but not always!) have a more expensive menu presentation than do their lower-price counterparts. Decisions about the menu cover and all other aspects of the menu are very important because they tie together the numerous components of the foodservice operation, which, as a whole, create the guests' dining experience.

## Menu Dimensions

The cover is just one of several physical factors that must be addressed by the menu designer. Consider, for example, the menu's overall dimensions. The menu's sheets or panels can be very small (8.5 inches by 11 inches or smaller) or very large (15 inches by 20 inches or larger). The number of items to be included on the menu will impact its size, but so will other factors such as the number of pages, spacing, graphics, and type styles (which are discussed later in this chapter). If a menu panel is too small, the print is typically small and often difficult to read; if a menu panel is too large, guests can knock over glassware while reading the menu. Also, what should guests do with large menus after they have decided what to order but before they give them back to the food server?

## Menu Materials

The construction material of the menu is also important because it affects its durability and the ability of staff to clean the menu. Menu designers must understand that menus cannot be effective in-house marketing and advertising tools if they do not properly reflect the cleanliness and professionalism of the foodservice operation. Service and other front-of-the-house staff must notice soiled menus and clean or remove them before the guests notice the dirty menus. If a menu cannot be cleaned, it must be discarded, regardless of its cost. The time to consider the cost and ease of cleaning of menu construction materials is *before* the menu is constructed.

## Menu Copy and Descriptions

Menu descriptions must be interesting, appetizing, and accurate, as we noted in Chapter 6. Descriptions should include the primary ingredients and the principal preparation method, when applicable, for each item. Menu copy need not be limited to listing food items and their descriptions. Copy about the restaurant and its history, interesting anecdotes about the origin of the restaurant's name, and a wide range of other topics can be included to add interest and to create a particular image. Pictures can add interest if they have significance.

The actual menu copy for menu items can be very simple or quite complex. Consider these two descriptions of a New York strip steak:

**New York Strip**                              $17.95

**New York Strip**: 14 ounces of succulent beef. We use only USDA Prime strip loins for our steaks. These are seasoned to perfection, and then seared over our real charcoal grills until they are cooked just to your liking. Always tender and delicious!
    $17.95

These two menu items could, of course, be the same item prepared in the same manner. In the first, the menu planners have chosen to give the guests only minimal information about the menu item. In the second, the detail is extensive, including the steak's weight, quality level (USDA Prime), and preparation method. Note that, as mentioned in Chapter 6, for complete accuracy the menu writers would also state, somewhere apparent on the menu, that "the weight for all meat items is before cooking; some weight loss occurs during the cooking process." The level of description that should be used by menu planners will vary with the space available on the menu, as well as with the number of menu items offered. If extensive menu copy is to be used, however, it is imperative that the writers

- describe the item accurately,
- use terms that are familiar to the reader,
- spell accurately,
- use proper grammar, and
- avoid wordy descriptions.

Good menu copy can make a menu more fun to read. Well-written copy also more effectively communicates the restaurant's offerings to guests and enhances the dining experience because guests will know exactly what they will be served before they order. Of course, poorly written, confusing, or (even worse) inaccurate menu copy does not reflect well on the restaurant and will result in decreased guest satisfaction.

## Menu Typography

Appealing menu item descriptions will not be useful if the menu type is difficult to read. There are dozens of attractive typefaces, but the primary consideration in choosing one for a menu is its readability. Multiple sizes of type on a single page can distract the reader and distort the image that the menu is designed to create. Type that is too small or too closely spaced can create confusion; instead of the ordering process being a pleasurable introduction to a fine meal, it becomes a less-than-hospitable experience.

Menu type is measured in points. There are 72 points to the inch, and for readability, type smaller than 12 points (one-sixth of an inch) should not be used. Also, experts in the printing business advise that copy set primarily in lower-case type is easier to read than type set with all upper-case letters. (This is probably because most readers are accustomed to the type used in the books, magazines, and newspapers they read daily.) Use of all upper-case type for words should be limited to headings and subheadings. Variations in type, such as italics, for emphasis are effective if done sparingly. (If too much copy is set in italics, it tires the eyes because it becomes more difficult to read.) Figure 7-4 illustrates several typefaces, all in the same size (11 points).

Varieties of Roman typeface are frequently used because of their readability; however, in ethnic or "Early American" restaurants or those with some other theme, the appropriate type should be used. Care should be taken to ensure that the color of the paper and type enhance readability. Black type on white paper is the most easily read. If you choose to use colors, make sure that the contrast is as close as possible to black and white.

## Menu Layout

The term **"menu layout"** refers to how menu items will be placed on the menu. Menu item categories were discussed in Chapter 6 when we presented menu-planning procedures. Normally, these categories will drive (or at least significantly influence) the menu's layout. For example, if menu planners have identified items to be included in appetizer, soup and salad, and entrée categories, the menu layout must obviously include space for these three categories.

---

*Glossary Terms*
**Menu layout.** The manner and location in which menu item categories are placed on the menu.

Figure 7-4. **Type Samples**

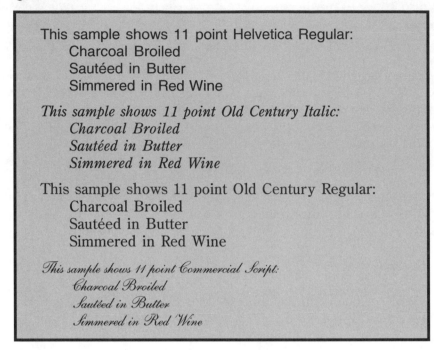

This sample shows 11 point Helvetica Regular:
Charcoal Broiled
Sautéed in Butter
Simmered in Red Wine

*This sample shows 11 point Old Century Italic:*
*Charcoal Broiled*
*Sautéed in Butter*
*Simmered in Red Wine*

This sample shows 11 point Old Century Regular:
Charcoal Broiled
Sautéed in Butter
Simmered in Red Wine

*This sample shows 11 point Commercial Script:*
*Charcoal Broiled*
*Sautéed in Butter*
*Simmered in Red Wine*

Some restaurants feature "California-style" menus that list breakfast, lunch, and dinner items on the same menu. All items are available at any time the property is open (and many do not close!). These restaurants offer at least as many different menu item categories as do any other type of food and beverage operation. They might, for example, offer several menu items under several categories. Space to accommodate each of these categories must be available, and several pages will likely be required. California-style menus might include the following categories:

- Buttermilk pancakes
- French toast
- Waffles
- Healthy-choice breakfasts
- Eggs
- Omelets
- Side orders
- Children's items
- Fruits
- Breads

- Burgers
- Salads
- Other sandwiches
- Appetizers
- Specialty sandwiches
- Chili and soups
- Chicken specialties
- Dinners
- Beverages
- Desserts

Contrast the numerous menu item categories in this California-style menu with those frequently used by a high-check-average theme restaurant that is open for dinner only. This type of property might offer only three categories on its main menu (appetizers, soups and salads, and entrées), and offer separate menus featuring desserts and wines. (Entrées may be divided into beef, seafood, poultry, or other classifications.)

Frequently, menu designers place categories on the menu by the order in which each is normally served. (For example, appetizers will be listed before soups and salads, which will be listed before entrées, which will be followed by desserts.) However, it is also important to recognize that menus have **"prime real estate"** areas in which the most popular and highly profitable items should be located. Where these areas are depends on their format (see Figure 7-1).

> *Glossary Terms*
> **Prime real estate.** A phrase used to define the areas on a menu that are most visible to guests and, therefore, should contain the items the menu planners most want to sell.

Figure 7-5 identifies where these areas are on three types of menus. As you review Figure 7-5, note that the prime real estate on a single-sheet menu is in the center of the upper half of the menu. On a two-sheet (folded) menu, the prime real estate is in the top center of the right hand page. The prime real estate for a two-folded (three panel) menu is in the center of the middle sheet when the menu is open.

The concept of a menu's prime real estate provides a challenge to menu designers. Yes, it is rational to place appetizers and soups and salads before entrées, and entrées before desserts. In fact, most menu readers would probably expect this presentation. However, it is important to recognize the location of the menu's prime real estate and to use this limited space wisely. (More information about the redesign of menus to recognize prime real estate concerns is presented in Chapter 9).

As mentioned, menu designers sometimes use subheadings within menu item categories. If the restaurant features several seafood, beef, chicken, and pork entrées, subheadings to identify the type of entrée can be helpful. If subheadings are not used, many menu designers list items of a like type (for example, beef items or poultry items) together in the entrée category rather than

list the beef and poultry items intermittently throughout the entrée list.

The relationship between the spaces allocated for menu item categories is very important. However, available space on the menu must also be used for other purposes, including the following:

- *Supplemental menu item descriptions.* For example, what accompaniments, if any, are provided with the entrées? What description of the "help-yourself" salad bar, which is provided as part of the entrée purchase, is necessary? What types of sauces are available with pasta products?
- *Cross-selling opportunities.* Effective menus cross-sell. Menu copy on a dinner menu that promotes Sunday brunches and copy on a lunch menu that describes banquet capabilities are examples.
- *Property information.* Property information (name, address, telephone and fax numbers, e-mail address, and hours of operation) should be included, especially if guests are likely to take menus with them (as occurs with souvenir, take-home, and carry-out menus).
- *Special information.* For example, warnings about the consumption of under-cooked meats (mandated by law in some areas) and an explanation of management-imposed gratuities for parties of a specified size may also be included. Some menus *tactfully* review incentives for a member of a guest party to serve as a designated driver in efforts to more responsibly serve alcoholic beverages.
- *Other information.* The history of the organization, its mission and philosophy, and other general information thought to interest the reader might be included.
- *Blank space.* A menu should not appear cluttered. (Some experts suggest that approximately 50 percent of the surface space on a menu should be left blank! While this seems like a lot of "wasted" space, wide borders around the outside edges of the

Figure 7-5. **"Prime Real Estate" Areas on the Menu**

Used with permission of Lani Sill, Hilo, Hawaii

menu and between categories and the items within them do help to make menus easy to read.)

---

*Glossary Terms*
**Cross-selling.** Tactics used by the menu designers to advertise other products and services offered by the food and beverage operation in addition to those offered on a specific menu. For example, a dinner menu may alert readers about the property's Sunday buffet; a college menu planner may use signage in the cafeteria to alert students that they can order pizzas for delivery to the residence hall rooms.

---

## Menu Mechanics

Menu mechanics include the use of color, decorative design details, and clip-ons. The use of color in menu design is an important consideration. Light colors typically suggest a warm atmosphere; darker colors can help emphasize selected menu items. Menu designers should consider the use of colors to create moods and to sell products. Assistance from a professional menu designer or a printer can help assure that a menu's color adds to rather than distracts from the image that the menu planners hope to portray.

Decorative details must be carefully considered to make a menu appealing. Pictures, drawings, and designs are details that when appropriately used will add to the menu's appeal. The overall graphic design of the menu helps assure that the menu is attractive and that everything on it is well spaced. For "do it yourself" menu planners, inexpensive clip art is available. Figure 7-6 illustrates samples of clip art that might be used in a menu.

In addition, many restaurant menus feature **clip-ons**. When properly used, clip-ons can be very effective. If used improperly, however, they can significantly detract from an otherwise effective menu. Clip-ons should not cover existing menu copy. It is inconvenient for a guest to turn the clip-ons up to read what is underneath them. But if guests do not lift up the clip-on, they will not learn

about the items that are described below the clip-on. A better approach is to design a space on the menu where the clip-on will be applied. In a well-designed clip-on menu, this space will not, however, be left blank. An illustration, a picture, or information about the restaurant should be included. Then, if a clip-on is not used on a specific date, the menu will still look complete and well designed.

---

*Glossary Terms*
**Clip-ons.** An insert in or an attachment to a menu that advertises daily specials or emphasizes other menu items that menu designers wish to sell.

---

## Menu Shapes

Using an unusual shape on a menu may be effective in projecting a particular image. Paper can easily (but not inexpensively!) be cut into shapes different from the usual rectangular form most commonly seen. In a family restaurant, for example, breakfast, luncheon, and dinner are sometimes included on one menu. The usual division is by panel, but a division that involves a change in menu shape adds interest. For example, consider a breakfast menu in the shape of a coffee cup, a luncheon menu shaped like a salad bowl, and an oval steak-platter-shaped dinner menu. Each says something about the meal listing that is described.

Hotel room service is a foodservice offering that can benefit from the interest that unusual menu shapes can generate. Recall that the room-service menu is usually read by the guest in his or her room, without a server to supply additional information. Likewise, guests ordering room service are not in a dining area where tempting food odors from nearby tables can be smelled. Therefore, the room-service menu has a difficult selling task. Consider, for example, that it is expected to sell breakfast, lunch, and dinner meals along with wines, cocktails, and hors d'oeurvres. In addition, it is sometimes placed in a folder with other materials selling laundry and va-

Figure 7.6.   Examples of Clip Art Drawings

Clip art courtesy of Softcafe@www.SOFT-CAFE.com

let services, car rentals, and so on. Designers of room-service menus should consider anything that attracts attention to the menu. One appropriately shaped menu for room-service breakfast is the key form. An example is shown later in this book (see Figure 10-13).

Another example of a creative menu for room service is shown in Figure 7-7. The menu is shown here in its actual size. Its dimensions allow it to fit in the door lock mechanism of an exterior room door that unlocks with a credit-card-sized "key." Guests must remove the menu before inserting their key card. This innovative menu cannot become "lost" in the stack of other in-room information. The menu illustrated has four panels; it is placed in the door lock, cover side out. It then opens like a matchbook to reveal two inside panels; the back side can also list additional menu items.

## Menu Printing

The many processes involved in printing a menu can make this stage of menu design seem more difficult than menu planning and design. After the menu-planning team has agreed on what items are to be included on the menu and how they are to be laid out, the menu can be printed. Traditionally, this has been a time-consuming process because several steps involving external printers were required. We will discuss these because there are times (when multiunit organizations print menus for many units, for example) that external printers are used. Recall, however, that menu designers can now create very professional menus in-house with desktop publishing technology. (This will be discussed in Chapter 8.)

Figure 7-7.　**Menu Insert for Modern Hotel Room Door Locking System**

Used with permission of Lani Sill, Hilo, Hawaii

***Working with Printers.*** Menu formats sent to printers require much coordination between menu designers and the printers. It is important to take time to carefully review proofs of the menu, because it is at this point that menu designers can correct errors or make necessary changes. The proofs should present an exact image of what is expected. However, this does not always happen. A new perspective is gained by studying the menu copy in the context of the overall design, and, therefore, changes are often made at this time.

Spelling, punctuation, and spacing must also be reviewed carefully, and changes should be marked on the proof, which is then sent back to the printer. After reviewing proofs and making corrections as necessary, menu designers often approve the menu for final printing. This is not always so, however, because an additional reading (to "proof the proofs") is sometimes necessary. Printers expect two readings of proofs, but additional proofs and further delays can result (with additional printing charges being incurred). Any extra charges or delays in scheduling that result from proof revisions should be clarified with the printer before work begins.

When menu layouts are done in-house, designers should be aware that many general programs such as Microsoft Publisher, Word, or other off-the-shelf design software programs may not be "printer-friendly" when it comes to outputting film when a commercial printer prints the work. Generally, printers prefer working with publishing programs such as Quark and PageMaker. A big problem is that of font compatibility. True Type fonts are what the general public has installed on their computers, and there are also numerous Roman True Type fonts in use. When printers receive files with these desk-top publishing fonts, there can be spacing issues that cause the document to look totally different because of reflow problems (that is, when margins from one publishing program differ from those of another). Graphic artists often use PostScript fonts that they send along with the document to the printer.

Normally, printers will not do menu layouts unless they have an extensive prepress department. If improperly laid out or designed (especially using the software programs noted above), the files can cause problems for the printer. The best rule of thumb is to contact a printer, let him or her know what layout programs will be used, and ask in advance if problems are likely. Sometimes, even when menu designers already have a layout in an incompatible program, the printer may be able to take the files (copy and general layout) and then reformat them into a compatible program. Be prepared, however, to pay more for this because the reformatting will take extra time. It is always better to ask questions first, get prices, and then weigh the options. Professional graphic designers know about design; they know what works well and what printers can do. A good graphics designer will handle the printing at a cost but usually will place the printing with a good printing company that he or she knows will print a quality product that will make the design look the best. The best-designed product can look very unattractive if not printed well or printed on the wrong type of equipment. (The use of professional menu designers is addressed later in this chapter.)

***Determining How Many Menus to Print.*** If inserts are used, the number of covers to order can be determined, in part, by evaluating printing quantity price break points. Printers typically charge a lower per-unit price as the number of printed copies increases. This amount should be tempered, however, by investment (cash flow) and storage considerations, and the operation's proposed menu revision schedule.

The number of copies to order is also influenced by the number of seats in the restaurant and the estimated discard rate. Two often overlooked but important factors are (1) is the restaurant clientele made up of a high percentage of repeat business (who may have no need to look at menus when they order "the usual")? and (2) do the prices change frequently? "Yes" to either or both of these questions indicates that fewer menus or inserts should be printed than, for example, in a resort property with relatively little repeat business or in a restaurant whose menu

features items with seldom-changing prices. Menus should be reviewed frequently and may be revised two or more times annually. Therefore, an approximate three-month supply of inserts is a basic figure with which to begin calculations.

If copy is printed directly on the menu cover, use the same reasoning to determine the number of covers to order. This number should be modified by the same considerations that were listed above for inserts. (However, the rate of discard between inserts and imprinted menu covers can vary quite widely. Consider, for example, our previous discussions about expensive covers with replaceable inserts and "wipe clean" covers that will last almost indefinitely.)

The use of clip-ons and partial inserts provides great flexibility in the menu, which allows a larger and presumably more economical number of menus to be printed. As we have noted, the menu design should include a place for inserts and clip-ons so that they do not cover a part of the regular menu.

All foodservice operations need copies of the menu for the cooks and cashiers and for staff members working in control and other supporting jobs. A number of copies of the menu should be printed on inexpensive paper for these uses.

After the order for printing the menus is placed, everything that needs to be done to prepare the menu has been done. Printing and delivery times vary, depending in part on what has been negotiated. Getting a menu printed can be a time-consuming activity, but one that is important to the menu's success. Experienced menu designers with a clear picture of what foods will be attractive to the potential clientele may find it easy to develop the items to be featured. However, as seen throughout this and the previous chapter, presenting these foods in a menu that will sell is never a simple task.

## MENU MERCHANDISING _____

A well-designed menu does more than just clearly and accurately inform guests about menu options. It also helps to sell those items the menu planners desire to sell. Some menus contain many pages (we have seen menus with 20—or more—pages!). Guests must review such extensive menus for some time before ordering. Guests may, on the one hand, be very impressed with menu variety and can be very entertained with the creative artwork, photographs, and other written and pictorial images. On the other hand, guests may be less sure about what to order, questions can arise (they may ask the server "What do you recommend?"), and extra time may be needed for first-time or infrequent guests to flip through pages looking for what they want to order. This can slow down the ordering process, creating a slow **seat turnover rate**.

---

*Glossary Terms*
**Seat turnover rate.** The number of times a seat is used for guest service during a meal period. For example, if 225 guests are served during lunch in a restaurant with 100 seats, the lunch seat turnover rate is 2.25 (225 guests divided by 100 seats).

---

While a many-paged menu can offer some marketing advantages to the restaurant (there is something for almost everyone, and the sheer variety of items offered may be a competitive edge for the property), how an extensive menu affects speed of service is a very important consideration. Most guests spend only several minutes reviewing the menu to make a choice. Because this time period is a very short window of opportunity to market to guests, the menu must be carefully designed to provide the desired advertising message. The menu planners' goal, then, must be to maximize the impact of the menu during this limited time, for the benefit of both the guest and the property.

Figure 7-8 presents a list of menu-design "don'ts" that menu planners should avoid. In effect, poor design means the menus

- are not friendly to read,
- do not adequately represent the property and help it to attain its objectives,
- do not focus on items the property wishes to sell, and
- are simply unattractive and present a poor "professional first impression."

What can menu planners do to influence the sale of products the establishment wants to sell? Using colors, boxes, special typefaces, illustrations, and photos will focus the guests' attention on specific items. Figure 9-5 in Chapter 9 shows four examples. Take a look ahead at this figure, which we will discuss in Chapter 9 in our review of menu-revision principles.

While truth-in-menu concerns must be kept in mind, creative descriptions can be helpful in selling desired items. Descriptions of menu items should be clear but concise—try to use as few words as possible. The position of the menu item within a list of similar items can also impact sales. Guests tend to see and recall items at the top.

Use common sense for effective menu design. For example, menu planners do not typically need to devote significant space to describe common products such as roast beef or deep-fried chicken. If these are items menu planners want to sell, graphics—not prose—is probably the preferred technique to increase sales. And photos, while expensive, can be used to draw attention to specific menu items, as can pencil or colored drawings and clip art. On the other hand, less-common items, such as piccata milanese (pan-fried veal scallops with macaroni) and pompano en papillote (pompano fin fish with a velouté or cream sauce served in a parchment paper bag) may require a brief, enticing description.

Figure 7-8. **Common Menu Design Problems**

- Type is too small.
- The menu appears cluttered.
- Words are printed on top of graphics (or vice versa).
- Decorative script and typeface are difficult to read.
- The menu cannot be easily read in dimly lit dining areas.
- Menus are not designed to sell items that the facility wants to sell (that is, the popular *and* profitable items).
- Foreign or unusual culinary words are used without explanation.
- Inadequate design fails to help the guests' eyes follow from category to category and from item to item.
- Graphics do not contribute to the menu's aesthetic appeal nor do they help to sell items.
- Selling prices are placed so that the guests focus on the price—not on the menu item.
- Printing is expensive, which makes it more difficult to justify frequent menu replacement
- Menus are physically too large or too small to handle or read.
- Menus are printed on too lightweight a paper stock and, therefore, lack durability.
- Menus do not accurately represent the actual items to be served to the guests.

How should the menu item's selling price be listed? Menu items should not be listed sequentially by ascending or descending selling prices. Menu designers should de-emphasize selling prices by making them unobtrusive rather than overt and eye-catching.

Some menu-design consultants suggest that the price *not* be listed in a separate column connected to the menu item by leader dots. Likewise, they suggest that dollar signs and bold type be avoided. A better approach is to list prices at the end of the menu item's description and in the same typeface. (See Chapter 5, and Figure 5-4 in that chapter,

for additional information about the listing of selling prices on menus.)

In summary, wise menu planners think about their guests as they design the menus. What do the guests want? The answer is fairly simple and obvious. Guests want menus to be

- legible (understandable),
- organized (and "friendly") to enable decision making, and
- well designed (with pictures and drawings that help them choose their meal and with an overall design that is in concert with the dining experience they will enjoy).

## WORKING WITH PROFESSIONAL MENU DESIGNERS

Chapter 8 discusses "do-it-yourself" menu design software available to menu planners. However, the use of copyright-permitted clip art, colorful borders and attractive scripts, and menu-design software does not automatically result in an effective menu that attracts guests and meets the establishment's profit goals. Easy-to-use and inexpensive generic desktop publishing or more specific menu planning and design software cannot replace creative

talent and the experience of those who understand the psychology of menu design.

Menus designed on site are less expensive than those created by a professional menu design service. In addition, as with the purchase of any other product or service, the least expensive menu designer is not necessarily the "best" for the food and beverage operation.

If a foodservice operation wants to use a professional menu designer, menu planners should review the following steps for initiating and coordinating a menu-design project, which will help develop a quality menu.

- *Establish a menu-development budget.* Menus can range from the simple to the extravagant. Establishing a budget for the menu-design project helps the menu planners select a professional menu designer who is affordable and who will stay within the budget range established.
- *Review the work of the professional menu designers under consideration.* Fortunately, it is easy to review samples of menus created by professional menu designers. Menu planners can quickly see the quality of work in these projects and determine if the menus represent the quality they desire.
- *Determine in-house versus contracted responsibilities.* As we have seen, there are many tasks involved in creating a menu. Depending on the skill and experience level of the menu planners, some or all of these tasks will become the responsibility of the professional menu designer. For example, the writing of menu copy for each entrée item may be assigned to the professional menu designer, or the menu planners may retain this responsibility. In either case, each party should clearly understand its responsibilities.
- *Interview potential design partners in person or by telephone.* The hiring of a professional menu designer creates a "menu partnership" between the designer and the menu planners. As with any partnership, it is best if the partners display mutual respect and real affinity for each other. This can best be established in a face-to-face setting in which both parties can evaluate the desirability of working together.
- *Determine all aspects of "final product" ownership.* While it might appear straightforward, the question of final product ownership can be complex. For example, if artwork is supplied on the menu (see, for example, Figure 7-9a), does the designer retain rights to use the artwork for other clients, or does

it become the exclusive property of the foodservice establishment? Likewise, if the menu is designed and loaded on a computer disk or file, do the menu planners "own" or have easy access to the file or is it the property of the designer? These questions can be important, especially in the situation where, for whatever reason, the partnership between the professional menu designer and the menu planners is dissolved. Menu planners should know what the professional menu designer will deliver when the project is completed and the ownership of what is delivered.

- *Keep communication lines open.* The best professional menu designers listen carefully to the intentions of menu planners. This is really the only way that an acceptable menu can be produced. It is the responsibility of the menu planners to communicate, in as much detail possible, the intended uses, goals, and objectives of the menu. Only then can professional menu designers design to the "needs" of the restaurant.
- *Sign a written contract.* Just as with any other purchase agreement, the buyer and seller of menu-design services must clearly understand their respective responsibilities. The details of the project including hourly or project rates to be charged, timetables, and final delivery dates should be clearly indicated. Also, the format (final printed version or computer file, for example) in which the work will be delivered should be specified.
- *Contribute to the project in a timely manner.* If a menu-design project is to be efficiently completed, menu planners must carry out their own assignments in a time frame that allows the menu designer to proceed with minimal delay or interruption. While all decisions to be made by the menu planners must be carefully considered, unnecessary postponement in editing menu copy, approving proofs, or supplying needed information will hinder (or, at least, slow) the project's success.

- *Be open to input.* While the final menu remains the responsibility of the menu planners, experienced designers can be extremely helpful in the development process. Menu planners should keep an open mind about suggestions that menu designers make and then use the best of these suggestions for the benefit of the operation.
- *Maintain control of the design process.* In the final analysis, menu planners, not the professional menu designer, are responsible for the menu's successful implementation. Menu planners must ensure that its final design is compatible with the operation's concept, clientele, equipment, and service levels. If the design project appears to stray from intended operational goals, the menu planners must refocus the designer's efforts to the original project objectives.

Figure 7-9a is an example of the front cover of a four-page menu produced by a professional menu designer in conjunction with, in this case, the hotel's food and beverage department general manager, food and beverage director, chef, and others. Attractive menus such as these are often the result of a collaborative effort between a professional menu designer and the foodservice manager or restaurant owner and others involved in menu planning.

The two inside pages (left and right) as well as the back cover of the professionally designed menu are included in, respectively, Figures 7-9b and 7-9c. Note that, in this instance, the sports theme introduced on menu's cover is carried throughout the menu, as are the simple line-art graphics and the overall "casual" style.

## MENU-DESIGN RESOURCES

A variety of resources are available to the foodservice professional responsible for menu design. These resources consist of web sites that offer free and "for purchase" information, as well as organizations and individuals who are professional menu designers.

### Web Sites

- www.menumaker.com. This site provides menu samples, menu covers, pricing information, and assistance in designing your own menu.
- www.mugjoint.com/oswalt/wgi2.html. This site of the Oswalt Menu Company provides information on menu covers, menu design, custom food photography, color printing, and binding.
- www.softcafe.com/menupro.htm. This site provides information on "Menupro," a software program on compact disk that includes over 100 predesigned menu styles, hundreds of food illustrations and watermark menu backgrounds, 50 type fonts, and a culinary spell-checker.

- www.exit109.com/~mstevens/menus. This interesting site contains menus from hundreds of restaurants. Each menu has been scanned onto the site and can provide ideas on what can be done in your own situation.

### Professional Designers and Assistance

- www.fcsi.org. This site of the Foodservice Consultants Society International lists contact address and e-mails for professional foodservice consultants.
- www.chrie.com. This site lists two- and four-year colleges who have faculty members that may provide menu-design and consulting services at reduced rates.
- www.creativemenus. This web site has been developed by a professional chef (Gunter Wiesmann) to provide expert menu-development assistance.
- http://armsco.com/paper/menpaper.-htm. This web site, sponsored by a paper company, provides printing and publication services completely on-line.

Figure 7-9a. **Front Cover of a Professionally Designed Menu**

**SIGEE'S sports Zone**

Clarion Hotel &
Conference Center

3600 Dunckel Drive, Lansing, Michigan
**517-351-7600**

## And on the Starting Line...

**Basket o' Fries** - A heaping bounty of our seasoned shoe-strings...............................$1.92

**Basket o' Onion Rings** - Steak cut, breaded and deep fried golden. ..........................................$3.92

**Wing Ding Zingers** - Choose from hot buffalo style, barbecue, or traditional. Served with snappy celery sticks and bleu cheese sauce for dipping...............$5.92

**Fried Mozzarella Sticks** - Served with a zesty marinara sauce............ $5.92

**Chicken Fingers** - Everybody has chicken fingers, but we have three different kinds! Buffalo style, traditional, or our special grilled style; you make the call. Each is served with dipping sauce of your liking.... $5.92

**Breaded Mushrooms** - A big basket of golden fried mushrooms, with your choice of ranch or marinara sauce. ..................................................... $5.92

Figure 7-9b.  **Inside Pages of a Professionally Designed Menu**

## On the Green

**Field of Dreams Salad** - A bottomless bed of lettuce tossed with a wide variety of fresh vegetables and our distinct house vinaigrette, finished with crisp croutons. If we build it, you will come... back! ............................... $3.92

**Baja Chicken Caesar** - Born in... Mexico? That's right, Mexico. Crisp romaine, Parmesan cheese, and crunchy croutons. Tossed with our own Caesar dressing and topped with a fresh grilled chicken breast. It's a classic reborn! .......... $6.43

**Chicken Taco Salad** - Fresh lettuce, tomato, onion, black olives and cheese, topped with your choice of grilled or blackened chicken breast. Served in a flour tortilla bowl. ...... $6.43

**Island Breeze** - A refreshing change from the ordinary! We take a quarter pineapple shell and fill it with grilled chicken breast, then surround it with the freshest melon, grapes, and pineapple chunks. ............................... $6.92

**Soup of the Day** - Whatever our chef is in the mood for, it's guaranteed to please..Cup $1.92 ................................................... Bowl $2.92

**Clarion's Custom Chili** - A robust blend of meat, beans and tomatoes, accentuated by the chef's secret blend of award winning herbs and spices will bring your taste buds to life. .........Cup $1.92 ......................................... Bowl $2.92

## Full Court Sandwiches

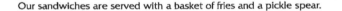

Our sandwiches are served with a basket of fries and a pickle spear.

**The Reuben** - Grilled rye piled high with corned beef, sauerkraut, thousand island, and Swiss cheese. Not too keen on corned beef, then try Reuben's sister. . ......................................... $5.92

**The Rachel** - We substitute shaved turkey for the corned beef, but there is still plenty of goodness to go around ............................................. $5.92

**Tour de France** - A heaping portion of roast beef smothered with provolone cheese on a crusty roll. Au jus on the side for dipping... Everyone comes home with the yellow jersey here! ............. $5.92

**Home Run Club** - We stack ham, turkey, bacon, cheese, lettuce, and tomato between three slices of toast. It'll knock you out of the park!............................................$5.92

**Spartan Sub** - Have a tailgate party any time! Your choice of ham, turkey, roast beef, or corned beef stacked with cheese, lettuce, tomato, and onion. .................................................................... $5.92

**San Diego Chicken Sandwich** - Tender marinated chicken breast grilled on an open flame with melted cheddar. Served on a rye bun with lettuce and tomato garnish (The real San Diego chicken was not harmed in the making of this sandwich!) Also available blackened ......................................... $5.92

**Gridiron Grinder** - As American as football! Shaved ham, Swiss and American cheeses, all piled high on a big submarine bun and finished in the oven .......... $5.92

Figure 7-9b.　(continued)

## The Burger Zone

Our burgers are served with a basket of fries and a pickle spear.

We start you out with a full half-pound of the finest lean ground beef, and you take the handoff and run with it! We have enough selections to make your burger as individual as you are! Included are the first two items, then it's just $.25 per item after that.

***Suggestions include:***

American, Swiss, cheddar, provolone, bleu cheese sauce, sauteed onions, peppers, or mushrooms, ham, bacon, jalapeno peppers. If you don't see something you like, just check with your server - 'cause we've probably have it. Lettuce and tomato garnish included.

$5.92

## Sports Zone Knock-Outs

(Available after 5:00 Monday - Saturday)
Dinner entrees served with salad, our famous smashed redskins, veggie of the day, and texas toast.
Soup available with meal for just .92ᶜ.

**Triple Play Sirloin** - 10 ounce juicy sirloin served up three ways! Choose from: 1.) smothered with sauteed onions, peppers and mushrooms, 2.) finished with a rich mushroom demi glace, or 3.) it's also available blackened for a real Cajun treat! ........................................... $11.92

**Stuffed Whitefish Supreme** - Tender, flaky whitefish filled with a crabmeat stuffing and baked to perfection ............................................... $10.92

**Sigee's Catch and Release Special** - Forget about the one that got away; your server will tell you tales of the ones that stayed on the hook! ....................................... Market price.

**St. Louis Ribs** - We take the best cuts, slow roast them to tender perfection, then slather them with our secret barbecue sauce and finish them over an open flame. ................................................. $11.92

**Margarita Chicken** - Two chicken breasts marinated in our own blend of tequila, lime and southwestern seasonings; flame broiled and finished with a zesty pineapple salsa .......................... $9.27

**Veggie Lasagna** - Layers of fresh veggies piled high with lasagna noodles, alfredo sauce, and parmesan cheese, then finished with marinara sauce. Served with the vegetable of the day and garlic toast. ............................................. $7.92

Please note that consuming raw or undercooked meat, poultry or seafood could be hazardous to your health.

Figure 7-9c.  Back Cover of a Professionally Designed Menu

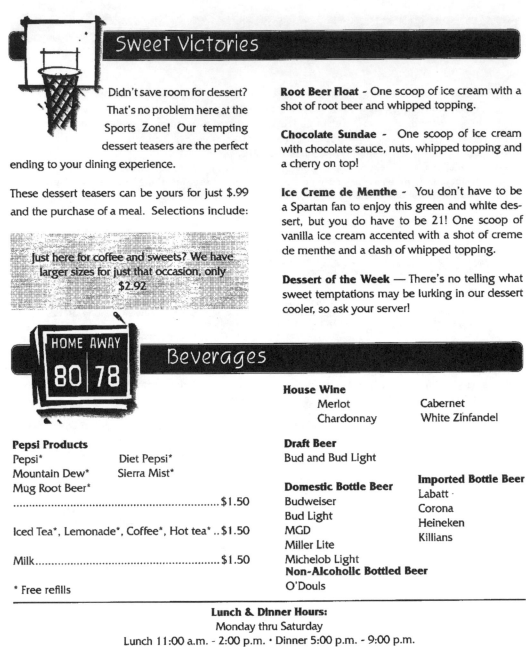

## Sweet Victories

Didn't save room for dessert? That's no problem here at the Sports Zone! Our tempting dessert teasers are the perfect ending to your dining experience.

These dessert teasers can be yours for just $.99 and the purchase of a meal. Selections include:

Just here for coffee and sweets? We have larger sizes for just that occasion, only $2.92

**Root Beer Float** - One scoop of ice cream with a shot of root beer and whipped topping.

**Chocolate Sundae** -  One scoop of ice cream with chocolate sauce, nuts, whipped topping and a cherry on top!

**Ice Creme de Menthe** -  You don't have to be a Spartan fan to enjoy this green and white dessert, but you do have to be 21! One scoop of vanilla ice cream accented with a shot of creme de menthe and a dash of whipped topping.

**Dessert of the Week** — There's no telling what sweet temptations may be lurking in our dessert cooler, so ask your server!

## Beverages

HOME AWAY
80 | 78

**Pepsi Products**

Pepsi*             Diet Pepsi*
Mountain Dew*      Sierra Mist*
Mug Root Beer*

..........................................................$1.50

Iced Tea*, Lemonade*, Coffee*, Hot tea* .. $1.50

Milk........................................................$1.50

* Free refills

**House Wine**

Merlot            Cabernet
Chardonnay        White Zinfandel

**Draft Beer**
Bud and Bud Light

**Domestic Bottle Beer**          **Imported Bottle Beer**
Budweiser                         Labatt
Bud Light                         Corona
MGD                               Heineken
Miller Lite                       Killians
Michelob Light
**Non-Alcoholic Bottled Beer**
O'Douls

**Lunch & Dinner Hours:**
Monday thru Saturday
Lunch 11:00 a.m. - 2:00 p.m. • Dinner 5:00 p.m. - 9:00 p.m.
**Lounge Hours:**
Friday & Saturday: Noon — 11:00 p.m. • Sunday: Noon - 5:00 p.m.
Monday thru Thursday from Noon to 10:00 p.m.
**Holiday Hours for Restaurant and Lounge:** Noon — 5:00 p.m.

## SIGEE'S MENU: A CASE STUDY

"Our concept and vision . . .," began David Berger, the food and beverage director at the hotel where Sigee's full service restaurant was housed, "is to be more casual, less expensive and, hopefully, popular!"

David was talking to Otto Pinskey, a restaurant menu design specialist who had produced some excellent menus for other restaurateurs. Their meeting had just begun in Sigee's lounge. David wanted Otto to take the menu ideas that the Sigee's menu-planning team had developed and create the actual Sigee's menu.

David had been very thorough in his selection of Otto's company. He had first exchanged e-mails, then talked to Otto by telephone after viewing Otto's work on the Internet and had been immediately impressed with Otto's knowledge of the business, his experience, and most of all, his practice of asking important questions and then listening carefully to David's answers. After discussing the budget that would dictate the extent of the project and reviewing hard copy of some of Otto's most recent work, David selected Otto's company from among three others he had considered.

"The restaurant looks great. Tell me about your guests," began Otto, as his eyes swept quickly across the bar and restaurant areas. David began to talk about the hotel's guests who used the restaurant, as well as the local guests who simply visited Sigee's but did not stay in the hotel.

For the next two hours, Otto asked David many questions about the restaurant, its staff, the equipment, décor changes David still had planned for the dining room and lounge, and how David envisioned using the menu itself.

The last question caught David a bit off guard. "What do you mean," asked David in response to Otto's question of how David would "use" the menu.

"Well," began Otto, "I know you will use the menu in the dining room, but where else?"

"Where else?" asked David.

"Yes. You've said you are going for a complete concept change, right?" asked Otto.

"Correct, the old concept just wasn't working for us," said David.

"Okay, then you want to use this new menu to get the word about Sigee's change out to as many people as possible."

"Exactly," replied David.

"Well, then," said Otto, "how about a menu designed to be taken away from the restaurant with each guest."

"Each guest?" asked David.

"Well, we know that not every guest will take a menu, but the idea is that the menu could be designed in such a way that they could be easily given away."

"I don't know," said David, "this sounds like a plot by a certain design company to sell me more menus."

"No," Otto laughed, "I know what you could be thinking, but consider this: What if we, within the budget we have, created a menu that was portable enough to be given way, could be folded for mailing to people in the community and yet, at the same time, looked nice enough to be used in the guest rooms as a room service menu?"

"Sure," replied David, "that would be great."

"Okay," said Otto, "I think I have the beginnings of a design idea, but first let's talk about the menu items you really want to feature, and what those items will communicate about Sigee's."

## CHAPTER 8

# Technology and Menu Planning and Design

## MENU TERMS USED IN THIS CHAPTER

Cost of goods sold
Hardware
Home page
Instant message program
Intranet
Purchase order system

Revenue
Sales history
Selling price
Software
World wide web

## CHAPTER OVERVIEW

Most readers have been dramatically affected by computer technology, both at home and at work. Menu planning and design have been made easier and more efficient by computer systems that provide the current and accurate information about the foodservice operation, which is necessary for menu planning. In addition, computer software allows designers to "experiment" with numerous layouts, typefaces and sizes, color, and other design variables.

This chapter begins by looking at specific ways that technology affects menu development. Menus cannot be developed without knowing the answers to questions such as the following:

- What should be served?
- What will the items cost?
- How often should the item be served (in many noncommercial foodservice operations)?
- What price should be charged?
- How effective is the menu?

Information to answer these questions can be developed manually, and has been done so through the years. Today, computers can be used to compile this information, which enables menu planners to access all the information they need to make menu-planning decisions when they need it.

The second major section in this chapter focuses on technology and menu design. We will discuss how each major design decision (layout, type style and size, color, photos and illustrations, and wording) can be evaluated before the final menu design is printed. "Yesterday" this process was typically "trial and error"—a print shop might print several possible versions of a menu, often at great expense. Today, increasingly, possible menu designs can be evaluated on site using word-processing programs on personal computers. With technology, menus can be printed in-house. They can change daily (or more frequently), and today's inexpensive black and white and color printers give the menus an incredibly professional look.

Our chapter concludes with a review of technology and how menus can help to sell an operation's products and services. Many foodservice operations have Internet web sites (home pages), and their menu is typically an integral part of it. Web sites can be used for direct sales (carry-out, nonfood and beverage product sales, and banquet advertising, for example). Internet search engines help viewers quickly learn about restaurant and menu alternatives, and numerous directories are available for this purpose. Other creative uses of technology for advertising will also be presented in this chapter to help readers keep up with the fast-changing ways that technology can help menu planners and designers perform their jobs more effectively.

## THE COMPUTER AND MENU PLANNING

In Chapter 6 we discussed the basic steps involved in the menu-planning process. The computer can help the menu planner with many of these steps. Figure 8-1 presents a schematic of these steps, and we will discuss in detail how technology can help with these menu-planning steps.

- *Step 1—Recognize menu-planning priorities.* Marketing surveys can be used to determine the guests' needs and desires. If oral or written ("hard copy") surveys are used, results can be input into a computer, and the results can be electronically tabulated. Reports can be generated to provide detailed information about guest preferences, sorted by numerous demographic factors such as age,

vocation, disposable income, and gender.

Today, food and beverage operations increasingly conduct consumer-opinion research directly on their **home page**. For example, viewers can be asked questions about their preferences regarding preparation methods, service styles, and beverage consumption. Increasingly, hotels offer guests the option to evaluate their products and services on the in-room television. Both of these venues provide feedback about foodservices, which can help with menu revisions.

Product quality is a menu-planning priority that can be enhanced by using a computer. For example, there is an increased assurance that food ingredients will be fresh when the purchaser and the supplier electronically share procurement and inventory information. In some large operations, optical scanning devices are helping track the amount of time that products are stored on site. Reduced storage times will yield higher-quality ingredients for use in preparing menu items.

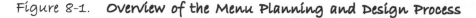

*Glossary terms*
**Home page (sometimes referred to as a web site).** Refers to a specific URL (Universal Resource Location) that offers the reader (viewer) information, data, graphics, or entertainment. Home pages may be established or maintained by organizations or by individuals.

Figure 8-1. **Overview of the Menu Planning and Design Process**

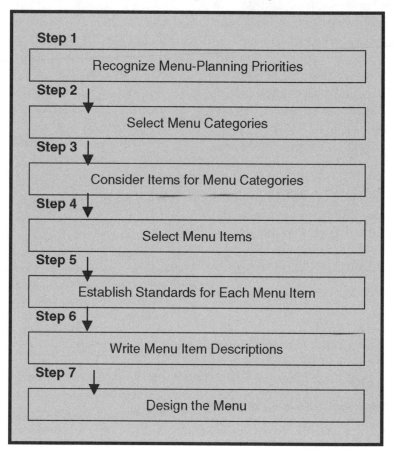

Other important menu-planning concerns relate to operating resources and financial goals. The property's operating resources are greatly impacted by technology. For example, computers may design preparation and dining areas, computers can schedule food production and service labor, and "high-tech" controls on production equipment accurately monitor time-temperature relationships during the cooking process.

Financial goals relate in many ways to financial-management practices. Almost all foodservice operations use personal computers or back-office accounting systems to develop operating budgets; to track revenue, expenses, and income (profit); and to develop financial statements. This data is of critical importance to menu planners.

- *Step 2—Select menu categories.* Marketing data gathered in Step 1 can help menu planners determine the food categories desired by guests. As well, menu evaluation (see Chapter 9) is frequently computer assisted and uses sales history information (also computer generated) to objectively determine the profitability and popularity of alternative menu items. This analysis could indicate, for example, that the number of menu item categories should be either expanded or reduced.

- *Step 3—Consider items for menu categories.* As noted, electronically generated sales history information for each menu item is very helpful when a menu is revised. Entire data banks are available to help menu planners as they evaluate potential items to add to menus. Food vendors frequently offer their customers electronic files consisting of the vendor's menu items. In addition, the Internet contains a wealth of information about new products and preparation methods that can result in new menu items. The following are just a few examples from hundreds of helpful web sites:

| For information on . . . | Go to |
|---|---|
| Beef recipes | www.beef.org |
| Pork recipes | www.otherwhitemeat.com |
| Poultry recipes | www.ichef.com |
| Pasta recipes | www.ilovepasta.com |

- *Step 4—Select menu items.* Information gathered through surveys (see Step 1) can be used to select items for new or revised menus; electronically generated menu evaluation data (see Chapter 9) can be used when deciding whether to keep or delete items on an existing menu.

- *Step 5—Establish standards for each menu item.* Standard recipes and standard food purchase specifications (see Chapter 5) are examples of tools used to implement menu item standards. Increasingly, commercial and noncommercial foodservice operations are using computerized standard recipes for food and beverage items. (A sample set of chained recipes generated by a computer was shown in Chapter 4.) Computerized standard recipes permit electronic adjustments of the number of portions and portion sizes needed, which can help reduce arithmetic errors that occur when busy food production personnel hurriedly make these calculations.

In Chapter 5 we noted that objective menu pricing methods were driven by product costs. Computerized precosting systems are widely used to calculate the cost of the ingredients that make up a menu item. If, for example, the purchase cost of ground beef changes, the menu planners can easily adjust the product cost for all menu items containing ground beef. Electronic versions of purchase specifications are also increasingly used as part of a **purchase order system**.

---

*Glossary terms*
**Purchase order system.** A procurement method in which prices for products in specified quantities meeting quality requirements outlined in purchase specifications are solicited from suppliers. Buyers make supplier-selection decisions for specific orders based on price quotations received and are assured that incoming products will be of the proper quality, since they will be checked against purchase specifications.

---

- *Step 6—Write menu item descriptions.* Computer software is available to help menu planners write item descriptions. While these programs will not tell menu planners how to describe an item, they will check the descriptions for correct spelling and grammar.

- *Step 7—Design the menu.* Software is available to help planners design the menu. This step will be discussed at length later in this chapter.

As this discussion shows, technology has a direct impact on each of the steps involved in menu planning and design. This is true today and will be increasingly true tomorrow as operating managers team up with software designers to develop additional applications.

# MENU DEVELOPMENT AND TECHNOLOGY

As explained throughout this text, the word "menu" can mean two very different things. First, it can indicate what items are offered for sale. Second, it can refer to the visual way in which information about those items is communicated to the guests. Advances in technology have had a great impact on both of these aspects of the menu. In this section, we will examine how advances in technology affect the menu planners' decision making as the menu is planned and designed.

## Technology and Menu Planning

As you have learned, it is critical to make good decisions about what menu items to offer. Some menu items are more popular than others. Some items are more profitable than others. Menu planners must consider both popularity and profitability to construct a menu with optimal item offerings, and they must analyze an extensive amount of information to make informed decisions about what should be served. Today, advances in **software** and **hardware** technology allow menu planners to make better decisions about what to serve; computers can now be used to manipulate the extensive data required to make those good decisions.

> *Glossary terms*
> **Hardware.** Point-of-sale system terminals, personal computers, inventory and bar code reading devices, printers, and other computer equipment items.
> **Software.** Computer programs that gather, sort, and report information.

Software developed for menu planning consists of the computer programs that gather, sort, and report management information. Menu-planning software has been developed for specific segments of the hospitality industry such as health care, quick service, and table service. The amount of information that can be collected by a powerful software program is vast,

but there are also significant economic, staff, training, equipment, material, and management costs associated with accumulating data by computer. Thus, only software programs that are truly critical to the menu-planning process should be purchased.

The hardware required for menu planning consists of the point-of-sale system terminals, personal computers (PCs), inventory and bar code reading equipment, printers, and other devices required to run the menu-planning software. The best software should be selected first, and then the hardware required to operate it. The hardware should facilitate the entering, storage, and retrieval of the information required by the software programs.

Software designed specifically for food-service operations, using data applicable to the individual property or facility, will allow the menu planners to easily

- select menu items,
- cost recipes for the selected items,
- compute each item's contribution margin,
- compute each item's food cost percentage,
- compute each item's profitability based on known costs,
- estimate sales of future items based on historical sales patterns, and
- assign prices to menu items.

Computer software designed to assist menu planners with these tasks has been developing rapidly within the past twenty years. Today, software programs that help managers plan menus may be "stand alone" programs that interface with other data that menu planners collect and enter into the computer system. Alternatively, menu-planning components may be integrated into larger computerized food-service management programs that include features related to labor cost control, nutrition, purchasing, inventory, and accounts payable, as well as to other areas of interest to management.

## Questions Addressed by Menu-Planning Technology

While the ability of a specific program to generate menu-related data is great, the ability of menu planners to actually use that data may be limited. When selecting software, it is easy to get sidetracked by the many interesting but perhaps unnecessary features of the software programs. Any good menu-planning software program should help managers answer a few specific questions, including the following:

- What should be served?
- What will the item cost?
- How often should the item be served?
- What price should be charged?
- How effective is the menu?

***What Should Be Served?*** One of the best features of quality menu-planning software relates to tracking what has been sold in the past. This information is known as a **sales history**. Effective menu-planning programs allow menu planners to track sales daily, weekly, or monthly by guest count, by date, and by sales type (cash, credit card, or debit card), if desired. Of course, the most important sales record is the tally of actual menu items sold during these time periods. Additional data helpful in determining what to sell are the guest check average and the number of each menu item sold in a period of time versus the number sold during prior, but similar, time periods.

---

*Glossary terms*
**Sales history.** The number of each menu item sold during a specific period of time (daily, weekly, or monthly, for example).

---

With a very clear understanding of what guests have purchased in the past, menu planners can begin to make good decisions about what should be served in the future. Less popular items may be removed from the menu in favor of others that are more popular. Good menu-planning programs also help forecast sales. Forecasting sales helps to establish appropriate inventory levels for the ingredients needed to prepare the items and assists in developing production schedules and, therefore, employee scheduling.

***What Will the Item Cost?*** Quality menu-planning programs include a component designed to tell the menu planners how much it costs to produce each proposed menu item. To achieve this, managers enter data related to standardized recipes (ingredient amounts and costs, for example) into the program, and the program calculates the cost of producing a single serving of the menu item. In the past, maintaining a standardized recipe file with up-to-date and accurate ingredient costs was a time-consuming and often tedious process. Computerized menu-planning programs make the process very easy. In addition to costing recipes, advanced menu design programs can calculate recipe quantity conversions.

Variations and enhancements of menu-planning software include components designed to make ingredient lists for purchase or issue from the storeroom, to supply color pictures of the finished menu item, and to create production forecasts based on sales forecasts. For operators that use cycle menus, the programs can suggest quantities of ingredients to order based on future needs, as well as provide a daily breakdown of what to order and when to pull items from the freezer to ensure that they are thawed in time for production.

***How Often Should the Item Be Served?*** While the popularity and production costs of menu items are very important menu development considerations, equally important to many operations is how often the menu items should be served. For example, in college residence halls, hospitals, and correctional and extended care facilities, foodservice managers must be aware of nutritional concerns when they plan menus. Most menu-planning software is designed to perform a nutrition-related analysis of menu items, and can generate reports that analyze recipe nutrients, diabetic exchanges, and weight management. For those foodservice managers responsible for the complete dietary intake of the establishment's consumers, this component of the menu-planning program is extremely critical. Advanced menu-planning programs also allow managers to track each diner's food preferences, calorie intakes, food allergies, and relevant medical history information.

***What Price Should Be Charged?*** Quality menu-planning programs can assist managers in determining the appropriate selling price of the menu items. To do this, the program should be able to analyze costs and compare the forecasted **cost of goods sold** to the actual cost of goods sold as well as make adjustments for other factors, such as employee meal costs. In addition, the relative popularity of the menu items should be considered. When managers know how much it costs to make items, along with the items' popularity and how often to sell them, menu prices can be determined.

Menu planners who do not fully understand the costs of producing their menu items might find that their selling prices are too low. Often they have underestimated their true production costs. Alternatively, some menu planners raise menu prices to increase revenue. It is critical to remember, however, that **revenue** and **selling price** are not synonymous terms. "Revenue" refers to the money collected from the sale of menu items; "selling price" is the amount charged for the purchase of one menu item.

Total revenue, then, consists of the selling price of a menu item multiplied by the number sold of that item, summed for all menu items. If prices are raised too high, the total number of menu items sold may actually decrease (because fewer guests buy the higher-

priced items). As a result, there is a decrease, rather than an increase, in total revenue.

***Glossary terms***
**Cost of goods sold.** The product costs incurred to generate the revenue produced from the sale of the product. A simplified formula is: Beginning Inventory Value + Purchases - Ending Value. (Numerous adjustments to this basic equation can be made to more closely match product costs with the revenue generated from their sale.)
**Revenue.** The amount of money generated from the sale of food and beverage products and other services offered by the food and beverage operation. (Note: The term "revenue" should not be confused with "sales," which refers to the number of units of product sold to guests. For example, a restaurant will have revenues of $25 if it sells five sandwiches at a selling price of $5 each.)
**Selling price.** The amount charged to purchase one menu item.

While there are exceptions, a general rule is that when the price of any item is increased, the sales of that item will likely decrease. For this reason, price increases must be evaluated by their impact on total revenue and not on price alone. Good menu-planning programs recognize this.

Some menu-planning software approach menu pricing with the goal of reducing the overall food cost percentage; the software's designers assume that the best menu price structure minimizes the food cost percentage. Other programs are based on each menu item's contribution margin (the amount remaining after the product [food] cost is subtracted from the item's selling price), in the belief that the average contribution margin per item is a more important consideration in pricing decisions than is the food cost percentage. There are good reasons for either of these approaches to menu pricing.

Many large foodservice organizations have established highly sophisticated computer-driven formulae for determining appropriate menu prices. However, for the average food-service operator, a menu-planning program that emphasizes food cost percentage, contribution margin, or a combination of both is typically most useful. Buyers must understand, though, the underlying pricing philosophy of the menu-planning software they select.

The best programs analyze menu-pricing data by menu category (for example, appetizers, salads, entrées, and desserts). Additional components of the pricing portion of a menu-planning program may include comparisons to competitors' menu prices, to prices within a geographic area, or to predetermined check average goals.

***How Effective Is the Menu?*** Another component of a quality menu-planning program relates to analyzing the menu's effectiveness. It is in this area that a computer-driven menu-planning program can be most helpful because of the sheer amount of data that can be reviewed. Typical analyses include those that consider individual menu item profitability based on food cost percentages, popularity, contribution margin, and menu price. This software may also provide a menu matrix analysis, break-even analysis, or performance-to-budget analysis. Very sophisticated programs can even perform cash-flow projections based on forecasted revenue.

### Technology and Menu Planning: Some Final Thoughts

A computerized menu-planning system allows menu planners to easily gather, sort, and analyze information. This is true not only in a single foodservice unit, which by itself produces a significant amount of such information, but especially in multiple service units, where data-collection systems in each service unit can be networked to send data to a central computer for analysis.

For example, a college foodservice consisting of multiple residence halls serving meals would likely find that a single menu for a given day is best developed by considering historical and cost data from all the residence halls collectively, rather than by considering the data from each unit individually. Likewise, menu planners in a multiunit quick-service restaurant would want to consider the data from each of its units before planning the menu for all of its units. Using menu-planning software housed in a central location, the individual units can send (download) data via the Internet (or **Intranet**) to the central server. Well-designed data-collection systems enable multiunit collection.

---

*Glossary terms*
**Intranet.** A network (much like the Internet) of linked computers, except that access is restricted to only those computers specifically designated as part of the network.

---

Even the best software programs, however, do not decide what items should be included on the menu or their price. These decisions are still made by foodservice managers, but a good computer program can help managers make good decisions by manipulating vast amounts of data to supply important information.

## TECHNOLOGY AND MENU DESIGN

Once menu planners know the items they want to sell and how much should be charged for each item, a physical menu is developed. The goal of a properly designed physical menu is to increase sales, especially of the operation's most profitable items. Since a restaurant uses the physical menu to communicate its offerings to guests, an effective menu design is critical to the ultimate success of the operation.

Creative and effective menu designs can be achieved without using computerized menu-design systems. After all, imaginative foodservice managers have been creating such menus for many years. Properly used, however, computers can be extremely helpful in improving menu quality, in reducing menu production costs, and in significantly speeding up the menu-design process.

There is a growing selection of menu-design software, and menu planners will find that they can select programs with very specific functions (for example, some software will offer only menu artwork or print-style choices, while others will assist with all aspects of producing the menu).

## Background

Before computer-assisted menu-design programs were available, menu planners took their ideas to an artist, printer, or menu-design specialist and then worked with these individuals, through trial and error, to produce the menu they envisioned.

A very clear example of how menu-design software can save time and money is found in our case study of Sigee's. Assume that Sigee's menu designers wished to evaluate the effect of changing the type style of the menu. Before menu-design software was available, Sigee's menu (or a significant part of it) would need to be typeset in the new type style by a professional printer, who would send a proof copy to the menu designer. The menu designer would then proofread the text, evaluate the type style, and return the corrected copy to the printer. Finally, the printer would make the changes to the proof and send the final copy back to the menu designer. This process is costly and time-consuming. In comparison, by using a basic word-processing program, Sigee's menu designers can now change the menu's type style by simply highlighting the text to be changed and selecting an alternative type style from the list of type styles available on the word-processing program.

In addition to providing alternative design components quickly, menu-design programs facilitate changing menu items and prices. When management decides to add new menu items or to eliminate old ones, it is critical that these changes be made cost-effectively. In some cases, such as in a college foodservice program, these changes may be easily accomplished, because the menu is not extensive. Alternatively, however, it may be a tremendous expense to change the physical menu in a large chain restaurant with hundreds of units, all of which use the same menu.

The capabilities of the numerous menu-design programs available today vary greatly. Some programs allow menu planners to design the menu and then send the design to a professional printing company; others actually create a menu that can be printed on a standard black and white or color office printer. It is important to understand that no software can completely "design" the menu. Rather, these programs allow menu designers to do their work quickly and more creatively.

The following are some traditional menu-design functions that can be accomplished using menu-design programs.

- Layout
- Type style
- Menu size
- Color
- Photos and illustrations
- Menu copy
- Printing

## Layout

One of the most important menu-design decisions is the menu's layout. Layout is the menu-design component people notice when they look at a menu. Since menus can be printed on anything from a wine bottle to a web page, the layout decision is the foundation for subsequent menu-design decisions.

Menu layout refers to the placement and space given to each segment of the menu. For example, many restaurants devote a section of the menu to appetizers. Menu designers must decide where to place this segment on the menu. One choice might be a space before and separate from the entrée section. Or, this segment could be placed on top of or along the side of the page that includes the entrées. A menu-design program allows the designer to quickly evaluate these alternative locations by simply "trying them out" on the computer and viewing them on the computer monitor.

Another layout decision involves determining the number of menu pages. Some menus are printed on a single page; others require ten or more pages. Effective design programs allow menu designers to quickly determine the amount of space each section of the menu requires and where that section can best be placed; efficient use of space can reduce the number of pages needed (which reduces printing costs) and allows guests to read the menu and make selection decisions more quickly (which reduces the time needed to serve guests).

## Type Style

The style of type used on a menu has a big impact on how that menu is perceived by the reader. Type style consists of two basic components: size and font. The size of type affects its readability because type that is too small is difficult for many diners (especially the elderly) to read. While smaller type allows more

to be printed on the menu, type that is too small detracts from the overall menu design and readability. As well, dim lighting in many upscale restaurants makes it very difficult for many guests to read menus with small type sizes and thin-lined fonts.

As discussed in Chapter 7, type size is measured in points. Each point is approximately 1/72 of an inch. Therefore, 12-point type is approximately 12/72 of an inch. This book is printed in 11-point type. The pica is another measuring unit used in software and by some printers. There are 12 points in a pica. Most word-processing and menu-design software allow the menu designer to use different type sizes in the same menu by simply highlighting text and then selecting the desired point size.

Menu designers can select from the virtually hundreds of type fonts available on menu-design programs. Font samples were shown in Figure 7-4. Fonts can make the menu fun to read, can follow the theme of the restaurant, or can simply provide visual variety. Consider the five different font types shown in Figure 8-2. Each is shown in 12-point type. Does the type font affect your perception of the menu item?

Figure 8-2. **Five Type Fonts**

## Size

While menu size is related to both layout and type style, it is a distinct design element. Even for those traditional menus that are held by the guest and read, the physical size of the

menu is important and is a design element that can be easily manipulated by the computer. A menu placed on 8.5" x 11" paper will have a different impact than the same menu placed on a 15" x 24" page.

In some cases, menu designers want to duplicate the menu layout and type style used in the restaurant menu in a smaller version that may, for example, be used for mailing or for guests to take away. The mailed menu may be designed to fit in a standard-size business envelope; the take-away menu may be larger than the menu to be mailed and yet smaller than the menu used in the dining room. Computer-assisted menu-design programs are perfect for such resizing issues.

## Color

One of the most convenient features of any menu-design program is that of alternative color selection. Color can be used for print, for boxes containing menu items, or for shading. Even the least expensive menu-design programs available today offer many color and shading selections. The impact of this design feature on the menu is shown by the following simple black and white shading patterns, each of which has a unique effect on the look of this menu item's title.

It is easy to see how, with hundreds of available colors and shading blends available, menu designers can create thousands of different color combinations that can be used to enhance the menu's overall design.

A great strength of computer graphics is the ability to create a nearly infinite number of colors. Food can be colorful, so it makes sense that many menu designers would like to show their products in color rather than in black and white. As in most other visual arts, the colors available to a menu designer using graphics are called a *palette*. In some programs, the palette is called a CLUT (Color Look-Up Table). On a computer screen, the palette displayed is usually only a portion of all the colors available in the software program. For example, a SVGA (Super Video Graphics Array) system used to provide the color in many software programs consists of 16 million unique colors. However, a computer screen may only display 256 at a time if the display is in 256-color mode. The computer's palette, therefore, would consist of the 16 million colors, but the program's palette would contain only the 256-color subset. All menu-design programs allow the designer to highlight text or art and then to choose from among the many alternatives to actually "color" the selected material.

## Photos and Illustrations

Most menu designers agree that pictures, artwork, and line drawings can positively affect the guests' perceptions of the menu and, by extension, the food and beverage operation. In addition, guests like to "see," whenever possible, a representative picture of what they are ordering. Recall that a menu seeks to communicate to the guests; therefore, it is easy to understand why it is helpful for the menu to be "a picture that speaks a thousand words."

Although menu designers agree that photos and illustrations enhance the menu, in the past these graphics have been very expensive

10 percent shading

| **Roast Breast of Turkey with Cranberry Dressing** |
| --- |

25 percent shading

| **Roast Breast of Turkey with Cranberry Dressing** |
| --- |

50 percent shading

| **Roast Breast of Turkey with Cranberry Dressing** |
| --- |

to produce and print. Computer programs, however, enable menu designers to choose from thousands of pictures, line drawings, and symbols that help to better communicate with the guests and also to enhance the aesthetic value of the menu.

Computer monitors display electronic pictures through the use of pixels. Short for "picture element," a pixel is a single point in a graphic image. Graphics monitors display pictures by dividing the display screen into thousands (or millions) of pixels, which are arranged in rows and columns. On color monitors, each pixel is actually composed of three dots—a red dot, a blue dot, and a green dot. Ideally, the three dots should all converge at the same point, but all monitors have the tendency to blur the pixels somewhat and, as a result, create a picture that appears fuzzy. The better the software program, hardware capability, and display monitor quality, the less this effect is noticed.

Electronic artwork of all types is available for purchase on the Internet, and this includes thousands of menu-related photos, illustrations, line drawings, and symbols. They can be inserted into the menu without changes (for example, when the menu designer feels the unaltered original will have the most impact) or modified by special software programs designed to allow users to change the color, shape, size, and other attributes of the artwork.

## Menu Copy

One of the most challenging aspects of creating a menu is developing the menu copy that describes the items sold. Not only is it difficult to write this copy creatively, some words are difficult to spell and may be missed in a normal proofreading of the menu. Computerized word-processing programs will identify menu copy spelling errors. The program's thesaurus can suggest alternative words that can be used

to enhance menu descriptions. In addition, grammatical errors can be identified and eliminated through the use of "grammar check" programs. Quality menu development software programs always include these features.

## Printing

Once a final menu has been developed, menu-design software enables menu designers to either print the menu directly or create a file that can be e-mailed or delivered on disc to a printer. It is in this area that some difficulties can occur. This is because, traditionally, those individuals (including printers) working in the arts use software programs that are different from individuals such as menu designers who work in business. As a result, it is possible that the electronic files developed by the menu designer may not be compatible with those of a printer. This is important and may dictate the decision about which printer should be used.

Depending on the design of the menu and the print quality desired, it is possible for the menu designer to complete the menu-design process and print the menu in-house. The price of quality color printers is now very low (less than $200.00) and, therefore, quality menus that could not have been created in-house as recently as five years ago can easily be produced today.

The ability to actually print the menu can truly pay off for foodservice operations. Simple selling-price changes can be made rapidly, as can the insertion or deletion of entire menu items. Also, because the menus have been created electronically, it is easy to change their size prior to printing. This makes it simple to create menus of various sizes, including credit-card-sized menus, envelope-sized menus for mailing, bar or tabletop menus, and clip-on menus and menu inserts.

## PURCHASING MENU-DEVELOPMENT TECHNOLOGY

Purchasing technology products such as menu-design programs and services at the proper price can be just as difficult as buying quality food products. Fortunately, however, the purchase of menu-planning or menu-design software can be evaluated in exactly the same way as the purchase of any other piece of foodservice equipment or service.

A proposed investment in menu technology should result in one of more of the following:

- Faster development time
- Reduced production costs
- Improved quality of the final menu
- Greater guest satisfaction

An overreliance on technology can result in wasted time and money. Properly selected, however, menu-related technology can make the entire menu-development process easier. Quality menu-development products should be evaluated based on the following:

- *Purchase price*—Cost plays an important role in the decision of how much technology menu designers should buy. When it is possible to demonstrate that the menu-design assistance will pay for itself relatively quickly, the decision can be an easy one. If, however, the cost of the tool exceeds its value to the operation, its purchase becomes questionable.
- *Complexity*—Some software systems are so advanced that using them effectively requires special skills and much experience. An effective menu-design system should be easy enough to use so that excessive training time is not required.
- *Assistance available*—Companies selling the best menu-design programs provide either for free or for a modest fee technical experts who can help menu designers when difficulties with the menu-design program. This is an especially important service when the program is first used.
- *Warranty*—Quality software programs include a warranty. It should be reviewed carefully to determine covered items, the length of the warranty, the hourly rate charged for repair service, and the guaranteed response time of service or repair technicians.
- *Reliability*—Two areas of reliability are important: the reliability of the product and the reliability of the vendor. To help ensure that menu designers select a reliable product, vendors should supply a list of customers who have designed menus using the software program. Obviously, if these references do not speak highly of the program's quality and its simplicity of use, the purchase decision should be carefully reconsidered. When selecting menu-design products, vendor reliability is nearly as important as product reliability. Stability, experience, and reputation are important when buying from any foodservice vendor, and the purchase of technology-related products, including menu design software, is no exception to this rule.

## TECHNOLOGY AND MENU ADVERTISING

In the "old days," menu planners talked about the power of the menu as an in-house marketing and advertising tool. This is still correct; however, today technology allows menu planners to use the menu as an advertising tool to reach a worldwide audience.

Many commercial and noncommercial foodservice operations have a home page to alert users of the **world wide web** to their operation. Home pages for a food and beverage operation may provide, in addition to the menu, information about

- location,
- contact information,
- private party opportunities,

- a virtual tour (with pictures),
- background information about the property,
- on-line sale of gift certificates,
- career opportunities,
- the operation in general and answers to questions,
- reviews (sometimes these can be provided in real time through discussion or chat room sections),
- management and the food production staff,
- links to related sites,
- on-line reservation service (these can be implemented either through an e-mail system; the guest requests a reservation via e-mail and the reservation is confirmed by the restaurant in the same manner) or an **instant message program,** and
- gift shop sales.

---

*Glossary terms*

**World wide web.** The interconnection (web) of various computers located "worldwide," frequently referred to as the Internet. Specifically, the world wide web refers to the portion of the Internet that can be navigated through the use of a browser (programs or software that enable a person to view the web) such as Internet Explorer, Netscape, Lynx, Opera, or Cello.

**Instant message program.** Refers to a "computer" conference using the computer's keyboard (a "keyboard chat") to communicate over the Internet. Two or more people, on-line at the same time, can type messages to each other in real time. AOL's Instant Messenger (AIM), Microsoft Network Messenger Service (MSNMS), ICQ, and Yahoo! Messenger are the major instant messaging services used by restaurants.

---

## The Menu on the Home Page

Following are several examples of how restaurants use their home pages to effectively convey menu information.

The home page of **Don & Charlie's Restaurant** (see Figure 8-3) displays the restaurant's menu in a traditional style, with menu categories laid out in a traditional sequence. Readers can scroll through, first, appetizers to salads, pasta ("and other good things"), and then through several categories of entrées.

The menu on **Damon's** home page (see Figure 8-4) first lists each menu category. The reader can then click on a category (let's select chicken!), and the menu items offered in this menu category appear.

The home page for the **Olive Garden Italian Restaurant** (see Figure 8-5) offers a unique "food-wine" matchmaker. Assume, for example, you are interested in recommendations for a wine to accompany the entrée "calamari alla marinara"; a click on this entrée choice brings up a frame that briefly describes the entrée and then indicates one wine that is an "ideal match" and two wines that are "other matches."

The menu on the home page for **Buffet's Inc.** (see Figure 8-6) indicates some of the menu features planned for each day of the week. (Note that it indicates the menu is "subject to change without notice.") For example, the frame for Tuesday's menu indicates both lunch and dinner features, and shows accompaniments that are included with each meal.

Some restaurants use their home page to advertise specialty menus for specific dates. For example, **Manna's Vegetarian Restaurant** (see Figure 8-7) posts its special menu for Valentine's Day weekend on its home page.

Food is not the only item emphasized on restaurant home pages. Consider, for example, the information about wine presented on the home page of **The Herb Farm**, in Woodinville, Washington. Traditionally, wine lists have been used for two reasons: to inform guests about available selections and to help (suggestively) sell these beverage items. However, wine lists can also be great educational resources to help guests better understand more about the "art and science" of wines. As this occurs, the guests will incorporate increased knowledge into their selection decisions, and their enjoyment of the dining experience will increase.

Figure 8-8 illustrates selected pages from the seventy-one page wine library (wine list) used by The Herb Farm, which is available on its

Figure 8-3. **Don & Charlie's Home Page Menu**

Entrees and specialties include chopped liver, bread basket, cole slaw (deli-style or creamy) or salad, with your choice of dressing (House Anchovy Dressing, 1000 Island, Creamy Garlic, Bleu Cheese, Vinaigrette or Lo-Cal Spa Vinaigrette), and choice of au gratin, baked, double-baked, french fries or pasta with marinara sauce. (*does not include potato)

### APPETIZERS

| | |
|---|---|
| Onion Strings (great for sharing) | 5.95 |
| Fried Calamari, Lemon Wedges, Cocktail Sauce | 7.95 |
| Don's Garlic Cheese Toast | 4.95 |
| Jumbo Shrimp Cocktail, Cocktail Sauce | 9.95 |
| Baked Spinach-Artichoke Dip with Crostini | 5.95 |
| French Onion Soup topped with Cheese | 4.95 |
| Shrimp De Jonghe | 9.95 |
| Frogs' Legs, Garlic Butter | 9.95 |
| Fried Jumbo Shrimp, Cocktail Sauce | 9.95 |

### SALADS

| | |
|---|---|
| Don's Special Salad Red Onions, Tomato, Cucumber, Egg, Bacon* | 5.95 |
| Caesar Salad* | 7.95 |
| with entree | 2.50 |
| Cajun Chicken Caesar Salad* | 10.95 |
| Caesar Salad with Shrimp* | 12.95 |
| Salmon Pasta Salad* | 12.95 |

Used with permission of Don Carson, Don & Charlie's, Scottsdale, Arizona

**Figure 8-3   (continued)**

Fresh salmon, sun-dried tomatoes, hearts of palm, artichoke hearts, fresh asparagus, capers, black olives, roma tomatoes, and rainbow pasta.

## PASTA AND OTHER GOOD THINGS

| | |
|---|---|
| Pasta Primavera* | 12.95 |
| Pasta Primavera (with shrimp)* | 15.95 |
| Chicken and Pasta* | 13.95 |
| Pasta Marinara* | 11.95 |
| Chicken Schnitzel, Lemon Butter Sauce | 14.95 |
| Sautéed Calves Liver, Peppers, Onions, Mushrooms | 14.95 |
| Frogs' Legs, Garlic Butter | 18.95 |
| Shrimp De Jonghe, served Chicago style | 20.95 |
| Fried Shrimp, Cocktail Sauce | 20.95 |

## SIDE DISHES/VEGETABLES

| | |
|---|---|
| Pasta Marinara | 3.95 |
| Baked Macaroni and Cheese | 3.95 |
| Sautéed Mushrooms | 3.95 |
| Sautéed Onions, Peppers & Mushrooms<br>  Great with steaks or garlic chicken | 3.95 |
| Creamed Spinach topped with cheese | 3.95 |
| Cauliflower Au Gratin | 3.95 |
| Cajun Rice | 2.95 |
| Roquefort Cheese Crumbles | 2.50 |

Figure 8-3 **(continued)**

## OUR FAMOUS BARBECUE

(Slow smoked over hickory wood)

| | |
|---|---|
| B.B.Q. Baby Back Ribs (full slab) | 19.95 |
| B.B.Q. Baby Back Ribs (half slab) | 15.95 |
| B.B.Q. Rib and Chicken Combination | 19.95 |
| B.B.Q. Rib and Filet Mignon Combination(8oz) | 27.95 |

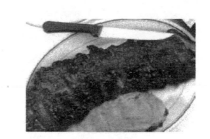

## CHICKEN

| | |
|---|---|
| B.B.Q. Chicken (whole chicken) | 14.95 |
| B.B.Q. Chicken (1/2 chicken) | 12.95 |
| Garlic Chicken, Cajun Rice (whole chicken) | 14.95 |
| Garlic Chicken, Cajun Rice (1/2 chicken) | 12.95 |

Don and Charlie's Famous Barbecue
is available either with our Original or
Southwestern Style Sauce
Pick up a bottle to take home!

## PRIME RIB

(carefully selected and aged 21
days, then slow roasted to
perfection)

| | |
|---|---|
| Carson Cut, au jus-creamed horseradish (20 oz.) | 28.95 |
| Large Cut, au-jus-creamed horseradish (16 oz) | 25.95 |
| Medium Cut, au-jus-creamed horseradish (12 oz) | 22.95 |
| Beef Ribs( B.B.Q. or Plain) | 14.95 |

Roasted fresh daily - served until
we run out.

## PRIME STEAKS AND CHOPS

Figure 8-3  (continued)

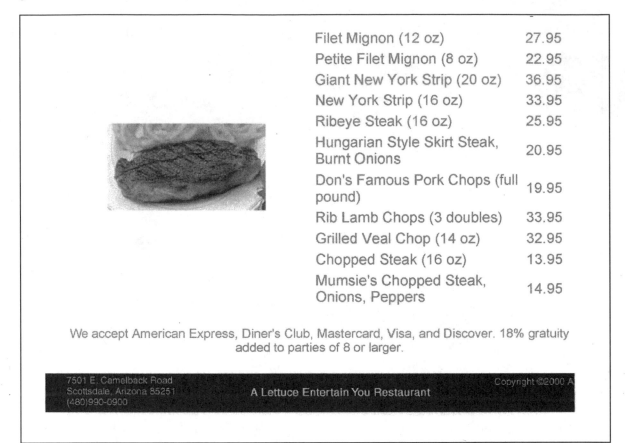

| Filet Mignon (12 oz) | 27.95 |
| Petite Filet Mignon (8 oz) | 22.95 |
| Giant New York Strip (20 oz) | 36.95 |
| New York Strip (16 oz) | 33.95 |
| Ribeye Steak (16 oz) | 25.95 |
| Hungarian Style Skirt Steak, Burnt Onions | 20.95 |
| Don's Famous Pork Chops (full pound) | 19.95 |
| Rib Lamb Chops (3 doubles) | 33.95 |
| Grilled Veal Chop (14 oz) | 32.95 |
| Chopped Steak (16 oz) | 13.95 |
| Mumsie's Chopped Steak, Onions, Peppers | 14.95 |

We accept American Express, Diner's Club, Mastercard, Visa, and Discover. 18% gratuity added to parties of 8 or larger.

7501 E. Camelback Road
Scottsdale, Arizona 85251
(480)990-0900                    A Lettuce Entertain You Restaurant                    Copyright ©2000 A

web site. (Among other honors, this restaurant, which features nine-course fixed price dinners, is ranked by Gourmet Magazine as one of the fifty best restaurants in America. It is the only AAA 5-star restaurant in America north of San Francisco and west of Chicago.)

A wide range of information is provided. Diners can learn much about the property's featured wines (those of the Pacific Northwest) and about wines from other regions of the United States and from around the world as well.

Wide left-hand margins make the wine list easy to read. As well, this allows the menu designer to provide interesting information such as backgrounds of area winemakers (see "Pacific Northwest Sparkling Wines") and historical information (see "French Champagne").

Other examples of educational information provided in the columns of the wine list relate to the following:

- Brief histories of famous wineries.
- Wine-related quotations from famous persons.
- Interesting facts about specific wines and categories of wine.

Several other features can be noted:

- The Table of Contents includes caveats about underage drinking and a "not responsible for typographical errors" disclaimer (with an extensive wine cellar, this statement is important).
- The "By the Glass" (aperitifs and after-dinner wine) page lists opportunities for guests to enjoy wines and nonalcoholic beverages during their meal.

Figure 8-4. **Damon's Home Page Menu**

Used with permission of Damon's International, Inc.

Figure 8-4   (Continued)

## • CHICKEN •

*Add a Damon's House Salad for only 1.99.*

*New!*   **Apple-Bourbon Grilled Chicken**   *Chardonnay*
Juicy, boneless chicken breasts, covered with melted Jack and
Cheddar cheese, plus smoked bacon and delicious apple-bourbon
sauce, served on rice pilaf with your choice of a side dish.  11.49

**Flame-Grilled Chicken Dinner**   *White Zinfandel*
Boneless chicken breasts, hot from the grill and finished to your
taste - choose plain, teriyaki glaze, or our famous barbecue
sauce ... comes with rice pilaf, crispy onion straws, and your
choice of a side item.  10.99

**Chicken Tenders**
Golden brown chicken strips - delicious plain, or tossed with
Buffalo hot, or spicy sweet & sour sauce - served with French
fries and your choice of a side item.  9.99

**Caribbean Grilled Chicken**   *Chardonnay*
*New!*   Flame-grilled boneless chicken in a rich teriyaki glaze, with grilled
pineapple, rice pilaf, and a flavorful green peppercorn sauce ...
now pick a side item.  11.49

**Chicken Parmigiana**   *Chardonnay*
Golden brown, breaded chicken breast, topped with real marinara
and melted Provolone cheese ... all resting on plenty of fettuccini
tossed with our sun-dried tomato alfredo sauce.  11.49

**Grilled Chicken Fettuccini**   *White Zinfandel*
Savory grilled chicken breast, presented on a bed of our
sun-dried tomato fettuccini alfredo ... finished with real
Parmesan cheese.  11.49

## • MORE DAMON'S SPECIALTIES •

*Add a Damon's House Salad for only 1.99*

**Grilled Meatloaf Stack**
Classic meatloaf served our way, topped with mushrooms,
onions and rich beef gravy, all on cheese -covered potatoes, with
crispy onion straws.  8.99

**Damon's Pot Roast**
Lean and tender pot roast, in beef gravy with mushrooms and
onions, piled on a plate of cheese-covered potatoes and crispy
onion straws.  8.99

Figure 8-5. Olive Garden Italian Restaurant Home Page

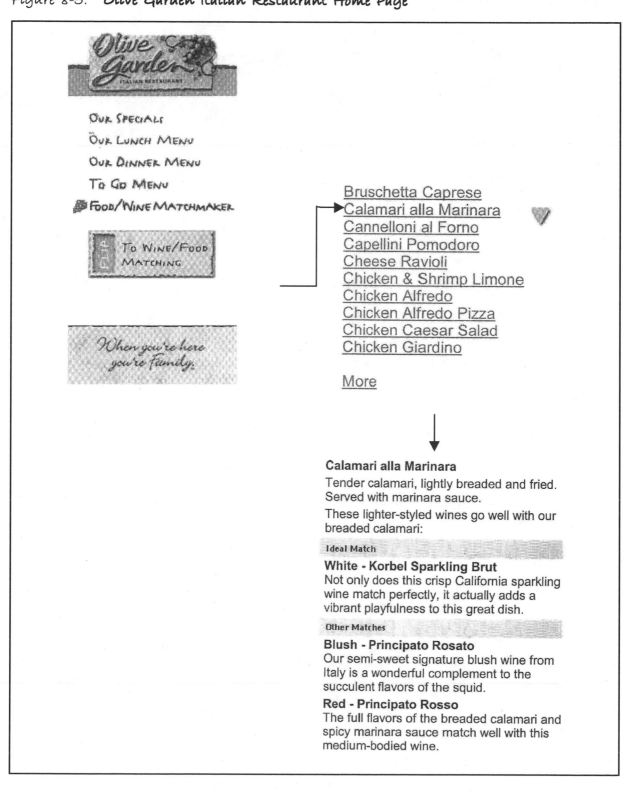

Used with permission of Olive Garden Restaurants, Orlando, Florida

Figure 8-6.  **Buffets, Inc.'s, Home Page**

Used with permission of Buffets, Inc.

• The "Half Bottles" page has a "Make Your Own" service option for less-than-full-bottle sales.

This wine list provides much information to readers visiting the property and to visitors to its web site. In the latter case, it is likely that some of these viewers will be attracted to the restaurant partly because of the wine information provided.

Wines are not the only beverages cited on restaurants' home pages. Figure 8-9 shows a sample page from **Clydz's Martinis and Cock-**

**tails**, which shows a few of the approximately one hundred drinks, presented in alphabetical order.

Kids' menus are shown on the home pages of some restaurants. An example from the **Sunnyside Restaurant** is shown in Figure 8-10.

Catering companies use home pages to show world wide web users their buffet menus. See the example for **Fairview Catering** in Figure 8-11.

Some restaurants feature food items on their home pages other than those offered on their table-service menus. Figure 8-12 shows a frame

Figure 8-7. **Manna's Vegetarian Restaurant Home Page for Valentine's Day**

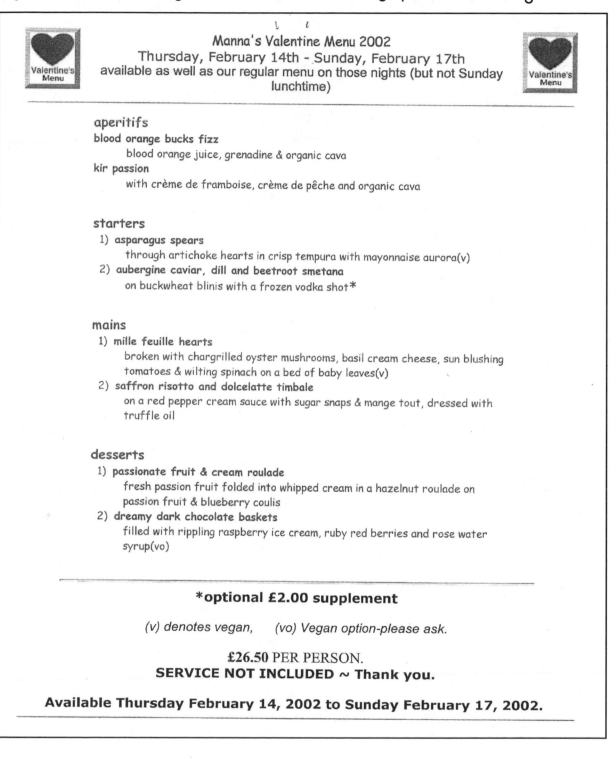

Manna's Valentine Menu 2002
Thursday, February 14th - Sunday, February 17th
available as well as our regular menu on those nights (but not Sunday lunchtime)

### aperitifs

**blood orange bucks fizz**
  blood orange juice, grenadine & organic cava
**kir passion**
  with crème de framboise, crème de pêche and organic cava

### starters

1) **asparagus spears**
  through artichoke hearts in crisp tempura with mayonnaise aurora(v)
2) **aubergine caviar, dill and beetroot smetana**
  on buckwheat blinis with a frozen vodka shot*

### mains

1) **mille feuille hearts**
  broken with chargrilled oyster mushrooms, basil cream cheese, sun blushing tomatoes & wilting spinach on a bed of baby leaves(v)
2) **saffron risotto and dolcelatte timbale**
  on a red pepper cream sauce with sugar snaps & mange tout, dressed with truffle oil

### desserts

1) **passionate fruit & cream roulade**
  fresh passion fruit folded into whipped cream in a hazelnut roulade on passion fruit & blueberry coulis
2) **dreamy dark chocolate baskets**
  filled with rippling raspberry ice cream, ruby red berries and rose water syrup(vo)

**\*optional £2.00 supplement**

*(v) denotes vegan,*     *(vo) Vegan option-please ask.*

£26.50 PER PERSON.
**SERVICE NOT INCLUDED ~ Thank you.**

**Available Thursday February 14, 2002 to Sunday February 17, 2002.**

Figure 8-8.  **The Herb Farm's Home Page Wine List**

# THE WINE LIBRARY
## CELEBRATING THE WINES OF
## THE PACIFIC NORTHWEST
### AND FINE VINEYARDS OF THE WORLD

## APÉRITIFS & SMALL BOTTLES
By the Glass................................................5
Half Bottles: Hundreds of selections..............6
Exploring wineries around The Herbfarm ..... 71

## BUBBLES
Sparkling Wines............................................7
Champagne..............................................8-11

## WHITE WINES
Chardonnay..............................................12-14
Pinot Blanc & Mélon......................................15
Sauvignon Blanc............................................16
Sémillon.......................................................17
Pinot Gris.....................................................18
Riesling........................................................19
Gewürztraminer............................................20
Aligoté.........................................................20
Arneis...........................................................20
Chenin Blanc................................................20
Müller-Thurgau............................................20
Muscat Blanc................................................20
Sake..............................................................21
Viognier........................................................21
White Rhône..................................................57
Other Whites ..............................................21

## RED WINES
Pinot Noir: Nearly 300 selections..............22-31
Red Burgundy............................................32-33
Cabernet Sauvignon: 290 selections ..... 34-38
California Cabernet....................................39-41
Red Bordeaux............................................42-45
Merlot.......................................................46-48
Syrah.............................................................49
Rhône Valley..............................................50-56
Australian Shiraz........................................58-59
Cabernet Franc..............................................60
Gamay Noir & Pinot Meunier..............55 & 56
Grenache Noir................................................55
Malbec...........................................................60
Mourvèdre.....................................................60
Nebbiolo.....................................................60-61
Lemberger......................................................61
Sangiovese.....................................................61
Tempranillo....................................................61
Zinfandel.......................................................62

## AFTER DINNER
Dessert Wines............................................63-64
Sauternes, & French Dessert Wine ........64-65
Port & Port-Style Wines............................66-67
Old Madeiras by the Glass........................68-70

Wines may be sold, consumed, or delivered only to persons who are at least 21 years old.
Not responsible for typographical errors.

Used with permission of Ron Zimmerman, The Herb Farm, Woodinville, Washington

**Figure 8-8.** **(continued)**

THE WINE LIBRARY AT THE HERBFARM

## WE BELIEVE

The Herbfarm Restaurant believes that no dish can be better than its ingredients, and that the best ingredients are usually local.

Freshness is ephemeral and geography expresses itself in the taste of the food—sometimes subtly and sometimes profoundly. The foods and wines of our region share a similar motherhood of soil and weather, making for happier culinary marriages than those from dissimilar climates.

The Herbfarm believes that chefs who cook with local ingredients—season by season, year after year—develop a more complete understanding of their foods than chefs who do not. This understanding can give rise to greater expressions of the food, its preparation, and enjoyment.

The Herbfarm believes that supporting local farmers, foragers, cheesemakers, wineries, and fishermen helps preserve and promote the foundation of regional cuisines.

## FINE WINE—FINE STEMWARE

The Herbfarm stocks 15 or more different shapes of stemware from Riedel, Spiegelau, and Schott-Zwiesel, all of which are designed to enhance your wine and dining experience.

## OUR LIST SHOWCASES THE BEST OF THE PACIFIC NORTHWEST

Because The Herbfarm showcases the foods of the Northwest, we belive that the wines of this region are typically the best accompaniments to the flavors of the foods on our menus. Therefore, the majority of our wines are chosen from the best and most-interesting producers of the Pacific Northwest. We define this region as from the Russian River in California to British Columbia to the north, and from Puget Sound and the Willamette Valley in the west to the high vineyards of Idaho to the east.

## OLD & RARE WINE

Our cellar of more than 12,000 bottles encompasses what is perhaps America's largest selection of Northwest wines, as well as rare and hard-to-find bottles from throughout the world. To the best of our knowledge, the wines in our collection have been kept under controlled temperate and humidity since their release. *We will replace any corked or spoiled wine of less than 25 years of age.* Though we believe our older bottles to be sound, each wine has its own history. For wines of this age, there are no good wines or vintages *per se*, just good bottles.

## CORKAGE

We encourage the exploration and enjoyment of all wine. We will gladly open any standard-size bottle *not on our list* for $20 per bottle. We ask that you make advance arrangements, if possible, for bringing your special bottle so that we may prepare the appropriate stemware and decant the wine, as necessary. Please call **206-784-2222** (or e-mail) to speak with one of our helpful and friendly sommeliers.

**For your cellar**
*The Herbfarm is rare among Washington State restaurants. Our liquor license also allows us to sell bottles for you to take home. If you see something you're interested in for your home cellar or as a gift, let us know.*

**E-mail**
*You may use e-mail to discuss you wine needs with our sommeliers. Address inquiries to:* **christine@theherbfarm.com** *and copy the email to* **ron@theherbfarm.com**

Figure 8-8.   (continued)

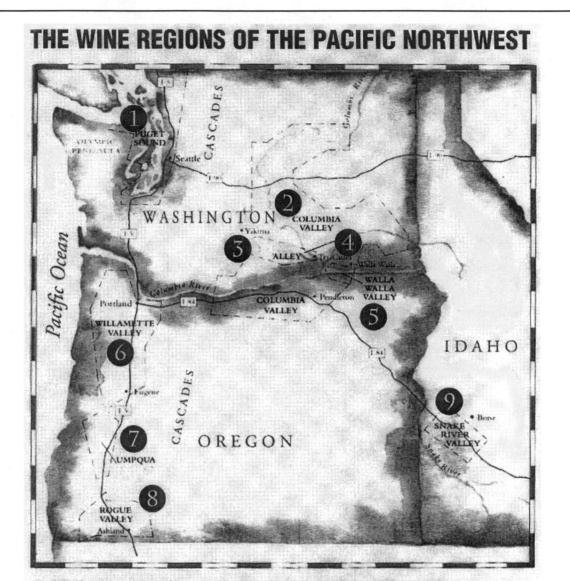

# THE WINE REGIONS OF THE PACIFIC NORTHWEST

## OFFICIAL AMERICAN VITICULTURAL APPELLATIONS OF THE NW

1 **Puget Sound** *Maritime climate. Cool climate vinifera varieties and French hybrids*

2 **Columbia Valley** *Washington's largest appellation*

3 **Yakima Valley** *Cabernet, merlot, chardonnay*

4 **Red Mountain** *Warmest Yakima Valley region, powerful but approachable cabernets and merlots*

5 **Walla Walla** *Washington's warmest appellation. Cabernet, syrah, merlot & sangiovese dominate*

6 **Willamette Valley** *Warmer than Puget Sound. A maritime-influenced region. Pinot noir, pinot gr.*

*pinot blanc, chardonnay are the major grapes. Very food friendly wines.*

7 **Umpqua Valley** *Warmer than upper Willamette Valley. Pinot noir, merlot, gewurztraminer*

8 **Rogue Valley** *Oregon's warmest region. Cabernet and merlot will ripen here.*

9 **Snake River Valley** *Warm continental climate with high-elevation vineyards; cool nights preserve lively grape acidity.*

Figure 8-8. **(continued)**

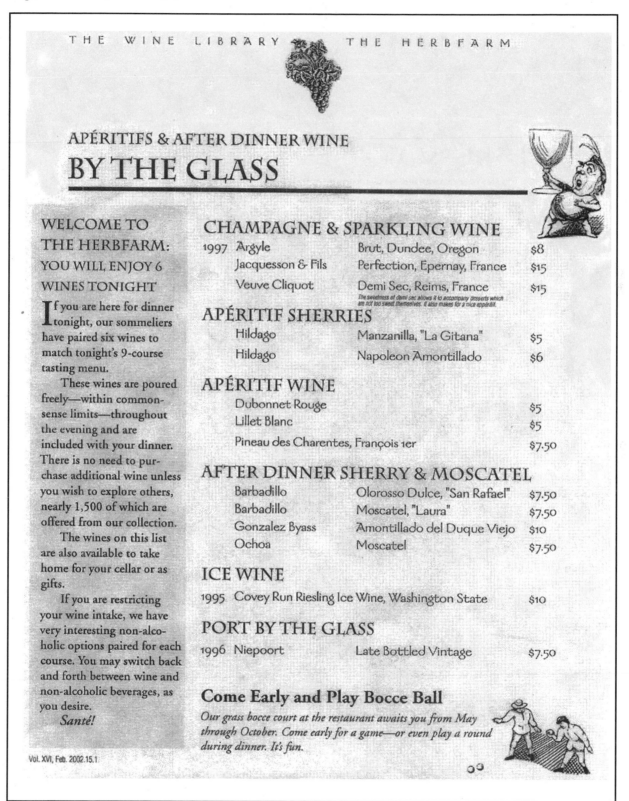

THE WINE LIBRARY · THE HERBFARM

## APÉRITIFS & AFTER DINNER WINE
# BY THE GLASS

**WELCOME TO THE HERBFARM:** YOU WILL ENJOY 6 WINES TONIGHT

If you are here for dinner tonight, our sommeliers have paired six wines to match tonight's 9-course tasting menu.

These wines are poured freely—within common-sense limits—throughout the evening and are included with your dinner. There is no need to purchase additional wine unless you wish to explore others, nearly 1,500 of which are offered from our collection.

The wines on this list are also available to take home for your cellar or as gifts.

If you are restricting your wine intake, we have very interesting non-alcoholic options paired for each course. You may switch back and forth between wine and non-alcoholic beverages, as you desire.

*Santé!*

### CHAMPAGNE & SPARKLING WINE

| | | | |
|---|---|---|---|
| 1997 | Argyle | Brut, Dundee, Oregon | $8 |
| | Jacquesson & Fils | Perfection, Epernay, France | $15 |
| | Veuve Cliquot | Demi Sec, Reims, France | $15 |

*The sweetness of demi sec allows it to accompany desserts which are not too sweet themselves. It also makes for a nice apéritif.*

### APÉRITIF SHERRIES

| | | |
|---|---|---|
| Hildago | Manzanilla, "La Gitana" | $5 |
| Hildago | Napoleon Amontillado | $6 |

### APÉRITIF WINE

| | |
|---|---|
| Dubonnet Rouge | $5 |
| Lillet Blanc | $5 |
| Pineau des Charentes, François 1er | $7.50 |

### AFTER DINNER SHERRY & MOSCATEL

| | | |
|---|---|---|
| Barbadillo | Olorosso Dulce, "San Rafael" | $7.50 |
| Barbadillo | Moscatel, "Laura" | $7.50 |
| Gonzalez Byass | Amontillado del Duque Viejo | $10 |
| Ochoa | Moscatel | $7.50 |

### ICE WINE

| | | |
|---|---|---|
| 1995 | Covey Run Riesling Ice Wine, Washington State | $10 |

### PORT BY THE GLASS

| | | | |
|---|---|---|---|
| 1996 | Niepoort | Late Bottled Vintage | $7.50 |

### Come Early and Play Bocce Ball

*Our grass bocce court at the restaurant awaits you from May through October. Come early for a game—or even play a round during dinner. It's fun.*

Vol. XVI, Feb. 2002.15.1

Figure 8-8.    **(continued)**

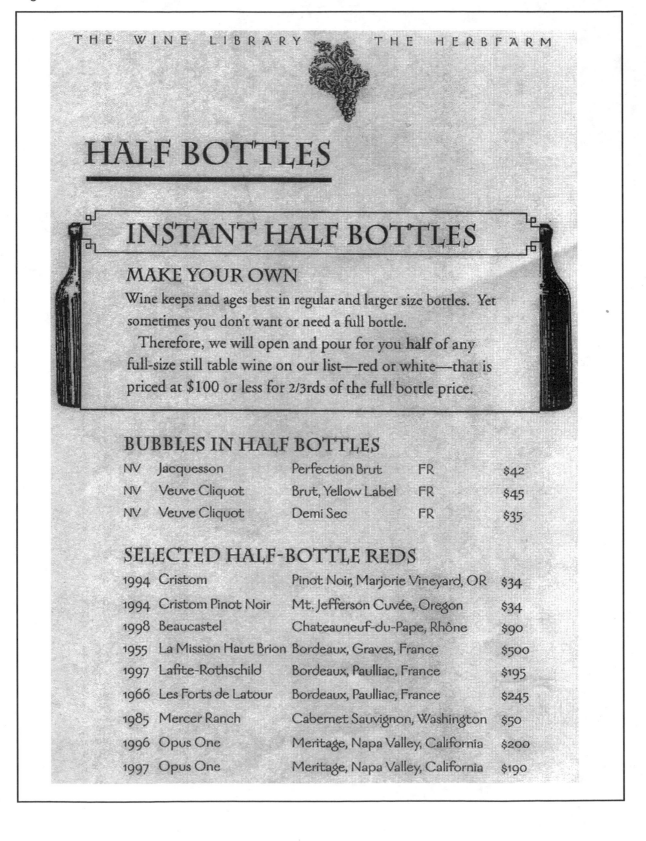

THE WINE LIBRARY     THE HERBFARM

# HALF BOTTLES

## INSTANT HALF BOTTLES

### MAKE YOUR OWN

Wine keeps and ages best in regular and larger size bottles. Yet sometimes you don't want or need a full bottle.

Therefore, we will open and pour for you half of any full-size still table wine on our list—red or white—that is priced at $100 or less for 2/3rds of the full bottle price.

### BUBBLES IN HALF BOTTLES

| NV | Jacquesson | Perfection Brut | FR | $42 |
| NV | Veuve Cliquot | Brut, Yellow Label | FR | $45 |
| NV | Veuve Cliquot | Demi Sec | FR | $35 |

### SELECTED HALF-BOTTLE REDS

| 1994 | Cristom | Pinot Noir, Marjorie Vineyard, OR | $34 |
| 1994 | Cristom Pinot Noir | Mt. Jefferson Cuvée, Oregon | $34 |
| 1998 | Beaucastel | Chateauneuf-du-Pape, Rhône | $90 |
| 1955 | La Mission Haut Brion | Bordeaux, Graves, France | $500 |
| 1997 | Lafite-Rothschild | Bordeaux, Paulliac, France | $195 |
| 1966 | Les Forts de Latour | Bordeaux, Paulliac, France | $245 |
| 1985 | Mercer Ranch | Cabernet Sauvignon, Washington | $50 |
| 1996 | Opus One | Meritage, Napa Valley, California | $200 |
| 1997 | Opus One | Meritage, Napa Valley, California | $190 |

Figure 8-8. **(continued)**

THE WINE LIBRARY ☙ THE HERBFARM

# PACIFIC NORTHWEST SPARKLING WINES

## OREGON

| | | | | |
|---|---|---|---|---|
| 1989 | Argyle | Brut | OR | $65 |
| 1989 | Argyle | Brut (jeroboam) | OR | $150 |
| 1989 | Argyle | Millenium, Extended Tirage | | $59 |
| 1991 | Argyle | Brut | OR | $55 |
| 1995 | Argyle | Brut, Knudsen Vineyard | OR | $55 |
| 1995 | Argyle | Blanc de Blanc, Knudsen | OR | $55 |
| 1996 | Argyle | Brut | OR | $45 |
| 1997 | Argyle | Brut | OR | $40 |
| 1994 | Silvan Ridge | Sparkling Early Muscat | OR | $35 |
| 1998 | Silvan Ridge | Sparkling Early Muscat | OR | $35 |
| 1991 | Secret House | Northern Silk | OR | $40 |
| 1989 | St. Innocent | Sparkling Brut | OR | $60 |
| 1990 | St. Innocent | Brut | OR | $50 |
| 1991 | St. Innocent | Brut | OR | $50 |
| 1996 | St. Innocent | Brut | OR | $40 |
| 1996 | St. Innocent | Blanc des Noirs | OR | $40 |
| 1997 | St. Innocent | Blanc des Noirs | OR | $40 |

## WEST-COAST SPARKLING WINES

| | | | | |
|---|---|---|---|---|
| 1996 | Alexia | Brut | WA | $40 |
| NV | Blue Mountain | Brut Rosé | BC | $40 |
| 1985 | Chinook | Sparkling Riesling | WA | $40 |
| NV | Korbel | Brut (375 ml) | CA | $15 |
| 1980 | Schramsberg | Reserve | CA | $50 |
| 1985 | Schramsberg | Cuvée de Pinot Rosé | CA | $50 |
| NV | Ch. Ste-Michelle | Brut | WA | $29 |
| 1987 | Whittlesey-Mark | Oregon Brut | WA | $40 |
| NV | Venturi-Schulze | Brut Naturel | BC | $50 |

*Argyle Winery's **Roland Soles** has a master's degree in enology from UC Davis. He crafts some of the finest sparkling wines in America. His wines have been served on a number of occasions at the White House.*

*St. Innocent Winery's **Mark Vlossak** was reading Esquire magazine years ago. The great California winemaker André Tchelistcheff was quoted as saying that Oregon might one day produce America's best sparkling wines. Inspired by the article, Mark threw his lot to Oregon and now makes excellent sparkling wines as well as crafting superb pinot noirs at both St. Innocent and Panther Creek.*

Figure 8-8.    (continued)

THE WINE LIBRARY · THE HERBFARM

# FRENCH CHAMPAGNE

*"I only drink Champagne when I'm happy—and when I'm sad. When I have company, I consider it obligatory. I trifle with it if I am not hungry and drink it when I am. Otherwise, I never touch it — unless I'm thirsty.*
**Madame "Lily" Bollinger (1899-1977)**

**Bollinger**, founded in 1829, is one of Champagne's few remaining family-owned Grande Marque houses. It is renowned for the high percentage of Pinot Noir and for the extra aging on the lees that its Champagnes receive.

**Dom Pérignon** (1639-1715), first Champagne master blender and first to use corks as stoppers for Champagne

| | | | |
|---|---|---|---|
| NV | Billecart-Salmon | Brut Réserve (magnum) | $180 |
| NV | Billecart-Salmon | Rosé | $99 |
| 1995 | Billecart-Salmon | Cuvée Elisabeth Salmon Rosé | $175 |
| NV | Bollinger | Special Cuvée Brut | $77 |
| 1979 | Bollinger | R.D. | $450 |
| 1981 | Bollinger | R.D. | $375 |
| 1981 | Bollinger | R.D. (magnum) | $800 |
| 1982 | Bollinger | R.D. | $300 |
| 1985 | Bollinger | R.D. | $400 |
| 1988 | Bollinger | R.D. | $250 |
| 1988 | Bollinger | Grand Année | $145 |
| 1989 | Bollinger | Grand Année | $120 |
| 1990 | Bollinger | R.D. | $300 |
| 1990 | Bollinger | Grand Année Prestigue Cuvée | $120 |
| 1990 | Bollinger | Grand Année (mangum) | $250 |
| 1990 | Bollinger | Grand Année Rosé (magnum) | $400 |
| 1969 | Bruno Palliard | Première Cuvée | $225 |
| 1969 | Bruno Palliard | Brut | $175 |
| 1991 | Georg Breuer | Brut (Germany) | $75 |
| 1990 | Nicolas Feuillatte | Cuvée Palmes d'Or | $200 |
| 1964 | Dom Pérignon | | $650 |
| 1966 | Dom Pérignon | | $450 |
| 1973 | Dom Pérignon | | $350 |
| 1975 | Dom Pérignon | | $650 |
| 1976 | Dom Pérignon | | $400 |
| 1980 | Dom Pérignon | | $400 |

Figure 8-8. **(continued)**

## THE 1975 EYRIE VINEYARDS SOUTH BLOCK PINOT NOIR MEETS THE PARIS WINE OLYMPICS

David "Papa Pinot" Lett, The Eyrie Vineyards

In Paris in 1979, the French food and wine magazine *Gault/Millau* sponsored an "Olympics of the Wines of the World." Thirty three of the world's wine regions entered 586 wines. In the final blind-tasting competitions, The Eyrie Vineyards 1975 Oregon Pinot Noir placed third in the Burgundy category.

For the French, there was a good deal of consternation concerning the number of foreign wines which had outscored the "home team" in the Olympiads. Twelve of these winners were challenged to a rematch to take place in the heart of Burgundy itself.

On the 8th of January 1980, twenty French, English, and American wine judges gathered in Beaune at the thousand-year-old Hall of Justice of the Dukes of Burgundy. The six top-scoring foreign Pinot Noirs and Chardonnays from the Olympiads were judged again, this time against the finest Burgundies of the best vintages.

The Eyrie Vineyards 1975 South Block Pinot Noir finished just two-tenths of a point behind the 1959 Joseph Drouhin Chambolle-Musigny. The result was seen (at least at the time in America) as a far-reaching victory for the vision of Eyrie's founder, David Lett, who as a young winemaker had, against strong advice, moved from California to Oregon to pursue his vision of Pinot Noirs grown and nurtured in cool climatic conditions.

As a result of these Wine Olympics, others took notice, and the seeds of the modern era in Oregon viticulture were planted. With the help of David Adelsheim and David Lett, Robert Drouhin—scion of the 120 year-old French *négociant* firm Maison Joseph Drouhin—invested ten-million dollars in the 1980s to create Domaine Drouhin Oregon, which is now overseen by his bright, energetic, and charismatic daughter, Véronique Drouhin-Boss.

*The Willamette Valley is considered America's promised land for Pinot Noir. Although there are many that dispute Oregon's excellence with the grape, the best producers here make Pinot Noir as good as or better than any in America.*
—Doug Frost, M.S., M.W.

Figure 8-8.   **(continued)**

THE WINE LIBRARY          THE HERBFARM

# OUR COLLECTION OF RARE, OLD MADEIRAS
## OFFERED BY THE OUNCE

Many years have gone into securing these examples of fine, old Madeira. Bottles have come from auction houses, rare wine dealers, great European cellars, and in some cases directly from private library collections of the producers on the island of Madeira.

A fire at The Herbfarm on the night of January 6, 1997 destroyed much of what had been one of America's largest collections of vintage Madeira. Among these were many century-old bottles and some irreplaceable rarities.

But, fortunately, other bottles were stored off-site and survived . . . and through the good graces of friends and wine dealers we are making progress in restoring the collection of these fascinating bits of vinous history.

The Six Grapes of Madeira

Four principal grape varieties are grown on Madeira.

The original, the Malvazia or Malmsey, makes the richest; the Bual a less rich, more elegant but equally fragrant wine; Verdelho a soft, much drier wine with a faintly bitter finish; the Sercial a fine light wine with a distinct acid 'cut'. Sercials make fine pre-dinner aperitifs.

Two other very rare varieties were also grown: Terrantez and Bastardo. Both of these varieties were shy bearers which were not replanted when the vineyards were devastated by the root louse phylloxera in the mid- to late-19th century. Bastardo is closest in style to Malmsey; Terrantez tends to be between Bual and Verdelho.

Figure 8-9. **Sample from Clydz's Martinis and Cocktails Home Page**

**CLYDZ**

**MARTINIS & COCKTAILS**

**absolut mess** - absolut mandarin, citron and kurant, triple sec, lime juice & cranberry juice

**almond joy** - luksusowa vodka, malibu rum and amaretto

**anabanana martini** - vanilla vodka, creme de banana, honey and pineapple juice

**b&b stinger** - b&b and white creme de menthe

begnini martini - vodka, sambuca and espresso

**berry white** - berry vodka, chambord, godiva white chocolate liqueur & just a touch of cream

**the bloody ear** - vincent van gogh orange vodka, licor 43, campari, orange and lemon juice

**bloody martini** - pepper vodka and a splash of out homemade bloody mary mix

**blue c in the sky with diamonds** - skyy vodka, blue curacao, licor 43 & oj with cubes afloat

**blue sapphire** - bombay sapphire, dry vermouth & blue curacao

**brandy alexander** - brandy, brown creme de cacao and cream brentini - berry vodka, midori and lime juice

**caipirinha** - cachaca (brazilian sugar cane liqueur) with muddled limes and sugar

**cajun martini** - pepper vodka, dry vermouth, tabasco & old bay seasoning

Used with permission of Clydz Restaurant, New Brunswick, New Jersey

Figure 8-10. **Sunnyside Restaurant's Kids' Menu Page**

# Sunnyside Restaurant
850 N. Hanover Street-Carlisle, Pennsylvania
717- 243-5712

**Home▸ Menus▸** Kid's Menu

Pizza by Pappou
7 inch, just cheese, sauce and seasoning, served with salad - - - - - - - -          4.95

Breaded Chicken Strips
Salad and Potato or Vegetable - - - - - - - - - - - - - - - - - - - - - - - - - -          4.95

Chicken Parmesian with Pasta
Served with Salad - - - - - - - - - - - - - - - - - - - - - - - - - - - - - - - - - -          4.95

Spaghetti with Sauce
Choice of sauce - Alfredo or Marinara served with salad - - - - - - - - - - -          4.95

Sirloin Steak 5 oz.
Salad and Potato or Vegetable - - - - - - - - - - - - - - - - - - - - - - - - - - -          5.95

Fish Sticks "in the shape of sharks"
Salad and Potato or Vegetable - - - - - - - - - - - - - - - - - - - - - - - - - - -          4.95

Bunch of Breaded Shrimp
Salad and Potato or Vegetable - - - - - - - - - - - - - - - - - - - - - - - - - - -          4.95

Sandwich and Fries
Grilled Cheese, Hamburger or Cheeseburger served with salad - - - - - -          4.95

Kid's Soft Drink or Milk - - - - - - - - - - - - - - - - - - - - - - - - - - - - -          .50

Kid's Sunnyside Chocolate Sundae - - - - - - - - - - - - - - - - - - - -          .75

\* Prices are subject to change

**Menus | Banquets | Directions | Gift Certificates | E-mail**
©1998-2000 Sunnyside Restaurant. All Rights Reserved

Used with permission of Sunnyside Restaurant, Carlisle, Pennsylvania

Figure 8-11. **Fairview Catering's Buffet Menu Page**

## BUFFET SELECTIONS

### HOT BUFFET

Fruit Cup
Tossed Salad/Dressing

(Choice of 2 Meats)
Roast Sirloin   Baked Ham
Roast Turkey Breast
Roast Pork   Roast Chicken

(Choice of 1 Potato)
Mashed Potatoes   Filling
Parsley Potatoes   Rice Pilaf
Sweet Potatoes

Vegetable
Rolls & Butter
Coffee

**$9.50 Per Person**

### COLD BUFFET

Roast Beef
Roast Turkey Breast
Baked Ham
Ring Bologna
Assorted Cheese

(Choice of 2 Salads)
Potato      Macaroni
Coleslaw    Broccoli

Baked Beans
Pickles
Chips & Pretzels
Bread & Condiments
Coffee

**$8.00 Per Person**

### HOT & COLD BUFFET

(Choice of 2)
Pasta      Barbecue*
Swedish Meatballs/over Rice

Ring Bologna
Assorted Cheese

(Choice of 1 Salad)
Potato      Macaroni
Broccoli    Pasta

Baked Beans
Pickles
Chips & Pretzels
Rolls
*Pork, Chicken, Turkey,
Hamburger, Beef
**$8.00 Per Person**

### PRIME RIB & SHRIMP BUFFET

Prime Rib of Beef (Au Jus)
Large Chilled Shrimp

(Choice of 1 Potato)
Mashed
Potatoes      Filling
Rice Pilaf    Parsley Potatoes

Salad/Dressings
Vegetable
Rolls/Butter
Desert
Coffee
Condiments

**$18.00 Per Person**

### OPTIONS

| | |
|---|---|
| Stuffed Chicken Breast Dinners | |
| Shrimp Cocktails (per person) | $6.00 |
| Hors d'oeuvre (per person) | $5.00 |
| Fruit Pies (per person) | $2.00 |
| Cheese Cake/topping | $2.75 |
| Yams & Apples | $1.50 |

Buffets are priced for 2 hours of service. Prices do not include china and flatware rental. Add 6% sales tax and 15% gratuity to all prices.

Used with permission of Fairview Catering, Whitehall, Pennsylvania

Figure 8-12.  **Robin's Restaurant's Home Page Featuring Specialty Cakes**

Used with permission of The French Caines Bakery, Robin's Restaurant, Inc., Cambria, California

from the home page for **Robin's Restaurant,** which sells elaborate wedding cakes and cakes for other occasions. **Damon's Restaurant's** home page, shown in Figure 8-4, provides site visitors with the opportunity to purchase barbecue sauce.

### Web Sites and Direct Sales

Some home pages allow viewers to do more than study menus before visiting the restaurant. Figure 8-13 shows a frame from **Don's Express**. Viewers are invited to print the page, select desired menu items, and place their orders by fax or telephone. Figure 8-14 shows registration information and the first page of a seven-page on-line menu for **Michael's** delicatessen. Part A of Figure 8-14 shows the personal (contact) information needed to register for this electronic ordering system. Part B shows the viewer "clicks" to select menu items and options and to checkout. As well, viewers can specify the time by which they want take-out

Figure 8-13.  **Don's Express Home Page**

# Express Yourself!

## SERVED 7 NIGHTS A WEEK FROM 5 - 8:30 PM

EXPRESS YOURSELF TONIGHT! PRINT THIS PAGE TO ORDER BY FAX! 480-994-0364
OR PHONE IN YOUR ORDER! 480-990-RIBS (7427)

Don't wait for a special occasion to enjoy the best food in town... Tailgate party,
family get-together, or just "don't wanna cook" means it's a night for Don's Express.

| Appetizers | | | Sandwiches | | | Entrees | |
|---|---|---|---|---|---|---|---|
| ☐ Onion Strings | 4.95 | ☐ | BBQ Pork Sandwich | 7.95 | ☐ | BBQ Chicken (whole) | 9.95 |
| ☐ Fried Shrimp with Cocktail Sauce | 7.95 | ☐ | BBQ Beef Sandwich | 7.95 | ☐ | BBQ Baby Back Ribs | 15.95 |
| ☐ Fried Chicken Tenders | 4.95 | ☐ | The Giant Burger | 6.95 | ☐ | Roasted Prime Rib | 16.95 |
| with BBQ Sauce | | ☐ | Chicken Schnitzel Sandwich | 6.95 | ☐ | Chopped Steak (16oz) | 9.95 |

| Salads | | | Sides | | | | |
|---|---|---|---|---|---|---|---|
| ☐ Creamy Cole Slaw (serves 2) | 2.95 | ☐ | Mashed Potatoes (serves 2) | 2.45 | ☐ | Texas Baked Beans | 2.95 |
| ☐ Caesar Salad | 6.95 | ☐ | Potato Salad (serves 2) | 2.45 | ☐ | Cajun Rice | 2.45 |
| ☐ Chopped Salad with Roasted Chicken | 6.95 | ☐ | French Fries (serves 2) | 2.45 | ☐ | Vegetable of the Day | 2.45 |

*Fill out your ORDER then FAX or CALL Don's Express! Fax: 480-994-0364 Tel: 480-990-RIBS (7427)*

_____     _____     _____     _____

(name)                                (pick-up time)                        (vehicle/color)                          (phone number)

**Don's Express**
**7501 E. Camelback Rd.**
**480-990-RIBS (7427)**
(Just East of Scottsdale
Road)

Look for the specially marked "Don's
Express" parking stalls right up front at
Don & Charlie's! Our "Express Crew"
will be right out to your car in a flash and
have your order ready-to-go so you can be
on your way in just a few minutes...
hope you're hungry!

Used with permission of Don Carson, Don & Charlie's, Scottsdale, Arizona

Figure 8-14, Part A.   **Michael's Registration Page**

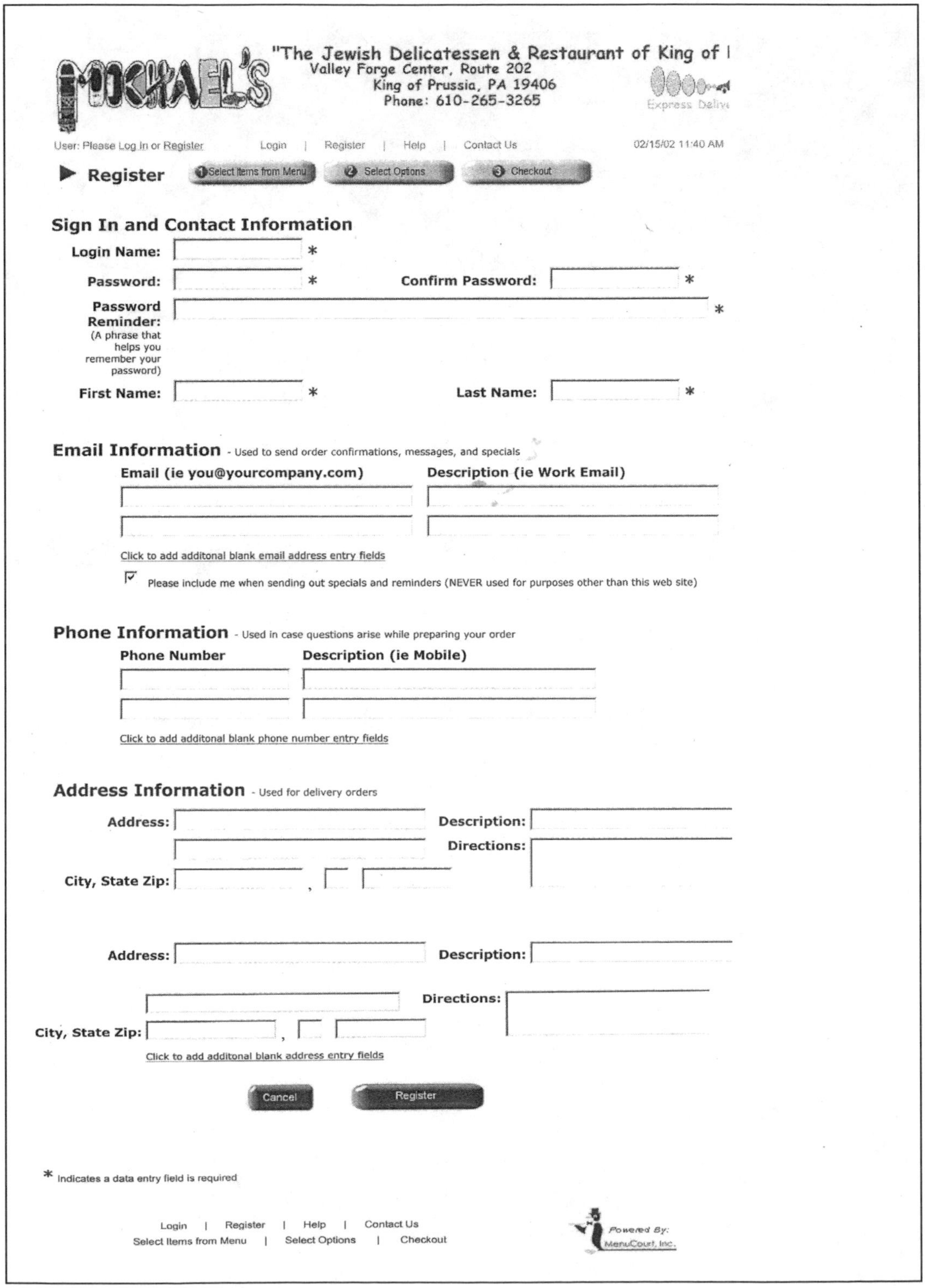

Used with permission of Michael's, King of Prussia, Pennsylvania

Figure 8-14, Part B. **Sample Page from Michael's Menu**

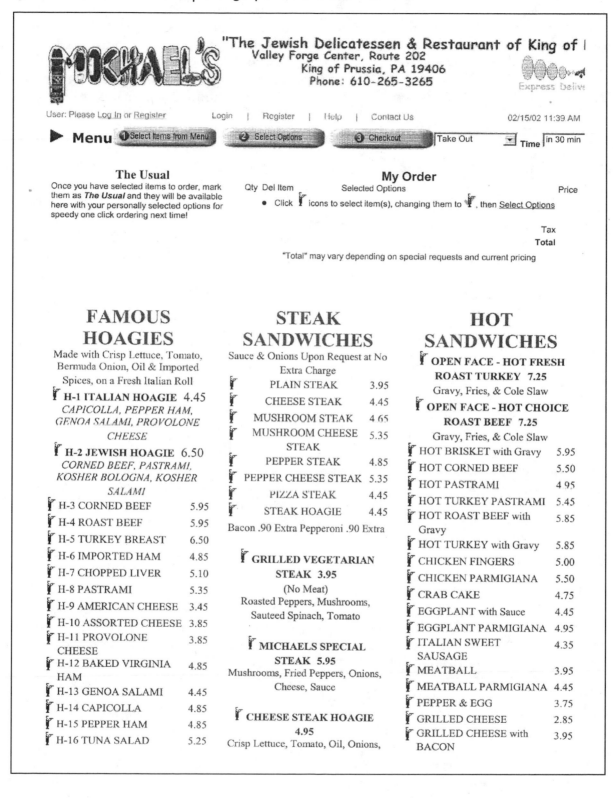

"The Jewish Delicatessen & Restaurant of King of I
Valley Forge Center, Route 202
King of Prussia, PA 19406
Phone: 610-265-3265

Express Delive

User: Please Log In or Register    Login | Register | Help | Contact Us    02/15/02 11:39 AM

▶ Menu   ❶ Select Items from Menu   ❷ Select Options   ❸ Checkout   Take Out ▾   **Time** | in 30 min

**The Usual**
Once you have selected items to order, mark them as *The Usual* and they will be available here with your personally selected options for speedy one click ordering next time!

**My Order**

Qty Del Item     Selected Options      Price

• Click 🍴 icons to select item(s), changing them to 🍴 , then Select Options

Tax

**Total**

"Total" may vary depending on special requests and current pricing

## FAMOUS HOAGIES

Made with Crisp Lettuce, Tomato, Bermuda Onion, Oil & Imported Spices, on a Fresh Italian Roll

**H-1 ITALIAN HOAGIE 4.45**
*CAPICOLLA, PEPPER HAM, GENOA SALAMI, PROVOLONE CHEESE*

**H-2 JEWISH HOAGIE 6.50**
*CORNED BEEF, PASTRAMI, KOSHER BOLOGNA, KOSHER SALAMI*

| | |
|---|---|
| H-3 CORNED BEEF | 5.95 |
| H-4 ROAST BEEF | 5.95 |
| H-5 TURKEY BREAST | 6.50 |
| H-6 IMPORTED HAM | 4.85 |
| H-7 CHOPPED LIVER | 5.10 |
| H-8 PASTRAMI | 5.35 |
| H-9 AMERICAN CHEESE | 3.45 |
| H-10 ASSORTED CHEESE | 3.85 |
| H-11 PROVOLONE CHEESE | 3.85 |
| H-12 BAKED VIRGINIA HAM | 4.85 |
| H-13 GENOA SALAMI | 4.45 |
| H-14 CAPICOLLA | 4.85 |
| H-15 PEPPER HAM | 4.85 |
| H-16 TUNA SALAD | 5.25 |

## STEAK SANDWICHES

Sauce & Onions Upon Request at No Extra Charge

| | |
|---|---|
| PLAIN STEAK | 3.95 |
| CHEESE STEAK | 4.45 |
| MUSHROOM STEAK | 4.65 |
| MUSHROOM CHEESE STEAK | 5.35 |
| PEPPER STEAK | 4.85 |
| PEPPER CHEESE STEAK | 5.35 |
| PIZZA STEAK | 4.45 |
| STEAK HOAGIE | 4.45 |

Bacon .90 Extra Pepperoni .90 Extra

**GRILLED VEGETARIAN STEAK 3.95**
(No Meat)
Roasted Peppers, Mushrooms, Sauteed Spinach, Tomato

**MICHAELS SPECIAL STEAK 5.95**
Mushrooms, Fried Peppers, Onions, Cheese, Sauce

**CHEESE STEAK HOAGIE 4.95**
Crisp Lettuce, Tomato, Oil, Onions,

## HOT SANDWICHES

**OPEN FACE - HOT FRESH ROAST TURKEY 7.25**
Gravy, Fries, & Cole Slaw

**OPEN FACE - HOT CHOICE ROAST BEEF 7.25**
Gravy, Fries, & Cole Slaw

| | |
|---|---|
| HOT BRISKET with Gravy | 5.95 |
| HOT CORNED BEEF | 5.50 |
| HOT PASTRAMI | 4.95 |
| HOT TURKEY PASTRAMI | 5.45 |
| HOT ROAST BEEF with Gravy | 5.85 |
| HOT TURKEY with Gravy | 5.85 |
| CHICKEN FINGERS | 5.00 |
| CHICKEN PARMIGIANA | 5.50 |
| CRAB CAKE | 4.75 |
| EGGPLANT with Sauce | 4.45 |
| EGGPLANT PARMIGIANA | 4.95 |
| ITALIAN SWEET SAUSAGE | 4.35 |
| MEATBALL | 3.95 |
| MEATBALL PARMIGIANA | 4.45 |
| PEPPER & EGG | 3.75 |
| GRILLED CHEESE | 2.85 |
| GRILLED CHEESE with BACON | 3.95 |

or delivery, and pricing for the order is displayed. (Note the opportunity for viewers to order "the usual"; all information applicable to a preferred order can be stored and called up the next time a viewer logs on.)

### Restaurant and Menu Directories on the Web

Some for-profit companies have recognized that many potential guests do not search the web for home pages of specific restaurants, but rather they use internet directories for this purpose. These directory companies provide the home pages of subscribing restaurants for a nominal annual fee plus, usually, set-up costs. Many of these directories provide detailed information about subscribing restaurants, including their menus.

Menu planners may list (advertise) their restaurant in citywide, regional, and even national directories developed and sponsored by chambers of commerce, tourist and convention commissions, restaurant associations, news media food critics, for-profit advertising organizations, and even individuals. Frequently these web sites allow viewers to sort restaurants by cuisine, location, and price. Clicking on a specified restaurant will typically yield information about the restaurant itself or part of the restaurant's menus. For example, Figure 8-15 shows one frame of "The Restaurant Guide of Kansas City." Note that the viewer can search the Kansas City restaurant database by cuisine and by location. Clicking on a restaurant will yield information about the restaurant, including its menu.

## OTHER CREATIVE USES OF TECHNOLOGY _____

There are numerous other ways that technology helps menu planners to generate more business. Examples of those that involve the menu are included in this section.

"Dining out" discount books have been available in many communities for many years. The basic plan involves the sale (frequently by groups as a fundraiser) of books containing discount coupons that can be redeemed at participating restaurants (sometimes other businesses are included in an "entertainment" discount book). There are now "high-tech" versions of this model in which a card (similar in size to a credit card) is sold to bargain hunters, who can view the corresponding web site display and check discounts offered by the participating restaurants (and, in the process, view the restaurant's complete menus along with other information). These cards can offer local, regional, national, or even international choices. Among other services provided by the companies to restaurateurs is the ability to change menus and provide updated information about menu specials.

A variation of this external-property advertising occurs when a for-profit organization faxes lunch specials from subscribing restaurants to local businesses or dinner specials to individuals. On-line versions of this advertising medium allow restaurateurs to post detailed information including menus and links to their web site.

Third-party businesses also provide delivery services. In one variation, travelers can obtain a brochure from a hotel's front desk describing the "extended room service" organization. The traveler can review the business's home page on a laptop computer and find information that includes the complete menus of participating restaurants or their carry-out menus, if applicable. The traveler can then contact the third-party carry-out service to order a meal from a participating restaurant.

Professionals in the worldwide hospitality industry are well aware of the global impact of the industry. Travelers from all over the world travel all over the world. Technology increasingly allows them to make dining plans from their home thousands of miles away from their final destination. Figure 8-16 shows one page of the menu from the home page of the **Le Dôme Restaurant** in Aruba. Note that it indicates the selling price of each menu item in both United States dollars and Aruban guilders.

Figure 8-15.  **A Sample of the Kansas City Restaurant Guide**

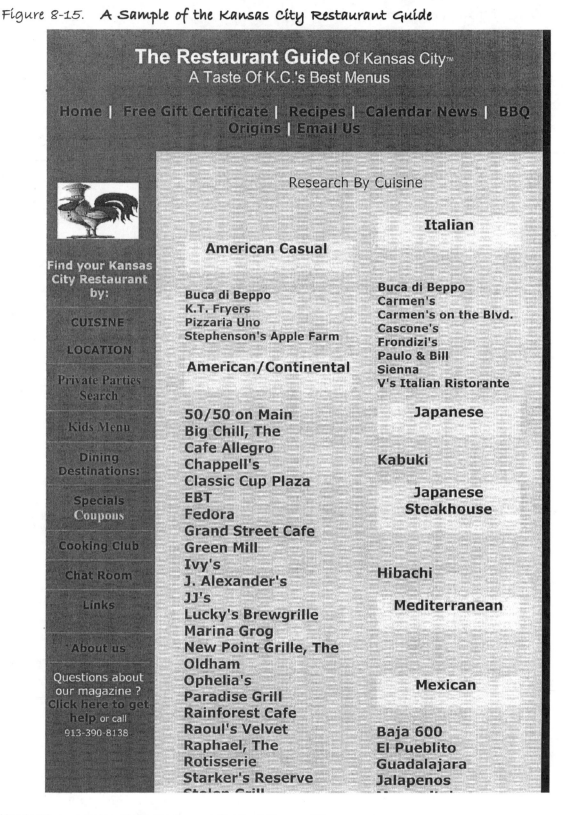

Used with permission of the Restaurant Guide of Kansas City

Figure 8-16. **Le Dôme Restaurant's Home Page**

| | | U.S. Dollar | AFL |
|---|---|---|---|

**Our Menu**

Cold Appetizers | Soups | Warm Appetizers | Our Salads | Fish | Kid's Menu | Meat | Poultry | Pasta's | Specialties

*Le Dôme Restaurant*

About Us
Dining Rooms
Our Menu
Reservations
Our Guestbook
News

**Cold Appetizers**

| | U.S. Dollar | AFL |
|---|---|---|
| **Trois petites Crevettes "Chaud Froid"** <br> A combination of North Sea Prawnisque, Prawn Croquette and a Tomato filled with Prawns | 11.00 | 20.00 |
| **Coctail au scampi** <br> Shrimp Cocktail with French cocktail sauce | 16.00 | 28.00 |
| **Jambon de Parme au Melon** <br> Thin sliced Parma Ham with Melon | 12.00 | 22.00 |
| **Saumon Fumé et sa Garniture** <br> Smoked Salmon with Tradition Condiments and toast | 19.00 | 35.00 |
| **Cocktail aux Fruits de Mer** <br> Seafood Cocktail with marinated Salmon, Baby Shrimp, Sea Scallops and Grouper filet, on a salad of Green Beans, and Pickled Red Onions | 17.00 | 30.00 |
| **Mousse de Cannard et Toast** <br> Mousse of Duck Liver with Toast | 12.00 | 22.00 |
| **La Symphonie deSaumon** <br> A Trilogy of Salmon | 19.00 | 35.00 |
| **Filet de Boeuf Cru au Parmesan** <br> Prime U.S. Beef Carpaccio with Parmesan and Olive Oil | 14.00 | 25.50 |
| **Salade Monteé d'Homard** <br> Caribbean Lobster salad with Sesame-Seed Vinaigrette | 19.00 | 35.00 |
| **Le Caviar Beluga Malossol avec Blinis** <br> Russian Beluga Malossol with Blinis and Condiments | 90.00 | 162.00 |

back to top

**Soups**

| | U.S. Dollar | AFL |
|---|---|---|
| **Potage du Jour** <br> Our Soup of the Day | 4.00 | 7.00 |
| **Crème de Tomates** <br> Tomato Soup with Cream | 4.00 | 7.00 |
| **Crème de Tomates au Cognac** <br> Tomato Soup with Cream and French Brandy | 5.00 | 9.00 |

Used with permission of Peter Balliere, Le Dôme Restaurant, Oranjestad, Aruba

## IN CONCLUSION

This chapter has presented information about ways in which technology impacts menu planners and their activities and their menu-planning and design activities. It has also indicated how the world wide web can present menus to creatively market the property. The future will see increased and more creative uses of technology in the foodservice industry. As always, the menu will be at the forefront of the "message" being communicated to current and potential guests.

## GO TO THE INTERNET FOR MORE INFORMATION

Since this chapter has addressed the impact of technology on menu planning and design, it is appropriate to include Internet addresses that provide additional information about many topics discussed in this chapter. Check out the following!

- To view the web site for a company that markets stand-alone menu-planning software, go to *http://www.calcmenu.com/chef/mainchef.htm*.
- To view the web site for a company that markets its menu-planning software as a component of a larger restaurant management program, go to *http://www.foodtrak.com*.
- To view the web site for a company whose menu-planning program contains excellent nutrition analyses, go to *http://www.computrition.com*.

- To view the web site for a company whose design program has excellent page layout capabilities and is easy to use, go to *http://www.adobe.com/products/pagemaker/main.html*.
- Additional help related to menu copy can be found in free-to-user food term dictionaries that can be found on-line. To view the web site of one such resource, go to *http://www.cafecreosote.com/dictionary.php3*.
- To view the web site and explore a sample program for a company whose software is used to modify the characteristics of photos and illustrations, go to *http://www.adobe.com/products/photoshop/tryreg.html*
- Complete menu development programs are available for review before you buy. To view the web site of one such program, go to *http://www.foodsoftware.com/PROGRAMS/MENUPRO/features.htm*.

# SIGEE'S MENU: A CASE STUDY

"Let me see if I get this straight," said Kathy Waller to David Berger, the food and beverage director at the hotel in which Sigee's restaurant was located. "You already have a computer in your office, but now you want a modem connection . . . and Internet access?"

"That's right," replied David. "We can use the Internet to retrieve a tremendous amount of information that will help us as we put the new menu in place." Kathy was the hotel's controller and was known for her ability to control expenses. David knew that if his request for additional departmental funding for the Internet access was to be approved, he was going to have to present a compelling case. He had been gathering information about how other restaurants in the area were using the Internet, and he was ready for Kathy's questions.

"Why not just go to the library?" asked Kathy. "It's free."

"We will," replied David, "but the most up-to-date information is posted on the Web."

"Like what?" asked Kathy.

"Well," replied David, "like new recipes from our vendors, clip art that we can use to produce our own in-house menus. . . ."

"In-house menus?" interrupted Kathy. "I thought that we used Wabash Printing for all of our menus."

"We have in the past," said David, "but with the color printers in the sales office, we can create our own tabletop and clip-on menus. That will save us money in the long run, and they will look very professional. I don't want to print our basic menu in-house, but I think there are a lot of times that we can quickly produce some specialty menus if I have Internet access."

"I don't know," said Kathy. "It is expensive to get on the Internet."

"The costs go down every month," replied David, "and the most important thing is that we can create our own menu website."

"Menu website?" asked Kathy "What is that?"

"Well, Kathy," replied David, "we can create a web address that will allow people who have Internet access to view our new menu before they come to the restaurant."

"So the menu would actually be posted on the Internet?" asked Kathy.

"That's right," said David. "We could even post specials on our website, advertise our Easter and Mother's Day brunches and, because we will have an e-mail address, we can actually solicit guest feedback—all from our own website."

"Okay," said Kathy. "We'll give it a try, but just for six months. Then we will get together again to see if your department really found the Internet useful."

"That's great," replied David. "Thanks, Kathy."

As he left Kathy's office he had no doubt about his department's ability to benefit from an Internet account for Sigee's. They would now have immediate access to a wealth of menu-development information, and he was determined to take advantage of all of it as he completed planning, designing, and promoting the new menu.

## CHAPTER 9

# Menu-Evaluation Strategies

## CHAPTER OUTLINE

**Menu Engineering**
  A Close Look at Popularity and Profitability
  The Menu-Engineering Worksheet
  Using Menu Engineering
    Plow Horses
    Puzzles
    Stars
    Dogs
  Is the Menu Any Better?
  Menu Engineering in Action

**Menu Engineering: A Noncommercial Example**
  Comparisons of Menu-Planning Objectives
  Menu-Engineering Worksheet
  Menu-Planning Tactics
**Menu Goal Value Analysis**
  Components of Goal Value Analysis
  Using Goal Value Analysis Components
**Menu Evaluation: Some Final Thoughts**
**Sigee's Menu: A Case Study**

## MENU TERMS USED IN THIS CHAPTER

Average contribution margin
Comfort food
Competitor analysis
Contribution margin
Food cost percentage
Menu engineering
Menu mix
Scramble system
Seat tax

## CHAPTER OVERVIEW

Assume that a menu has been planned and designed to incorporate the marketing and financial concerns of a foodservice property. You conclude that the menu-planning process is complete—right? Wrong! This process is *never* complete because of the ever-changing wants and needs of the guests and because the resources available to menu planners also change constantly. The menu is, then, an evolving tool that improves as it "keeps up" with the marketplace.

In this chapter we will review two models for the quantitative evaluation of menus: menu engineering and menu goal value analysis. Both of these evaluation models require menu planners to know the details of product costs and sales history information. In menu engineering, menu planners study sales histories (that is, the numbers and percentages of menu items sold) and contribution margins (that is, revenues less food costs) to determine each item's popularity and profitability relative to other items on the menu.

The menu goal value analysis model also addresses sales and contribution margins but considers two other variables as well: food cost percentage and the amount that a menu item contributes to fixed costs and profit. These additional variables are considered in efforts to address the fact that higher-priced items typically contribute more to the recovery of nonfood costs but, at the same time, may be

more difficult to sell because of their higher prices.

It is said that the work of a foodservice manager is never done. This is correct, and much of this ongoing work includes menu planning. Menu planners find that work on the menu is cyclical: A menu judged to be the "best" possible is implemented; over time, changes become necessary; these changes are incorporated into the next generation of menus; and the process continues.

This chapter provides insight into tactics that menu planners can use to best assure that their menus are up to date and are working to most effectively meet the marketing and financial goals for which the menu has been planned.

## MENU ENGINEERING

Menu planners must spend a significant amount of time and must be very creative when planning menus. The result of an effectively planned menu is a powerful in-house marketing tool that can help the operation succeed by pleasing guests as it attains financial goals. Unfortunately, the job of menu planners is never done. Guest preferences change over time and, as well, new food products and ingredients and new equipment enable the operation to offer new menu items. The current menu is the most recent version of a menu that has evolved from earlier versions. At the same time, the current menu will likely continue to change in the future as it is improved.

Sometimes, food fads lead to menu changes. For example, during the 1980's, "blackened redfish" (a fin fish from the Gulf of Mexico that is coated with pepper and other seasonings and seared in a very hot frying pan until blackened) became an almost overnight sensation. Many menu planners quickly added this item at the request of their guests. In a similar vein, the late 1990's saw the introduction of the "wrap." Because of their great popularity, these meat- and vegetable-filled

flour tortillas spread rapidly from the quick-service restaurants to very upscale restaurants.

More common than these dramatic menu additions are the subtle changes that focus on one or both of the following questions as menu planners evaluate their menu offerings:

- How can we increase the popularity of our menu items?
- How can we increase the profitability of our menu items?

A process called **menu engineering** allows the menu planners to address these two questions. This process provides tactics that menu planners can use to measure the popularity and profitability of their current menu items.

*Glossary Terms*
**Menu engineering.** A method of evaluation that focuses on the popularity and profitability of competing menu items with the goal of maximizing the sale of popular and profitable items and minimizing or eliminating, when practical, the sale of the less popular or less profitable items.

## A Close Look at Popularity and Profitability

Ideally, each menu item should sell its "fair share" of the total of all items sold. For example, assume that a menu has ten **competing menu items;** if all items were equally popular, then each would generate 10 percent of total sales (100 percent divided by 10 equals 10 percent). The menu-engineering model, however, defines an item as popular if it sells 70 percent of expected sales. In the example above, an item would be considered popular if it sold 7 percent of total sales (10 percent expected sales times 0.70 [the definition of minimum acceptability]).

---

*Glossary Terms*
**Competing menu items.** Those menu items that normally "compete" with one another for purchase by the guests. Consider, for example, menu items for children listed on the menu for the convenience of young persons brought to the restaurant by the adult guests. These items would normally be excluded in the menu-engineering process because they would not be among the menu items normally considered by the typical guests.

---

Historically, the concept of a menu item's profitability has focused on its food cost percentage (the food cost of menu item divided by the menu item selling price) with the belief that a lower **food cost percentage** yields a more profitable operation. The menu-engineering model, however, focuses attention on the **contribution margin** rather than on its food cost percentage. Figure 9-1 illustrates the difference between the two concepts.

---

*Glossary Terms*
**Contribution margin.** The menu item selling price less the menu item food cost; the amount of revenue that remains after product costs are subtracted from the product's selling price. For example, a sandwich selling for $5 with a product cost of $1 will yield a contribution margin of $4.
**Food cost percentage.** The percentage of a menu item's selling price required to purchase the ingredients for the item; it is the food cost of the menu item divided by the menu item selling price.

---

Let's look at the financial information for each menu item in the figure:

- The meat loaf dinner has a food cost of $4.50 and a selling price of $12.95. Its food cost percentage is, then, 34.7 percent ($4.50 divided by $12.95), and its contribution margin is $8.45 ($12.95 less $4.50).
- The pork chop dinner has a food cost of $10.00 and a selling price of $21.50. Its food cost percentage is 46.5 percent ($10.00 divided by $21.50), and its contribution margin is $11.50 ($21.50 less $10.00).

Figure 9-1. Which Is Better: A Low Food Cost Percentage or a High Contribution Margin?

| Menu Item | Menu Item | | | |
|---|---|---|---|---|
| | Food Cost | Selling Price | Food Cost Percentage | Contribution Margin |
| Meat loaf dinner | $ 4.50 | $12.95 | 34.7 | $ 8.45 |
| Pork chop dinner | $10.00 | $21.50 | 46.5 | $11.50 |
| Steak and lobster dinner | $15.00 | $27.90 | 53.8 | $12.90 |

- The steak and lobster dinner has a food cost of $15.00 and a selling price of $27.90. Its food cost percentage is 53.8 percent ($15.00 divided by $27.90), and its contribution margin is $12.90 ($27.90 less $15.00).

Figure 9-1 shows that the meat loaf dinner has a lower food cost percentage (34.7 percent) than does either the pork chop dinner (46.5 percent or the steak and lobster dinner (53.8 percent). If menu planners had a financial goal of minimizing the food cost percentage, then they should try to maximize the sale of the meat loaf dinner.

However, let's take a look at the contribution margins of the three competing items. The meat loaf dinner, the item with the lowest food cost percentage, also has the lowest contribution margin ($8.45). By contrast, the steak and lobster dinner, the item with the highest food cost percentage (53.8 percent), has the highest contribution margin ($12.90). Since, by definition, the contribution margin is what remains from an item's selling price after deducting its food cost, menu planners will want to maximize sales of the steak and lobster dinner. There is $4.45 more remaining from the revenue generated from the sale of the steak and lobster dinner than from the sale of the meat loaf dinner ($12.90 less $8.45) after product costs are deducted from the selling price. This remainder (the contribution margin) can be used to pay for all other categories of allocated expenses and to then contribute to the operation's net income.

A review of Figure 9-1, then, makes it clear that the goal of the menu planners should be to maximize the contribution margin and *not* to minimize the food cost percentage. Figures 9-2 and 9-3 explore this concept further by illustrating the concept of "**menu mix**."

---

*Glossary terms*

**Menu mix.** The sale (number of units) of a menu item relative to the total sale of all competing menu items. If 100 portions of chicken are sold on a day when 1,000 meals were served, the chicken's menu mix is 10 percent (100 divided by 1,000).

---

Figure 9-2. **Contribution Margin and Menu Mix: Menu Mix A**

| Menu Items | Menu Sales Mix | Item Food Cost | Total Food Cost | Item Sales Price | Total Revenue | Contribution Margin |
|---|---|---|---|---|---|---|
| Meat loaf dinner | 1,000 | $ 4.50 | $ 4,500.00 | $12.95 | $12,950.00 | $ 8,450.00 |
| Pork chop dinner | 400 | 10.00 | 4,000.00 | 21.50 | 8,600.00 | 4,600.00 |
| Steak and lobster dinner | 300 | 15.00 | 4,500.00 | 27.90 | 8,370.00 | 3,870.00 |
| Total | 1,700 | | $13,000.00 | | $29,920.00 | $16,920.00 |

$$\text{Food cost percentage} = \frac{\$13,000.00}{\$29,920.00} = 43.4 \text{ percent}$$

$$\text{Average contribution margin} = \frac{\$16,920.00}{1,700} = \$9.95$$

Figure 9-3. **Contribution Margin and Menu Mix: Menu Mix B**

| Menu Items | Menu Sales Mix | Item Food Cost | Total Food Cost | Item Sales Price | Total Revenue | Contribution Margin |
|---|---|---|---|---|---|---|
| Meat loaf dinner | 300 | $ 4.50 | $ 1,350.00 | $12.95 | $ 3,885.00 | $ 2,535.00 |
| Pork chop dinner | 800 | 10.00 | 8,000.00 | 21.50 | 17,200.00 | 9,200.00 |
| Steak and lobster dinner | 600 | 15.00 | 9,000.00 | 27.90 | 16,740.00 | 7,740.00 |
| Total | 1,700 | | $18,350.00 | | $37,825.00 | $19,475.00 |

$$\text{Food cost percentage} = \frac{\$18,350.00}{\$37,825.00} = 48.5 \text{ percent}$$

$$\text{Average contribution margin} = \frac{\$19,475.00}{1,700} = \$11.46$$

In Figure 9-2, the sales of the meat loaf, pork chop, and steak and lobster dinners were, respectively, 1,000, 400, and 300 portions, for a total of 1,700 portions sold. Figure 9-2 also includes each item's food cost and selling price as well as the total food cost and total revenue. For example, the total food cost for the meat loaf dinners is $4,500 (1,000 units sold times $4.50 per item food cost). Information about total revenue is also provided. For example, the sale of 1,000 meat loaf dinners generated revenue of $12,950 (1,000 units sold times $12.95 per item). The total contribution margin is shown in the last column. For the meat loaf dinner, the contribution margin of $8,450 is determined by subtracting the total food cost ($4,500) from the total revenue ($12,950). When these calculations are made for the three items, the total food cost ($13,000), the total revenue ($29,920), and the total contribution margin ($16,920) for the sale of all 1,700 items can be calculated.

Menu planners can calculate the food cost percentage in Figure 9-2 ($13,000 [total food cost] divided by $29,920 [total revenue] equals 43.4 percent). They can also calculate the **average contribution margin** ($16,920 [total contribution margin] divided by 1,700 total meals sold equals $9.95). Some managers refer to the average contribution margin as the **"seat tax."** While each guest pays a different amount for the food cost (a steak dinner has higher product costs than does a hamburger sandwich), after these costs are deducted from the selling price, the seat tax (average contribution margin) remains to pay the guest's "fair share" of other allocated expenses and profits.

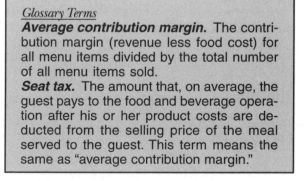

*Glossary Terms*
**Average contribution margin.** The contribution margin (revenue less food cost) for all menu items divided by the total number of all menu items sold.
**Seat tax.** The amount that, on average, the guest pays to the food and beverage operation after his or her product costs are deducted from the selling price of the meal served to the guest. This term means the same as "average contribution margin."

In Figure 9-3 the total number of menu items sold (1,700) has not changed from Figure 9-2. Rather, the menu sales mix has changed. The sale of meat loaf has dropped from 1,000 dinners to 300 dinners. At the same time, the sale of pork chop dinners increased from 400 meals to 800 meals, and the sale of steak and lobster dinners increased from 300 meals to 600 meals. This change in sales mix resulted in a higher total food cost ($13,000 in Menu Mix A to $18,350 in Menu Mix B). However, both the total revenue and the total contribution margin from the sale of all items also increased. (Total revenues generated by Menu Mix A were $29,920; the total revenue generated by Menu Mix B increased to $37,825.) The total contribution margin from Menu Mix A ($16,920) was exceeded by Menu Mix B ($19,475). Note that in Figure 9-3 the food cost percentage from the sale of all 1,700 items increased to 48.5 percent—an increase of 5.1 percent (48.5 percent [Menu B] less 43.4 percent [Menu A]) from Menu Mix A.

Traditionally, menu planners would perceive that this new menu mix would hurt the operation's profitability because the food cost percentage increased. In fact, however, note that the average contribution margin also increased by $1.51 ($11.46 [Menu B] less $9.95 [Menu A]). In other words, the revised number of portions sold in Menu Mix B generated an additional $1.51 contribution margin for each of the 1,700 items sold. The menu planners have an additional $2,555 ($19,475 [Menu Mix B] less $16,920 [Menu Mix A]) remaining after product food costs are deducted from revenue in Menu Mix B to pay for all other applicable expenses and to contribute to the operation's income.

## The Menu-Engineering Worksheet

Figure 9-4 is a spreadsheet that menu planners can use to manually evaluate the menu. (*Note*: While menu-engineering software is available, the menu planners must understand the basic concepts of and procedures for evaluating the menu regardless of whether they use a manual or an automated evaluation system.)

Let's review how to complete the menu-engineering worksheet.

- *Column A (Menu Item Name).* The names of competing menu items are listed here. To simplify, we will assume that a menu has only six competing items. Since the menu-engineering process analyzes competing items, when properties have more than one menu (for example, different menus for breakfast, lunch, and dinner), a separate menu-engineering analysis is required for each menu. Likewise, if a hotel has more than one dining outlet open for dinner (for example, a low-check-average coffee shop and a high-check-average fine-dining restaurant), it is necessary to do a separate menu-engineering analysis for each item.

- *Column B (Number Sold [MM]).* The number sold (menu mix) of each item listed in Column A is shown here. The data is taken from sales history information that tallies the number sold over the previous fiscal period. What is the preferred length of the time period for the analysis? The best answer is "as long as possible!" In practice, though, this is the amount of time necessary for menu item sales patterns to average out. Menu planners with at least one month of sales history information probably have sufficient data to use the property's menu mix data.

- *Box N.* This is the sum of all menu items sold during the period covered by the analysis. Note that in this example 2,000 total portions of the six menu items were sold.

- *Column C (Menu Mix [%]).* The percentage of total sales represented by each menu item (Column A) is listed here. For example, note that 350 portions of beef stew were sold (see Column B). This represents (in Column C) 17.5 percent of the total items sold as tallied in Box N: 350 portions divided by 2,000 total portions equals 17.5 percent.

Figure 9-4. **A Menu-Engineering Worksheet**

Date: ______

Restaurant: ______ Meal Period: ______

| A | B | C | D | E | F | G | H | L | P | R | S |
|---|---|---|---|---|---|---|---|---|---|---|---|
| **Menu Item Name** | **Number Sold (MM)** | **Menu Mix (%)** | **Item Food Cost** | **Item Selling Price** | **Item CM (E–D)** | **Menu Costs (D x B)** | **Menu Revenues (E x B)** | **Menu CM (F x B)** | **CM Category** | **MM Percentage Category** | **Menu Item Classification** |
| 1. Beef stew | 350 | 17.5 | $4.10 | $10.00 | $5.90 | $1,435.00 | $3,500.00 | $2,065.00 | Low | High | Plow Horse |
| 2. Chow mein | 210 | 10.5 | 4.40 | 11.25 | 6.85 | 924.00 | 2,362.50 | 1,438.50 | High | Low | Puzzle |
| 3. Ham and cheese sandwich | 100 | 5.0 | 4.80 | 10.50 | 5.70 | 480.00 | 1,050.00 | 570.00 | Low | Low | Dog |
| 4. BLT sandwich | 450 | 22.5 | 4.90 | 12.50 | 7.60 | 2,205.00 | 5,625.00 | 3,420.00 | High | High | Star |
| 5. Hamburger platter | 510 | 25.5 | 4.45 | 11.45 | 7.00 | 2,269.50 | 5,839.50 | 3,570.00 | High | High | Star |
| 6. Chicken sandwich | 380 | 19.0 | 2.75 | 8.50 | 5.75 | 1,045.00 | 3,230.00 | 2,185.00 | Low | High | Plow Horse |
| | | | | | | | | | | | |
| | | | | | | | | | | | |
| | | | | | | | | | | | |
| | | | | | | | | | | | |
| Column total | N | | | | | I | J | M | | | |
| | 2,000 | | | | | $8,358.50 | $21,607.00 | $13,248.50 | | | |
| Additional computations: | | | | | | | | O = M/N | Q = 100% / Number of Items x 70% = 11.7% | | |
| | | | | | | | | 6.62 | | | |

- *Column D (Item Food Cost)*. This is the per-portion cost for every ingredient in the menu items listed in Column A when (a) they are prepared according to standard recipes and (b) when the recipes have been precosted with current ingredient costs. For example, beef stew (Column A) has a food cost of $4.10 (Column D) if it is prepared according to currently precosted standard recipes..

- *Column E (Item Selling Price)*. This is the amount listed on the menu that a guest must pay to purchase the menu item. For example, the selling price of beef stew (Column A) is $10.00 (Column E).

- *Column F (Item CM [E-D])*. This column is used to report the contribution margin (an item's selling price less the item's food cost) for each item in Column A. For example, beef stew has a contribution margin (Column F) of $5.90 (the item's selling price [$10.00] less its cost [$4.10]).

- *Column G (Menu Costs [D x B])*. This column indicates the total food cost incurred to produce all portions of each menu item sold. For example, 350 portions of beef stew were sold (see Column B). Each portion of beef stew has a $4.10 food cost (see Column D). The total food cost incurred to produce all portions of beef stew was, then, $1,435 (in Column G: 350 portions times $4.10 equals $1,435.00).

- *Box I.* This box indicates the total menu (food) cost to produce the total number of portions of all menu items. For example, the total food cost to produce all 2,000 items (Box N) is $8,358.50 (the sum of Column G as reported in Box I).

- *Column H (Menu Revenues [E x B])*. This column indicates the total revenue generated from the sale of all portions of each menu item. For example, if 350 portions of beef stew were sold (see Column B) at a per-portion selling cost of $10.00 (see Column E), then the total revenue generated from the sale of all portions of beef stew would be $3,500 (350 portions times $10 in Column H).

- *Box J.* This box indicates the sum of all revenues generated from the sale of all menu items. For example, $21,607.00 in revenue was generated from the sale of all 2,000 menu items reported in Box N.

- *Column L (Menu CM [F x B])*. This column indicates the total contribution margin generated from the sale of all portions of each menu item. For example, beef stew generated a total contribution margin of $2,065 (menu revenues [in Column H] of $3,500 less menu costs [Column G] of $1,435).

- *Box M.* This box indicates the total contribution margin generated from the sale of all menu items. For example, the 2,000 menu items sold (in Box N) generated a total of $13,248.50 in contribution margin.

- *Box O (M ÷ N)*. This box indicates the average contribution margin (seat tax) generated from the sale of all menu items. For example, the total menu contribution margin ($13,248 in Box M) divided by the total number of meals (2,000 in Box N) equals $6.62. The menu planners now know the "definition" of profitability for this menu; they desire to sell those items with a contribution margin of $6.62 or more.

- *Box Q (100 % ÷ the Number of Items x 70 %)*. This box is used to calculate the "popularity" factor for the menu: 100 percent divided by 6 (the number of menu items in Column 1) times 70 equals 11.7 percent. The menu planners now know the most popular items—those with a menu mix (Column C) of 11.7 percent or higher.

- *Column P (CM category)*. This column is used to indicate whether the contribution margin of each item listed in Column A is lower or higher than the average contribution margin reported in Box O. For example, beef stew has an item contribution margin (Column F) of $5.90, which is lower than the average contribution margin ($6.62 in Box O); therefore, it is reported as a low contribution margin item in Column P. By contrast, chow mein has an item contribution margin of $6.85 (Column F), which is higher than the average contribution margin ($6.62 in Box O); therefore, chow mein is reported to have a high contribution margin in Column P.

- *Column R (MM % Category)*. This column is used to indicate whether the menu mix (popularity) of each menu item is higher or lower than the menu's average popularity. For example, beef stew has a menu mix of 17.5 percent (see Column C). This is higher than the menu's popularity index (11.7 percent in Box Q). Therefore, it is reported to have a high menu mix in Column R. By contrast, chow mein has a menu mix of 10.5 percent (see Column C), which is lower than the menu's popularity index (11.7 percent in Box Q). Therefore, chow mein is reported to have a low menu mix percentage in Column R.

- *Column S (Menu Item Classification)*. This column is used to classify (name) each menu item listed in Column A. The traditional names assigned by the menu-engineering model for each classification are as follows:
  1. *Plow Horse.* Unprofitable (low contribution margin) but popular (high menu mix) menu items; beef stew and chicken sandwich are Plow Horses.
  2. *Puzzle.* Profitable (high contribution margin) but unpopular (low menu mix) items; chow mein is a Puzzle.
  3. *Dog.* Unprofitable (low contribution margin) and unpopular (low menu mix) items; ham and cheese sandwich is a Dog.
  4. *Star.* Profitable (high contribution margin) and popular (high menu mix) items; BLT and hamburger platter are Stars.

Classifications can be assigned after reviewing each item's contribution margin category (Column P) and menu mix category (Column R). For example, beef stew is a Plow Horse (Column S) because it has a low contribution margin (Column P) and a high menu mix percentage (Column R).

## Using Menu Engineering

Menu planners can use the results of the menu-engineering analysis to better manage the menu. Objective information about each item's profitability relative to its popularity can be used to make decisions about menu content (product availability) and menu design. Without this information, the menu-revision process is much more subjective, leaving the menu planners to use intuition and trial and error to make decisions, which will not be as accurate as those based on menu-engineering analysis. Let's look at tactics that menu planners can use to manage each classification of menu items.

*Plow Horses.* Recall that Plow Horses are items that have a low contribution margin (profitability) but high popularity. Plow Horses may be very popular because guests view their relatively low prices as a value. Perhaps prices can be increased gradually and carefully without affecting demand. As this is done, the contribution margin increases, and the item becomes more profitable.

It may also be possible to shift demand away from Plow Horses. Menu planners can relocate Plow Horses to lower-profile "real estate" on the menu. ("Prime real estate" areas of menus were discussed in Chapter 7). The space vacated by the Plow Horses can, then, be used to promote more profitable and popular items. In addition, point-of-sale advertising and suggestive selling by service staff can emphasize other items. Another way to shift demand is to provide alternatives with better value. For example, a Puzzle (high contribution margin and low popularity) may be offered with a "free" dessert. This may increase sales of the Puzzle (which will shift demand away from the Plow Horse), and, even though a dessert is now provided, the Puzzle may still have a higher contribution margin than the Plow Horse.

Plow Horses can also be combined with items that have a lower food cost in efforts to increase contribution margins. Perhaps, for example, a relatively high-cost twice-baked potato would be eliminated as a potato choice and relisted on the menu as an à la carte item. Perhaps, especially during times when they are high priced, garnishes such as fresh fruits can be replaced with lower-cost alternatives.

The direct labor costs incurred to produce Plow Horses should also be examined, since menu engineering analyzes food costs alone. Plow Horses that require significant preparation labor will be much more costly to produce than Plow Horses that require little or no preparation labor. Menu planners might rationalize that a Plow Horse that requires little or no labor to produce it is acceptable, while more significant management tactics are needed for Plow Horses that require extensive labor for preparation.

Plow Horses might also be repackaged in efforts to increase their contribution margins. Perhaps, for example, a dessert costing $0.50 could be added to the Plow Horse item for an add-on selling price of $1.00. This approach will yield a $0.50 increase in contribution margin, which will make the Plow Horse a more profitable item. If guests view the $1.00 add-on price as a value incentive to order the Plow Horse, then the item will become more popular.

***Puzzles.*** Puzzles are menu items that have a high contribution margin but low popularity. Menu planners like these items but, unfortunately, guests do not. What can menu planners do to more effectively manage Puzzles? Several tactics may be useful.

First, Puzzles can be repositioned on the menu to "prime real estate" areas. As well, they can be featured by highlighting them (with boxes, colors, shades, photos, or drawings) and by providing more extensive menu descriptions. Figure 9-5 shows samples of this approach.

Note that the same menu items are listed four times in this figure. (We have taken them from the sample menu in Figure 7-9b.) Notice how the clip-art drawing, shading, elegant

box, and simple box draw your eyes to different items in each list.

Renaming the item may also help to sell it. (Which sounds more appealing: "tenderloin on a skewer" or "filet mignon brochette"?) Menu planners may also decide to decrease the price of Puzzles. (These items may be less popular because they are higher priced and perceived by guests as less of a value.) If the selling price is decreased to a point that still generates at least an average contribution margin, the item will still be "profitable."

Increased sales of Puzzles might also be generated by point-of-sale advertising and suggestive selling by service staff. Increasing an item's visual presentation at service, such as by serving a steak on a sizzling platter, by tableside flambéing, or by the use of very creative garnishes may also help to influence sales. Guests seated at a nearby table may ask a server, "What did those guests order?" That item might be a Puzzle—and additional sales can be generated.

***Stars.*** Stars are profitable and popular items. The best tactic for managing a Star is often to do nothing! Purchase specifications for ingredients should remain the same to help assure that quality is not altered. As well, the menu planners can assure that Stars are located in highly visible menu locations, and that merchandising such as point-of-sale advertising and suggestive selling by servers is consistently done. In some instances, prices might be increased when the item or the experience of which it is a part is unique. That is, it is not or cannot be offered by competitors and cannot be duplicated at home. Examples of opportunities to turn Stars into "superstars" are when the dining experience is unique (such as a view of Diamondhead on Oahu, Hawaii) and when there is entertainment provided by a famous singer or musician.

***Dogs.*** Dogs are unprofitable and unpopular items. Menu planners can use a few tactics with Dogs. Dogs should probably be eliminated

Figure 9-5. **Examples of Menu Item Highlighting**

**The Reuben**- Grilled rye plied high with corned beef, sauerkraut, thousand island, and Swiss cheese. Not too keen on corned beef, then try Reuben's sister................................................................. $5.92

**The Rachel** - We substitute shaved turkey for the corned beef, but there is still plenty of goodness to go around................................................................. $5.92

**Tour de France** - A heaping portion of roast beef smothered with provolone cheese on a crusty roll. Au jus on the side for dipping... Everyone comes home with the yellow jersey here!............................................ $5.92

**Home Run Club**
We stack ham, turkey, bacon, cheese, lettuce, and tomato between three slices of toast. It'll knock you out of the park!............................................ $5.92

---

**The Reuben**- Grilled rye plied high with corned beef, sauerkraut, thousand island, and Swiss cheese. Not too keen on corned beef, then try Reuben's sister................................................................. $5.92

**The Rachel** - We substitute shaved turkey for the corned beef, but there is still plenty of goodness to go around................................................................. $5.92

**Tour de France** - A heaping portion of roast beef smothered with provolone cheese on a crusty roll. Au jus on the side for dipping... Everyone comes home with the yellow jersey here!............................................ $5.92

**Home Run Club** - We stack ham, turkey, bacon, cheese, lettuce, and tomato between three slices of toast. It'll knock you out of the park!............................................ $5.92

---

**The Reuben**- Grilled rye plied high with corned beef, sauerkraut, thousand island, and Swiss cheese. Not too keen on corned beef, then try Reuben's sister................................................................. $5.92

**The Rachel** - We substitute shaved turkey for the corned beef, but there is still plenty of goodness to go around................................................................. $5.92

**Tour de France** - A heaping portion of roast beef smothered with provolone cheese on a crusty roll. Au jus on the side for dipping... Everyone comes home with the yellow jersey here!............................................ $5.92

**Home Run Club** - We stack ham, turkey, bacon, cheese, lettuce, and tomato between three slices of toast. It'll knock you out of the park!............................................ $5.92

---

**The Reuben**- Grilled rye plied high with corned beef, sauerkraut, thousand island, and Swiss cheese. Not too keen on corned beef, then try Reuben's sister................................................................. $5.92

**The Rachel** - We substitute shaved turkey for the corned beef, but there is still plenty of goodness to go around................................................................. $5.92

**Tour de France** - A heaping portion of roast beef smothered with provolone cheese on a crusty roll. Au jus on the side for dipping... Everyone comes home with the yellow                    jersey here!................................................................. $5.92

**Home Run Club** - We stack ham, turkey, bacon, cheese, lettuce, and tomato between three slices of toast. It'll knock you out of the park!............................................ $5.92

or, at least, prices should be raised to equal those of Puzzles. Limited menu space and operating problems that are incurred with Dogs, including unnecessary purchasing, preparation, or service requirements, do not justify keeping most Dogs on the menu.

## Is the Menu Any Better?

How do menu planners answer this question if they have not done menu engineering before revising the menu? Typical responses might include, "The guests seem to like the new menu" or "The new menu hasn't created any production bottlenecks; the cooks like it." Compare those responses to remarks that can be made by menu planners who have used menu engineering as the menu was revised: "Our new menu is significantly better than the previous one; we have been able to increase the contribution margin by $1.25 without a reduction in guest count."

Profitability (what the food and beverage operation desires) and popularity (what the guests desire) are important variables that should be considered as menus are initially planned and subsequently revised. Menu engineering is a strategy that can help make both of these processes more objective.

## Menu Engineering in Action

The value and power of menu engineering does not come as the menu planners identify the classifications of each menu item. Rather, the benefits arise when they use item-classification information to improve the menu.

Let's assume that Sigee's Restaurant has been using the menu shown in Figures 7-9a-c and that sales history information for a four-week operating period is available. Since precosted standard recipes for each menu item are always used and since the purchase cost for the ingredients in each menu item have not changed over the last month, the menu planners have the required information available to do a menu-engineering analysis.

Recall that menu engineering is used to analyze competing items. Therefore, items on the front page of this four-panel menu (appetizers) and on the back page (desserts) are not included in the analysis. Figure 9-6 shows the original menu after results of menu engineering are incorporated into its redesign. Note when reviewing Figure 9-6:

- The revised menu looks very similar to the original menu; it incorporates the sports theme, which is consistent with the atmosphere of the restaurant.
- Menu items are divided into the same basic classifications (salads and soups, sandwiches, burgers, and entrées), and the "odd cents" pricing tactic is still used
- A new menu classification (Special Spartan Salute Sandwiches) has been added. This tactic is more than just a menu change. The restaurant manager will work with the marketing and sales director to do extensive and consistent advertising related to the many athletic events in which the local university participates. **Competitor analysis** has indicated that while many local restaurants and sports bars tie promotions to sporting events, none of Sigee's off-campus competitors offers a menu item section focusing on the team and its name.

> *Glossary Terms*
> **Competitor analysis.** The study of the competitions' products, prices, promotional and advertising efforts, and other factors to assure that one is doing as well as (or better than!) competitors to attract guests in the same market.

Figure 9-7 presents information derived from the menu-engineering analysis about the profitability, popularity, and classification for each item on Sigee's original menu (Figures 7-9b). The menu planners used this information to make changes in the revised menu shown in Figure 9-6. We will next look

Figure 9-6. **Revised Sigee's Menu**

## On the Green

**Field of Dreams Salad** - A bottomless bed of lettuce tossed with a wide variety of fresh vegetables and our distinct house vinaigrette, finished with crisp croutons. If we build it, you will come back!...............................$3.92

**Baja Chicken Caesar** - Born in...Mexico? That's right, Mexico. Crisp romaine, Parmesan cheese, and crunchy croutons. Tossed with our own Caesar dressing and topped with a fresh grilled chicken breast. It's a classic reborn!................................................................$6.23

**Chicken Taco Salad** - Fresh lettuce, tomato, onion, black olives, and cheese, topped with your choice of grilled or blackened chicken breast. Served in a flour tortilla bowl.........................................................$6.43

**Island Breeze** - A refreshing change from the ordinary! We take a quarter pineapple shell and fill it with grilled chicken breast, then surround it with the freshest melon, grapes, and pineapple chunks!...............................$6.52

**Soup of the Day** - Whatever our chef is in the mood for, it's guaranteed to please.....................................Cup $1.92
.........................................................Bowl $2.92

**Clarion's Custom Chili** - A robust blend of meat, beans, and tomatoes, accentuated by the chef's secret blend of award winning herbs and spices will bring your taste buds to life.....................................................Cup $1.92
.........................................................Bowl $3.22

## Full Court Sandwiches

Our sandwiches are served with a basket of fries and a pickle spear.

**The Reuben** - Grilled rye piled high with corned beef, sauerkraut, thousand island, and Swiss cheese. ......................................................................$5.92

**The Rachel** - Reuben's sister, we substitute shaved turkey for the corned beef, but there is still plenty of goodness to go around....................................$5.92

**Tour de France French Dip** - A heaping portion of roast beef smothered with provolone cheese on a crusty roll. Au jus on the side!............................................. $5.92

**Home Run Club** - We stack ham, turkey, bacon, cheese, lettuce, and tomato between three slices of toast. It'll knock you out of the park!.......................................$5.42

### SIGEE'S SPECIAL RECIPE!!
### San Diego Chicken Sandwich
Tender marinated chicken breast grilled on an open flame with melted cheddar. Served on a rye bun with lettuce and tomato garnish (The real San Diego chicken was not harmed in the making of this sandwich!)  Also available blackened
.........................................................................$5.92

Figure 9-6.   (continued)

## Special Spartan Salute Sandwiches

**Spartan Sub -** Have a tailgate party any time! Your choice of ham, turkey, roast beef, or corned beef stacked with cheese, lettuce, tomato, and onion.................$5.92

**Spartan Grinder -** As American as football! Shaved ham, Swiss and American cheeses, all piled high on a big submarine bun and finished in the oven........$5.92

Our Spartan sandwiches are served with a basket of fries, pickle spear, a Spartan souvenir flag garnish and special good wishes to our Spartan sports teams.

## The Burger Zone

Our burgers are served with a basket of fries and a pickle spear.

We start you out with a full half-pound of the finest lean ground beef, and you take the handoff and run with it! We have enough selections to make your burger as individual as you are! Included are the first two items, then it's just $.25 per item after that.

***Suggestions include:***

American, Swiss, cheddar, provolone, bleu cheese sauce, sautéed onions, peppers, or mushrooms, ham, bacon, jalapeno peppers. If you don't see something 'you like just check with your server 'cause we've probably have it. Lettuce and tomato garnish included.

$5.92

## Sports Zone Knock–Outs

(Available after 5:00 Monday - Saturday)
Dinner entrees served with salad, our famous smashed redskins, veggie of the day, and Texas toast.
Soup available with meal for just .92¢

**Triple Play Sirloin -** 10 ounce juicy sirloin served up three ways! Choose from: 1.) smothered with sautéed onions, peppers and mushrooms, 2.) finished with a rich mushroom demi glace, 3.) it's also available blackened for a real Cajun treat!......................................... $14.92

**St. Louis Ribs -** We take the best cuts, slow roast them to tender perfection, then slather them with our secret barbecue sauce and finish them over an open flame................................................................... $11.92

**Sigee's Catch and Release Special –** Forget about the one that got away; your server will tell you tales of the ones that stayed on the hook!..................Market price.

**Margarita Chicken -** Two chicken breasts marinated in our own blend of tequila, lime and southwestern seasonings; flame broiled and finished with a zesty pineapple salsa.......................................... $9.27

 Please note that consuming raw or undercooked meat, poultry or seafood could be hazardous to your health.

**Veggie Lasagna -** Layers of fresh veggies piled high with lasagna noodles, alfredo sauce, and parmesan cheese, then finished with marinara sauce. Served with the vegetable of the day and garlic toast............ $7.92

Figure 9-7.  **Sigee's Restaurant: Menu-Engineering Results**

| | Contribution Margin (Profitability) | Menu Mix (Popularity) | Item Classification |
|---|---|---|---|
| **Salads and Soups (On the Green)** | | | |
| Field of Dreams Salad | High | Low | Puzzle |
| Baja Chicken Caesar | High | Low | Puzzle |
| Chicken Taco Salad | High | High | Star |
| Island Breeze | High | Low | Puzzle |
| Soup of the Day | Low | High | Plow Horse |
| Clarion's Custom Chili | Low | Low | Dog |
| **Sandwiches (Full Court)** | | | |
| The Reuben | High | Low | Puzzle |
| The Rachel | Low | High | Plow Horse |
| Tour de France | Low | High | Plow Horse |
| Home Run Club | High | Low | Puzzle |
| San Diego Chicken Sandwich | High | High | Star |
| **Spartan Salute Specials** | | | |
| Spartan Sub | High | Low | Puzzle |
| Spartan Grinder | High | High | Star |
| **Burgers (Burger Zone)** | | | |
| Burgers | High | High | Star |
| **Entrées (Sports Zone Knock Outs)** | | | |
| Triple Play Sirloin | High | Low | Puzzle |
| Stuffed Whitefish Supreme | Low | Low | Dog |
| Sigee's Catch and Release Special | Low | High | Plow Horse |
| St. Louis Ribs | High | High | Star |
| Margarita Chicken | Low | High | Plow Horse |
| Veggie Lasagna | High | Low | Puzzle |

at each menu item, note the changes that have been made, and discuss the reasons for the changes:

- *Field of Dreams Salad.* This item is a Puzzle (high in profitability but low in popularity). The menu planners are not surprised with this finding: It is profitable because of the relatively low-cost vegetable ingredients used to prepare the salad; it is relatively unpopular because guests at the sports-themed restaurant typically select more "hearty" items. The menu planners have decided to retain the item on the menu because, while it is not typically selected as

a main course, it is sometimes ordered as an accompaniment to a soup or sandwich.
- *Baja Chicken Caesar.* This Puzzle (high in profitability but low in popularity) is addressed by lowering the selling price by $0.20 (from $6.43 to $6.23). This pricing tactic leads guests to perceive a better value. At the same time, the average contribution margin will remain above average.
- *Chicken Taco Salad.* This item is a Star (high in profitability and popularity). The menu planners have decided to change nothing except to add shading to the menu description in efforts to attract the interest of more guests.

- *Island Breeze.* This Puzzle is addressed in two ways. Its shading is removed so that attention is not drawn away from the Chicken Taco Salad (a Star), and its price is reduced by $0.40 to add value (and perhaps sales).
- *Soup of the Day.* This is a Plow Horse (low in profitability but high in popularity). Several tactics will be used to manage it, but they will not appear on the menu. First, recipes will be reviewed to determine if high-priced ingredients (fresh seafood, for example) can be better managed. Also, serving staff will be requested to properly emphasize (suggestively sell) the soup as an "add on" to other items as they are taking guests' orders.
- The menu planners note that *Clarion's Custom Chili* is a Dog (low in profitability and popularity). Perhaps this item should eventually be removed from the menu. However, the menu planners recall that for the first several months that Sigee's was open (the time period covered by the menu-engineering analysis), the temperatures were relatively hot. Perhaps guest preferences will change during the upcoming colder fall and winter seasons. The selling price for a bowl of chili has been increased by $0.30 (from $2.92 to $3.22) to bring its contribution margin closer to the status of a Puzzle.
- *The Reuben* sandwich is a Puzzle. In efforts to increase its sales, the menu planners have decided to shade the menu description. Also, they have omitted a cross-selling reference to The Rachel sandwich, which is low in profitability.
- *The Rachel* sandwich will stay on the menu while menu planners study the impact of the menu description change for the Reuben. (They want its popularity to decrease and sales to be diverted to more profitable items.)
- The *Tour de France* sandwich is a Plow Horse. It is managed by changing its name (adding the term "French Dip") and by reducing the wording in the menu description. Efforts will be made to increase the contribution margin by reducing the food cost: The roll will be replaced with a smaller, less expensive roll that, while reducing the food cost, will give the impression of a more generous portion of roast beef.
- Efforts will be made to increase the popularity of the *Home Run Club* by reducing the selling price by $0.50 (from $5.92 to $5.42). This price reduction will still yield a contribution margin significantly above average and should increase sales by increasing guests' perception of value.
- The menu planners believe that sales of the *Spartan Sub* and its counterpart (the Gridiron Grinder, renamed "Spartan Grinder"; see below) will increase significantly because of its increased emphasis on the menu. The very high contribution margin will be offset by only about $0.10 (for the special flag garnish that will be added). With the relocation of the burgers (see below), the menu planners hope that the Sub and Grinder will be able to take advantage of their better location on the upper edge—just outside of the menu's "prime real estate."
- The menu planners are very excited about the *San Diego Chicken Sandwich*, which is a Star. They have emphasized it with shaded space and with a special heading, "Sigee's Special Recipe!" The labor cost associated with this item is relatively low (only the marinade must be made, and the sandwich must be assembled), so the menu planners are aware of the significant profit potential of this item.
- The *Spartan Grinder* is a Star. The menu planners have the same positive outlook that sales of this Star will increase due to the additional emphasis on it within the menu.
- Not surprisingly, *Burgers* are Stars. The only changes made on the revised menu involve moving the burger section further down on the page to take better advantage of the "prime real estate" area on this two-page (single-fold) menu. Note that on the original menu (see Figure 7-9b) the burger "add-ons" with a selling price of only $0.25 per item occupied much of the "prime real estate."

Before discussing the entrées, some discussion about selling prices is in order. Guests visiting Sigee's Restaurant will have access to the exciting sports theme and high-quality service and will be part of the "in the place to be" atmosphere during sporting events regardless of whether they order the least- or most-expensive menu item. Therefore, the menu planners are concerned that raising prices for Plow Horse items may be counterproductive; this tactic may skew check averages downward as guests select lower-price alternatives. Unless selling prices for salads and soups and sandwiches can be raised (and this is not judged to be a practical alternative), the menu planners are reluctant to raise the prices of these "high-end" menu items.

We will next study the revisions to the entrées on Sigee's menu.

- During the evening meal period, the *Triple Play Sirloin* is a great competitor of the burgers. This is good because its contribution margin is higher. The menu planners decide to shade this item in efforts to increase sales.
- The *Stuffed Whitefish Supreme* is a Dog and has been eliminated from the revised menu. The menu planners will consider offering white fish occasionally as the seafood special (see below).
- *Sigee's Catch and Release Special*, a Plow Horse, will be better managed in ways not seen on the menu. First, the purchase cost and selling price of the daily special will be closely examined in efforts to raise the contribution margin closer to average. As well, while the item must be suggestively sold (because the special changes daily), the servers will be trained to suggestively sell the ribs, which are Star items.
- The *St. Louis Ribs* are a Star, and nothing will be done to this item except that its menu description will be shaded. As in the original menu (see Figure 7-9b), the ribs are located next to the sirloin, and this is the only place on the menu where the

menu planners will "experiment" with shading that extends across both columns.
- The *Margarita Chicken*, a Plow Horse, will be managed by attempting to focus attention on the sirloin and ribs by removing the current shading (see Figure 9-5).
- The *Veggie Lasagna* is low in product cost, which makes it a high-profit item. While it has a low popularity (relatively few guests desire vegetarian meals), the menu planners decide to keep it on the menu until at least the next revision: Sigee's does attract some guests desiring the vegetarian alternative and its few sales do result in high contribution margin returns to the restaurant.

Sigee's menu planners are enthusiastic about implementing the revised menu, which has no real downside and many positive new features. Guests will perceive little change, and the revised menu will require almost no change in operations that impact purchasing, production, or service personnel. (Servers will, however, need to be trained in effective suggestive selling techniques to properly emphasize the soup of the day, the seafood special, and the Star items in each category of menu items during the appropriate meal period.)

The menu planners realize that this new menu is not a "final" menu; few, if any, menus are. Rather, the new menu is simply the newest generation of Sigee's menus. The menu will continue to evolve over time as menu planners incorporate changes in what the guests want while trying to proactively manage for increased profitability. The menu planners will continue to use their common sense and experience, guest input from numerous sources, and menu engineering, among other tactics, to gather information helpful in the ongoing process of menu improvement.

## MENU ENGINEERING: A NONCOMMERCIAL EXAMPLE[1]

To this point we have been examining the traditional menu-engineering model used primarily in commercial foodservice operations. Since guests pay an identifiable amount for each item selected, "profitability" relates to contribution margin (menu item revenue less menu item food cost). This is a convenient definition because, almost without exception, commercial food and beverage operations establish a selling price for each menu item so that contribution margins can be easily calculated.

How, if at all, can the menu-engineering model be applied in a noncommercial foodservice operation that does not establish a selling price for each specific item? Consider, for example, a college or university foodservice program that sells a meal plan to students that allows them to purchase many meals over a period of many months. Consider also that same operation when it sells a single "meal ticket" that is good for only a specified meal period. In both cases, the guests (students or other consumers) pass through a serving line or **scramble system**. They may request desired items from among those portioned by cafeteria serving personnel or help themselves to items available on a "serve yourself" serving counter.

---

*Glossary Terms*

**Scramble system.** A cafeteria serving system in which foods in specific menu item categories (soups and salads, cold entrées, hot entrées, sandwiches, and desserts, for example) are offered on separate serving lines in different parts of the serving area. This system avoids the long waiting in line that often occurs in a traditional cafeteria serving line arrangement. Instead, guests can move in front of others or between serving lines, depending on their preferences. Guests in scramble system cafeterias spend less time waiting in line.

---

[1] The authors acknowledge Ms. Rose Jaffer, Operations Supervisor, Auxiliary Services, Division of Housing and Food Services, Michigan State University, East Lansing, Michigan, for her assistance with this section.

College and university foodservice administrators, like their counterparts in all other segments of the noncommercial foodservices industry, are just as concerned about controlling costs, meeting budget goals, and retaining their market share as are food and beverage managers in the commercial segment of the industry. It is, therefore, just as critical for menu planners in these operations to monitor the effectiveness, efficiency, and popularity of menu items offered. This can be done through a modification of the basic menu-engineering model.

### Comparisons of Menu-Planning Objectives

Menu planners in a college and university foodservice typically have different objectives in mind when planning the menu than do planners in a commercial foodservice operation. Some of these objectives are contrasted in Figure 9-8.

When reviewing Figure 9-8 note that it contrasts the importance of selected menu-planning factors between commercial and college and university foodservices. Let's look at these factors more closely.

- *Financial concerns.* The goal of the menu planners in a commercial operation is to maximize the contribution margin (profit); the financial goal of college and university menu planners is to minimize (or, at least, to stay within specified budget parameters of) food costs.
- *Recipe (ingredient) concerns.* Commercial menu planners select recipes based on the perceived ability to generate profit; college and university menu planners select recipes based on the resulting food costs.
- *Popularity.* Popularity concerns in commercial operations require the menu planners to search for signature items (with the goal that they will be Stars in the menu-engineering model). By contrast, menu planners in college and university foodservices address

Figure 9-8. **Important Factors in Menu Planning for Commercial and Noncommercial Foodservice Operations**

| | HOW ADDRESSED | |
|---|---|---|
| **Menu-Planning Factors** | **Commercial Foodservices** | **College and University Foodservices** |
| Financial concerns | Contribution margin (profit) | Food cost |
| Recipe (ingredient) costs | Profit-based | Budget-based (food cost) |
| Popularity | Search for signature items | Ability to produce and serve |
| Service | Impact on profits | Mission of department |
| Volume of production | Customized demand | Equipment and labor considerations |
| Menu mix | Contribution margin (profit maximization) | Cost-sensitive (cost minimization) |

perceived popularity by confirming that they have the ability to produce and serve enough of the popular items to meet the demand for them. They are especially interested in adding low-cost popular items because sales of these items offset higher-cost items.

- *Service.* The commercial operator's concern focuses on service because it impacts profits; service is typically part of the mission of the college and university foodservices department.
- *Volume of production.* In commercial operations, there is typically more customized demand. Orders are placed one (or a few) at a time, and cooking is done made-to-order or in small batches. By contrast, large-volume production requirements set significant limitations on college and university menu planners. Menu planners must select menu items while keeping in mind the equipment and labor requirements unique to large-volume production, in order to prevent a maximum of operational difficulties. For example, items requiring use of a deep fryer can be planned for a specific meal period.
- *Menu mix.* Commercial menu planners are concerned about the overall contribution margin generated by menu items with differing contribution margins. They desire to maximize profits. By contrast, col-

lege and university foodservice menu planners are very cost-sensitive; they are more concerned about minimizing the costs to produce all the menu items required.

Earlier in this chapter we noted four basic menu categories into which the traditional menu-engineering model places all items:

- *Stars.* Popular and profitable items.
- *Plow Horses.* Popular but not profitable items.
- *Puzzles.* Not popular but profitable items.
- *Dogs.* Neither popular nor profitable items.

Experienced menu planners in college and university foodservice operations know cafeterias offer a fifth category of menu items that are very important to their consumers: **comfort foods.** Comfort foods affect the demand of other items offered on the menu, and together they determine the production, cost, popularity, and financial success of many college and university foodservice operations. Figure 9-9 illustrates the impact of these items on food cost.

Figure 9-9.  **The Power of Comfort Foods**

| Lunch Menu Entrée Costs | | | |
|---|---|---|---|
| **Menu #1** | | **Menu #2** | |
| Chicken tenders | $1.25 | Chicken tenders | $1.25 |
| Beef stew | $1.00 | Beef stew | $1.00 |
| Eggplant lasagna | $2.00 | Grilled cheese | $0.50 |
| Food cost (three entrées) | $4.25 | Food cost (three entrées) | $2.75 |

*Glossary Terms*

**Comfort foods.** Food items that college and university students desire regardless of other items that may be offered. Comfort foods are familiar items frequently served at home and help to remind one of family and the familiar home environment. Examples include hot dogs, hamburgers, French fries, soups, and cold cereal.

Two objectives for college and university foodservice operations are to minimize costs and, at the same time, to provide good service. Let's assume that a student takes an equal portion of each item as he or she passes through the "help yourself" cafeteria line during the lunch period. If grilled cheese is a comfort food for many of the students, they will prefer it (menu #2) rather than eggplant lasagna (menu #1) The foodservice operation will do well to offer grilled cheese because its cost is much lower than the cost of a portion of lasagna. Menu planners who offer the grilled cheese sandwich, in this example, please the students and minimize food costs. In so doing, two of the most important goals of the foodservice operation are attained.

From a financial perspective, a $1.50 per-student difference in food cost is very significant. For example, a residence hall feeding 1,000 students will reduce its food cost by about $1,500 for that single lunch period. If this menu were offered twice monthly, the food cost savings would be $3,000 per month. College and university foodservice menu planners who incorporate the tactic of frequently offering comfort foods can reduce food costs significantly while, at the same time, providing maximum customer acceptance.

## Menu-Engineering Worksheet

To this point we have noted that one of the several financial goals of college and university foodservices is to minimize food costs. The definition of "profitability," then, should focus on minimizing food costs rather than on maximizing the contribution margin. How can this be done? The menu-engineering worksheet shown in Figure 9-10 makes suggestions. Note that the format of this worksheet is similar to that shown in Figure 9-4 for commercial, or "pricing," operations. However, since there are no menu item selling prices, information about menu item selling price, revenues from the total number of units of each menu item sold, and contribution margin are omitted. Instead, an additional column, "cost category" (see column 6), has been added.

Let's look at Figure 9-10 more closely.

• Assume that the items listed in Column 1 are those typically served together on a cycle menu. (Assume, for example, that they generally rotate every 35 days [a 5-week period] in a dinner cycle.) Note (in Column 2) the number of each menu item sold. Column 3 (Menu Mix Percentage) indicates the percentage of the total sales

Figure 9-10. **Menu-Engineering Worksheet: Nonpricing Operations**

| Menu Item | Number Sold | Menu Mix Percent age | Item Food Cost | Menu Costs | Cost Category | Popularity Category | Item Classification |
|---|---|---|---|---|---|---|---|
| (1) | (2) | (3) | (4) | (5) | (6) | (7) | (8) |
| Chicken | 420 | 42 | $2.21 | $ 928.20 | Low | High | Star |
| Pork chop | 360 | 36 | 2.75 | 990.00 | High | High | Plow Horse |
| Roast beef sandwich | 150 | 15 | 3.15 | 472.50 | High | Low | Dog |
| Lasagna | 70 | 7 | 2.40 | 168.00 | Low | Low | Puzzle |
| Total | 1,000 | | | $2,558.70 | | | |

$$\text{Average (standard food cost)} = \frac{\text{Menu costs (Column 5)}}{\text{Number. sold (Column 2)}} = \frac{\$2,588.70}{1,000} = \underline{\$2.59}$$

$$\text{Popularity} = \frac{100\,\%}{\text{Number of items}} \times .70 = \frac{100\,\%}{4} \times .70 = 17.5\,\%$$

represented by each menu item.

• Note that the item food cost for one serving of chicken (see Column 4) is $2.21. Like the menu-engineering worksheet for commercial foodservices, this represents the cost to produce one portion of chicken when it is prepared according to the applicable standard recipes that are precosted with current ingredient costs.

• Note that the total menu cost (Column 5) to serve all chicken entrées is $928.20 (420 servings [in Column 2] times $2.21 [the per-portion cost in Column 4]).

• The total menu cost (sum of Column 5) for all menu items sold is $2,558.70.

• The average food cost for all entrées sold is $2.59 (total menu cost [sum of Column 5] divided by 1,000 entrées sold [total of Column 2]). The financial goal of the menu planners, then, becomes one of increasing the sale of menu items with a food cost of $2.59 or less. As with the commercial menu-engineering model, the popularity goal is the same: to maximize the sale of items that sell at least 70 percent of the expected menu mix (100 percent divided by 4 times .70 equals 17.50 percent). (Note that a major difference in college and university foodservices is that the basic meal plans are priced with a built-in expected "no-show" (missed meal) rate. This allows college and university menu planners to generate revenues that are not offset by food costs; a cushion is, therefore, built into the costing process.)

When reviewing Figure 9-10, observe the cost category (Column 6) and popularity category (Column 7) for each item classification (in Column 8), keeping in mind our previous definitions of Stars, Plow Horses, Dogs, and Puzzles.[2] The goal of the menu planners is to maximize the number of Stars and Puzzles served and to minimize the number of Plow Horses and Dogs.

Let's look at how menu planners in a nonpricing foodservice operation might use menu engineering when there is no per-person or per-portion revenue and, therefore, no menu item contribution margin. Let's assume that the foodservice program operates for post-secondary school students who "help themselves" to menu items as they pass through a serving line.

The menu planners have in place a financial benchmark (a food cost of $2.59 or lower) and a popularity benchmark (17.5 percent or more of all items sold). Menu planners can now use tactics to influence students to select low-cost, popular items.

## Menu-Planning Tactics

Let's look at some of the tactics menu planners can use:

- *Stars.* Chicken has a low food cost and is very popular. Several tactics used to manage stars in pricing operations can help manage Stars in nonpricing operations. For example, the food purchase specifications for ingredients in the chicken recipe should not be altered. The Star items can be placed in a highly visible location on the menu, if a menu is used. (For example, if there is a menu board, this item can be placed high on the list. If there are electronic or hard copies of the menus, then boxing, different colors, or other techniques to draw the guests' eyes to these items can be helpful.)

Perhaps the steam table or other pan into which these items are placed for service can be attractively garnished and, if applicable, can be placed in front of other items on the serving line. As well, serving staff can be asked to suggestively sell: "Everything is good today, you know that; however, why don't you try the chicken [Star] because the chef said it is especially good today.") Stars are often served on specialty food bars for faster service, especially since they are low in cost. However, caution must be taken because waste increases on self-serve food bars. Examples of Stars often include hamburgers, hot dogs, grilled cheese sandwiches, and deli bars.

- *Plow Horses.* Pork chops have a high food cost and are popular. First, relocate the item to a less-convenient location (such as to the end of the serving line) on the serving counter, if applicable. Use suggestive selling techniques to influence students to select other (Star and Puzzle) items. Reduce the portion size. (In many nonpricing operations, guests can return to the serving line for second portions if they desire.) Evaluate the labor cost for the Plow Horse; labor is a fixed cost (at least to a certain extent) in many noncommercial foodservice operations. However, if there is no significant additional labor required (for example, perhaps the cooks need only place portions on a baking pan as opposed to preparing a stew or casserole from scratch), then the menu planners might be better able to justify the selection of Plow Horses that require no or little labor.

- *Dogs.* Roast beef sandwiches are high in food cost and unpopular. The menu planners should attempt to discover why the item is not popular or profitable. For example, perhaps the quality of the product should be improved. Plow Horses often become Dogs because they lose quality during preparation or while holding before serving, which will reduce their popu-

---

[2] Earlier in this chapter we identified the names of items that are in popular use. College and university foodservice administrators might see other names to be more relevant to their operations, such as the following: Stars = Comfort Foods; Plow Horses = Homestyle Foods; Puzzles = Health-Kick Foods; Dogs = No-Way Foods.

larity. (Items such as baked spaghetti, tuna fish casserole, and other casserole and stew items are often examples.) Perhaps the portion size of the roast beef sandwich can be reduced, especially when students can help themselves to additional quantities. Consider ways to reduce food costs without sacrificing quality. For example, if the Dog is a casserole dish, perhaps less cheese could be sprinkled on top of the item before baking. This would reduce the item's food cost. As well, this could please some students; additional shredded cheese could be available for others who want it. If food costs can be reduced, then tactics such as repositioning the item in a more visible location on the serving line with enhanced garnishes, better accompaniments, and improved quality might help increase sales. As well, the menu planners could consider marketing this item by offering samples on the serving line or in the dining room. The item could be renamed and given a new "look." If tactics to reduce food costs and to increase popularity do not succeed, it would be wise to eliminate this item from the menu. Examples of Dogs often include Tex-Mex items, some pasta, and numerous casserole dishes.

- *Puzzles.* Lasagna has a low food cost and is unpopular. The menu planners should attempt to increase the selection of this item. For example, perhaps it could be repositioned to a more visible location on the serving line. Renaming, using suggestive selling techniques, developing point-of-service advertising campaigns, garnishing, and using other techniques to create "eye appeal" can be helpful. (For example, a salad featured with assorted greens, tomatoes, and red cabbage topped with cheddar cheese may look more appealing than a tossed "salad of the day.") Typical examples of Puzzles in college and university foodservices are vegetarian items, stir fries, salad bars, and many pasta items.

To this point, we have discussed the use of a modified menu-engineering model for nonpricing operations. Experienced menu planners in these segments sometimes note that some products are "trendy"; they have short-term popularity and, often, low variable costs. Students request these "trendy" items, which (at the time of this writing) include gyros, wraps, and ethnic food items including Mexican, Chinese, Japanese, and East Indian. However, as other items become popular (trendy), preferences change (sometimes rapidly). It is, therefore, important for menu planners to continually track sales and to revise menus as necessary to keep up with changing student choices.

Wise menu planners should conduct sufficient research and testing of new items in order to yield the best production and most consistent delivery of them. For example, consumers may lose interest in many ethnic foods because the foodservice operation cannot accurately and consistently recreate an authentic product. It may be advisable to offer samples of these items to increase their popularity. As well, the items can be marketed on the menu, and information about their origin can be used, in part, for suggestive selling efforts. Properly executed, "trendy" items may become mainstays on the menu and may rise to a Star classification.

Menu planners in nonpricing operations and their counterparts in commercial foodservices with "help yourself" salad bars and buffets can do several things to help minimize food costs:

- Keep track of the variety and volume of items that are produced, transported to self-service stations, and left over. Production and leftover records should be reviewed when developing production forecasts and when considering menu changes.
- Assure that the menu is flexible. Perhaps some items should not offered, for example, when market prices increase dramatically

(either seasonally or during times of temporary shortages).

- Consider how, if at all, leftovers can be reused. (Sanitation and quality are critical issues that must be considered first when these decisions are made.) The ability to use leftovers is one of many planning considerations that confront the menu planners who plan to include self-service items on the menu.

Menu planners in noncommercial foodservice operations such as those provided in universities and colleges are just as concerned about financial and marketing issues as are their counterparts in hotels and restaurants. The use of a modified menu-engineering approach to menu evaluation and management can be one tactic to better control costs and please customers.

## MENU GOAL VALUE ANALYSIS

One reason the menu-engineering model is popular is because it is simple to use. A matrix that relates two factors—profitability (contribution margin) and popularity (menu mix)—gives menu planners information about the profitability and popularity of each menu item, which menu planners can compare with those of the average of the menu. A criticism of this approach, however, is that it emphasizes items with higher selling prices because they typically have higher contribution margins. Another disadvantage may be that some items must always be below average and, as these items are replaced, other items will then fall below the average point. However, some menu planners want to continuously replace below-average menu items: it can help the menu to evolve with each revision to yield higher profitability (contribution margin). If this occurs without the guest count decreasing, the menu will, over time, be improved.

Another approach to menu evaluation, goal value analysis, can also be used. With this method, each menu item is compared to an exemplary menu item rather than to the other menu items with which it competes.[3]

Goal value analysis creates an ideal goal value for all competing menu items on the menu, and then allows menu planners to calculate the goal value for each competing menu item. Those menu items that yield goal values greater than the goal value for the entire menu are the items the menu planners want to sell.

Let's look more closely at goal value analysis to see how it works.

### Components of Goal Value Analysis

Menu planners using this evaluation model assess four financial factors for the entire menu and for each specific menu item. These factors are

A. contribution margin percentage (100 percent less food cost percentage),
B. popularity (the total number of all competing menu items sold),
C. selling price (as stated on the menu), and
D. fixed cost percentage plus profit percentage (100 percent less variable cost percentage).

We will next show how goal value analysis can be used for menu evaluation, using the data in Figure 9-4.

---

[3] Readers interested in detailed information about goal value analysis are referred to: David Hayes and Lynn Huffman, "Menu Pricing: A Better Approach," *The Cornell Quarterly*, Vol. 25, no. 4 (1985) and "Value Pricing: How Low Can You Go?" *The Cornell Quarterly*, February 1995.

<u>*Step 1.*</u> *Calculate the Goal Value for the Entire Menu.* This is done by multiplying the four elements discussed above:

A                  B                  C                  D

Total menu goal value = Contribution x Average no. x Check x Fixed cost percentage
margin percentage    items sold    average    + Profit percentage

Using the data from Figure 9-4, the amounts are:

A. *Contribution Margin (CM) Percentage:*

$$\frac{\text{Total menu CM (Box M)}}{\text{Total menu revenue (Box J)}} = \frac{\$13,248.00}{\$21,606.50} = \underline{61.1\%}$$

B. *Average Number of Items Sold:*

$$\frac{\text{Box N}}{\text{Number of menu items}} = \frac{2000}{6} = \underline{333.3}$$

C. *Check Average:*

$$\frac{\text{Total menu revenue (Box J)}}{\text{Number sold (Box N)}} = \frac{\$21,606.50}{2000} = \underline{\$10.80}$$

D. *Fixed Cost Percentage plus Profit Percentage:*

To determine the fixed cost percentage plus profit percentage, one must understand the basic profit equation:

$$\text{Revenue} - \text{Costs} = \text{Profit}$$

There are three types of costs:
- food costs (a variable cost)
- nonfood variable costs[4]
- fixed costs[5]

---

[4] Examples of nonfood variable costs include controllable expenses such as labor (salaries, wages, and benefits), direct operating expenses, music and entertainment, and marketing.
[5] Examples of fixed costs include rent, occupation costs, interest, and depreciation.

Said another way, then:

$$\text{Revenue} - [\text{Food} + \text{Nonfood} + \text{Fixed}] = \text{Profit}$$
$$\text{costs} \quad \text{variable costs} \quad \text{costs}$$

We can revise the above equation for the purposes of menu goal value analysis as follows:

$$\text{Revenue} - [\text{Food} + \text{Nonfood}] = \text{Fixed costs} + \text{Profit}$$
$$\text{costs} \quad \text{variable costs}$$

The goal value analysis model requires that the elements in this equation be expressed as a percentage.

- Revenue is 100 percent. The total of all costs must be less than revenue (100 percent) if there is to be a profit.
- The food cost percentage in Figure 9-4 can be easily calculated:

$$\text{Food cost percentage} = \frac{\text{Menu costs (Box I)}}{\text{Menu revenue (Box J)}} = \frac{\$\ 8{,}358.50}{\$21{,}606.50} = 38.7\% \text{ (rounded)}$$

- The menu planner's nonfood variable costs cannot be determined from information in Figure 9-4. The income statement must be studied to obtain this information.[6] Let's assume that the income statement shows nonfood variable costs (all available costs *except* food) of 31 percent.

We can now calculate the menu's fixed cost percentage plus profit percentage:

$$\text{Revenue} - [\text{Food cost} + \text{Nonfood}] = \text{Fixed cost} + \text{Profit}$$
$$\text{percentage} \quad \text{percentage} \quad \text{variable} \qquad \text{percentage} \quad \text{percentage}$$
$$\text{cost percentage}$$

$$100\% - [38.7\% + 31.0\%] = 30.3\%$$

Now let's use the four elements we have calculated to determine the total menu goal value:

| Contribution margin percentage | x | Average number items sold | x | Check average | x | Fixed cost percentage plus profit percentage |
|---|---|---|---|---|---|---|
| 61.1% | x | 333.3 | x | $10.80 | x | 30.3% = |

$$\underline{\underline{666.4}} \text{ (rounded)}$$

---

[6] For more information about the income statement, see R. Schmidgall et al., *Restaurant Management Basics: Financial Management.* New York: John Wiley & Sons, Inc., 2002.

Note that the total menu goal value has been calculated to be 666.4. This is a numerical goal that is neither a dollar amount nor a percentage. It is, instead, a numerical score to help the menu planners evaluate the menu. Menu items whose specific goal value equal or exceed 666.4 will, then, have a profitability that equals or exceeds that of the total (average) menu.

## Using Goal Value Analysis Components

Figure 9-11 calculates the goal value for each of the six menu items noted in Figure 9-4.

Recall that to undertake goal value analysis for each menu item, the following four elements must be known:

- Contribution margin percentage
- Number of items sold
- Item selling price
- Fixed cost percentage and profit percentage

Two of these, the number of each item sold and the item selling price, require no calculations. The number of items sold is a simple tally of the sales volume of each menu item for a recent fiscal period. The item selling price can be taken right from the menu. The remaining two elements required for goal value analysis (contribution margin percentage and fixed cost and profit percentage) must be calculated; the worksheet in Figure 9-11 helps with this calculation.

Let's look at the first menu item (beef stew) to see how the contribution margin percentage and fixed cost and profit percentage are calculated. To calculate the item's contribution margin percentage (column D), the menu planners must divide the item contribution margin (column B) by its selling price (column C). For example, the contribution margin percentage for beef stew is 59 percent ($5.90 divided by $10.00). Note that the item contribution margin (column B) is calculated by subtracting the item's food cost from its selling price. This is done in column F of Figure 9-4; it can also be calculated from the data in Figure 9-11 (menu item selling price [$10 in column C] less item

food cost [$4.10 in column G]).

To calculate the fixed cost and profit percentage for each item in Figure 9-11, it is necessary to know the food cost percentage and the nonfood variable cost percentage. To calculate the food cost percentage, the menu planners must divide the food cost by the item's selling price. For example, to calculate the food cost percentage for beef stew in Figure 9-11, the menu planners divide the item's food cost ($4.10 in column G) by its selling price ($10.00 in column C).

How does one calculate the food cost (column G)? It is the cost listed in column D in the menu-engineering worksheet (Figure 9-4). It can also be calculated by adding the per-portion food cost for all of the menu components (entrées, vegetable, potato choice, and so on) of the menu item when they are prepared according to standard recipes that have been precosted with current food costs.

The nonfood variable cost percentage (column I) in Figure 9-11 is determined by the menu planners when they review a current income (profit and loss) statement. The total food cost percentage and nonfood cost variable percentage (column J) is calculated by adding the food cost percentage (column H) and the nonfood variable cost percentage (column J). For example, in the worksheet above, the menu planners add the food cost percentage (41 percent in column H) to the nonfood variable cost percentage (31 percent in column I) to yield the total food cost/nonfood cost variable percentage (72 percent in column J).

Once the total food cost percentage and nonfood cost variable percentage (column J) are known, the menu planners can calculate the fixed cost and profit percentage: Total revenue percentage (100 percent in column F) minus the total food cost percentage and nonfood cost variable percentage (72 percent in column J) equals the fixed cost and profit percentage (28 percent in column K). Data from Figure 9-11 can then be used to calculate the specific goal value for each menu item. This is shown in Figure 9-12.

| | Contribution Margin | | | | | Fixed Cost plus Profit Percentage (FCP%) | | | | | |
| Menu Item | Item CM | Selling Price | Item CM Percentage | Number Sold | Total Revenue % | Food Cost Percentage | | Nonfood Variable Cost Percentage | Total Food Cost Percentage and Nonfood Cost Variable Percentage | Fixed Cost Percentage and Profit Percentage | |
| | | | | | | Food Cost | Food Cost Percentage | | | | |
| | | | B÷C | | | | G÷C | | H+I | F–J | |
| (A) | (B) | (C) | (D) | (E) | (F) | (G) | (H) | (I) | (J) | (K) |
| 1. Beef stew | $5.40 | $10.00 | 59 | 350 | 100 | $4.10 | 41 | 31 | 72 | 28 |
| 2. Chow mein | 6.85 | 11.25 | 61 | 210 | 100 | 4.40 | 39 | 31 | 70 | 30 |
| 3. Ham and cheese sandwich | 5.70 | 10.50 | 54 | 100 | 100 | 4.80 | 46 | 31 | 77 | 23 |
| 4. BLT sandwich | 7.60 | 12.50 | 61 | 450 | 100 | 4.90 | 39 | 31 | 70 | 30 |
| 5. Hamburger platter | 7.00 | 11.45 | 61 | 510 | 100 | 4.45 | 39 | 31 | 70 | 30 |
| 6. Chicken sandwich | 5.75 | 8.50 | 68 | 380 | 100 | 2.75 | 32 | 31 | 63 | 27 |

*Figure 9-11.* Goal Value Analysis Data Worksheet for Six Menu Items

Figure 9-12. **Results of Goal Value Analysis for Six Menu Items**

| Menu Item (A) | Contribution Margin Percentage (B) | Number Sold (C) | Selling Price (D) | Fixed Cost Percentage + Profit Percentage (E) | Goal Value (F) |
|---|---|---|---|---|---|
| 1 | 59 | 350 | $10.00 | 28 | 578.2 |
| 2 | 61 | 210 | 11.25 | 30 | 432.3 |
| 3 | 54 | 100 | 10.50 | 23 | 130.4 |
| 4 | 61 | 450 | 12.50 | 30 | 1029.4 |
| 5 | 61 | 510 | 11.45 | 30 | 1068.63 |
| 6 | 68 | 380 | 8.50 | 27 | 593.03 |

When reviewing Figure 9-12, note that the menu planners use information from Figure 9-11 to calculate the goal value of each item. For example, the contribution margin percentage (column B in Figure 9-12) is taken from column D in Figure 9-11; number sold (column C in Figure 9-12) is taken from column E in Figure 9-11; selling price (column D in Figure 9-12) is shown in column C in Figure 9-11; the fixed cost percentage plus profit percentage (column E in Figure 9-12) is shown in column K in Figure 9-11.

To calculate the goal value for each specific item (column F in Figure 9-12) the menu planners need only multiply contribution margin percentage (column B) by the number sold (column C), by the selling price (column D), by the fixed cost percentage plus profit percentage (column E). For example, to calculate the goal value of beef stew:

$$59\% \quad \times \quad 350 \quad \times \quad \$10.00 \quad \times \quad 28\% \quad = \quad 578.2$$

(column B)    (column C)    (column D)    (column E)    (column F)

Recall that the menu planners have calculated a total menu goal value of 666.4. This value, then, becomes the benchmark against which the goal value of each specific item in Figure 9-12 is measured. Items that are most profitable on the menu are those with a goal value equal to or above 666.4. Therefore, items 4 and 5 with goal values of, respectively, 1029.4 and 1068.63, are the most desired items. By contrast, item 3, with a goal value of 130.4, is the least-desired menu item. Items 1 and 6, with goal values of, respectively, 578.2 and 593.03, are somewhat below the total menu goal value, and item 2, with a goal value of 432.2, has even less profitability. Note that

the data from Figure 9-4 and from Figure 9-12 are very consistent. The similarity is not surprising because the information about product cost, selling price, and popularity used in both models are the same. For example, notice that in both instances, the items that the menu planners most want to sell are items 4 and 5 (they are Stars in the menu-engineering model) and the items with the highest goal value in the goal value analysis model. Likewise, item 3 is the least desired (it is a Dog), and it has the lowest goal value (130.4). Likewise, items 1 and 6 have similarities: they are both Plow Horses in menu engineering and have a similar goal value when goal value analysis is used. Finally, item 2 is similar in both models.

How do the menu planners use goal value analysis to evaluate and improve menus? Many of the procedures are the same as those used after menu engineering. For example, items with exceptionally high goal values should probably be managed in a way that is consistent with past practices: Neither purchase specifications, standard recipes, nor menu location should be changed. The same em-

phasis on suggestive selling and other point-of-sale techniques noted for Stars and Puzzles in the menu-engineering model can likewise be used. Procedures for managing Plow Horses (that is, increasing the contribution margin and shifting sales to more profitable items) are in order for items 1 and 6. Menu planners should consider tactics to increase the popularity of item 2 and, perhaps, the elimination of item 3.

## MENU EVALUATION: SOME FINAL THOUGHTS

This chapter has explored two objective methods (menu engineering and goal value analysis) to help evaluate menus. Neither of the methods provides a final and definite answer to the question: "What exactly can be done to improve the menu?" However, menu planners should be concerned about improving the menu and should try to assess how, if at all, the menu can be improved. To do anything less in the management of the single most important marketing and operational planning tool of a foodservice establishment will not allow the menu planners to achieve the two most important menu objectives: to satisfy those being served and to attain financial goals.

Unfortunately, some menu planners ignore menu evaluation. Reasons may include:

• They don't know how.
• They aren't aware of the importance of evaluation.
• They believe they understand "what the market wants."
• They don't want to change menus because "they have been successful in the past."
• They don't believe the time spent on the task is worth the required effort.

Wise menu planners recognize that these and other reasons for failing to evaluate menus will yield the same result: The foodservice establishment will have menus that diminish the likelihood that the operation can remain competitive (and almost all foodservice operations in both the commercial and noncommercial sectors have competitors!). Finding out what the guests want (menu planning) and determining how successful one has been in delivering what the guests want (menu evaluation) are two critical steps that no menu planner can overlook.

## SIGEE'S MENU: A CASE STUDY

"I'm not sure all the cooks have bought in 100 percent yet," said Samuel Ludwig, the executive chef at the full-service hotel that houses Sigee's restaurant, "but I think it's going to go great!"

"It" was the new menu being introduced at Sigee's. The result of a multistep process that included careful assessment of management's goals, guest preferences, equipment limitations, recipe evaluation, pricing strategies, evaluation of the existing menu, and extensive menu layout and design considerations, the "new" menu was in its final stages of production and would be placed into service on the first day of the next month.

Despite the fact that most of the work on the new menu was done, David Berger, the hotel's food and beverage director, knew that it was important to have everyone's enthusiastic support when the menu was actually launched. This final meeting of the menu planning committee was being held to address any concern the management staff had about the menu rollout, and to congratulate them publicly for a job well done.

"That's good to hear, Sam," replied David. "I want you all to know," he continued, "that I presented the menu to Peggy Sill and the rest of the hotel's Executive Operating Committee last week, and they absolutely love it. (Peggy Sill is the hotel's G.M, and it was at her request that the new menu project had been undertaken.) David was delighted that her response had been one of enthusiastic support, and he wanted to share that news with his food and beverage team.

"How about the dining room staff?" continued David.

"Well, I think some of the staff feel like the tips could be less because the menu prices are lower than before," said Reesie Davies, the dining room manager. Reesie had only recently joined the Sigee's staff, and David had appreciated her honesty and insightfulness during the entire menu redesign project.

"I can understand how they might feel that way," replied David. "And I think we need to address that with them, because I really do think we will see increased guest counts and sales, and that will make their tips go up, not down!"

"I agree," said Reesie. "And I also think it's important that we managers show our support for this menu. If we are proud of it, the staff will be also, and that's good for the guests! I've been watching some of the sample plates Samuel has been producing, and I think the guests will love them. I know if my staff saw the same thing, they would really get excited."

"Why not show 'em?" said Samuel. "My team has been working hard to perfect the taste and presentation of all the new items. I'm sure they would love to 'show off' a bit."

"That's a great idea!" said David. "We'll have a 'staff-only' menu tasting. I think it would go a long way toward making our service team, and our cooks, comfortable with the new concept. We'll hold it right here in the dining room."

David listened as the group excitedly finished the plans for the menu sampling. The redesign process, had, he believed, gone well. He was truly proud of the new Sigee's menu and the staff effort that had gone into the new re-design. The guest counts, he was sure, would go up, as would the profits. He could hardly wait to see the results!

*Author's note:* The new Sigee's menu was indeed introduced. The result was a sustained 40 percent increase in the restaurant's total sales within the first three months of its introduction.

## CHAPTER 10

# Learning by Example: Commercial and Noncommercial Menu Review

## CHAPTER OUTLINE

## MENU TERMS USED IN THIS CHAPTER

Blood alcohol concentration (BAC)
Folio

## CHAPTER OVERVIEW

It is not possible to present all of the variations in menus that commercial (for-profit) and noncommercial menu planners and designers use to communicate, inform, and sell to their guests. One reason is simply the vast number of food and beverage outlets providing products and services to a very wide range of guest markets. Another—and more important—reason is that menu planners are incredibly creative. While few, if any, menu planners develop completely "brand new" or never-before-seen menu concepts, many menus, if one looks carefully enough, contain something that is new and different from other menus.

Menu planners will always learn something new from at least some of the existing menus they review. Some menus may not represent a new way of presenting information, but have value because they reinforce a menu-planning principle or "truth" that should always be remembered. Menu planners who can evaluate existing menus and learn from them are assets to any foodservice operation.

In this chapter, we will examine a variety of commercial and noncommercial menus in order to illustrate points that have been discussed in this book. These representative menus have been selected to demonstrate how menu planners in both the commercial and noncommercial foodservice segments creatively (or sometimes inappropriately!) develop menus.

Many menu planners and others in the hospitality industry enjoy looking at different menus and asking questions such as these:

• Is there something here that I can use in my operation?

• Is there something here that I notice that causes a problem that might also appear in my menus?
• How would I improve this menu?
• What makes this menu appeal to guests?
• What, if anything, about this menu can be distracting for guests?
• Can I (or the guest) determine what items the planners of this menu *really* want to sell?

Our list of questions could continue. However, the point is that just as a menu in a specific operation continues to evolve, so should menu planners continue to learn more about this critical marketing and sales tool so that their own skills can evolve and improve. The menu used by a property should already be a "good" one; radical changes are not necessary for further improvements. Still, menu planners can practice their continuous quality improvement (CQI) efforts by making small changes that move them ever closer to an "ideal" menu—one appreciated by the guests and most profitable for the operation. (*Note:* menu engineering and menu goal value analysis were discussed in Chapter 9. They are examples of tactics that menu planners can use to update and assure that their most powerful in-home selling tool is as effective as it can be.)

In this chapter, we will highlight sections of commercial and noncommercial menus that present some important learning points. Most of the examples suggest positive tactics that menu planners might want to use in their own operation. Some, however, illustrate potential problems that menu planners should avoid.

## HOW TO BENEFIT FROM THIS CHAPTER

Review the information in this chapter carefully. Assess how it relates to the basic principles discussed earlier in the text. Think about points being made by the menu planners, who have popularity and profitability goals in mind, and at the same time consider the impact that the information will have on the guests. Careful study will help to enforce the learning points discussed here. As important, however, will be the development of the attitude that menu planning and design are critical, and that both the "small things" and the major problems can have a dramatic impact on a menu's success. This attitude should carry over to the ongoing question of every good menu planner: How can I improve the menu to make it better for my guests and for my operation?

We use "Key Learning Points" in this chapter to illustrate and describe some of the "dos and don'ts" of menu planning and design. As you review each figure and the discussion about it, recall how the "little things count" in effective menu planning and design. Most of the figures that follow the key learning points illustrate positive tactics that can improve menus. Some, however, present images that may distract from the menu's effectiveness. When planning and designing menus, remember the learning points of menus that use positive tactics and try to avoid those tactics that are not.

## KEY LEARNING POINTS—COMMERCIAL MENUS

### Learning Point One: Menus Can Be Used for On-Site Orders

This book has emphasized throughout that menus can be used for multiple purposes. We have noted, for example, that they can be used to communicate menu offerings ("what's available") to guests. As well, they can serve as a sales tool to help advertise those items the property desires to sell. They can also be used for off-site ordering (an example of a menu format that can be e-mailed or faxed to a restaurant by guests who place orders from remote sites is shown in Chapter 8).

Menus can also be used for on-site ordering, as illustrated by the example in Figure 10-1. In this property, guests who want a "serve-to-order" entrée from a pasta bar can pick up a pencil and a menu ordering form at the beginning of the serving line. (The property uses a modified scramble-type cafeteria system so that guests who want another item need not stand in line behind those ordering from the pasta bar.) As noted in Figure 10-1, guests can indicate the type of pasta, sauce, and toppings they desire. The menu order form is then given to a foodservice staff member who portions the preprepared ingredients that have been ordered.

Figure 10-1.  **Menu Order Form**

▼ ▼ ▼ ▼ ▼ ▼ ▼ ▼

Nº    9169

# River Cafe
# Pasta Bar

Pasta Type: _____

Please Circle Options

Sauce:

Marinara
Pesto Cream
Alfredo
Garlic Herb Butter

Toppings:

| | |
|---|---|
| Tomato | Chicken |
| Broccoli, | Italian Sausage |
| Red Onions | Daily Seafood |
| Mushrooms | White Wine |
| Zucchini | Fresh Garlic |
| Yellow Squash | Olive Oil |

Nº    9169

▲ ▲ ▲ ▲ ▲ ▲ ▲

Used with permission of Kellogg Hotel and Conference Center, Michigan State University, East Lansing, Michigan.

## Learning Point Two: Be Creative but Careful with Alcoholic Beverage Sales

Figure 10-2 shows a portion of a menu that features "Beer and Bevs." Menu planners have been creative in their packaging and promotion of "sampler packs." Many guests are likely to enjoy the opportunity to sample several relatively small portions of house beers. When reviewing Figure 10-2 consider the following:

• What is the size of the "sampler" glass that is sold for $0.75? Should the menu reader assume it is four ounces, since that is the size of the portions in the sample pack? Should serving size be stated?

• There is no "discount" for "volume" purchase. Note, for example, that an eight-sample pack priced at $6 is twice the cost of a four-sample pack priced at $3. Likewise, assuming the "sampler" glass priced at $0.75 is a four-ounce sample, it is priced at 25 percent of the four-sample pack's price of $3.

Menu planners in this operation have a tough problem: How can they encourage consumption (offering a "discount" might do that!) and at the same time encourage *responsible* drinking in efforts to manage the risks that can occur with excessive alcohol consumption.

**Figure 10-2. An Alcoholic Beverage Sampler Pack Menu**

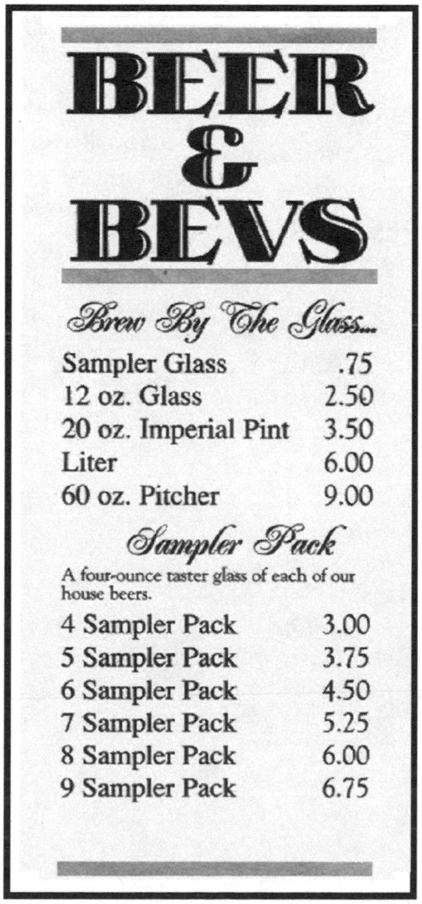

## BEER & BEVS

### Brew By The Glass...

| | |
|---|---|
| Sampler Glass | .75 |
| 12 oz. Glass | 2.50 |
| 20 oz. Imperial Pint | 3.50 |
| Liter | 6.00 |
| 60 oz. Pitcher | 9.00 |

### Sampler Pack

A four-ounce taster glass of each of our house beers.

| | |
|---|---|
| 4 Sampler Pack | 3.00 |
| 5 Sampler Pack | 3.75 |
| 6 Sampler Pack | 4.50 |
| 7 Sampler Pack | 5.25 |
| 8 Sampler Pack | 6.00 |
| 9 Sampler Pack | 6.75 |

Implementation of this menu must be tied closely to server training. For example, a guest who orders an eight-sample pack will consume 32 ounces of beer (8 samples at 4 ounces each). Information provided by the Distilled Spirit Council of the United States, Inc.,[1] indicates that a 160-pound person will have **a blood alcohol concentration (BAC)** of approximately 0.07 at the end of one hour if 32 ounces of beer are consumed. (This BAC represents the initial consumption, which must be reduced by approximately 0.02 during the 60-minute period.) In most jurisdictions, this BAC is below the limit for driving-while-intoxicated. However, persons who weigh less, who drink more or faster, or who also take medication, for example, fall within the BAC limits, and what shall be done if the guest orders a second sampler pack after quickly consuming the first one? A sampler pack of 32 ounces might be ordered and consumed by a group of guests, which will appreciably reduce potential problems associated with high BAC levels. You can see that menu planners are introducing the potential for abuse, lawsuits, and even physical harm to guests and others. Should the creative planning that led to this menu section be rethought? Probably! Is server training needed before this menu is implemented? Absolutely! Server training is necessary to consider the many potential problems that can arise when these sampler packs are ordered.

> *Glossary Terms*
> **Blood alcohol concentration (BAC).** The amount of alcohol in one's bloodstream. In many states, for example, a person with a BAC of 0.08 percent (8/100 of 1 percent) is considered legally drunk.

## Learning Point Three: Room Service Menus Are on In-Room Television

Technology has caught up with room service! Increasingly, hotels are allowing guests the option to order room service breakfast meals on their guestroom television sets. This interaction is similar to the opportunities that guests may have to use their in-room televisions to check their **folio** status during their stay and to check out at the end of their stay. While guests may some day order any meal in this manner, most properties today offer the service for breakfast only, since this menu is less complex than are lunch and dinner.

> *Glossary Terms*
> **Folio.** A financial statement maintained at the front desk that details all of a guest's transactions (payments and charges) since checking into the hotel.

Note that the property offering this option also allows guests to "place a pre-order for breakfast personally with one of our friendly sales representatives." Menu planners recognize that some guests may be less familiar with and more anxious about using technology for this purpose. To help maximize room-service revenues, the establishment encourages these guests to order with the traditional (telephone) method.

---

[1] Distilled Spirit Council of the United States, Inc. "Know Your Limits Chart," in: *Controlling Alcohol Risks Effectively (CARE)*. East Lansing, Mich.: Educational Institute of the American Hotel & Lodging Association, 1993.

Figure 10-3. *"Order-by-T.V." Room-Service Menu*

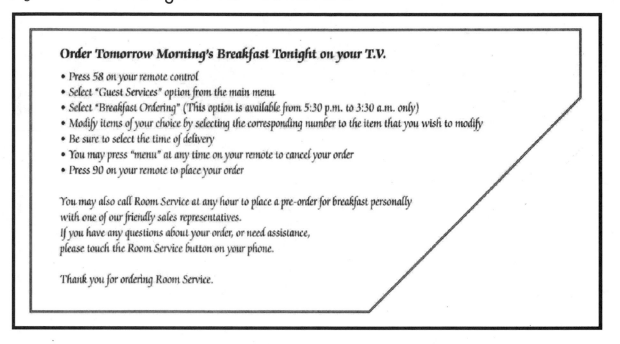

## Learning Point Four: Alert Guests About Spiced Foods

The range of guest preferences for spicy foods is from very mild (almost no seasonings) to as "spicy as you can make it." Figure 10-4 illustrates how one Asian restaurant recognizes and informs guests about a menu item's taste. Note, for example, that Bulgolgi is available in both a spicy and a less-spicy sauce. The menu further indicates that Daegi-Gogi-Bokum is "spicy" and the Kampungi is "mildly spicy." These descriptions, while subjective, can provide some help to guests. Does the property allow guests to sample sauces before ordering a particular entrée? If so, there will be further assurance that the guests will be pleased rather than displeased with the item offered.

Three other points about information provided on this menu can be noted:

- The "homemade Korean sauce" served with the Kalbee and Daegi-Gogi-Bokum might be described in order to better inform the readers about what they will receive.
- The descriptions about the menu items are helpful; if you were a guest unfamiliar with Korean food, would you want still more information?
- Recall from Chapter 5 that some menu planners believe that prices listed in a column separated from the menu item description focuses attention on the prices and away from the menu descriptions. What did you first notice on this menu? Does the listing of prices in this location negatively impact the menu? (Your responses to these questions may or may not differ from those of the guests reading the menu. However, menu planners should consider potential consequences of their decisions when the menu is designed.)

Figure 10-4.  **A Menu with Descriptions of "Spiciness"**

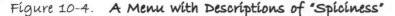

## Korean Dishes

**BULGOLGI.** 불고기 ...................................................................... 8.25
Thinly sliced beef marinated in homemade Korean sauce with green and
white onions. **(available in a spicy sauce)**

**KALBEE** 갈비 ........................................................................... 9.50
Beef short rib steak marinated in homemade Korean sauce.

**DAEGI-GOGI-BOKUM** (spicy) 돼지고기 볶음 ......................... 8.25
Sliced pork marinated with green peppers and onions in a hot sauce.

**KAMPUNGI** (mildly spicy) 깜풍기 ...................................... 7.25
Fried chicken wings in sweet and spicy sauce. **(Boneless $7.75) (Shrimp $9.75)**

### Learning Point Five: Team Up with Name Brands

Figure 10-5 illustrates a banner at the bottom of a menu that indicates the brand names of beverages served at the property. Guests will likely be familiar with many of these brands and should connect them with high quality. This connection with high quality should in turn give guests the impression that this is a "quality" property.

Note also that the property invites guests to learn about other draft beers available, and that the menu planners suggestively sell a "big beer draft" for an additional dollar. Will guests want to know the portion size of the "big beer draft?" Do they also need to know the portion size and selling price of the featured draft beers to make a decision about the value of the special (Big Beer Draft) being suggested? It does take space on the menu to indicate this type of information; however, it also takes the server's time to provide details. Menu planners must recognize this trade-off between menu space and server time. Both are valuable and limited. These are among the many details that must be considered as menus are planned.

Figure 10-5. Name Brands on a Beer Menu

### Learning Point Six: Sometimes Spelling Errors Are Acceptable!

We noted in Chapter 7 that menus must be carefully designed to professionally represent the property offering it. Menus must be proof-read, sometimes several times, for spelling and typographical errors. Sometimes, however, the intentional misspelling of words can be part of a restaurant's theme. Consider, for example, the menu in Figure 10-6, which has a "Hillbilly" theme. Here the misspelling of egg (aig) and biscuits (biskits) is part of that theme.

While reviewing Figure 10-6, consider whether menu readers will want to know the number of pieces of toast in the French Toast or the difference between a "½ order" and "full order" of griddle cakes. These omitted details may distract from the simple and "down-home" message that the menu planners are attempting to convey.

Figure 10-6. A Menu with Intentional Misspellings

### SAMMY'S BREAKFAST

| | |
|---|---|
| 1 Hen Aig | 2.25 |
| 2 Hen Aigs | 2.50 |
| Steak 'n Aigs | 3.85 |
| French toast | 2.85 |
| ½ Order griddle cakes | 2.00 |
| Full order griddle cakes | 2.50 |
| Sausage biskits | 1.95 |

### Menu Learning Point Seven: Banquet Guests Appreciate Menus

Many commercial operations allow guests at small banquet functions to order off the menu, which helps guests know what they will receive. However, as groups get larger, the need for a pre-established banquet menu becomes important. Today, with on-site desktop publishing increasingly available to properties of all sizes, it is no longer necessary to say "chicken" or "beef" when a guest asks a banquet server what is on the menu.

Figure 10-7 shows a banquet menu that is placed on a base plate or otherwise incorporated into the table setting for a banquet event. It can be placed under the guest's plate or can be folded and placed into a guest's pocket or purse for reference during the meal or as a take-home souvenir, if desired. What's on the menu? It depends on that menu course, and each item in each course is listed.

Figure 10-7.   **A Banquet Menu**

Used with permission of the University Club of Michigan State University, East Lansing, Michigan.

### Learning Point Eight: Cross-Sell; Capitalize on Common Names

Figure 10-8 shows a portion of a menu that invites guests to visit the property's bar. Nu- merous properties have "Mai-Tai," "Martini," and other bars named to evoke positive im- ages for the guests.

Figure 10-8. **A Menu that Uses a Common Name to Evoke a Positive Image**

> *Visit Our Mai Tai Bar*
> *for our World Famous Mai Tai*
>
> **mai tai bar**

### Learning Point Nine: Take-Home Menus Advertise Group Functions

Many properties make take-home menus available to guests. Generally, these menus inform guests about single meal (per guest) dining alternatives.

Figure 10-9 illustrates part of a take-home menu that focuses on the sale of banquet func- tions rather than à la carte dining. Note, for example, that the hosts of group functions are invited to purchase from a choice of three differ- ent entrées with accompaniments at three sepa- rate package prices. As well, two buffets with a choice of two entrées each are offered by the property for a minimum of 50 guests.

The information in Figure 10-9 is included as part of an attractive brochure with a map showing specific details about the restaurant's location and other necessary information (telephone number, an invitation to develop special plans for specific events, and the avail- ability of off-site catering), which will likely enable this property to generate new busi- ness from a new market of potential guests.

Figure 10-9.  **A Take-Home Menu for Single-Order Dinner Packages and Buffets**

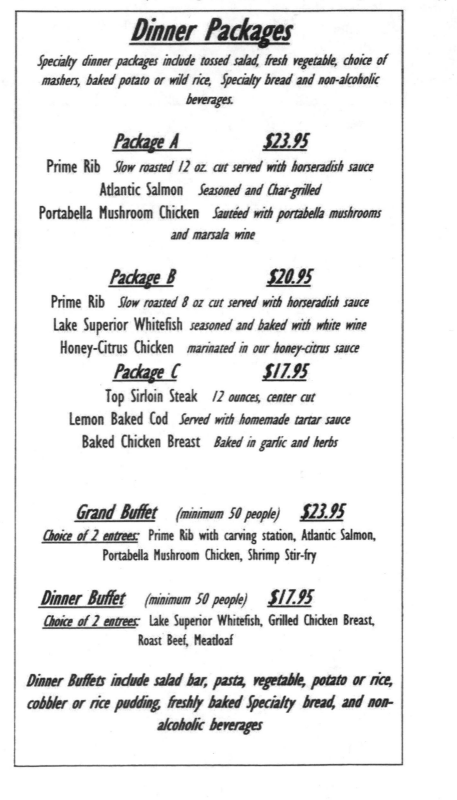

# Dinner Packages

*Specialty dinner packages include tossed salad, fresh vegetable, choice of mashers, baked potato or wild rice, Specialty bread and non-alcoholic beverages.*

### Package A                $23.95

Prime Rib  *Slow roasted 12 oz. cut served with horseradish sauce*

Atlantic Salmon  *Seasoned and Char-grilled*

Portabella Mushroom Chicken  *Sautéed with portabella mushrooms and marsala wine*

### Package B                $20.95

Prime Rib  *Slow roasted 8 oz cut served with horseradish sauce*

Lake Superior Whitefish  *seasoned and baked with white wine*

Honey-Citrus Chicken  *marinated in our honey-citrus sauce*

### Package C                $17.95

Top Sirloin Steak  *12 ounces, center cut*

Lemon Baked Cod  *Served with homemade tartar sauce*

Baked Chicken Breast  *Baked in garlic and herbs*

### Grand Buffet  *(minimum 50 people)*  $23.95

*Choice of 2 entrees:*  Prime Rib with carving station, Atlantic Salmon, Portabella Mushroom Chicken, Shrimp Stir-fry

### Dinner Buffet  *(minimum 50 people)*  $17.95

*Choice of 2 entrees:*  Lake Superior Whitefish, Grilled Chicken Breast, Roast Beef, Meatloaf

*Dinner Buffets include salad bar, pasta, vegetable, potato or rice, cobbler or rice pudding, freshly baked Specialty bread, and non-alcoholic beverages*

### Learning Point Ten: "Elaborate" Menus Can Be Simple

We noted in Chapter 7 that sufficient blank space must be provided on the menu so that it does not appear cluttered. Figure 10-10 is an example of the accompaniments section of an à la carte menu that illustrates this principle. This section (like others on the menu) is boxed in separate menu categories. Each self-explanatory item is listed without further description. (*Note:* Do you seem to focus on any area of this box when you gaze at the menu? If, for example, your eyes focus on the Fresh, Sautéed Mushrooms and Roquefort Mashed Potatoes, this may be the "prime real estate" area of the menu category box; the most popular and profitable accompaniments should be placed in this center area.)

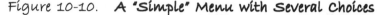

Figure 10-10.  A 'Simple' Menu with Several Choices

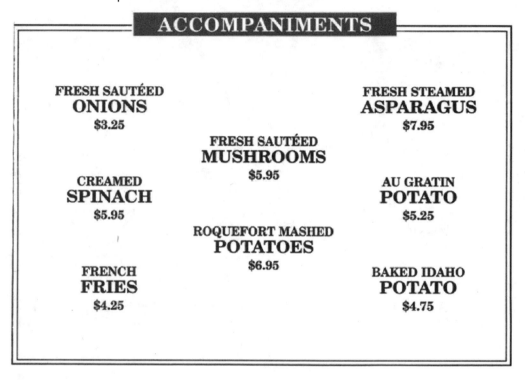

### Learning Point Eleven: Assure that Menus Are Readable

The menu in Figure 10-11 is not nearly as easy to read as the menu illustrated in Figure 10-10. This portion of the beverage menu is crowded and therefore difficult to read. It is good to let guests know about the extensive variety of products available, and the menu does this. At the same time, however, it can slow down service, as guests need more time than usual to read menu.

Figure 10-11.  **A Hard-to-Read Beverage Menu**

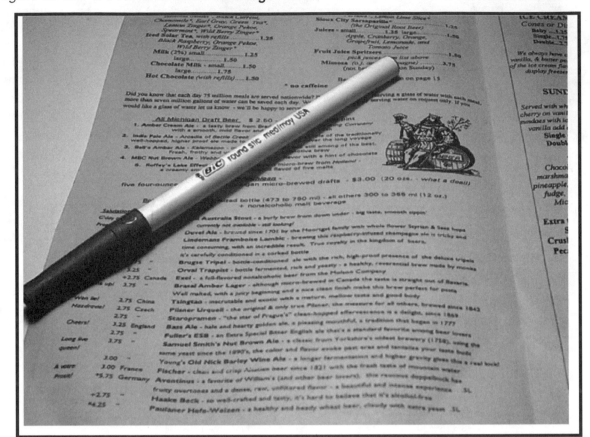

## Learning Point Twelve: Room-Service Menus Must Communicate!

All menus must, of course, communicate. However, room-service menus in hotels with guests from different countries have special challenges. Figure 10-13 illustrates part of a room-service menu designed to be placed on the room's exterior door handle. You will note that it is written in four languages (English, French, Spanish, and German) in efforts to make it easy for guests who speak these languages to order their breakfast without assistance.

Figure 10-12.  **A Key-Shaped Room-Service Menu**

## Learning Point Thirteen: Room Service Menus Can Sell Beverages

Figure 10-13 shows a portion of a room-service menu featuring red wine. Note the following important points:

- Wines are available in different portions (glass, bottle, and half-bottle).
- The pricing encourages the sale of bottles. (A 750-ml bottle of wine holds approximately five glasses. Note that it is a better value to buy a bottle than four or more glasses.)
- The government warning is clearly stated on the menu.
- Information is provided, including the telephone extension number (which makes it easy to order) and service charges and sales tax to be added to the check (which makes "communication problems" less likely).

Figure 10-13.  **A Room-Service Beverage Menu**

| Red | Glass/Bottle |
|---|---|
| Meridian Cabernet Sauvignon | $6.00/$22.00 |
| Robert Mondavi Coastal Cabernet | $7.50/$29.00 |
| Rosemount Estate Merlot | $6.50/$24.00 |
| Clos du Bois Merlot | $32.00 |
| | $21.00 Half Bottle |
| Robert Mondavi Coastal Pinot Noir | $5.75/$21.00 |
| St. Francis Old Vine Zinfandel | $37.00 |

GOVERNMENT WARNING: According to the Surgeon General, women should not drink alcoholic beverages during pregnancy because of risk of birth defects.

Beverages

( Ext. 1681

*A service charge and appropriate sales tax will be added to your check.*

## Learning Point Fourteen: Don't Forget the Children

Some restaurants use paper placemats to provide children's menus that include space for children's games. Figures 10-14 and 10-15 show, respectively, two graphics that can be part of the placemat: the menu and tic-tac-toe grids. Games will help keep the children occupied while waiting for their meals. As well, if the placemat is properly designed with the property's name, hours of operation, and address, the placemat can make an excellent take-home advertisement tool if additional copies are given to the families when they depart.

Figure 10-14. **Children's Menu**

**MEALS**     Children 12 years and under

| | |
|---|---|
| Dinosaur Nuggets | $2.95 |
| Kid's Cheeseburger w/fries | $2.95 |
| Corn Dog 'N' Fries | $2.95 |
| Tortilla Cheese Melt | $1.95 |
| Kid's Nachos | $2.95 |
| Cheese Pizza | $2.95 |
| Kid's Fish & Fries | $2.95 |

Figure 10-15. **Game on Children's Menu**

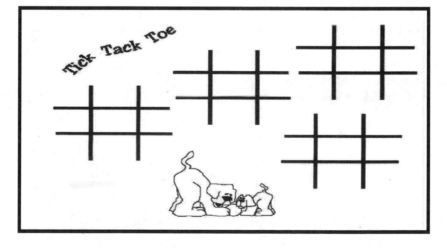

Tick Tack Toe

## Learning Point Fifteen: The Menu Can Cross-Sell Properties

We have suggested throughout this book that menus can help to sell other products, services, and meal periods within a property. They can also promote, or "cross-sell," the operation itself. Figure 10-16 shows part of a take-home menu for "Tony's" (a fictitious restaurant) that lists the addresses and telephone numbers for all the properties that are part of that multiunit restaurant organization. With today's increased travel within cities and regions, a guest enjoying a meal at a Tony's property in one community might well be interested in visiting another location in another community.

Figure 10-16.  **A Menu that Cross-Sells the Foodservice Operation**

**SAGINAW:** Address: xxxxxxxx / Phone: xxx-xxx-xxxx
**BRIGHTON:** Address: xxxxxxxx / Phone: xxx-xxx-xxxx
**LUBBOCK**: Address: xxxxxxxx / Phone: xxx-xxx-xxxx
**TROY**: Address: xxxxxxxx / Phone: xxx-xxx-xxxx
**DETROIT:** Address: xxxxxxxx / Phone: xxx-xxx-xxxx
            Address: xxxxxxxx / Phone: xxx-xxx-xxxx
**RHINELANDERS:** Address: xxxxxxxx / Phone: xxx-xxx-xxxx
**OKEMOS**: Address: xxxxxxxx / Phone: xxx-xxx-xxxx
**YPISLANTI**: Address: xxxxxxxx / Phone: xxx-xxx-xxxx

### Learning Point Sixteen: Menus Can Relate Your Nutrition Concerns

We discussed in Chapter 6 the growing interest among guests for nutritious meals. Figure 10-17 shows menu wording that communicates the menu planners' concern for their guests' nutrition.

Figure 10-17.  **A Menu Section that Conveys Nutrition Information**

FOR YOUR HEALTH & DINING PLEASURE
— WE USE CHOLESTEROL-FREE —

HOT DOG BUNS
HAMBURGER BUNS
BREADS

AND

SUPREME FRY-ON CORN & CANOLA OIL
(LOW IN SATURATED FATS)

### Learning Point Seventeen: All Menus Should Reflect the Operation

The importance of the menu as the primary marketing and advertising tool for the food and beverage operation has been stated consistently throughout this book. Figure 10-18 shows a graphic reproduced on the cover of a take-home menu. The menu itself appeared copied from the menu used in the à la carte dining restaurant of the same property, which has a good menu and excellent food and beverage products and service. The copied menu does not accurately portray the appropriate image to guests who order take out. If they haven't eaten in the main restaurant, they might judge the property by this menu alone.

All menu planners should objectively look at the menus used for all dining venues and ask, "Does this menu portray my foodservice operation in a professional manner?"

Figure 10-18. **A Poorly Reproduced Take-Home Menu**

### Learning Point Eighteen: Fax Menus Encourage Sales

Food and beverage operations are increasingly using their fax machines to advertise their property, and their menu is the medium. In Chapter 8 we noted that an increasing number of restaurants allow guests to fax in their orders for later pick-up or delivery. Our current learning point addresses the reverse of this; restaurants can, for example, fax copies of their lunch or other menus to nearby office buildings. Figure 10-19 shows an example; a sandwich operation has faxed a listing of individual sandwiches and group lunch menus to encourage lunch sales of these items.

When reviewing Figure 10-19 and its excellent concept, note also the spelling of "Oatmeal Raison" (should be "Oatmeal Raisin") in the cookie tray offering. This type of error must be caught and corrected before distributing the menu.

Figure 10-19.  **Faxable Menu**

### Learning Point Nineteen: Menus Should Provide Necessary Information

While this learning point is obvious, it is sometimes overlooked. Figure 10-20 shows an example of helpful information. You will note, for example, the "steak ordering guide"; a statement about credit cards, personal property, and minimum checks; and another statement about gratuities (from a menu marketed to international travelers that has been written in five languages).

Figure 10-20. A Menu that Provides Important Information

**STEAK ORDERING GUIDE** ▶ RARE—very red, cool center, MEDIUM RARE—red, warm center, MEDIUM—hot, pink center, MEDIUM WELL—slightly pink center, WELL—cooked throughout, no pink.

SORRY — NO CREDIT CARDS
NOT RESPONSIBLE FOR PERSONAL PROPERTY
MINIMUM CHECK $12.50 PER PERSON

We are often asked about gratuities...No service charge or gratuity has been added to your bill. Quality service is customarily acknowledged by a gratuity of 15%. Parties of 6 or more, the gratuity is included. Thank you.

On nous questionne souvent au sujet du pourboire... Aucun service ou pourboire n'a été ajouté à votre addition. Un service de qualité est généralement récompensé par un pourboire de 15%. Pour les tables de 6 ou plus, le service est déjà inclus dans le total. Merci.

Con frecuencia nos preguntan sobre las propinas. No añadimos a su factura ni el servicio ni las propinas. Es costumbre gratificar al camarero con un 15% sobre la factura por la calidad de su servicio. La propina para grupos de 6 personas ó más está incluida, gracias.

Wir werden oft auf Trinkgelder angesprochen: In Ihrer Rechnung ist kein Trinkgeldzuschlag enthalten. Es ist jedoch landesweit üblich, 15% des Rechnungsbetrages als Trinkgeld zu gewähren. Ab einer Gruppe von 6 Personen ist der Trinkgeldzuschlag bereits in Ihrer Rechnung enthalten. Vielen Dank.

チップに関して：サービスチャージは、
伝票に含まれておりませんが、良好なサービスに対して
15%のチップを支払って頂くのが習慣となっております。
6名様以上の場合は、料金の中にチップは含まれ
ております。有難うございます。

### Learning Point Twenty: Menus Should Provide Food-Safety Information

Laws in some states require that guests be alerted to potential food-borne illness concerns associated with certain menu items. Examples of wording include:

- "Consuming raw or undercooked meats, poultry, seafood, shellfish, or eggs may increase your risk of food-borne illness."
- "Consuming raw or undercooked meats, poultry, seafood, shellfish, or eggs may increase your risk of food-borne illness, especially if you have certain medical conditions."
- "Regarding the safety of these items, written information is available upon request."
- "When eating out or cooking at home, thorough cooking of foods of animal origin reduces the risk of food-borne illness."

It is important that menu planners comply with applicable requirements. To do this, of course, it is necessary that adequate space be allocated on the menu for this food safety information. The use of an asterisk (*) or other symbol will likely be required to direct guests to footnotes.

### Learning Point Twenty-One: Allow Your Menu to Make a Quality Statement.

Menu planners hope to develop a menu that consistently offers quality products and services to guests. Menus can subtly deliver this message of quality through their creative, well-thought-out, and accurately portrayed listings of menu items. It is also possible, however, to make an overt statement about quality, as shown in Figure 10-21. Note that it makes a quality promise about food, beverages, and service. It also makes a pledge of genuine concern about the dining experience and the property's reputation.

Figure 10-21. A Menu's Quality Statement

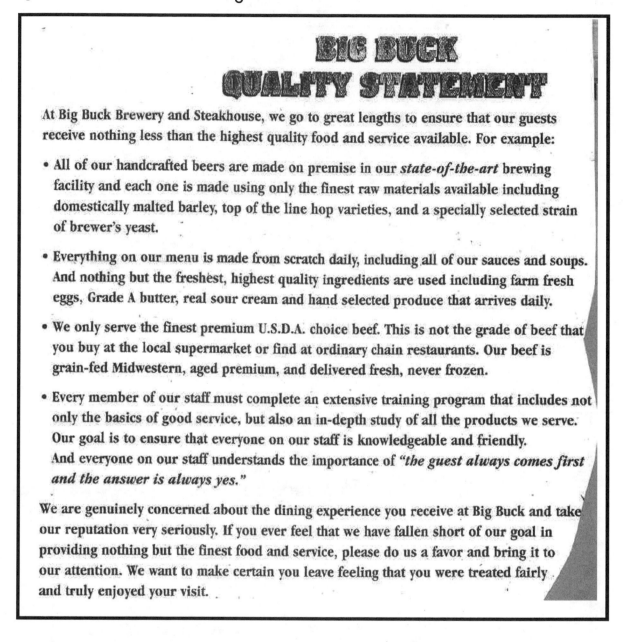

## BIG BUCK QUALITY STATEMENT

At Big Buck Brewery and Steakhouse, we go to great lengths to ensure that our guests receive nothing less than the highest quality food and service available. For example:

- All of our handcrafted beers are made on premise in our *state-of-the-art* brewing facility and each one is made using only the finest raw materials available including domestically malted barley, top of the line hop varieties, and a specially selected strain of brewer's yeast.

- Everything on our menu is made from scratch daily, including all of our sauces and soups. And nothing but the freshest, highest quality ingredients are used including farm fresh eggs, Grade A butter, real sour cream and hand selected produce that arrives daily.

- We only serve the finest premium U.S.D.A. choice beef. This is not the grade of beef that you buy at the local supermarket or find at ordinary chain restaurants. Our beef is grain-fed Midwestern, aged premium, and delivered fresh, never frozen.

- Every member of our staff must complete an extensive training program that includes not only the basics of good service, but also an in-depth study of all the products we serve. Our goal is to ensure that everyone on our staff is knowledgeable and friendly. And everyone on our staff understands the importance of *"the guest always comes first and the answer is always yes."*

We are genuinely concerned about the dining experience you receive at Big Buck and take our reputation very seriously. If you ever feel that we have fallen short of our goal in providing nothing but the finest food and service, please do us a favor and bring it to our attention. We want to make certain you leave feeling that you were treated fairly and truly enjoyed your visit.

Used with permission of Big Buck Restaurant, Grand Rapids, Michigan.

### Learning Point Twenty-Two: Sell! Sell! Sell! (Even on a Cocktail Napkin)

Figure 10-22 illustrates how a fictitious restaurant uses a menu on its beverage napkin to sell appetizers. Note how the napkin appears when it is closed—it looks like any other beverage napkin. When opened, though, the napkin reveals a list of appetizers. As guests enjoy their before-dinner beverage they will also likely see and react positively to this creative point-of-sale selling tool. Is the point being made just a minor one? No, because it suggests that several minor improvements can have a major impact on an operation's success.

Figure 10-22.  **An Innovative Beverage Napkin**

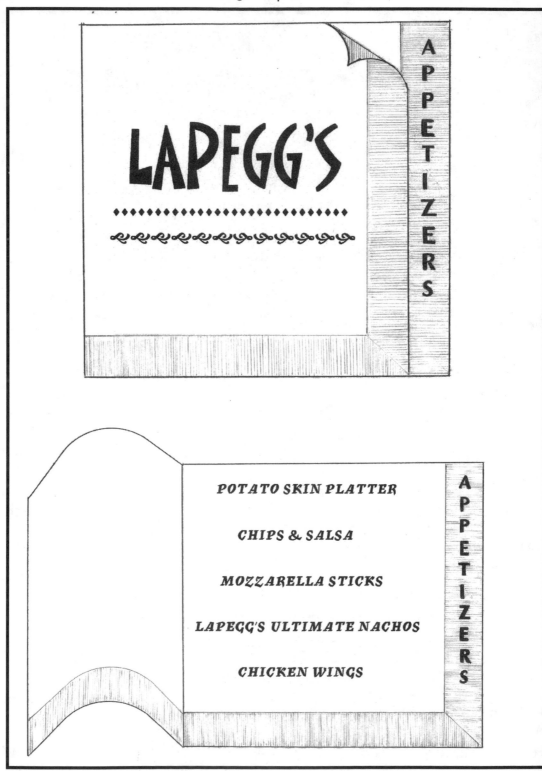

Drawing Courtesy of Lani Sill, Hilo, Hawaii

## KEY LEARNING POINTS—NONCOMMERCIAL MENUS

As stated earlier in this chapter, menu planners can learn what to do—and, sometimes, what not to do—when they carefully study menus. The examples already given in this chapter suggest the types of details that should be looked at and addressed in commercial menus. We will next review menus used in noncommercial facilities.

Throughout this book we have emphasized that there are many more similarities than dissimilarities in menu-planning activities for commercial establishments and for noncommercial foodservice operations. For example, the important purposes of the menu as a list of available items and as a physical tool to communicate the availability of items to guests are the same in commercial operations and in noncommercial ones. Likewise, the menu-planning steps are the same, beginning with thinking first about guests, product quality, operating resources, and financial goals; then selecting menu categories and items in each category while establishing standards for each menu item.

Procedures for the design of the physical menu—when used—are also the same. For example, menu boards used in cafeteria operations should be designed according to the same principles used to design menu boards in, for example, quick-service properties. As well, à la carte menus in sit-down commercial restaurants and in executive dining rooms in the business and industry segment will be very similar.

In all cases, the physical menu, however it is presented, should always be an evolving medium for the message. Continual improvements to the menu to address changes in guests' preferences is always necessary.

As in commercial operations, menu planners for noncommercial establishments must be concerned with details. Almost every menu can be improved. It is, therefore, an ongoing challenge for menu planners to evaluate what to improve and to implement those improvements. The process described for commercial operations—that is, to stay alert for new menu ideas and be able to recognize them—is just as important in the noncommercial sector. Experienced menu planners should review menus offered by other noncommercial operations and by those in the commercial sector as they look for new ideas that might improve their own menus. The remainder of this chapter presents learning points applicable to noncommercial menus. Since there are no "secrets" in foodservices of any type, it is hoped that the generic ideas suggested will benefit most foodservice operations.

### Learning Point Twenty-Three: Menus Can and Should Be Appealing

Unfortunately, some observers of the noncommercial foodservices industry have an incorrect and negative stereotype of the industry. They perceive these operations as "stainless steel islands" (unattractive cafeteria lines in public areas)—with a "captive" audience that has few, if any, dining alternatives (which encourages mediocrity in foodservice management)—that de-emphasizes financial concerns (since budgeted deficits will pick up the slack). In fact, experts realize that these and related perceptions are totally inaccurate. Menu planners and other managers in noncommercial foodservices are just as concerned about the same basic types of goals as are their peers in commercial foodservices.

Figure 10-23a through 10-23d show physical menus offered by one contract foodservice management company in one healthcare facility. You will note that these menus are just as attractive and creative in their design and content as are the most attractive hotel or restaurant menus.

Figure 10-23a.  **A Package of Catering Menus Available to the Facility's Clients**

Used with permission of AVI Foodsystems, Inc., Warren, Ohio.

Figure 10-23b. **A Catering Menu for a Sit-Down Lunch or Dinner**

AVI FOODSYSTEMS

*Catering Menus*

**First Course**
Lobster Bisque
En Croute

**Second Course**
Belgian Endive and
Goat Cheese Salad with a Hundred
Year old Balsamic Vinaigrette

**Third Course**
Walnut and Stilton Blue
Cheese Crusted Filet Mignon
Wild Mushroom Risotto
Oven Roasted Winter Vegetables

**Fourth Course**
Lemon Berry Linzer Tart with
Black Berry Coulis

Used with permission of AVI Foodsystems, Inc., Warren, Ohio.

Figure 10-23c.   **Hors D'oeuvre Selections**

AVI FOODSYSTEMS

*Catering Menus*

## Hors D'oeuvre Selection

___*Atlantic Blue Crab Tarts*
*Blue Crab and Fresh Herbs Tossed in Garlic butter Served in a Phyllo Shell*

___*Brie and Raspberries*
*French Brie and Fresh Raspberries Wrapped in Phyllo and baked*

___*Portabella Mushroom Tarts*
*Portabella Mushrooms and Imported Cheeses Baked and Served in a Phyllo Shell*

___*Smoked Chicken Quesadilla*
*Smoked Grilled Chicken and Zesty Mexican Cheese Rolled in a Flour Tortia*

___*Mini Cal zone Triangles*
*Mini Puff Pastry Triangles Filled with a Blend of Italian Cheeses and Sauce*

___*Spicy Cheese and Salsa Tarts*
*Monterey Jack Cheese and Spicy Salsa Baked in a Phyllo Tart Shell*

___*Mini Quiche Lorain's*
*Assorted Mini Quiche Flavored with Bacon and Cheddar, Broccoli and Swiss*

___*Lobster and Mushroom En Crout*
*Bites of Lobster and Wild Mushrooms Sautéed in Garlic Rolled in Puff Pastry*

___*Artichokes and Cheese Tarts*
*Marinated Artichokes and Herbed Cheese Baked in a Phyllo Shell*

Used with permission of AVI Foodsystems, Inc., Warren, Ohio.

Figure 10-23d. **Hors D'oeuvres for Group Functions**

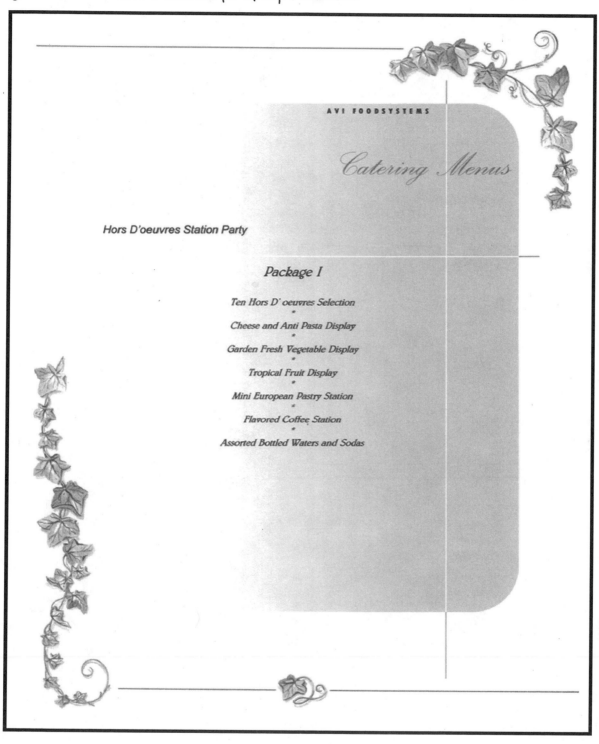

AVI FOODSYSTEMS

*Catering Menus*

Hors D'oeuvres Station Party

*Package I*

*Ten Hors D' oeuvres Selection*

*Cheese and Anti Pasta Display*

*Garden Fresh Vegetable Display*

*Tropical Fruit Display*

*Mini European Pastry Station*

*Flavored Coffee Station*

*Assorted Bottled Waters and Sodas*

Used with permission of AVI Foodsystems, Inc., Warren, Ohio.

Figure 10-23d   **(continued)**

AVI FOODSYSTEMS

*Catering Menus*

Hors D'oeuvres Station Party

## Package VI

Seafood Display Station

*

Choice of Two Chef Carved Item

*

Chef Grilling Station

*

Chef Sautee Station

*

Ten Hors D'oeuvres Selection

*

Cheese and Anti Pasta Station

*

Glazed Apricot Mustard Kosher Salami

*

Whole Baked Glazed Brie Wrapped in Puff Pastry

*

Fresh Tropical Fruit Display

*

Mini European Pastry Station

*

Gourmet Flavored Coffee Station

*

Selection of Bottled Beverages and Sodas

These figures show a large range of offerings and innovative marketing of products and services that are just as impressive as those of commercial foodservices. For example, the foodservice operation

- provides products for vending machine units throughout the healthcare campus,
- offers products and services for elegant parties hosting heads of state (who might be residents at the facility for several months or longer),
- offers and creatively advertises products for departmental meetings and parties,
- accepts credit cards,
- allows customers to e-mail or fax pizza orders and prepares the products and delivers them to the department (the healthcare campus is eight square blocks in size), and
- offers sit-down and cafeteria services at several locations throughout the healthcare campus.

Consumers in many types of noncommercial foodservices have dining alternatives ranging from competitors within the facility (a quick-service franchise operation located in the same building as the self-operated foodservice program, for example), to nearby commercial foodservice operations, to vending machines, to bringing their meals from home. Therefore, menu planners in these facilities must be just as creative in attracting and retaining their base of foodservice customers.

### Learning Point Twenty-Four: Menus Can and Should Be Exciting

Figure 10-24 illustrates a menu developed by a for-profit contract management company for use in a business and industry foodservice operation. It is available in both hard copy format and electronically. Note that for each of the five work days, daily specials are listed for several of the following menu item categories:

- Morning editions (entrée)
- A luncheon special (market carvery)
- Nutritious (balanced-choice alternative)
- Sandwich special
- Sandwich wrap (grill special)
- Daily soup special
- Italian cuisine special
- Other items ("menutainment," "panini fresca," and "wild greens")

Figure 10-24.  **A Business and Industry Cafeteria Menu**

## SAP America Café

Menu for week of:
June 18, 2001

COMPASS
GROUP

### Monday

*Today's Soup*

Eurest

| | | |
|---|---|---|
| Monday | | |
| Seafood Okra Gumbo | | |
| $1.59/1.89/2.29 | | |

| | | |
|---|---|---|
| **Morning Editions:** | Vanilla French Toast | $2.49 |
| **Market Carvery:** | Hearty Beef Stew | $3.29 |
| **Nurture Our World:** | Baked Fish with Lemon Pepper Crumbs | $3.99 |
| **Sandwich Central:** | Italian Deli Sub Romeo | $4.29 |
| **Wrap-a-bles:** | Southern Fried Chicken Wrap | $4.29 |
| **The Fresh Grille:** | Shaved Smoked Ham, Cheese & Tomato | $4.29 |
| Menutainment! | Spicy Buffalo Chicken Salad | $4.99 |

Tuesday
Pasta Fagoli
$1.29/1.59/1.99

### Tuesday

Wednesday
Iowa Corn Chowder
$1.29/1.59/1.99

| | | |
|---|---|---|
| **Morning Editions:** | Corned Beef Hash & Poached Egg | $2.99 |
| **Market Carvery:** | Chicken Cordon Bleu | $3.59 |
| **Terra Ve:** | *New* Vegan Mushroom Casserole | $3.29 |
| **Sandwich Central:** | Smoked Turkey Baguette Club | $4.29 |
| **Panini Fresca:** | Fresh Mozzarella, Tomato, Basil | $4.29 |
| **The Fresh Grille:** | Open Faced Roast Beef Sandwich | $4.79 |
| **Origins:** | Szechwan Green Beans & Beef | $4.79 |

Thursday
Mushroom Beef Barley
$1.29/1.59/1.99

Friday
New England Clam
Chowder
$1.59/1.89/2.29

### Wednesday

Chili Available Daily
$1.79/2.09/2.49

| | | |
|---|---|---|
| **Morning Editions:** | Smoked Bacon & Cheese Omelet | $3.29 |
| **Market Carvery:** | Creole Jambalaya | $3.59 |
| **Nurture Our World:** | Morroccan Chicken with Cous Cous | $3.79 |
| **Sandwich Central:** | Maple Ham, Smoked Gouda, Bacon Kaiser | $4.29 |
| **Wrap-a-bles:** | Fajita Chicken Wrap | $4.59 |
| **The Fresh Grille:** | Cowboy Steak with Tumbleweed Onions | $4.79 |
| Menutainment! | Mu Shu Pork Wrap | $5.29 |

*Trattoria*

| | | |
|---|---|---|
| Monday | | |
| Three Cheese Pizzette | | |
| $2.59 | | |

### Thursday

Tuesday
Sicilian Pepperoni & Plum
Tomato
$2.99

| | | |
|---|---|---|
| **Morning Editions:** | Blueberry Pancakes (3) | $2.49 |
| **Market Carvery:** | Tender Beef Liver & Onions | $2.99 |
| **Nurture Our World:** | Pork Loin with Roasted Peppers & Penne | $4.29 |
| **Sandwich Central:** | Smoked Salmon, Bermuda Onion and Tomato | $4.99 |
| **Wrap-a-bles:** | Athens Vegetarian Wrap | $4.29 |
| **The Fresh Grille:** | Grilled Corned Beef Rueben | $4.59 |
| Menutainment! | Ali's Chicken Curry | $5.29 |

Wednesday
Sweet Italian Sausage
Pizzette
$2.99

Thursday
Mesquite Grilled Chicken
Pizzette
$3.29

### Friday

Friday
Grilled Veggie Pizzette
$2.99

| | | |
|---|---|---|
| **Morning Editions:** | Cat Fish & Cheese Grits | $3.29 |
| **Market Carvery:** | Battered Fried Fish | $3.59 |
| **Terra Ve:** | Tofu & Broccoli in Peanut Sauce | $3.29 |
| **Sandwich Central:** | Tarragon Chicken Salad Croissant | $4.29 |
| **Wrap-a-bles:** | *New* Turkey Bacon Club Wrap | $4.59 |
| **The Fresh Grille:** | Tuna Melt | $4.29 |
| **Wild Greens:** | Grilled Shrimp Lo Mein Salad | $5.29 |

A Balanced Choice

Note how the menu attracts the guest's attention to specific items with the "nurture our world" symbol, and with phrases and icons for "new" and "extra value." It is easy to see that guests who buy breakfast or lunch at the facility several times each week are not likely to be bored with a monotonous, unappealing, unexciting menu when they visit the SAP Cafeteria.

### Learning Point Twenty-Five: Use a Theme.

Figure 10-25 shows samples of on-site advertising that features menu items included in a "Field of Dreams" theme within a "creative cuisine" developed by a for-profit contract management company. Themes can also be noted in Figure 10-24, where menu items are listed within themes such as "market carvery," "nurture our world," "trattoria," "the fresh grill," and "menutainment." Diners, especially those who eat frequently at a foodservice operation, want variety; themes provide a structure within which menu varieties can be featured.

Figure 10-25. **Creative Menu Advertising**

Used with permission of AVI Foodsystems, Inc., Warren, Ohio.

## Learning Point Twenty-Six: "Show Your Guests Where to Go."

Noncommercial foodservice menu planners are just as concerned as their commercial counterparts about assuring that guests are aware of their location. An example of this is shown in Figure 10-26, which is an insert from a portfolio of banquet menus that is sent with

other information to meeting planners. It helps to emphasize the centralized location of the facility offering the meeting services. Figure 10-27 shows the locations for residence hall cafeterias offering "green" or "white" menus that essentially double students' menu choices. (See the next Learning Point, Twenty-Seven.)

Figure 10-26.  **Insert Showing a Facility's Location**

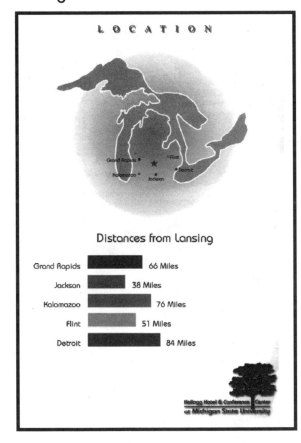

Used with permission of Kellogg Hotel and Conference Center, Michigan State University, East Lansing, Michigan.

Figure 10-27.  **Residence Hall Cafeteria Locations**

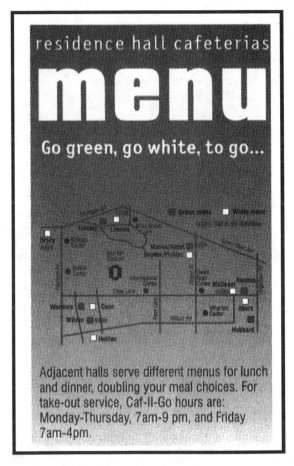

Used with permission of Division of Housing and Food Services, Michigan State University, East Lansing, Michigan.

## Learning Point Twenty-Seven: Double the Menu Choices

Figure 10-28 shows part of a "green and white" menu offered at a major university.

Menu planners have planned two cycle menus, each of which features different items. One menu (the green menu) is implemented in one residence hall, and the sec-

Figure 10-28.   **Cycle Menu Featuring Two Different Venues—"Green" or "White"**

| Tuesday • Feb 19 | Wednesday • Feb 20 | Thursday • Feb 21 | Frida... |
|---|---|---|---|
| **BREAKFAST** | | | |
| Eggs to Order, Sausage Pattie | Eggs to Order, Bacon | Eggs to Order, Smoked Sausage | Eggs to O... |
| Ham & Cheese Bagel | Egg Cheese Muffin ✲ | Caramel Apple Raisin French Toast | Biscuit wi... |
| Cranberry Biscuit Sticks ✲ | Blueberry Pancake/Hot Syrup ✲ ▼ | /Hot Syrup ✲! | Sausage/C... |
| Home Fries ✲ | Assorted Danish Butterflies | Hash Browns ✲, Blueberry Muffins | Home Fr... |
| Sweet Rolls, Jelly Donut | Cinnamon Sugar Fried Cakes | Glazed Plain Fried Cakes | Glazed St... |
| Banana Muffins | Carrot Muffins | Glazed Fried Cinnamon Rolls | Cherry A... |
| Chocolate Iced Cherry Fried Cakes | Apple Fritter | Cherry Almond Coffee Cake | Orange B... |
| **LUNCH • green** | | | |
| Beef Barley Soup ▼ 76K 2.0g | Matzo Ball Soup 97K 5.5g | Split Pea Soup ▼ 73K 1.5g | Clam Chow... |
| Cream of Cauliflower Soup ✲ 97K 5.9g | Lo Fat Minestrone Soup ✲ ▼ 108K 1.2g | French Onion Soup +60K 2.5g | Tabasco Sh... |
| Fish Nuggets/Dips +363K 27.0g | Tex-Mex Spicy Chicken Sand. 235K 7g | Italian Grinder | +320... |
| Szechuan Chicken Noodle | Corn Dog 194K 14.3g | Baked Spaghetti 388K 13.6g | Baked Fish... |
| Bacon Lettuce & Tomato Sandwich | Veggie Corn Dog ✲ ▼ 264K 6.1g | Breakfast Bar | Club Wrap... |
| 308K 16.3g | Tacos ±395K 22.3g | Baked Beans ✲ ▼ 191K 6.0g | Rotini & Ve... |
| Vegetarian Lentil Stew with | Nacho Bar ✲ ±448K 25.4g | Meatless Baked Spaghetti ✲▼ 248K 2.7g | Smiley Fri... |
| Rice ✲ ▼ 309K 0.6g | Red Beans & Rice ✲ ▼ 211K 1.4g | Seasoned Wedge Cut Fries ✲ 220K 16g | Veggie D'jo... |
|  | Veggie D'jour ✲ ▼ | Italian Green Beans ✲ ▼ | |
| **white** | | | |
| Cream of Broccoli Soup ✲ 155K 10.5g | Vegetable Beef Soup 75K 3.2g | Low Fat Minestrone Soup ✲▼ 108K 1.2g | Cream of T... |
| Navy Bean Soup ▼ 160K 5.0g | Pizza Calzone 435K 18.8g | Washington Chowder 103K 6.7g | Sour Crea... |
| Chicken Teriyaki Sandwich 250K 5g | General Tso's Chicken/ | Chimichanga 362K 25.0g | Baked Fish... |
| Beef Ravioli 284K 9.8g | Jasmine Rice 599K 23.3g | Hot Turkey Sandwich ▼ with Mashed | Grilled Ham... |
| Hot Dog Bar +220K 16.4g | Gourmet Cod/Baked Fish ±200K 13.4g | Potatoes ✲ ▼ and Gravy 367K 14.7g | Grilled Chee... |
| Hot Baked Beans/Sausage ▢ | Mushroom & Cheese Calzone | Bean Chimichanga ✲ 227K 13.0g | Veggie Chix... |
| Cheese Ravioli ✲ 284K 9.8g | ✲ 355K 13.8g | Koushari ✲ ▼ 294K 4.7g | Onion Petal... |
| Steak Fries ✲ 279K 14.7g | Asparagus ✲ ▼ 22K 0.3g | Nacho Bar✲ +448K 25.4g | Veggie D'jo... |
| Veggie D'jour ✲ | | Mexican Rice ✲ 150K 5.9g | |
| **DINNER • green** | | | |
| Soup D'jour | Soup D'jour | Homestyle Chicken Noodle Soup 75K 3.1g | Soup D'jo... |
| Lasagna 528K 23.9g | Golden Swiss Chicken 331K 18.3g | House Sub 522K 25.7g | Pasta Ba... |
| Grilled Rainbow Trout 234K 18.0g | French Dip ▼ 524K 16.4g | Cod Baked Florentine 416K 14.1g | Mozzarella... |
| Chicken Pattie Sandwich 371K 19.1g | Vegetable Wrapper ▼ ✲ 130K 2.7g | Beef Bulgogi/Sauteed Veggie | BC Chicken... |
| Vegetable Lasagna ✲ 301K 14.7g | Slim Fries ✲260K 20g | /Jasmine Rice 347K 15.1g | Baked Fish... |
| or Spinach Lasagna ✲ 293K 13.6g | Long Grain Wild Rice Blend▼148K 4.1g | Wing Bar ! +432K 26.7g | Bread Stick... |
| Seasoned Diced Potatoes ✲ 343K 18.0g | Fried Zucchini/Tiger Sauce | Bulgogi Veggie/Jasmine Rice ✲ | Confetti Ric... |
| Steamed Peas & Carrots ✲ ▼ 44K 0.4g | Normandy Mix ✲ ▼ 24K 0.2g | Baby Carrots ✲ ▼ 26K 0.1g | Broccoli Ra... |
|  | | | 60K 2... |
| **white** | | | |
| Soup D'jour | Soup D'jour | Philly Steak Stromboli 306K 13.4g | Soup D'jo... |
| Beef Tacos +320K 17.7g | Pasta Bar ✲±346K 6.9g | Turkey Dijon ▼ 262K 6.2g | Fried Clam... |
| Chicken Fajitas ▼ +341K 8.7g | Chicken Fillet Sandwich Bar +384K 13.1g | Fried Catfish 341K 19.8g | Burger Ba... |
| Vegetable Burrito ✲ 237K 11g | Grilled Salmon 262K 11g | Veggie Philly Stromboli ✲339K 17.7g | Turkey Bu... |
| Nacho Bar ✲+448K 25.4g | Lemon Rice ! | Crinkle Cut Fries or Hash Browns ✲ | Spicy Black... |
| Mexican Rice Ala Cruz ✲ 196K 6.2g | Sour Cream Seasnd. Fries ✲ 279K 14.7g | 257K 14g/170K 9g | Macaroni &... |
| Fiesta Corn 69K 1.7g | Classic Sicilian Blend ✲ ▼ 30K 0g | Broccoli Almondine Rice ▼ 210K 3.5g | Slim Fries ... |
|  | Brussels Sprouts ✲ ▼ 38K 0.4g | Capri Mixed Vegetables ✲ ▼ 30K 0g | Vegetable D... |

Used with permission of Division of Housing and Food Services, Michigan State University, East Lansing, Michigan.

ond menu (the white menu) is implemented in a nearby residence hall. Students residing in either hall can visit either cafeteria (or any other residence hall cafeteria on campus featuring the green or white menu!), depending on what they prefer to eat.

The green and white menu model is one tactic to encourage residence hall students to stay on campus to eat (there are many other dining alternatives nearby) and to create favorable rather than unfavorable opinions about campus dining options. Note also that nutrition information (number of calories and grams of fat) is provided for lunch and dinner menus for both green and white venues.

### Learning Point Twenty-Eight: Advertise Like "Downtown"

Figure 10-29 shows a widely distributed advertisement for an on-campus café. Note that it indicates recurring menu items (soups, salads, and sandwiches) as well as special menu items offered each weekday. As with any commercial property, location is very important. This café outlet is located in a busy area of a large residence hall in a central location on the campus.

Figure 10-29. **College Café Menu**

Used with permission of Division of Housing and Food Services, Michigan State University, East Lansing, Michigan.

### Learning Point Twenty-Nine: Add Specials on Cycle Menus

Cycle menus, regardless of how extensive and creative, can still have room for daily specials. Figure 10-30 illustrates an advertisement in a campus foodservice publication that alerts readers to special dinners available to residence hall students. (At this university, students are permitted to dine in any associated campus location; special dinners are, however, limited to residents of the specified residence hall.)

Figure 10-30.  *Menu of Special Dinners at a Particular Residence Hall*

Used with permission of Division of Housing and Food Services, Michigan State University, East Lansing, Michigan.

### Learning Point Thirty: Clip Art Can Be Effective

Figure 10-31 shows how clip art is used to enhance a menu used in a physician's dining room in a healthcare facility. The actual menu uses color printing to make the menu interesting and appealing to its readers.

Figure 10-31. **Clip Art on a Noncommercial Foodservice Menu**

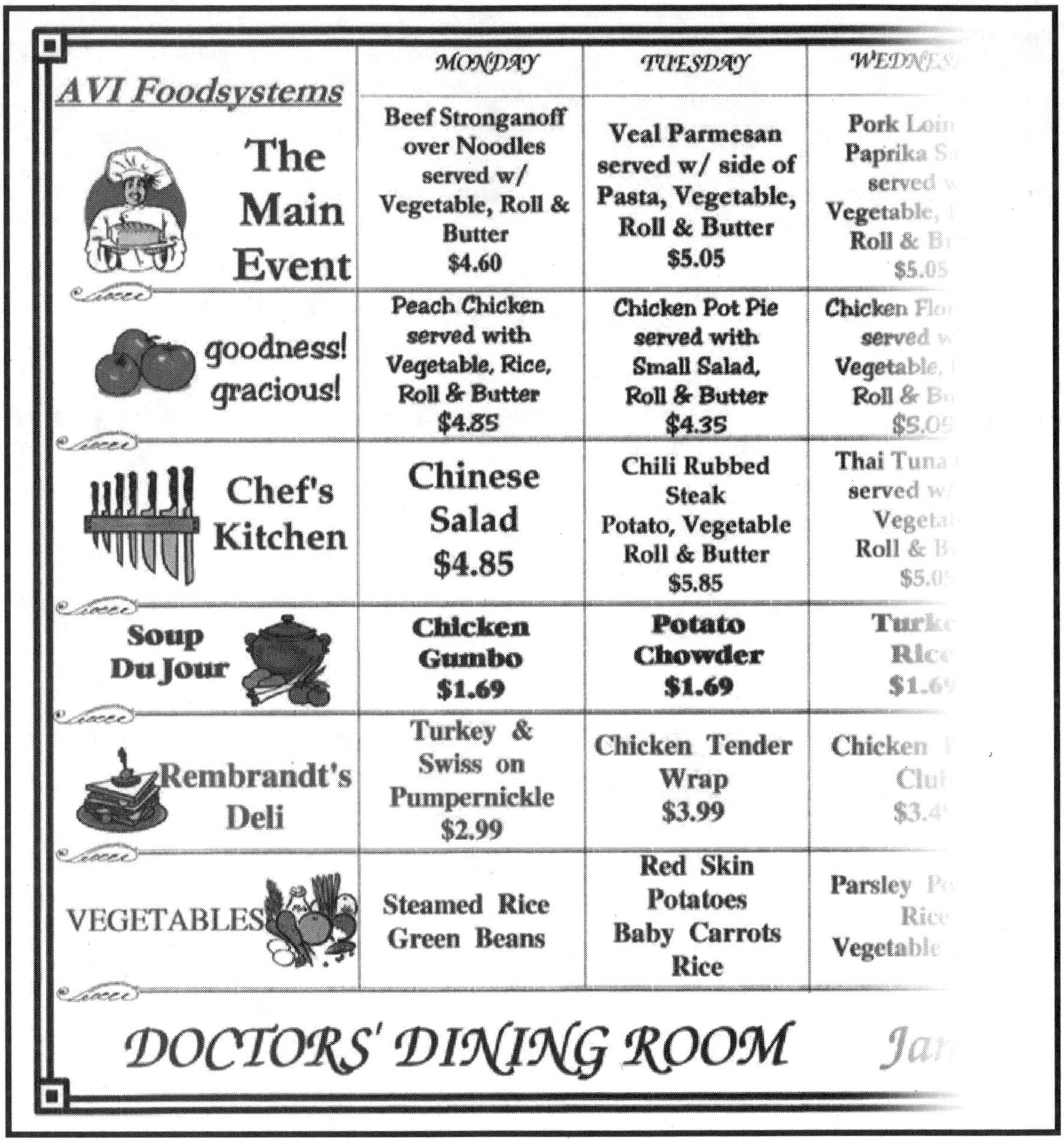

| AVI Foodsystems | MONDAY | TUESDAY | WEDNES |
|---|---|---|---|
| The Main Event | Beef Stronganoff over Noodles served w/ Vegetable, Roll & Butter $4.60 | Veal Parmesan served w/ side of Pasta, Vegetable, Roll & Butter $5.05 | Pork Loin Paprika S served Vegetable, Roll & B $5.05 |
| goodness! gracious! | Peach Chicken served with Vegetable, Rice, Roll & Butter $4.85 | Chicken Pot Pie served with Small Salad, Roll & Butter $4.35 | Chicken Flo served Vegetable. Roll & B $5.05 |
| Chef's Kitchen | Chinese Salad $4.85 | Chili Rubbed Steak Potato, Vegetable Roll & Butter $5.85 | Thai Tuna served w Vegeta Roll & B $5.0 |
| Soup Du Jour | Chicken Gumbo $1.69 | Potato Chowder $1.69 | Turke Rice $1.69 |
| Rembrandt's Deli | Turkey & Swiss on Pumpernickle $2.99 | Chicken Tender Wrap $3.99 | Chicken Clu $3.4 |
| VEGETABLES | Steamed Rice Green Beans | Red Skin Potatoes Baby Carrots Rice | Parsley P Rice Vegetable |

**DOCTORS' DINING ROOM**    Jar

Used with permission of AVI Foodsystems, Inc., Warren, Ohio.

## Learning Point Thirty-One: Pizza Delivery Menus in Noncommercial Operations

Will only commercial restaurants deliver pizza to your office? No—not at the healthcare facility whose pizza menu is illustrated in the brochure shown in Figure 10-32. A nice variety of pizza, Italian salads, and chicken wings are available. Note the well-written menu descriptions, the photos, and the attractive menu layout and design.

**Figure 10-32.** Pizza Delivery Menu

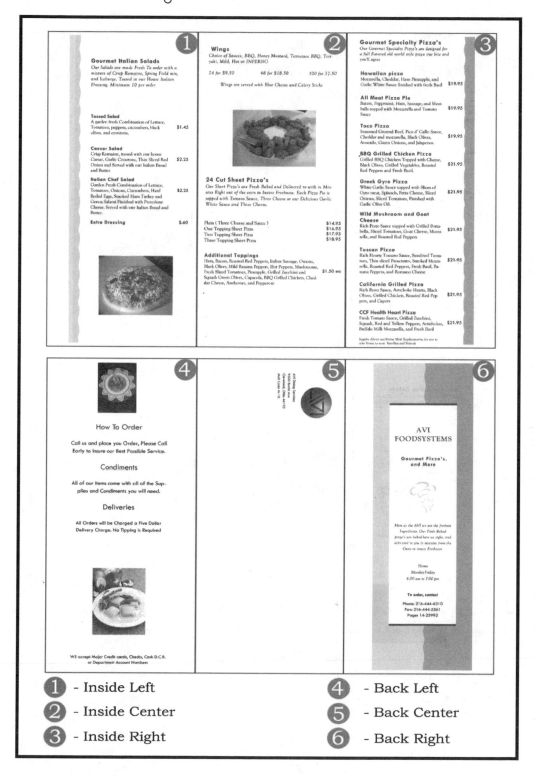

Used with permission of AVI Foodsystems, Inc., Warren, Ohio.

Figure 10-32   (continued)

**1**

### Gourmet Italian Salads

*Our Salads are made Fresh To order with a mixture of Crisp Romaine, Spring Field mix, and Iceburge. Tossed in our House Italian Dressing. Minimum 10 per order*

**Tossed Salad**

A garden fresh Combination of Lettuce, Tomatoes, peppers, cucumbers, black olives, and croutons.     $1.45

**Caesar Salad**

Crisp Romaine, tossed with our house Caesar, Garlic Croutons, Thin Sliced Red Onion and Served with our Italian Bread and Butter.     $2.25

**Italian Chef Salad**

Garden Fresh Combination of Lettuce, Tomatoes, Onions, Cucumbers, Hard Boiled Eggs, Smoked Ham Turkey and Genoa Salami Finished with Provolone Cheese. Served with our Italian Bread and Butter.     $2.25

**Extra Dressing**     $.60

**2**

### Wings

*Choice of Sauces, BBQ, Honey Mustard, Tennessee BBQ, Teriyaki, Mild, Hot or INFERNO*

24 for $9.50      48 for $18.50      100 for 37.50

*Wings are served with Blue Cheese and Celery Sticks*

### 24 Cut Sheet Pizza's

*Our Sheet Pizza's are Fresh Baked and Delivered to with in Minutes Right out of the oven to Insure Freshness. Each Pizza Pie is topped with Tomato Sauce, Three Cheese or our Delicious Garlic White Sauce and Three Cheese.*

| | |
|---|---|
| Plain ( Three Cheese and Sauce ) | $14.95 |
| One Topping Sheet Pizza | $16.95 |
| Two Topping Sheet Pizza | $17.95 |
| Three Topping Sheet Pizza | $18.95 |

### Additional Toppings

Ham, Bacon, Roasted Red Peppers, Italian Sausage, Onions, Black Olives, Mild Banana Peppers, Hot Peppers, Mushrooms, Fresh Sliced Tomatoes, Pineapple, Grilled Zucchini and Squash Green Olives, Capacola, BBQ Grilled Chicken, Cheddar Cheese, Anchovies, and Pepperoni     $1.50 ea

Figure 10-32 **(continued)**

## Gourmet Specialty Pizza's

*Our Gourmet Specialty Pizza's are designed for a full flavored old world style pizza one bite and you'll agree*

**Hawaiian pizza**
Mozzarella, Cheddar, Ham Pineapple, and Garlic White Sauce finished with fresh Basil     $19.95

**All Meat Pizza Pie**
Bacon, Pepperoni, Ham, Sausage, and Meatballs topped with Mozzarella and Tomato Sauce     $19.95

**Taco Pizza**
Seasoned Ground Beef, Pico d' Gallo Sauce, Cheddar and mozzarella, Black Olives, Avocado, Green Onions, and Jalapenos.     $19.95

**BBQ Grilled Chicken Pizza**
Grilled BBQ Chicken Topped with Cheese, Black Olives, Grilled Vegetables, Roasted Red Peppers and Fresh Basil.     $21.95

**Greek Gyro Pizza**
White Garlic Sauce topped with Slices of Gyro meat, Spinach, Fetta Cheese, Sliced Onions, Sliced Tomatoes, Finished with Garlic Olive Oil.     $21.95

**Wild Mushroom and Goat Cheese**
Rich Pesto Sauce topped with Grilled Portabella, Sliced Tomatoes, Goat Cheese, Mozzarella, and Roasted Red Peppers     $21.95

**Tuscan Pizza**
Rich Hearty Tomato Sauce, Sundried Tomatoes, Thin sliced Prosciutto, Smoked Mozzarella, Roasted Red Peppers, Fresh Basil, Banana Peppers, and Romano Cheese     $21.95

**California Grilled Pizza**
Rich Pesto Sauce, Artichoke Hearts, Black Olives, Grilled Chicken, Roasted Red Peppers, and Capers     $21.95

**CCF Health Heart Pizza**
Fresh Tomato Sauce, Grilled Zucchini, Squash, Red and Yellow Peppers, Artichokes, Buffalo Milk Mozzarella, and Fresh Basil     $21.95

*Inquire About our Home Meal Replacements, for you to take Home to your Families and Friends*

③

④

## How To Order

Call us and place you Order, Please Call Early to Insure our Best Possible Service.

## Condiments

All of our Items come with all of the Supplies and Condiments you will need.

## Deliveries

All Orders will be Charged a Five Dollar Delivery Charge. No Tipping Is Required

WE accept Major Credit cards, Checks, Cash D.C.B. or Department Account Numbers

Figure 10-32   (continued)

### Learning Point Thirty-Two: Wine Menus In Noncommercial Operations

Some noncommercial foodservice operations sell wine and, therefore, develop and offer wine lists. An example is shown in Figure 10-33. This organization is somewhat unusual. Note, for example, that it offers three tiers of pricing; all wines (which are separated by type: white, blush, sparkling, and red) within a specific tier are offered at the same price. For example, note that several wines of each type are listed in "Tier One" for the same price—$20.00.

Figure 10-33.   **Wine Menu in a Noncommercial Operation**

Used with permission of Kellogg Hotel and Conference Center, Michigan State University, East Lansing, Michigan.

### Learning Point Thirty-Three: "Menus" for Vended Products

We have stressed throughout this book the need for careful placement of specific items on a menu. A similar approach is required for the placement of products within a vending machine. Figure 10-34 shows how products should be arranged within a specific unit in one company. This provides a "menu" for route persons as they fill or service the vending machines.

Figure 10-34. **Item Layout for a Vending Machine**

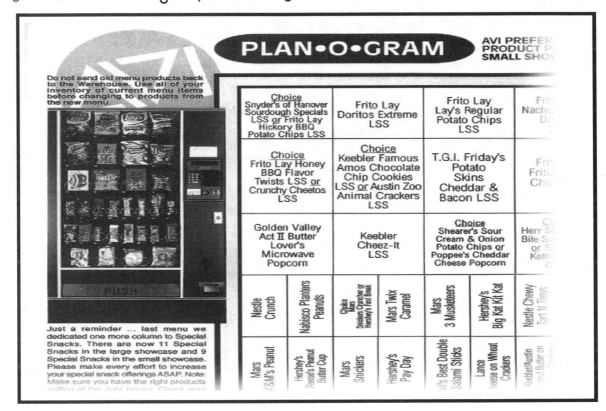

Used with permission of AVI Foodsystems, Inc., Warren, Ohio.

### Learning Point Thirty-Four: Hospital Special Diet Menus

Many patients in hospitals and nursing homes require special diets. Figure 10-35 shows a tray menu for a 2-gram sodium/low-sodium menu in a hospital. In this facility some patients are allowed menu choices. They record their preferences on a "menu checksheet" the day before each menu is served. This information is entered into a computerized system that produces tray slips such as the one illustrated in Figure 10-35. This slip is placed on the tray, which proceeds down a tray line where applicable portions are placed on the tray as it moves between stations on the serving line. (*Note:* In Figure 10-35, "SR/FR" refers to "Sodium Restricted/Fat Restricted"; "KK" means "Fat Free.")

Figure 10-35. **Hospital Menu for Special Diet**

**LUNCH**

SUN-14

Starters
Grey Diet Kit ........................................................................ 1 EACH

**Main Fare**
SR/FR Green Beans ............................................................. 1/2 CUP
Baked Chicken w/SR/FR Gravy ............................................ 3 OZ
SR Mshd Pot w/SR/FR Chckn Gravy ................................... I/2 CUP

**A la carte**
Orange Juice ....................................................................... 4 OZ
Margarine ............................................................................ 1 PC
Wheat Bread ....................................................................... 1 SLICE

**Accompaniments**
Garden Green Salad ........................................................... 1 SERVING
Applesauce ......................................................................... 1 SERV
Ranch Dressing, FF ............................................................ 1 PKT

PATIENT
202002          10 TH FLOOR

2 GRAM SODIUM/LOW SODIUM

## Learning Point Thirty-Five: Be Careful with Your Instructions to the Guests

There are tactful (and less tactful) ways to inform guests about the policies of the foodservice operation. Consider the following information taken from a banquet menu in a noncommercial foodservice operation.

### LUNCH AND DINNER BUFFETS

All lunch buffets require a minimum guarantee of 25 guests; if a guarantee of less than 25 is given, you will be charged for 25 guests. All dinner buffets require a minimum of 50 guests; if a guarantee of less than 50 is given, you will be charged for 50 guests.

Among the several problems with this information are the following two:

- Instructions are redundant; a "minimum guarantee of 25 guests" or "50 guests" should be self-explanatory.
- Guests should not be "required" to do almost anything. Could the menu planners have substituted words such as "Our lunch buffets are served for a minimum of 25 guests; if your group will involve fewer guests, we will be happy to serve a special plated menu for you" (and, perhaps, it would also be possible for the menu planners to offer a "help yourself" salad bar as a first course for a group slightly smaller than 25 guests).

Communication problems can also be avoided if menu wording is definitive. Consider the following example from a noncommercial dinner menu.

---

### DINNER SELECTIONS

Dinner selections include your choice of starter and dessert, chef's appropriate accompaniment, rolls and butter, and beverage.

---

What does the term "beverage" mean? Many operations may offer coffee, hot or iced tea, and milk. Water is almost never priced separately unless it is a bottled water. What about soft drinks? Are these considered "beverages" by the foodservice operation? Could some guests believe that "beverages" include alcoholic beverages such as wine or a cocktail? The time to answer these and related questions is, of course, at the time the menu is planned.

A banquet menu for another noncommercial banquet operation includes the following menu item description.

---

### CARIBBEAN CHICKEN

Citrus marinated Pierre-cut grilled breast, served on a bed of black bean chili with melon salsa.

---

What is a "Pierre-cut" of grilled chicken breast? At the least, service personnel must be taught this relatively uncommon term; at the most, the menu description might be revised to include a brief explanation. Another example of a menu item description can further make the point about the importance of careful wording.

---

### WEDGE OF ICEBERG

With tomato, chopped egg and parsley; served with blue cheese dressing.

---

It is probable that many—but certainly not all—guests reading this menu will recognize that "Iceberg" is a type of lettuce. Is it even remotely possible that a guest might think the term referred to frozen ice from the polar regions? While this may appear to be a small point, the addition of the term "lettuce" af- ter the term "iceberg" may clarify the menu. A final example of guest information ends on a positive note.

> Please accept our apologies if, because of previous selection by passengers, your menu choice is not available.

This, or similar, wording is available on the menus offered by many airlines. It alerts guests that the airline cannot guarantee that all menu item selections will be available to all passengers. It shows a concern for passen- gers and, at the same time, may eliminate problems that arise when a disappointed passenger wishes to voice displeasure with a cabin attendant.

# In Conclusion

We have maintained throughout this book that every foodservice operation, whether commercial or noncommercial, has a menu that ensures reaching a specified profit or some other budget goal. An effective menu helps to do this by reflecting the tastes, needs, and desires of guests. A menu must also reflect the vision and goals of the owners or managers of the foodservice operation.

Good managers know that a proper menu drives almost all the activities of the entire foodservice operation. It is not a static part of the foodservice, but rather a constantly evolving communication device that seeks to incorporate changing tastes, operational costs, and food trends for guests' enjoyment and for the financial health of the operation. As a marketing device, the menu, more than any other aspect of the foodservice operation, defines the style, clientele, potential prices, and even the service styles that are used. A menu is much more than a list of what the restaurant sells. It communicates the very essence and personality of the foodservice operation. In fact, when a well-designed menu can be shown to someone who has never been to the restaurant, that person should be able to understand almost everything about the restaurant, from price range to ambiance and service.

An appropriate menu can be developed after menu planners have thoroughly analyzed the space, equipment, and physical layout of the storage, kitchen, and service areas. During this analysis, menu planners will discover that production bottlenecks are avoided, service levels are increased, and guest satisfaction is enhanced. What a menu promises must be consistently delivered. Standardized purchase specifications, recipes, and production methods help to ensure this goal. In addition, profitable menus depend on consistent menu item costs. With the use of standard operating procedures, these costs are known and vary little. As a result, effective menu planners can use pricing strategies that incorporate what is known about each menu item's food cost, popularity, and contribution margin to establish appropriate selling prices.

One of the most challenging tasks in the entire menu-development process is creating the physical menu. Regardless of whether the menu planners work alone, employ a planning team from within the operation, or hire outside professionals, extensive resources are available. This is especially true for those menu planners who are proficient in the use of computers and desktop publishing programs. When the menu planners do not have these skills and must hire others to do some work on the menu, the development process must still be overseen and directed by the menu planners.

A well-designed menu is a real asset to management. When menu planners properly analyze the menu, they may gain insight into the items the guests will select, the foods that must be purchased, and the staffing levels required to ensure good service. Regardless of how good they believe their menus to be, effective menu planners are always alert to the many factors that could influence their menus.

As a result, they should carefully evaluate the menus from other foodservice operations. They identify menu characteristics and approaches that can help them to improve their own menus. In this way, menu planners learn constantly and use the knowledge they attain to improve their menus. The educational development of successful menu planners is an ongoing process. It is the hope of the authors that the contents of this book will contribute to that process.

## SIGEE'S MENU: A CASE STUDY

"I'm excited about it!" said David Berger, food and beverage director for Sigee's Sports Zone, the restaurant inside the hotel where he worked. "This revision process will really make our new menu stronger."

"David, your planning team certainly came through on the first revision, and I know they can do it again," said Peggy Sill, the hotel's general manager. "I'm glad to hear you are ready to finalize Sigee's new menu. What changes are you considering?"

David was meeting with Peggy to discuss his plans to revise the "new" Sigee's menu. He knew the menu would never be "finished" completely, because there would always be new menu items to try and improvements to be made. He was giving Peggy an update on how the new menu had performed in the six months that it had been in place. Because she saw the improvement in daily sales and monthly expense statements, she knew about its positive financial impact. David wanted her to know more about what the food and beverage department had discovered in the past six months that would help them enhance the new menu by making further changes.

"Well, pricing for sure," replied David. "The cost on most of our items is about the same as six months ago with the exception of some seafood items used on the daily specials. Those costs went sky high just after our printing."

"Do you want to take the seafood special off the menu?" asked Peggy.

"No," replied David. "We think it's a plus. We'll look at portion size, change the item's placement on the menu to de-emphasize it and then review the costs carefully to increase the price only enough to regain our original contribution margin."

"Sounds good," said Peggy. "What else are you evaluating?"

"Just about everything," replied David. "We'll look at sales patterns to see if we want to move items that don't sell so well off the prime real estate sections of the menu and put them in a less prominent spot. And, as you know, we did find one spelling error we missed in the first go-around."

Peggy laughed, "That does seem to happen, regardless of the number of times you proof—trust me, I know. Any new items to be added?"

"Yes," replied David, "The chef does want to try two new items, one sandwich and one dinner entrée. The problem is deciding what, if anything to eliminate! We'll also look at our pricing, placement and item descriptions, and we want to review the paper stock we selected. We may make some changes there. I've just purchased a new book on menu planning and its full of ideas we can use!"

"David, it sounds like your group is on the right track. Thanks for the hard work," Peggy said as she signaled the end of the meeting by getting up from the conference table. "Please keep me posted on your progress, and tell your team how proud I am of them for all they do to help the hotel."

"I will," promised David. As David left the meeting he thought back to the first menu revision meeting he had with Peggy. It was in that meeting that the term "excellent food at traveler friendly prices" had evolved. It was, he firmly believed, a great vision for Sigee's, and the revised menu had helped promote that vision. With this newest revision, he was sure the menu would communicate that vision even more clearly, more concisely and more professionally. He could hardly wait to get started!

# Glossary

*"A" ingredients.* The relatively few ingredients that make up 75 percent or more of the total purchase dollars; in other words, most purchase dollars are spent to purchase the relatively few "A" ingredients.

*À la carte menu.* A meal chosen item by item; each item is priced separately.

*Advertising.* The activities employed to bring menu item offerings to the attention of potential and current guests (consumers).

*As purchased.* The weight of a product before cooking; also known as "AP Weight."

*Average contribution margin.* The contribution margin (revenue less food cost) for all menu items divided by the total number of all menu items sold.

*Back-of-the-house.* The kitchen, storage areas, and other traditionally nonpublic spaces within a food and beverage operation; also referred to as "heart-of-the-house."

*Banquet.* Relating to setting the room for a group function and for preparing and serving the food required for the event.

*Base selling price.* The selling price of a menu item derived from the use of an objective pricing method. The base selling price is not necessarily the price advertised on the menu. Rather, it is a foundation selling price based on operating budget data. This price may be modified after menu planners consider factors including marketing issues, the competition, and psychological pricing.

*Benchmark.* The process of comparing the practices and methods of one's organization against those of others who are considered "world-class performers" and who compete for the same market of potential guests.

*Bidding.* The process by which foodservice contract management companies develop proposals that meet a noncommercial facility' requirements for its foodservices. These proposals are then analyzed, and a contract is negotiated with the company offering the best proposal.

*Bin lists.* A storage system for wine in which wines of a specific brand and type are stored in a specific place. Frequently, wine lists indicate the "bin number" in which the wine is located.

*Blind testing.* The process of evaluating items produced from standard recipes in such a way that the evaluators know neither the recipe nor its ingredients before or during evaluation. This method helps reduce biases that are formed when raters know they are assessing favorite or unpopular recipes and when they have formed perceptions (favorable or unfavorable) about recipe ingredients.

*Blood alcohol concentration (BAC).* The amount of alcohol in one's bloodstream. In many states, for example, a person with a BAC of 0.08 percent (8/100 of 1 percent) is considered legally drunk.

*Bottleneck.* One or more places in the production system where workflow is interrupted. Causes include too little or the wrong type of equipment and a production step such as breading or filleting that slows production output.

*Break-even analysis.* Also called cost-volume-profit (CVP) analysis, this process can be used to study the relationships between revenues, variable costs, fixed costs and profit. Its use includes, but is not limited to, menu-pricing decisions.

*Call brand.* A high-quality (and, therefore, more expensive) brand of liquor that, in many operations, is sold only when the specific brand name is requested. In addition to the house brand (sometimes called the speed rail, pour, or well brand), some properties offer a third tier—premium—of still higher quality (and cost) brands for their more discriminating guests.

*Cash cafeteria operation.* Foodservices in non-commercial operations in which some or all of the food and beverage products are sold for cash. For example, a college cafeteria may accept meal tickets with debit balances from students and cash for purchases by faculty members in the same cafeteria line. Alternatively, the cafeteria in a business and industry setting may accept cash only in a specific dining area even though all consumers must be employees of the organization.

*Catering.* Relating to selling a banquet event. In small operations, catering is a function of the marketing and sales department. In a large property, catering may be organized as a separate department.

*Center of the plate.* The tactic of positioning different portions of food on a plate by working from the center of the plate toward its rim while slightly overlapping each menu item. There is, then, no space in the center (eating) area of the plate exposed to the guest.

*Chained recipe.* A recipe that yields an ingredient in another recipe.

*Check average.* Food revenue divided by the number of guests served; the average amount spent by guests in the food and beverage operation.

*Clip-ons.* An insert in or an attachment to a menu that advertises daily specials or emphasizes other menu items that menu designers wish to sell.

*Cocktails.* Alcoholic beverages such as a martini or Manhattan that contain the liquor as the primary ingredient.

*Comfort foods.* Food items that college and university students desire regardless of other items that may be offered. Comfort foods are familiar items frequently served at home and help to remind one of family and the familiar home environment. Examples include hot dogs, hamburgers, French fries, soups, and cold cereal.

*Commercial operations.* A food and beverage operation (such as offered in a hotel or by a restaurant) that exists primarily to generate profits from the sale of food and beverages.

*Competing menu items.* Those menu items that normally "compete" with one another for purchase by the guests. Consider, for example, menu items for children listed on the menu for the convenience of young persons brought to the restaurant by the adult guests. These items would normally be excluded in the menu-engineering process because they would not be among the menu items normally considered by the typical guests.

*Competitive edge.* Any tactic, process, or procedure used by a food and beverage operation and desired by diners that is not offered by competitors (or is not offered as well by them).

*Competitor analysis.* The study of the competitions' products, prices, promotional and advertising efforts, and other factors to assure that one is doing as well as (or better than!) competitors to attract guests in the same market.

*Continuous quality improvement (CQI).* The process of determining ways to improve the foodservice operation to more consistently deliver products and services that meet (or exceed) the organization's standards (which, in turn, are driven by what the guests want and need).

**Contract food management company.** A for-profit foodservice organization retained by some noncommercial facilities to operate their foodservice program.

**Contribution margin.** Menu item selling price less menu item food cost; the amount of revenue that remains after product costs are subtracted from the product's selling price. For example, a sandwich selling for $5 with a product cost of $1 will yield a contribution margin of $4.

**Convenience food.** A food item that has some or all of the labor built into it that otherwise would need to be provided on site.

**Cost control.** A management responsibility that involves determining what costs should be, what they are, when they are excessive, and how to reduce them to planned levels without sacrificing quality standards.

**Cost effective.** Something that is worth more than it costs. For example, if menu planners introduce an item that requires expensive specialty production equipment but will generate relatively low revenue levels, then they are probably not making a cost-effective decision.

**Cost of goods sold.** The product costs incurred to generate the revenue produced from the sale of the product. A simplified formula is: Beginning Inventory Value + Purchases - Ending Value. (Numerous adjustments to this basic equation can be made to more closely match product costs with the revenue generated from their sale.)

**Cross-selling.** Tactics used by the menu designers to advertise other products and services offered by the food and beverage operation in addition to those offered on a specific menu. For example, a dinner menu may alert readers about the property's Sunday buffet; a college menu planner may use signage in the cafeteria to alert students that they can order pizzas for delivery to the residence hall rooms.

**Cuisine.** The style and range of menu items to be offered by the foodservice operation.

**Cyclical menu.** A menu in which items are offered on a repeating (cyclical) basis.

**Décor.** Decorations including window treatments, wall and floor coverings, and tablecloths within the dining area.

**Demographics.** Characteristics of a population (such as a restaurant's potential guests), which, if known, can help the menu planners to better meet that market's wants and needs.

**Design.** The manner in which space and dining areas are used. Typically, dining room furniture, bars, reception, and server areas are considered part of the design.

**Direct competitors.** Those foodservice operations that offer similar menu items, at similar prices, and in similar settings to guests with similar needs.

**Dram shop liability.** A legal concept that allocates responsibility to third parties such as commercial food and beverage operations for accidents and injuries caused by persons who consume alcoholic beverages in an operation. (By law, the "first party" is the person injured or harmed; the "second party" is the person causing the injury; the "third party" is anyone else contributing to the injury.)

**Du jour menu.** A menu featuring items that change daily.

**Electronic point-of-sale (POS) system.** A restaurant system used to control revenue and product usage. A POS consists of hardware, software, and an input device such as touchscreen, keyboard, keypad, or scanner.

**Excessive price spread.** The observation that guest check averages may be skewed downward when there is a significant range of menu item selling prices. Guests may select lower-priced items because they still receive many aspects of the total dining experience at a reduced cost.

*Finishing.* The task of providing additional ingredients or labor to a convenience food product before service. For example, shrimp can be purchased in a peeled and deveined market form, with additional on-site labor used to butterfly the product before breading and deep-frying.

*Folio.* A financial statement maintained at the front desk that details all of a guest's transactions (payments and charges) since checking into the hotel.

*Food cost percentage.* The percentage of a menu item's selling price required to purchase the ingredients for the item; it is the food cost of menu item divided by the menu item selling price.

*Food fads.* Food products, preparation methods, or cuisines that are extremely popular for a relatively short time period.

*Food trends.* Food products, preparation methods, or cuisines that, unlike a food fad, are ongoing, beginning slowly and more gradually increasing in popularity.

*Franchise.* An agreement between an organization that originally developed the business (franchiser) and a company that operates under the agreement (the franchisee). The franchise agreement specifies that the operating company can use the franchiser's brand name in return for complying with contractual requirements (many of which are related to helping assure consistency between units) and paying agreed-upon fees.

*From scratch.* The use of raw ingredients to prepare items on-site; for example, a stew made from scratch would require the purchase of beef (which would need to be cubed), celery, potatoes, carrots, and other ingredients that must be processed and cooked in the property's kitchen.

*Front-of-the-house.* The dining room, public rest areas, guest waiting area, and all other areas of the food and beverage operation that can be accessed by the establishment's customers.

*Hardware.* Point-of-sale system terminals, personal computers, inventory and bar code reading devices, printers, and other computer equipment items.

*High check average.* Relates to the average price a guest pays for a meal; a guest consuming a meal in a high check average restaurant (such as a hotel's roof-top dining room) pays more, on average, than a guest in that hotel's coffee shop.

*Highballs.* Alcoholic beverages made with one liquor to which water, juice, soft drink, or other nonalcoholic beverage is added.

*Home page (sometimes referred to as a web site).* Refers to a specific URL (Universal Resource Location) that offers the reader (viewer) information, data, graphics, or entertainment. Home pages may be established or maintained by organizations or by individuals.

*Income.* Also called "profit" (in a commercial operation) and sometimes "operating surplus" (in a noncommercial operation), income is the "bottom line"; it is the amount of money remaining after all expenses associated with or allocated to the foodservice operation are deducted from its revenue.

*Incremental sales.* Additional revenue generated by marketing efforts that yield more guests visiting the property, by suggestive selling, or by other techniques that increase the amount of revenue spent by guests.

*Indirect competitors.* Those operations that offer any type of food and beverage products and services.

*Ingredient room.* A space (ideally located between the storage and the preparation areas) used to weigh and measure ingredients required for recipes to be produced in preparation areas.

*Instant message program.* Refers to a "computer" conference using the computer's keyboard (a "keyboard chat") to communicate over the Internet. Two or more people, on-line at the same time, can type messages to each other in real time. AOL's Instant Messenger (AIM), Microsoft Network Messenger Service (MSNMS), ICQ, and Yahoo! Messenger are the major instant messaging services used by restaurants.

*Intranet.* A network (much like the Internet) of linked computers, except that access is restricted to only those computers specifically designated as part of the network.

*Just-in-time (JIT).* A relatively recent food purchasing and receiving system in which products are ordered for receipt on the day of preparation and service to maximize product freshness, to reduce on-site storage space, and to reduce inventory carrying costs. These systems require an effective communication system between the purchaser and supplier and relatively large volumes of products for which purchase commitments are made in order for them to be considered cost-effective for either the purchaser or food supplier.

*Liaison.* An employee of a noncommercial organization (often with commercial food-service training and experience) who represents the organization in interactions with a contract food management company.

*Line-ups.* Brief training sessions conducted before the start of employee shifts to update staff members about the current situation (daily specials, items to be emphasized, number of leftover portions to be served, and special functions going on within the property, for example).

*Make-or-buy analysis.* The process of objectively evaluating the quality and cost differences to the options of preparing a menu item on site, purchasing it in a convenience food form, or finishing it on site.

*Market research.* The process of identifying ways to improve the food and beverage operation to more consistently deliver products and services that meet (or exceed) the organization's standards.

*Menu.* A French term meaning "detailed list"; in common usage it refers to a listing of the foodservice establishment's available food and beverage products and to the way this list is provided to the guest.

*Menu engineering.* A method of evaluation that focuses on the popularity and profitability of competing menu items with the goal of maximizing the sale of popular and profitable items and minimizing or eliminating, when practical, the sale of the less popular or less profitable items.

*Menu layout.* The manner and location in which menu item categories are placed on the menu.

*Menu mix.* The sale (number of units) of a menu item relative to the total sale of all competing menu items. If 100 portions of chicken are sold on a day when 1,000 meals were served, the chicken's menu mix is 10 percent (100 divided by 1,000).

*Menu rationalization.* The use of a primary recipe ingredient such as shrimp or chicken for several (or more) different menu items to reduce the operational difficulties that arise when many different items for different recipes must be purchased.

*Niche marketing.* The tactic of focusing marketing attention on a more narrow subgroup within a major market. For example, a high-check-average restaurant may market primarily to after-theater diners or to business meeting groups rather than to anyone willing to pay more than a specified price for a meal.

*Noncommercial operations.* A food and beverage operation (such as in a school, hospital, or business or industry) in which food and beverage services must be provided incidental to the primary purpose of the organization. (For example, the school exists to educate, the hospital to cure illness, and the business and industry setting to make a product or offer a service.) Also commonly referred to as an "institutional foodservice operation."

*Operating budget.* A financial plan that estimates planned revenue, expenses, and income for a specific period. Budgets are usually planned for a twelve-month period on a bimonthly basis.

*Operating costs.* Expenses incurred by a food and beverage operation in the course of generating revenues. For example, an operation must pay for the food (one type of operating cost) that must be prepared and served.

*Penny profit.* An item's selling price less the combined food costs and paper costs; it is, then, a variation of the term "contribution margin" (selling price less food costs) that is used by commercial operators other than those in the quick-service segment.

*Point-of-sale.* Any on-site effort to influence the customer's purchase decision. This includes the use of table tents and suggestive selling.

*Portion control.* Any activity to help assure that the size (by weight or volume) of a menu item is consistent. Examples include the use of a scoop or ladle to serve foods prepared in batches or larger quantities and the use of a preportioned item (such as a 6-ounce hamburger patty) for items cooked to order.

*Potentially hazardous foods.* Generally, foods of animal origin or those that contain large amounts of foods of animal origin, which are most prone to contamination by microorganisms that might cause food-borne illness.

*Precosting.* The process of determining the cost to produce all portions and a single portion of a menu item when a standard recipe is accurately followed.

*Prime cost.* The sum of product (food and beverage) and labor costs. Prime costs can be calculated for a menu item or for the total of these costs (for example, in an operating budget). They can be expressed in dollars or as a percentage of total costs.

*Prime real estate.* A phrase used to define the areas on a menu that are most visible to guests and, therefore, should contain the items the menu planners most want to sell.

*Psychographics.* A system to measure the beliefs, opinions, and interests of consumers.

*Purchase order system.* A procurement method in which prices for products in specified quantities meeting quality requirements outlined in purchase specifications are solicited from suppliers. Buyers make supplier-selection decisions for specific orders based on price quotations received and are assured that incoming products will be of the proper quality, since they will be checked against purchase specifications.

*Purchase specification.* A definition of required quality that must be met by products purchased by the foodservice operation.

*Purchase unit.* The measurement unit normally used to purchase food products. For example, fluid whole milk may be purchased by the gallon; flour is purchased by the pound.

*Quality.* Suitable for intended use; the more suited that a product is for its use, the more appropriate the quality is for the product. A "quality" product, then, requires that it do what it is supposed to do better than any other product.

*Reconstitute.* To convert a food item from a nonedible to an edible form. Reconstituting occurs, for example, when water is added to a dry product or when heat is applied to a chilled product.

*Revenue.* The amount of money generated from the sale of food and beverage products and other services offered by the food and beverage operation. (*Note:* The term "revenue" should not be confused with another term, "sales," which refers to the number of units of a product sold to guests. For example, a restaurant will have revenues of $25 if it sells five sandwiches at a selling price of $5 each.)

*Sales.* The activities related directly to the delivery of menu offerings to potential and current guests (consumers).

*Sales history.* The number of each menu item sold during a specific period of time (daily, weekly, or monthly, for example).

*Scramble system.* A cafeteria serving system in which foods in specific menu item categories (soups and salads, cold entrées, hot entrées, sandwiches, and desserts, for example) are offered on separate serving lines in different parts of the serving area. This system avoids the long waiting inline that often occurs in a traditional cafeteria serving line arrangement. Instead, guests can move in front of others or between serving lines, depending on their preferences. Guests in scramble system cafeterias spend less time waiting in line.

*Seat tax.* The amount that, on average, the guest pays to the food and beverage operation after his or her product costs are deducted from the selling price of the meal served to the guest. This term means the same as "average contribution margin."

*Seat turnover rate.* The number of times a seat is used for guest service during a meal period. For example, if 225 guests are served during lunch in a restaurant with 100 seats, the lunch seat turnover rate is 2.25 (225 guests divided by 100 seats).

*Selling price.* The amount charged to purchase one menu item.

*Server station.* A work area often located in front-of-the-house areas, sometimes separated from a dining area by a screen or other room divider, that is used by service staff to store serviceware, condiments, table linens and other products and supply items needed for guest service.

*Service bar.* A bar used to produce beverages ordered by servers who subsequently provide the beverages to guests; guests do not, themselves, order drinks at service bars. Guests may order and directly receive beverages from public bars.

*Service.* The process of moving products (food and beverages) from service staff to the guests.

*Serviceware.* The plates, bowls, dishes, and flatware (knives, forks, spoons, and other eating utensils) for serving food, along with the cups and glassware used to serve beverages.

*Serving.* The process of moving products (food and beverages) from production (cook or bartender) to service staff.

*Shopper's service.* Assistance provided by trained foodservice professionals or by others employed by a foodservice operation who pose as guests and evaluate all front-of-the-house procedures (such as menu offerings, service techniques, products, and quality) offered by the foodservice operation.

*Signature items.* Food items that are unique to or are associated with a specific foodservice operation. Guests are attracted to the operation because of these items and frequently request them. Guests may associate a restaurant, for example, with a "one-pound pork chop," a "mile-high pie," or a "shrimp boat" (a loaf of French bread hollowed out and filled with deep-fried shrimp).

*Software.* Computer programs that gather, sort, and report information.

*Standard of identity.* A detailed description of ingredients that must be included in a food product for the item to be assigned a specific name. For example, "fruit cocktail" must contain a specified ratio of specific fruits; "mixed fruit" can contain whatever the manufacturer desires to put into the product.

*Standard recipe.* Information required to prepare a food or beverage item to consistently meet a foodservice operation's required quality and quantity standards. A standard recipe should indicate the type and quantity of each required ingredient, pre-preparation and preparation procedures including required large and small equipment, yield (number of portions and portion size), garnishes, and any other information needed to produce and serve the menu item.

*Subjective pricing methods.* Procedures to establish menu selling prices that do not consider, at least in part, the financial structure and requirements of the foodservice operation or the product costs of the menu items being priced.

*Suggestive selling.* Efforts made by a food and beverage server to increase sales of suggested items by offering these items to customers when orders are taken.

*Supply chain.* The channel of distribution through which products move from the initial grower, processor, or manufacturer through wholesalers, distributors, and brokers to the final user (the foodservice operation).

*Table d'hôte menu.* A meal composed of menu items offered at a fixed price.

*Table tents.* Advertising messages typically folded to stand on the tables (sometimes they are inserted in transparent plastic sleeves) to promote sales of specified products or services to a guest while seated at a dining table.

*Temperature danger zone.* The temperature range of 40° F to 140° F, within which microorganisms responsible for most food-borne illnesses best grow and reproduce.

*Trade puffing.* Boasting about a product as an advertising tactic. For example, "Mile-High Pie" is obviously not one-mile tall; "best hamburger in the world" is probably more merchandising than it is a fact. However, "Our bread is baked on-site daily" and "Our seafood is flown in fresh daily from the Pacific Coast" do imply information that should be true.

*Truth-in-menu.* The requirement that menu descriptions accurately portray the quantity,

quality, point of origin, and numerous other factors that help menu readers understand the items being described; also referred to as accuracy-in-menu.

*Value:* The relationship between price and quality. Guests desire value: the greatest quality of products, services, and environment for the least amount of money that they must pay for the dining experience.

*Wine list.* A menu indicating wines (often with explanations of them) and prices available for sale by the food and beverage operation.

*Workflow.* The movement of a product from receiving to storage, to pre-preparation and preparation areas, and on to service personnel. Ideally, there is a straight-line flow with little back-tracking. This enables processing to be done most efficiently and effectively.

*Workstation.* The space needed (including necessary equipment) to do work of a certain type. For example, the food and beverage manager needs space with a desk, computer, telephone, and other office equipment; a fry cook may need space for a refrigerator to store items to be prepared during the shift, a deep-fryer, space to bread or otherwise make ready items for deep-frying, space to hold the plates, pans, or other serviceware to serve or hold finished products, and space for numerous small equipment items.

*World wide web.* The interconnection (web) of various computers located "worldwide," frequently referred to as the Internet. Specifically, the world wide web refers to the portion of the Internet that can be navigated through the use of a browser (programs or software that enable a person to view the web) such as Internet Explorer, Netscape, Lynx, Opera, or Cello.

*"Wow factor."* Something unexpected and designed to increase a guest's interest in the dining experience.

# Index

Penny profit, defined, 40
Perdue, Joe, 139
Planet Hollywood, 36
Plow Horses, 225–226, 232, 233
  in noncommercial operations, 238
Point-of-sale advertising, 41
Point-of-sale systems, 41–43
  defined, 15, 42
  guest preferences and, 41–43
  in noncommercial operations, 43
Portion control
  in buffets and salad bars, 91, 92
  defined, 63
Potentially hazardous foods, defined, 58
Precosting
  defined, 87
  objective pricing and, 103
  recipes, 86–88
Preparing workstation, 56–57
Pre-preparing workstation, 56
Price increases
  incremental sales and, 116–117
  excessive price spread and, 117–118
  management of, 116–118
  niche marketing and, 117–118
Pricing items, 99–119. *See also* Menu
    pricing
  break-even analysis and, 111–114
  cost of goods sold and, 179
  daily specials as, 114–116
  in franchises, 40
  mark-up factors for, 105–108
  menu item classification and, 225–228
  objective methods for, 102–110
  price increases and, 116–118
  prime cost and, 109–110
  psychological aspects of, 118–119
  revenue and, 179
  software for calculating, 178
  strategy for, 31–32
  subjective methods for, 101–102
  target market and, 31–32
  of wine lists, 141–142
Prime cost
  defined, 109
  pricing, 109–110

Prime real estate,
  defined, 157
  examples of, 158, 261
Printing of menus, 160–162
  bar menus, 73
  quantity, 162
  poor, example of, 267
  printers for, 161–162
  professional, 161–162
  technology use and, 184
Prix fixe, 4
Profit. *See also* Income; Revenue
  goals, technology use and, 177–180
  menu evaluation and, 219–228
  menu mix and, 220–225
Psychographics
  defined, 29
  characteristics, 30–31
Psychological pricing factors, 118–119
  example of, 119
Purchase order system, defined, 176
Purchase specifications, 93–97
  "A" ingredients in, 94
  computer use and, 176
  defined, 93
  developing, 94–95
  format for, 96
  mechanics of, 95–96
  quality and, 93–94, 97
  standardization and, 96–97
  supply chain and, 94
  value and, 94–95
Purchase unit, 86–87
  defined, 87
Purchasing agent, on menu-writing team,
  13
Puzzles, 225, 226, 231, 232, 233
  in noncommercial operations, 238, 239

Quality
  defined, 94
  grades, 131
  philosophy, 35–36
  purchase specifications and, 94–95,
    96–97
Quantity foodservice, history of, 2–6

Quick-service restaurants
  advertising in, 41
  facility design of, 61
  franchise units, 39
  menu changes and, 63
  pricing in, 40
  penny profit in, 40
  packaging in, 39–40, 63
  packaging clean up, 61
  storage space for packaging, 55
  target market in, 31

Ratio pricing, 108–109
Real estate, menu item classifications and,
    225–228. *See also* Prime real estate
Receiving, 55
Recipe calculations
  for buffet costs, 90–92
  computer use and, 176
  for menu costs, 88–90
  precosting, 86–88
  portion number and, 85, 87
  portion size and, 85–86, 87
  for salad bars, 90–92
Recipe evaluation form, 84
Reconsituted, defined, 58
Restaurant Guide of Kansas City, 212, 213
Revenue. *See also* Profit
  defined, 10, 101, 179
  menu-planning software and, 179
Revision, of menus. *See also* Evaluation of
    menus; Menu changes; Menu
    engineering
Robin's Restaurant, 208
Room-service menu
  examples of, 262–264
  folios and, 254
  holding foods for, 58
  shape of, 159–160
  technology and, 212
  on television, 254–255
Rudd, Theda, 39

Salad bars
  calculating costs for, 90–92
  cost minimization in, 239–240

management philosophy for, 90–91
  menu analysis for, 91
  portion control for, 91, 92
  serviceware for, 92
  standard recipes for, 91
Sales, defined, 7
Sales history, 41–42
  defined, 178
  menu mix and, 222
Scappi, Bortolomeo, 5
Schmidgall, Raymond, 103, 242
Scramble system, defined, 234
Seat tax, defined, 221
Seat turnover rate, defined, 163
Self-service operations. *See* Buffets; Salad
    bars
Selling price
  defined, 179
  menu design and, 176, 180–184
  of menu items, 179–180
  menu-planning software and, 179
  product quality and, 174–175
Server station, defined, 61
Server training
  of alcoholic beverages, 254
  line-ups and, 13
Service, defined, 59
Service bar, defined, 58
Service workstation, 59
Serviceware
  for buffets and salad bars, 92
  defined, 70
Serving, defined, 58
Serving workstation, 58
Shapes of menus, 159–160
Shopper's service
  defined, 45
  report of, 46–48
Signature items
  defined, 41, 125
  in noncommercial operations, 234–235
Simmons, Amelia, 5
Simple mark-up pricing methods, 105–107
  entrée mark-up, 105–106
  markup with entrée and
      accompaniment cost as, 106–107